Musical Solidarities

The New Cultural History of Music

SERIES EDITOR   *Jane F. Fulcher*
SERIES BOARD
MEMBERS: Celia Applegate
Philip Bohlman
Kate van Orden
Michael P. Steinberg

The Politics of Appropriation:
German Romantic Music and the Ancient
Greek Legacy
Jason Geary

Defining Deutschtum:
Political Ideology, German Identity, and Music-
Critical Discourse in Liberal Vienna
David Brodbeck

Materialities:
Books, Readers, and the Chanson in
Sixteenth-Century Europe
Kate van Orden

Singing the Resurrection:
Body, Community, and Belief in Reformation Europe
Erin Lambert

Electronic Inspirations:
Technologies of the Cold War Musical Avant-Garde
Jennifer Iverson

Musical Solidarities:
Political Action and Music in Late
Twentieth-Century Poland
Andrea F. Bohlman

Musical Solidarities

Political Action and Music in Late Twentieth-Century Poland

ANDREA F. BOHLMAN

UNIVERSITY PRESS

Oxford University Press is a department of the University of Oxford. It furthers
the University's objective of excellence in research, scholarship, and education
by publishing worldwide. Oxford is a registered trade mark of Oxford University
Press in the UK and certain other countries.

Published in the United States of America by Oxford University Press
198 Madison Avenue, New York, NY 10016, United States of America.

© Oxford University Press 2020

All rights reserved. No part of this publication may be reproduced, stored in
a retrieval system, or transmitted, in any form or by any means, without the
prior permission in writing of Oxford University Press, or as expressly permitted
by law, by license, or under terms agreed with the appropriate reproduction
rights organization. Inquiries concerning reproduction outside the scope of the
above should be sent to the Rights Department, Oxford University Press, at the
address above.

You must not circulate this work in any other form
and you must impose this same condition on any acquirer.

Library of Congress Cataloging-in-Publication Data
Names: Bohlman, Andrea F. author.
Title: Musical solidarities : political action and music in late twentieth-century Poland /
Andrea F. Bohlman.
Description: New York, NY : Oxford University Press, [2019] |
Series: The new cultural history of music series | Includes bibliographical references and index.
Identifiers: LCCN 2019019358 | ISBN 9780190084080 (pbk.) |
ISBN 9780190938284 (hardback) | ISBN 9780190938291 (updf) |
ISBN 9780190938307 (epub) | ISBN 9780190938314 (online)
Subjects: LCSH: Music—Political aspects—Poland—History—20th century.
Classification: LCC ML3917.P58 B65 2019 | DDC 306.4/8420943809048—dc23
LC record available at https://lccn.loc.gov/2019019358

This volume is published with the generous support of the AMS 75 PAYS Endowment of the American
Musicological Society, funded in part by the National Endowment for the Humanities and the Andrew
W. Mellon Foundation.

For my parents,
who have always worked toward musical community

CONTENTS

Acknowledgments ix
List of Abbreviations xv
About the Companion Website xvii
Introduction: Action   1

1 Sound   23
2 Silence   67
3 Protest   107
4 Voice   145
5 Megaphone   192
6 Chorus   234

Selected References   281
Index   305

ACKNOWLEDGMENTS

If the materials at the heart of this book sing of hope and scream for change, it has perhaps been my duty as a scholar to be skeptical of such committed passions. After a decade of thinking about Solidarity's decade, however, I find myself overwhelmingly grateful for the models of committed political work, sustained artistic practice, and critical debate I encountered while asking questions during fieldwork and archival stays in Poland. I am indebted to the activists, musicians, and friends who have engaged me along these travels and who compel me to believe in community after all.

I began working on music in Poland at Harvard University, where Anne C. Shreffler modeled a care for language, open ears, and passion for learning as my dissertation advisor. Through the years since, I have continued to be thankful for her compassionate guidance and generous support. I am also grateful for Alexander Rehding's generous mentorship, which keeps me writing for many audiences. Many other teachers at Harvard shaped me as a scholar in innumerable ways. They supported the early stages of this research by asking hard questions and pushing me to be rigorous in a breadth of modes: Carolyn Abbate, Jonathan Bolton, Virginia Danielson, Christopher Hasty, Thomas Forrest Kelly, Lewis Lockwood, Ingrid Monson, Carol Oja, Kay Kaufman Shelemay, Jason Stanyek, Hans Tutschku, and Christoph Wolff. The Music Department's staff cheered me on, along with my graduate cohort, in ways that still give this project energy. I am grateful for the special opportunity of studying the Polish language with Anna Barańczak while thinking about musicality and political community. Finally, I owe a special debt to long conversations with Suzannah Clark, Joanna Niżyńska, and Sindumathi Revuluri, all of whom pushed me to be—to stay—myself, and whose compassion and creativity as teachers and friends I have cherished long past my time in Cambridge.

In Warsaw, many individuals gave their time and opened their homes to me. My research methods themselves, I hope, responded to the personal manner in which people shared their archives and listened (to radio, to records, to tape) with me while we ate and spoke about the past and present in no particular order. That Grażyna and the late Michał Bristiger lived around the corner from me in 2009–10 was foundational to my critical ear and, I hope, shaped a place for humor in my labor. I regret that Małgorzata Pietkiewicz did not live to read this book: her conviction was a source of inspiration. I am thankful for Bolesław Błaszczyk's enthusiasm for and encyclopedic knowledge of musical lives in Warsaw, and that he was willing to go digging through archives with me. Katarzyna Naliwajek-Mazurek's kindness and cutting edge as a humanist kept me on track and reminded me to look at undiscussed times in Polish history. Marta Ptaszyńska shared her creativity, curiosity, and support on both sides of the ocean. Longina Bychawska sang with me on many cherished occasions. Through the years, many, many others in Poland or visiting from Poland opened doors, picking apart Solidarity and sound with me: Jan Bokiewicz, Antoni Buchner, Marek Chimiak, Andrzej Chłopecki, Ryszard Cieśla, Greg Czarnecki, Anna Czekanowska, Piotr Dahlig, Jarosław Guła, Danuta Gwizdalanka, Jacek Jackowski, Robert Jarosz, Joanna Kaczyńska, Michał Klubiński, Krzysztof Knittel, Jerzy Kornowicz, Jan Kossakowski, Saba Krasoczko, Stanisław Krupowicz, Michał Kubicki, Roberto Kulpa, Krzysztof Kur, Mieczysław Litwiński, Krzysztof Meyer, Grzegorz Michalski, Adam Michnik, Andrzej Mitan, Beata Molak, Maciej Orłoś, Dominik Skrzypkowski, Judyta Szylar, Anna Tarnowska-Waszak, Piotr Wierzbicki, and Adam Marek Wojdak. Many others wished to keep their voices in this book off the record, a request I honor with gratitude.

Research for this book was undertaken with the generous support of a Fulbright-Hays Fellowship from the US Department of Education, an Alvin H. Johnson AMS 50 Fellowship, an Andrew W. Mellon Postdoctoral Teaching Fellowship at the University of Pennsylvania, a fellowship from the American Council of Learned Societies, and a Faculty Excellence Grant from the Institute for the Arts and Humanities at the University of North Carolina, Chapel Hill. I am thankful to Zbigniew Skowron and the University of Warsaw Department of Music for hosting me during my first research in Poland, 2009–10. I completed the manuscript with the instrumental support of a EURIAS Fellowship at the Wissenschaftskolleg zu Berlin.

Across the archives where I have read and listened, I was dependent on many generous workers without whom this research would have been impossible. At Harvard's Libraries Sarah Adams, Virginia Danielson, Joanna Epstein, Joseph Garver, Kerry Linklater, Bradley Schaffner, Liza Vick, Andrew Wilson, and, with his knowledge of *drugi obieg* tapes, Joseph Zajac responded to every query. At the Music Special Collections at the University of Warsaw's library, Magdalena Borowiec, Elżbieta Jasińska, Piotr

Maculewicz, and Barbara Kalinowska taught me the ins and outs of Polish archives and sent me off to talk to people, too. At the Polish Composers' Union, Beata Dźwigaj, Mieczysław Kominek, and Izabela Zymer welcomed my invasion of their offices and let me sit and listen. The staff at the Archive of Solidarity's National Commission in Gdańsk, Archiwum Akt Nowych, Biblioteka Narodowa in Warsaw (especially Mariola Nałęcz and Anna Romnianuk), Instytut Pamięci Narodu in Warsaw and Gdańsk, the Karta Organization, Muzeum Niepodległości (especially Emil Noiński), Stanford University's Hoover Institute, and Stowarzyszenie Wolnego Słowa all welcomed my search for music and surprised me with unexpected sources. Karina Garsztecka responded to numerous requests to hear the bountiful collection of opposition media at the Archiv der Forschungsstelle Osteuropa an der Universität Bremen. I remain astonished at the resourcefulness of and am indebted to the kindness of the library staff of the Wissenschaftskolleg zu Berlin.

The questions and material woven together here began to take shape as a book while I was a postdoctoral fellow at the University of Pennsylvania. I am thankful for the broad interdisciplinarity at the Penn Humanities Forum and in the Department of Music, particularly through the warm intellectual buzz cultivated by Emma Dillon, Rossen Djagalov, Emily Dolan, James English, Jeffrey Kallberg, Guthrie P. Ramsey, Timothy Rommen, Kevin Platt, and Anna Weesner. I am especially grateful that conversations with Amy Cimini, Joanna Dee Das, Mitch Fraas, and Naomi Waltham-Smith about writing books and artistic commitment begun during that year have grown in the time since. Sheila Kaufman and Brynn Utley made my temporary Philadelphia citizenship tremendously meaningful.

At the University of North Carolina, Chapel Hill, I am thankful for inspiring and engaging colleagues whose support was crucial to this book's development. As Department chairs, Mark Katz, Louise Toppin, and Allen Anderson advocated for me and always listened. I am thankful to Terri Rhodes in the Dean's Office and Robert Jenkins and Donald Raleigh at the Center for Slavic, East European, and Eurasian Studies. Evan Bonds, Tim Carter, Annegret Fauser, David Garcia, Mark Katz, and Jocelyn Neal have been the most generous and erudite senior colleagues; they have all scrutinized my prose, kept scholarly dialogue fun, and cared that this project mattered to me. Anne MacNeil and Severine Neff, when we were on campus together, reminded me to look at matters differently. Juan Álamo, Stephen Anderson, Jennifer Curtis, Nicholas DiEugenio, Stefan Litwin, Tommy Otten, Mimi Solomon, Lee Weisert, and Clara Yang gave their time and musical talents to concerts and conferences that brought the sounds of this research to campus. I am grateful to share an office wall and a penchant for long rants filled with big dreams with Michael Figueroa. I cannot imagine a kinder collection of interlocutors across campus and am thankful for long and short collaborations with Karen Auerbach, Chad Bryant, Adnan Džumhur, Jennifer Ho, Heidi Kim, Louise McReynolds, Michael Palm, Hana Píchová, Donald Raleigh, Julia Sherwood, Peter Sherwood, Silvia Tomášková, and Ewa Wampuszyc. At Duke, Beth Holmgren, Louise Meintjes, and Philip Rupprecht helped me build bridges. *Musical Solidarities* would not have been possible without the tremendous resources of UNC's Libraries; I am indebted to its experts, in particular Monica Figueroa, Carrie Monette, Diane Steinhaus, Kirill Tolpygo, and Philip Vandermeer. Gina Bombola provided much appreciated bibliographic assistance.

I am deeply inspired by the communities of scholars who have supported my research, whose work has compelled me to write, and whose fellowship I do not take for granted. I presented portions of this research at numerous venues at the University of North Carolina at Chapel Hill and to attentive and inquisitive audiences at Cape Breton University, the Harriman Institute at Columbia University, the Hoschule für Musik und Theater Hamburg, the Humboldt University in Berlin, Indiana University, the Institute for Advanced Study in Bucharest, the Polish Music Center at the University of Southern California, Universität Bremen, and the University of Pennsylvania. Major test runs of many key arguments and close readings occurred at numerous academic conferences. Certain sentences, ideas, and turns of phrase are the result of questions I can still remember—and for which I am obviously still thankful—asked by Michael Beckerman, Georgina Born, Seth Brodsky, Suzanne Cusick, Martin Daughtry, Eric Drott, Phil Ford, Danielle Fosler-Lussier, Jane Fulcher, Adriana Helbig, Kevin Karnes, Noriko Manabe, Nicholas Mathew, Barbara Milewski, Benjamin Piekut, Peter Schmelz, Richard Taruskin, Kirill Tomoff, and Justin Willliams. The mutual support among the fellows at the Wissenschaftskolleg zu Berlin transformed my sense of audience and kept me wondering: Asef Bayat, Hetty Berg, Rogers Brubaker, Phillipp Deines, Jennifer Fewell, Jon Harrison, Myles Jackson, Cornelia Jöchner, Barbara Kowalzig, Michael Lambek, Vivek Nityananda, Emily Sena, Jacqueline Solway, Katharina Volk, and Julia Voss.

Many of the subjects in this book felt they were living among an extraordinary network of people who, together, could make something out of ideas, even when they disagreed. If history has made it harder for me to get swept up in such idealism, my friends and colleagues have not. At Harvard, my graduate cohort formed social cohesion that is crucial to this scholarly ethos: Sofia Becerra, Louis Kaiser Epstein, Glenda Goodman, Michael Heller, Frank Lehman, Tom Lin, Danny Mekonnen, Rowland Moseley, Matthew Mugmon, and Meredith Schweig. Elizabeth Craft, Paavali Jumppanen, Evan MacCarthy, and Anna Zayaruznaya shared important passions, intellectual and otherwise. To colleagues who share their writing and teaching out of compassionate rigor despite institutional constraints and overloads, I am thankful for sustenance: Marié Abe, Catherine Appert, Jonathan De Souza, Ryan Dohoney, Wayne Marshall, Griffith Rollefson, and Maria Sonevytsky.

The study of music and sound under state socialism has (in a somewhat peculiar fashion) shaped a strikingly considerate—if quirky—network of scholars; their humor-filled collegiality has made this work all the more pleasurable and rewarding: Emily Abrams Ansari, Rachel Beckles Willson, Joy Calico, John Gabriel, Elaine Kelly, Nina Noeske, Emily Richmond-Pollock, Florian Scheding, Anne Searcy, Anne Shreffler, Martha Sprigge, Anicia Timberlake, Matthias Tischer, Nicholas Tochka, David Tompkins, Amy Wlodarski. Kevin Bartig and Leah Goldman, also crucial comrades, make writing about artistic power and social networks in the East a delight. The fierce group of scholars working on Polish music has been a rewarding audience for portions of this work: Bolesław Błaszczyk, Kasia Naliwajek-Mazurek, Nicholas Reyland, Adrian Thomas, David Tompkins. Sprawling email conversations with Lisa Cooper Vest and Lisa Jakelski energize me always.

Musical Solidarities developed out of a stubborn attempt to hear history out of cassette tapes. A number of shrewd interlocutors pushed my thinking broadly: Dariusz Brzostek, Zeynep Bulut, Delia Casadei, Amy Cimini, Wolfgang Ernst, Brian Kane, Michael Heller, Farzaneh Hemmasi, Alexandra Hui, Peter McMurray, Jens Papenburg, Alexander Rehding, Shayna Silverstein, Jason Stanyek, Jonathan Sterne, Benjamin Tausig, Viktoria Tkaczyk, Gregory Weinstein, and Gavin Williams. I am grateful for the model of attention that Brigid Cohen and Ben Steege have brought to ideas and arguments as loud and quiet sounding boards through the years. Joshua Walden has always brought my attention back to wordplay and humor.

Suzanne Ryan and Jane Fulcher kept asking me questions about this book; as it became more real, their support and vision were instrumental to its final shape. It was a delight to entrust this project to Victoria Dixon at Oxford University Press. The manuscript's three anonymous readers made the writing, structure, and concept tighter and stronger; I am particularly moved by the care these scholars put into their comments. Ryan Dohoney, Michael Figueroa, Glenda Goodman, Hannah Lewis, and Ben Trott put individual chapters under the looking glass: our conversations about writing helped me hear myself anew. I am tremendously grateful for the workshop on the final chapter hosted by graduate students at Cornell University, whose keen ear for critical discourse pushed me to think about big stories out of small details.

Chapter 3 is based on my article, "Solidarity, Song, and the Sound Document," *Journal of Musicology* 33, no. 2 (2016), 232–69. I am grateful to the publishers for their permission to reprint this material.

This book would be unimaginable without people who care for me and build their lives out of conviction. In North Carolina, I have been fortunate to have friends who sustain me with their commitment to working toward a better world while making art and food. Zach Aliotta, Karen Auerbach, Petna Ndaliko, Tim Stallmann, and Ben Trott kept me thinking about real world concerns with dark wit and sparkling fantasy. Chérie Rivers Ndaliko probably has superhuman strength and passion; I cherish all the puzzles we take on together—artistic, athletic, intellectual, and agricultural. And the love and laughter of Uzuri Nation. In Berlin, Erik Albrecht, Lydia Barnett, Chris Geissler, Menaka Guruswamy, Andrew Tompkins, Ben Trott, and meLê Yamomo have filled my life with brilliant crossfires, insistent laughter, and lessons in compassion. Tuesday Bhambry transformed how I listen to and for voices forever; I am thankful for the journeys of our friendship. Meredith Schweig has taught me what loyal laughter is, always lacing hers with a balance of sipping tea, extraordinary stories, and deep empathy. With their clever wisdom and profound kindness, Vanessa Agnew and Kader Konuk reminded me of travel's power and gave the last chapter of this book a mission. *Musical Solidarities* kept me on the move, talking and questioning, but Glenda Goodman and Thomas Hilder were there wherever I went: their support I cherish as family. From the beginning I have cooked and hiked my way through new and old communities with Thom, shaping our musical solidarity at highs and lows along the way. I never take for granted Glenda's infinite thoughtful curiosity, insistence that the simple is beautiful, and fierce friendship.

I am still sure that long afternoons with my grandfather, Vilas Bohlman, let me articulate this book's questions for the first time. His memory inspires me always. Ben and Danielle Bohlman are inspirational dreamers; I cherish our shared laughter. My parents, Christine and Phil Bohlman, work through music, but it is their love, support, and deep kindness for which I am so humbly grateful. I dedicate this book to them.

ABBREVIATIONS

KOR   Workers' Defense Committee (Komitet Obrony Robotników)
NOWa   Independent Publishing House (Niezależna Oficyna
        Wydawnicza)
SB   Security Service (Służba Bezpieczeństwa)
PZPR   Polish United Workers' Party (Polska Zjednoczona Partia
        Robotnicza)
ZKP   Polish Composers' Union (Związek Kompozytorów Polskich)

ABOUT THE COMPANION WEBSITE

www.oup.com/us
Username: Music1
Password: Book5983

Musical Solidarities issues an invitation to listen in a myriad of ways. Readers will find a selection of audiovisual materials relevant to the project of listening to the Polish opposition to state socialism at a password-protected accompanying website hosted by Oxford University Press. These excerpts from radio broadcasts, bootleg recordings, and state propaganda—along with more traditional musical examples—are conceived of as another reconfiguration of each chapter's sound world. The recordings and videos are cued up at particular moments in the text with the icon ▶. Readers are also encouraged to consult longer performances and commercial recordings online and in libraries.

Musical Solidarities

1 Introduction

Action

I was privileged to be among the two thousand people who thronged into the plush interior of the Teatr Wielki *{Great Theatre} that evening. A huge red* SOLIDARNOŚĆ *logo hung above an otherwise bare stage, like a crucifix over an altar.*
—Timothy Garton Ash, The Polish Revolution

A group of Polish protesters stands beneath a white flag that bears the word "Solidarity" (*Solidarność*) in red spray paint: this is the iconic image of the Polish opposition to state socialism in the 1980s.[1] The single word hangs stretched across the crowd, placing those assembled on a stage and positing their unity. The banner colors the politics in the red and white of the Polish flag. The emblazoned slogan reclaims the ideologically loaded language of the Communist Party to critique the socialist state that regulated the People's Republic of Poland from 1944 until its dissolution in 1989. The participants—performers and protesters at once—are an animated community of action.

In August 1980, in Gdańsk, such a collective occupied the Lenin Shipyards and demanded the rights to form an independent labor union and to strike. For four hours on March 27, 1981, workers and members of the recently legalized union known as Solidarity (Solidarność) manifested in this mode again, taking on a nationwide strike to protest violent attacks on three of its members by the police and Security Service (SB, Służba Bezpieczeństwa) in Bydgoszcz eleven days earlier. On December 16, 1981,

---

1 Epigraph from Timothy Garton Ash, *The Polish Revolution: Solidarity*, 3rd ed. (New Haven, CT: Yale University Press, 2002), 90.

coal miners in Katowice stood in formation to protest the declaration of martial law three days earlier: nine were killed by the paramilitary forces of the Motorized Reserves of the Citizens Militia (Zmotoryzowane Odwody Milicji Obywatelskiej). In late October 1984, mourners held vigil in the streets surrounding St. Stanislaus Kostka Parish in Warsaw after Father Jerzy Popiełuszko, "Solidarity's chaplain," had disappeared, to be confirmed dead on October 30 at the hands of the SB. In early June 1987, Pope John Paul II sermonized to crowds in Gdynia, "I said: solidarity must precede the fight. I will say more: solidarity can also release the fight."[2] In the weeks leading up to the free elections on June 4, 1989, campaign posters across the nation replicated this image of protest to rally support for candidates running as members of the now-registered Solidarity Party.

A tidy vision of dissent, the visual icon indexes the euphoric and devastating moments of 1980s Poland. It suggests that the story of the triumph of the Polish opposition to state socialism is one of collective might against tremendous adversity, that "revolutionary rehearsals" beget political change from below.[3] It also opens one tableau of the theater piece, *On Mother and Fatherland* (*Utwór o matce i ojczyźnie,* 2008), by feminist literary activist Bożena Keff.[4] As the scene begins, the piece's chorus stands on guard beneath a banner. This ensemble has performed the role of a Greek chorus, interjecting and exhorting as the protagonists, a mother and daughter, revisit storied moments of Polish history in the twentieth century. To flag, motto, and color, Keff adds sound. The chorus members' voices revitalize the sounds of Solidarity's masses into motion on stage, as they begin speaking, according to the stage directions, "in canon."

Through subtle musical instruction, Keff draws attention to the theatricality of the moment, interpreting popular protest as a mosaic of individual political actors. The chorus breaks the silence of the frozen image through cacophony. What is presented as a stoic image of unity becomes, through sound, a confusing and noisy din of catchphrases projecting instability.[5] The

---

2 *Mówię o was i za was: Trzecia pielgrzymka Jana Pawła II do Ojczyzny* (Warsaw: Wydawnictwo Pelikan, 1988), 144. Unless otherwise noted, translations from Polish are by Tul'si (Tuesday) Bhambry. In general I have quoted from published English translations when available.

3 Colin Barker, ed., *Revolutionary Rehearsals* (Chicago: Bookmarks, 1987).

4 The epigraph from the scene reads, "Trade unions against slavery: CHORUS with 'Solidarity' flag begins in canon." See Bożena Keff, *Utwór o matce i ojczyźnie* (Cracow: ha!art Corporation, 2008), 31.

5 René Lück's 2005 art installation at the contemporary art gallery housed at the Lenin Shipyards today similarly urges a reading of Solidarity as performative. In "Rock gegen Rechts" (Rock against the Right), he recalls the rock concerts hosted by trade unions in Germany in solidarity with Solidarity in the early 1980s. At the same time, the piece allows for a quirky reimagination of the assembled crowds of 1980; http://www.

chorus's text also creates friction of a particular nature: Keff assigns the chorus an anti-Semitic screed. They amplify a critique of Solidarity recapitulated across the far right in twenty-first-century Poland by calling out its Jewish leaders. Keff's instruction to organize in "canon" also highlights her technique as a playwright. She criticizes historical canons and the stronghold they exert on public consciousness by paying attention to—replicating, echoing, distorting, amplifying—the myths and symbols out of which they are constituted. Through blasphemous and aggressive poetic language, Keff emphasizes the danger of triumphant history and is frustrated with conventional interpretations of the recent Polish past across *On Mother and Fatherland*. In *Musical Solidarities*, I hear, heed, and echo such demands to re-examine, deconstruct, and complicate Polish history by letting its materials resound. I ask readers to listen with me.

When Keff adds sound to the iconic image, the stability of its symbolic language comes undone. The exclamation point at the end of the *Communist Manifesto* that rouses action—"unite!"—becomes a signal that is much more difficult to interpret, organize, and act upon. She grounds the powerful organizing force of "solidarity" for political action, with its legacy in Marxist thought, in the historical complexity of Poland's "Solidarity."[6] In doing so, she takes seriously the social movement's continued cultural meaning and pushes back against the kind of teleological narrative laid out in resistance-oriented narratives like the one I teased out of crowd scenes as I riffed on her tableau.[7]

It is easy to be enticed by such stories of grassroots power, particularly from a Western perspective, where the promise of movements like Solidarity fueled ideas about "living in truth" during the Cold War.[8] At the same time,

---

wyspa.iq.pl/index.php?picture_id=149&parent_id=44&menu_id=1. Unless otherwise noted, all web sources were last accessed July 10, 2018.

6 For an overview of theories of solidarity in European political theory, see Steinar Stjernø, *Solidarity in Europe: The History of an Idea* (Cambridge: Cambridge University Press, 2004), 42–59.

7 Keff's is far from the only voice to criticize a monolithic treatment of identity and Solidarity. Examples of critiques of homosocial treatments of the Polish opposition include Shana Penn, *Solidarity's Secret: The Women Who Defeated Communism in Poland* (Ann Arbor: University of Michigan Press, 2005); and Padraic Kenney, "The Gender of Resistance in Communist Poland," *American Historical Review* 104 (1999), 399–425. For the still understudied anti-Semitism of Polish politics in the 1980s, see, for example, David Ost, *The Defeat of Solidarity: Anger and Politics in Postcommunist Europe* (Ithaca, NY: Cornell University Press, 2005), 60–93; and Adam Michnik, ed., *Przeciw antysemityzmowi 1936–2009*, vol. 3 (Cracow: Towarzystwo Autorów i Wydawców Prac Naukowych Universitas, 2010).

8 Jonathan Bolton, *Worlds of Dissent: Charter 77, the Plastic People of the Universe, and Czech Culture under Communism* (Cambridge, MA: Harvard University Press, 2012), 3.

the harrowing totalitarian politics of the twentieth century—through which Poland sat on the European fault line—have also conditioned a certain unease about collective action. As Hannah Arendt wrote in *On Revolution*: "The political trouble which misery of the people holds in store is that manyness can in fact assume the guise of oneness, that suffering indeed breeds moods and emotions and attitudes that resemble solidarity to the point of confusion."[9] The power of nation to cohere, the ability of the chorus to organize, the potential of the slogan to simplify: these are some of the fundamental features of twentieth-century social movements in the West.[10] But they are also necessary myths to cohere heterogenous actors as they negotiate across difference while working toward political change, what sociologist Asef Bayat calls "imagined solidarities."[11]

Solidarity orients discussions of musical communities, large-scale organization, and social integration.[12] The concept can speak to performance, articulating, for example, the interaction among diasporic musical communities or the relationship between an individual musician and the ensemble. "Musical solidarity" in these cases might refer to music's exceptional place as a mediator of togetherness, or the existence of shared music in the absence of social unity—one thinks, for example, of the West-East Divan Orchestra.[13] In music, the term imbues positive attributes upon the case study to which it is applied, or it captures optimism among the musicians and listeners who invoke it. One of the defining aspects of solidarity as it is used in contemporary culture, then, is the open-ended possibility that it suggests. The simplistic social optimism resonates in the designs for and analyses of protest anthems as catalytic sparks for unity against oppression.[14]

See also David Eugster and Sibylle Marti, "Das Imaginäre des Kalten Krieges," in *Das Imaginäre des Kalten Krieges: Beiträge zu einer Kulturgeschichte des Ost-West-Konfliktes in Europa* (Essen: Klartext, 2015), 3–17.

9 Hannah Arendt, *On Revolution* (London: Penguin Books, 1990 [1963]), 94.

10 Alberto Melucci, *Challenging Codes: Collective Action in the Information Age* (Cambridge: Cambridge University, 1996), 20–34.

11 Asef Bayat, "Islamism and Social Movement Theory," *Third World Quarterly* 26, no. 6 (2005), 901–5.

12 Gaye Theresa Johnson, *Spaces of Conflict, Sounds of Solidarity: Music, Race, and Spatial Enlightenment in Los Angeles* (Berkeley: University of California Press, 2013).

13 Rachel Beckles Willson, "Whose Utopia? Perspectives on the West-Eastern Divan Orchestra," *Music and Politics* 3, no. 2 (2009), http://quod.lib.umich.edu/m/mp/9460447.0003.201?view=text;rgn=main.

14 Eric Drott tracks the emphasis in the popular press on anthems contra other "sounds of contention" in twenty-first-century movements like Occupy and the Jasmine Revolution. See Eric Drott, "Resistance and Social Movements," in *The Routledge Reader on the Sociology of Music*, edited by Kyle Devine and John Shepherd (New York: Routledge, 2015), 171–79.

In *Musical Solidarities*, I take inspiration from the method I read out of Keff's *On Mother and Fatherland*. I consider the sounds and musics of the Polish opposition to state socialism, a political history that has been examined and championed many times, but never from the perspective of music studies.[15] The many modes, sounds, and media across this study profile a significant musical presence on the political stage in the final decade of the People's Republic of Poland. At the same time, this is no traditional history of music in Poland. Since the Cold War, Polish music—whether the avant-garde, jazz, or punk rock scenes—has frequently been held up as the triumphant exception to the assumption that Soviet-style communism squelched creative freedoms. In recent years, scholars have made strides to explain the institutional mechanisms behind and creative effects of the dynamic scenes generated by, as examples, the Warsaw Autumn Festival, Jazz Jamboree, and Jarocin Festival to show the value of music for the Party's cultural diplomacy, aesthetics for the intelligentsia, and rock for a burgeoning market-driven economy.[16] This scholarship is illuminating for and invaluable to the present study, but my methods diverge. Rather than beginning with music, I position the opposition itself as a site for the creation, performance, and theorization of aural culture. I sound out the canonic narrative of Solidarity by returning to the opposition's archives (of sound recordings and written material), approaching its contemporary resonance through fieldwork (at concerts and protests in twenty-first-century Poland), and following its media networks (AP reports and cassettes) across borders.

I argue that sound mattered to the Polish opposition to state socialism in the 1980s: that music both unified and splintered Solidarity *at once*. It is this "at once," like the canonic recitation in Keff's scene, that keeps music's plurality and the social movement's contingent social formations in dynamic tension. Put differently, I draw out—but in the process underscore—what Eric Drott maintains as "the fragility of musical and political alliances."[17] My use of the term "political action" draws on the importance of action in social

---

15 Andrzej Paczkowski, *Revolution and Counterrevolution in Poland, 1980–1989*, translated by Christine Manetti (Rochester, NY: University of Rochester Press, 2015); Jack M. Bloom, *Seeing through the Eyes of the Polish Revolution: Solidarity and the Struggle against Communism in Poland* (Leiden: Brill, 2016); Ash, *The Polish Revolution*.

16 Lisa Jakelski, "Pushing Boundaries: Mobility at the Warsaw Autumn International Festival of Contemporary Music," *East European Politics and Societies and Cultures* 29, no. 1 (2015), 189–211; Lisa Cooper Vest, "Educating Audiences, Educating Composers: The Polish Composers' Union and *Upowszechnienie*," *Musicology Today* 7 (2010), 226–42; Raymond Patton, "The Communist Culture Industry: The Music Business in 1980s Poland," *Journal of Contemporary History* 47, no. 2 (2012), 427–49.

17 Eric Drott, *Music and the Elusive Revolution: Cultural Politics and Politics of Culture in France, 1968–81* (Berkeley: University of California Press, 2011), 8.

movement theory, from Marxian class action to Durkheim's fundamentally social collective action. But it also avoids discourses of intentionality that would fix certain individuals as more politically minded than others (i.e., activists, a term that is eschewed in Polish in favor of *działacz*, from the verb meaning to operate or work) or direct attention to the political efficacy of musical performances, compositions, or other events. *Musical Solidarities* is not a history of Polish music through its activist musicians or a history of the Polish opposition as it affected music in Poland. Instead, *Musical Solidarities* is a music history of a social movement.

The Polish Opposition

Western onlookers sought out and celebrated vocal nonconformists as dissidents, but the keyword in the Polish context is "opposition" (*opozycja*).[18] The founder of the Committee for Workers' Defense (Komitet Obrony Robotników), Jacek Kuroń, set the discursive tenor in the late 1970s. As a committed socialist, Kuroń redirected the efforts of those protesting the government's efficacy toward "rebuilding civil society and ignoring the state sphere."[19] In his pre-Solidarity articles, "The Political Opposition in Poland" (1974) and "The State's Status and the Program of the Opposition" (1979), it was Kuroń who co-opted the term "opposition" for the broad and culturally mobilized networks of church groups, humanitarian organizations, student radicals, underground presses, nationalist clubs, and dissident organizations.[20] As a gloss for a movement with its origins in humanitarian aid, the label "opposition" was inclusive and indicative of a vague allegiance—Maryjane Osa has characterized it as a "middle path" between right and left—rather than a specific action or politics.[21] The Culture Department of the Central Committee of the Polish United Workers' Party (Polska Zjednoczona Partia Robotnicza, PZPR) elided Solidarity with the "opposition" through the 1980s within its paperwork.[22] When the opposition coalesced to coordinate

18 Jonathan Bolton, *Worlds of Dissent: Charter 77, The Plastic People of the Universe, and Czech Culture under Communism* (Cambridge, MA: Harvard University Press, 2012).

19 David Ost, *Solidarity and the Politics of Anti-Politics: Opposition and Reform in Poland since 1968* (Philadelphia: Temple University Press, 1991), 39.

20 Reprinted as "Sytuacja w kraju a program opozycji" and "Polityczna opozycja w Polsce" in Jacek Kuroń, *Opozycja: Pisma Polityczne 1969–1989*, edited by Michał Sutowski, Maciej Kropiwinicki, and Sebastian Liszka (Warsaw: Wydawnictwo Krytyki Politycznej, 2010), 180–85 and 40–57.

21 Maryjane Osa, *Solidarity and Contention: Networks of Polish Opposition* (Minneapolis: University of Minnesota Press, 2003), 133.

22 See in particular the folders collated on artistic participation, LVI 1408–17, WK PZPR, Archive of Modern Acts (AAN), Warsaw, Poland.

nationwide strikes in the summer of 1980, it became, according to Andrzej Walicki, a "mass movement."[23] By the end of the decade, a veritable "carnival of revolutions," to use Padraic Kenney's term, dispelled any sense of a shared direction or target for Polish oppositional energy.[24] "Opposition" is thus a necessarily nebulous network—enacted and re-enacted—that I employ here as a gesture toward inclusion, rather than as a label that delineates boundaries, valorizes heroes, or privileges "direct action."[25] Jan Józef Lipski, another founding member of the Committee for Workers' Defense, valued the opposition's indistinct presence and porosity when he conceded in 1977: "Still, it is better that things be this way than that a wall exist cutting the active opposition off from those latent social energies which sooner or later will be released."[26]

The position of the People's Republic of Poland *between* the capitalist and communist spheres of influence is a symptom of historical trauma (see Figure I.1). The nation's location on the border between the West and the East has long challenged the notion of a clearly bounded European history. Already in the sixteenth century, Erasmus wrestled with contradicting barbarism and cultural productivity in the Polish kingdom on the peripheries of civilization.[27] As historian Larry Wolff has shown, Enlightenment travelers understood the land east of the Oder River and extending up the Baltic Coast as a space between the fortress of European civilization and the terrain of barbarism. From 1791 to 1918, the Russian, Prussian, and Austro-Hungarian imperial powers controlled Poland under partition. Following the Nazi and Soviet invasions of independent Poland in September 1939, the Molotov-Ribbentrop Pact divided the nation again. After the Second World War, the Iron Curtain defined this terrain both "in the mind and on the map."[28] Historian Tony Judt, noting the elision of East Central Europe—what

---

23 Andrzej Walicki, "The Three Traditions in Polish Patriotism and Their Contemporary Relevance" (Bloomington, IN: The Polish Studies Center, 1988), 15.

24 Padraic Kenney, *A Carnival of Revolution: Central Europe 1989* (Princeton, NJ: Princeton University Press, 2002), 10.

25 Padraic Kenney, "Opposition Networks and Transnational Diffusion," in *Transnational Moments of Change: Europe 1945, 1968, 1989*, edited by Gerd-Rainer Horn and Padraic Kenney (Lanham, MD: Rowman & Littlefield, 2004), 207–23. On politics and musical heroism, see Nomi Dave, "The Politics of Silence: Music, Violence and Protest in Guinea," *Ethnomusicology* 58, no. 1 (2014), 26–29. "Direct action" includes sit-ins, boycotts, civil disobedience; see T. V. Reed, *The Art of Protest: Culture and Activism from the Civil Rights Movement to the Streets of Seattle* (Minneapolis: University of Minnesota Press, 2005), xviii.

26 Quoted in Osa, *Solidarity and Contention*, 153.

27 Larry Wolff, *Inventing Eastern Europe: The Map of Civilization on the Mind of the Enlightenment* (Stanford, CA: Stanford University Press, 1994), 10.

28 Wolff, *Inventing Eastern Europe*, 1.

FIGURE I.I. 1982 CIA map of Poland, indicating provincial capitals.

Timothy Snyder calls the Bloodlands—from twentieth-century histories, stipulates that "the history of the two halves of post-war Europe cannot be told in isolation from one another."[29] My own focus on Poland, following Judt, underscores the place's potential to unsettle Europe's musical geography.[30] I also zero in on the Polish case, occasionally eschewing the temptation

---

29 Timothy Snyder, *Bloodlands: Europe between Hitler and Stalin* (New York: Basic Books, 2010); Tony Judt, *Postwar: A History of Europe since 1945* (New York: Penguin Press, 2005), 5.

30 Musicologists who have mentioned Judt explicitly include Rachel Beckles Willson in her *Ligeti, Kurtág, and Hungarian Music during the Cold War* (Cambridge: Cambridge University Press, 2007), 2; Kevin C. Karnes, "Recollecting Jewish Musics from the Baltic Bloodlands," *Acta Musicologica* 84, no. 2 (2011), 254; and Peter J. Schmelz, "Music in the Cold War," *Journal of Musicology* 26, no. 1 (2009), 8.

to spin the stories transnationally, to insist that local and everyday experiences shaped the symbolic work, discursive nuance, and aural cultures of Solidarity. In musicology, too, the hotspots of postwar music histories have focused, with their attention to the Axis and Allied powers of the Second World War—particularly West Germany, the Soviet Union, and the United States—on music as what Nicholas Tochka calls a "Cold War form of knowledge," a means of, first and foremost, constituting East and West as different and antipodal.[31]

For the opposition, nation mattered; the discourses of Polish nationalism push and pull through *Musical Solidarities*. As much as Poles' vision for civic reform was inspired by looking to the west—across the Iron Curtain—and to the south—to the rest of East Central Europe—the movement's core quest was for sovereignty. Likewise, administrators and cultural organizers developed projects focused on Polishness, carrying out the celebration of Nazi Germany's defeat and a rebuilt Poland as long as concatenations of national holidays would permit. This obsession with (re)defining and (re)confirming the self hides a troubling silence with respect to "contaminating" others, whether powerful Soviet military forces, ethnic minorities who laid claim to Polish lands, or the many individuals with Jewish heritage prominent in the opposition. Further work on the musical solidarities that animated alternative, anarchic, and queer subcultures—discourses frequently trampled out of the public spaces that are the focus of this book—remains to be done. A repeating mantra of Poland for Poland's sake focused discourse on the Self in some of the opposition's loudest moments. Through *Musical Solidarities* I take seriously this refrain's power, then and now, though I work to always be suspicious of their dominance. Crucial for this work is the juxtaposition—and inherent contradiction—of ethnographic and archival methods I employ to sound out Solidarity. Take the following sensationalist media assemblage—a song that connects Solidarity's high in August 1980 with its low in December 1981—as an example.

"Let Poland Be Poland"

On December 13, 1981, the Polish premier, General Wojciech Jaruzelski, set a police state into motion when he declared martial law in Poland. He did so out of what he framed as an "obligation to Poland's future."[32] The

---

31 Nicholas Tochka, "Pussy Riot, Freedom of Expression, and Popular Music Studies after the Cold War," *Popular Music* 32, no. 2 (2013), 303–11.

32 Wojciech Jaruzelski, "Nadeszła godzina ciężkiej próby!," address from December 12, 1981.

arrest and detainment of Solidarity's leaders, the imposition of a curfew, and the right to search individuals at will, Jaruzelski claimed, would forestall an invasion by Soviet tanks, a specter haunting the Eastern Bloc since the Prague Spring.[33] In his television address, which was also broadcast on the radio, printed throughout the country's papers, and stapled to public information boards, Jaruzelski concluded with a submission to "the whole Polish nation and the entire world" framed as subjunctive. He quoted the first lines of the Polish national anthem: "Poland has not yet perished as long as we remain alive" ▶.

The US Information Agency took Jaruzelski's gesture toward a global television audience for his address to the next level. They looked to the skies to stage a dramatic demonstration of solidarity with the Polish Solidarity movement. Charles Wick, the head of the Agency, saw the Polish government's intervention in "freedom" as an opportunity to produce what he called a "television spectacular"—to be live-broadcast (for the first time) on satellite around the world.[34] Wick, who had cut his teeth in the entertainment industry as an arranger and manager for the Tommy Dorsey Orchestra before making his way into politics via Ronald Reagan, envisioned a collaboration between Hollywood celebrities, Polish émigrés in North America, and world leaders.

The $500,000 production was broadcast to 184 million people in 46 countries on January 31, 1982.[35] The show bombards viewers with visual representations of Poland that gradually modulate from technicolor shots of charming palatial glory to gripping still portraits of everyday people and a productive industry ▶. Scenes of protests from Solidarity's successes—variations on the theme of Keff's tableau—are juxtaposed with those of citizens waiting in long lines to buy nothing from empty stores. Frédéric Chopin's A major Polonaise, "Military" (Op. 40, No. 1), scores the swift slide show. Then, a cannon shot is synchronized with the cut to black. A third martial sound, a pattering drum cadence, accompanies black-and-white images of tanks on streets, Jaruzelski in characteristic black glasses and military get-up presides over troops and weary citizens, their faces lined with wrinkles and bundled in winter scarves. Charlton Heston delivers a pathos-filled voice-over that morphs into direct address from a dark stage buttressed by candles:

---

33 A. Kemp-Welch, *Poland under Communism: A Cold War History* (Cambridge: Cambridge University Press, 2008), 302–32.

34 Alvin A. Snyder, *Warriors of Disinformation: How Lies, Videotape, and the USIA Won the Cold War* (New York: Arcade, 1995), 5–11.

35 The US Embassy in Warsaw has uploaded the complete video: https://www.youtube.com/watch?v=T5avzxLrBUY.

A light has been extinguished in Poland, but it still burns in the hearts of the Polish people. Tonight we are lighting a candle for the people of Poland. We're sending its light across the world to shine on their struggle and their suffering. To show them we believe their love of freedom will never die. As part of the International Day of Solidarity with the people of Poland we send them this message behind their wall of silence. In this time of despair we hold out this candle of hope. [*drum roll*] "Let Poland Be Poland": A program transmitted this evening across the world.

This is Cold War propaganda at its most obvious: the Polish people, Charlton Heston would have us believe, are frozen behind the Iron Curtain, trapped in silence. The belliphonic sounds position the people of Poland as "listening through war" and set the tone for that devastating metaphor: this is a message sent "behind the wall of silence."[36] A title screen drives the program's simple message home (Figure I.2).

A simple byproduct of this book—and indeed the now-established field of Cold War Studies within music—is to counter the cultural work of such loud and widely circulated rhetoric through close listening to historical materials in order to rebuke the notion of a Soviet veil of silence over Eastern Europe. In recent years, filling in the musicological blind spots brought about by the "Cold War" has been a fundamentally compensatory project of articulating activity, aesthetics, and agency in Eastern Europe and the Soviet Union. Historical musicologists have unearthed and examined the energy, values, and production of avant-garde scenes and art-music communities.[37] Ethnomusicologists and popular music scholars have taken the popular music engaged in socialist projects seriously on questions of circulation, subjectivity, and sentimentality.[38] Most follow György Peteri's suggestion that the Iron Curtain might be better imagined as cast in nylon: somewhat porous in both directions.[39] In step, this robust

---

36 J. Martin Daughtry, *Listening to War: Sound, Music, Trauma, and Survival in Wartime Iraq* (New York: Oxford University Press, 2015), 33–36.

37 Rachel Beckles Willson, *Ligeti, Kurtág, and Hungarian Music*; Joy H. Calico, *Arnold Schoenberg's* A Survivor from Warsaw *in Postwar Europe* (Berkeley: University of California Press, 2014); Elaine Kelly, *Composing the Canon in the German Democratic Republic: Narratives of Nineteenth-Century Music* (Oxford: Oxford University Press, 2014); and Peter Schmelz, *Such Freedom, If Only Musical: Unofficial Soviet Music during the Thaw* (New York and Oxford: Oxford University Press, 2009).

38 David MacFadyen, *Red Stars: Personality and the Soviet Popular Song, 1955–1991* (Montreal: McGill-Queen's University Press, 2001); Nicholas Tochka, *Audible States: Socialist Politics and Popular Music in Albania* (Oxford and New York: Oxford University Press, 2016).

39 György Peteri, "Nylon Curtain—Transnational and Transsystemic Tendencies in the Cultural Life of State-Socialist Russia and East-Central Europe," *Slavonica* 10, no. 2 (2004), 113–23.

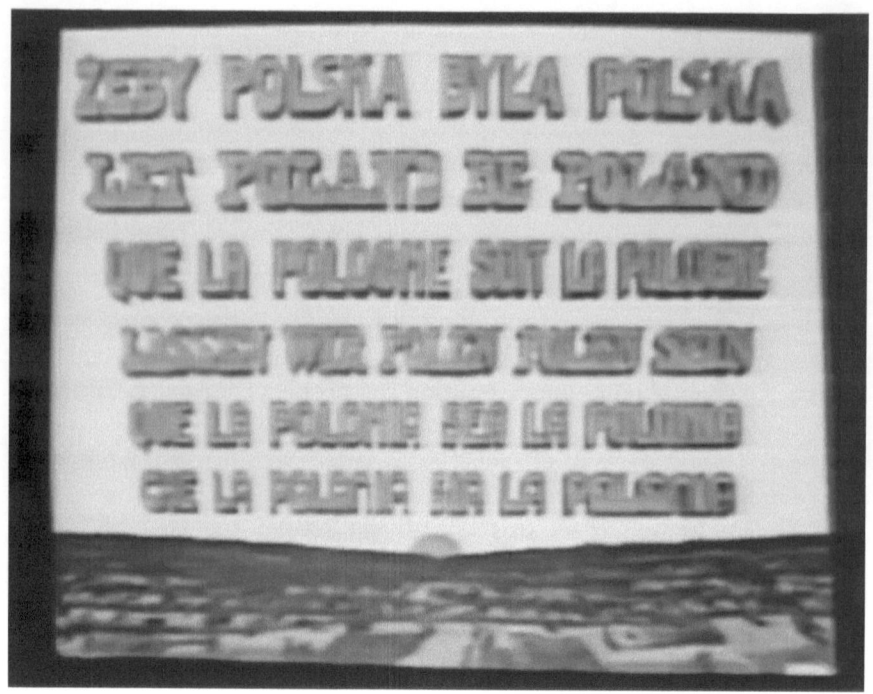

FIGURE I.2. Title screen for the US Information Agency's "Let Poland Be Poland" (1981).

scholarship has made a strong case that studying the Cold War is part and parcel of studying power in and through music—not to mention the power of music—into the twenty-first century.⁴⁰

Heard through Polish media networks, the American broadcast cues up some of the most cherished sounds of the 1980s. Chopin's warhorse polonaise had been the chime that heralded the evening news on Polish Radio from its first broadcast in 1925 through the twentieth century ▶. In the local context, these "well-known chords" were well-calibrated to pull at listeners' heartstrings.⁴¹ And Wick and his team lifted the very special episode's title,

---

40 A crucial example here is Guntis Šmidchens's study of the "Singing Revolution" to liberate the Balkan states from Soviet rule. This study, which draws on fieldwork, oral history, and literary analysis, positions song and song festivals as the driving motor of solidarity. While the Polish opposition did communicate and coordinate with (primarily) Lithuanian colleagues, the music and sound histories happened within the bounds of language. Guntis Šmidchens, *The Power of Song: Nonviolent National Culture in the Baltic Revolution* (Seattle and London: University of Washington Press, 2014).

41 Maciej Józef Kwiatkowski, *Wrzesień 1939 w Warszawskiej rozgłośni Polskiego Radia* (Warsaw: Państwowy Instytut Wydawniczy, 1984), 17.

EXAMPLE I.1. Jan Pietrzak, "So That Poland Will Be Poland" (1976), closing refrain.

"Let Poland Be Poland," from a cabaret anthem that, in many ways, has a history that captures the precarious oneness of Solidarity. Frank Sinatra balked at learning the song's text for that evening's program—instead, the credit music is his canned recording of "Ever Homeward/Wolne Serce," which he insisted was "based on a Polish folksong," for the 1948 film *The Miracle of Bells.*

Within the show we hear the sung refrain of the cabaret anthem, Jan Pietrzak's "Let Poland Be Poland," perhaps better translated as a rallying cry to enjoin people to stand together: "So That Poland Will Be Poland" ("Żeby Polska była Polską," 1976). As the gentle and a cappella chorus transcribed in Example I.1 swells, Heston stands in front of Solidarity's logo—another mediation of Keff's tableau (Figure I.3). The stately composition by Włodzimierz Korcz has a simple sincerity that stands out in a performance tradition that foregrounds irony and subversion. But Pietrzak's text also articulates the appeal of a collective, and the refrain's internal repetition (Poland as subject and object), as well as its obsessive rearticulation (five times at the end of each verse), implicates those singing in the nationalist cause. As a journalist who heard the song performed live by its author in Gdańsk in August 1981 recalled, "I stood at attention when Jan Pietrzak stood at attention and pleaded that Poland could be Poland."[42] Time marches through the song's narrative as Pietrzak aligns generations, dynasties, cities, and ideals, projecting a teleological vision of Polish history that, in a critical move, addresses his audience as a part of that fabric. Pietrzak gives inevitability a positive spin, implying that Solidarity is just the beginning, providing the opposition with utopian valence ▶.

---

42 Przemysław Ćwikliński, "Zembaty za kraty," *Nie* 37 (2001), 3.

FIGURE I.3. Charlton Heston while serenaded by Jan Pietrzak's "So That Poland Will Be Poland."

First verse:
Z głębi dziejów, z krain mrocznych,   From the depths of history, from the shadowy lands,
Puszcz odwiecznych, pól i stepów,   From primeval wildernesses, fields, and steppes,
Nasz rodowód, nasz początek,   Our origins, our beginning,
Hen od Piasta, Kraka, Lecha.   Far from Piast, Krak, and Lech.
Długi łańcuch ludzkich istnień   Long concatenations of human existence
Połączonych myślą prostą.   Joined through straight thought.

Refrain:
Żeby Polska, żeby Polska!   So that Poland, so that Poland!
Żeby Polska była Polską!   So that Poland will be Poland!

Final verse:
Matki, żony w mrocznych izbach   Mothers, wives in darkened homes
Wyszywały na sztandarach   Embroidered on flags
Hasło: "Honor i Ojczyzna"   The slogan: "Honor and Fatherland"
I ruszała w pole wiara.   And into the fields spread faith
I ruszała wiara w pole   And faith spread into the fields
Od Chicago do Tobolska.   From Chicago to Tobolsk.

Jan Pietrzak, the forty-something leader of Warsaw's "Cabaret Under the Aegis" (Kabaret pod Egidą), had experienced intermittent censorship because of his cabaret's bullying parody of the Party. In 1977 he was officially removed from the Party's blacklist.[43] It was at this point that he began concluding his cabaret evenings with the performance of "So That Poland Will Be Poland." In his autobiography, Pietrzak also draws attention to the dramaturgy of the refrain in these dark times: "The choral production, quite slow, with hushed voices, made the whole thing complete. The audience, who would bring tape decks to our performances, recorded the whole program. Thus our piece spread across Poland. Copied from tape to tape, the technological quality often suffered, but not the message."[44]

There is material history of this affective atmosphere.[45] During the strikes in August 1980 and through the months of the trade union's legal existence, Pietrzak's hit circulated on tape and in print (Figure I.4).[46] Video recordings from the Cabaret Under the Aegis from 1980 usher the collective into the limelight: as the melody descends in sequence, the band stops playing and the spotlight moves from Pietrzak to his ensemble, dressed in street clothes.[47] The gentle repetition of *"Polska"* and *"Polską"*—the Poland of the past and future—emerges as a metonymic insistence on their collective embodiment of the real nation. It was Pietrzak who capped the concert at the Grand Theatre in Warsaw on November 10, 1980, when the Supreme Court's ratification of the Gdańsk Agreement legalized Solidarity, solidifying the song as an anthem. Timothy Garton Ash's description of this event, the epigraph for this introduction, dwells on the powerful simplicity of the musical message.[48]

In August 1981 Pietrzak sang the song standing in the middle of Warsaw's busiest intersection, that of Marszałkowska Street and Jerozolimskie Avenue, just two blocks from the seat of the Party's Central Committee. In the crooner's own account, crowds flooded the streets and stopped traffic. "All of Warsaw sang with me," he described in a 2009 interview.[49] Julia Czarnecka remembered the performance as similarly momentous, but emphasized that

43 *The Black Book of Polish Censorship* (New York: Vintage Books, 1984), 405–8.

44 Jan Pietrzak, *Jak obaliłem komunę* (Łomianki: Wydawnictwo LTW, 2010), 91.

45 Ben Anderson, *Encountering Affect: Capacities, Apparatuses, Conditions* (London: Routledge, 2014).

46 "Flugschriften, Flugblätter, Dokumente aus dem poln. zweiten Umlauf," FSO-2-003, Archiv der Forschungsstelle Osteuropa an der Universität Bremen, Bremen, Germany.

47 *Kabaret pod Egidą: Sezon słynny '80.* DVD, Telewizja Polska S.A., 2009.

48 Garton Ash, *The Polish Revolution*, 90.

49 Quoted in "Prawda w żartach zawarta: Z Janem Pietrzakiem, twórcą Kabaretu pod Egidą rozmawia Patrycja Gruszyńska-Ruman," *Biuletyn IPN* 7 (2008), 16.

>   *Jan Pietrzak*
>
> ### ŻEBY POLSKA
>
> | | |
> |---|---|
> | *Z głębi dziejów, z krajów mrocznych,* | *Zrzucał uczeń portret cara,* |
> | *Puszcz odwiecznych, pól i stepów* | *Ksiądz Ściegienny wznosił modły,* |
> | *Nasz rodowód, nasz początek,* | *Opatrywał wóz Drzymała,* |
> | *Hen od Piasta, Kraka, Lecha.* | *Dumne wiersze pisał Norwid.* |
> | *Długi łańcuch ludzkich istnień* | *I kto szablę mógł utrzymać* |
> | *Połączony myślą prostą:* | *Ten formował legion, wojsko!* |
> | *Żeby Polska, żeby Polska,* | *Żeby Polska, żeby Polska,* |
> | *Żeby Polska, była Polską.* | *Żeby Polska była Polską.* |
> | | |
> | *Wtedy, kiedy los nieznany* | *Matki, żony w mrocznych izbach* |
> | *Rozsypywał nas po kątach,* | *Wyszywały na sztandarach* |
> | *Kiedy obce wiatry gnały* | *Hasło: „Honor i Ojczyzna"* |
> | *Obce orły na proporcach,* | *I ruszała wiara w pole.* |
> | *Przy ogniskach wybuchała* | *I ruszała w pole wiara* |
> | *Niezamożna nuta swojska,* | *Od Chicago do Tobolska,* |
> | *Żeby Polska, żeby Polska,* | *Żeby Polska, żeby Polska,* |
> | *Żeby Polska była Polską.* | *Żeby Polska była Polską.* |
>
> NSZZ „SOLIDARNOŚĆ"

FIGURE 1.4. "So That Poland Will Be Poland," in circulation by Solidarity. Archiv der Forschungsstelle Osteuropa an der Universität Bremen, FSO 02-003-K30-124.

the streets were just as much a staging area for the work of the opposition as they were a musical stage:

> The atmosphere in the square was like on a popular holiday. Jacek Fedorowicz and Jan Pietrzak performed on stage. Thousands of Varsovians were with us, despite the sweltering heat. We received huge amounts of food, from private individuals and from the nearby hotels, Metropol and Forum, which are always happy to help. The first Ikarus bus flanking the street had a well-stocked bar. The second Ikarus was a meeting room. For the managers and leaders of the action. Then came a Berliet—the press and information point. The next Ikarus was for first aid. Farther down the street the crowd got thinner, especially as a voice from the stage doesn't reach far.[50]

As for a trace of that loud performance that mythically unfurled through Warsaw's avenues, "the whole city was blocked off," Pietrzak claims, "[but] there is no record of it." In the wake of uncaptured sound, accounts like Pietrzak's and Czarnecka's continue to fuel the looming presence of the song.

---

50 Quoted in Agnieszka Dębska, "Niezależna Samorządna," *Karta* 46 (2005), 41.

As the US Information Agency grabbed Pietrzak's slogan to make a propaganda point, so did many in Poland—and some critically. The amateur singer Jan Krzysztof Kelus scoffed at the cabaret's basic language and politically stunted message in a 1981 song. He sneers: "Poland with Poland about Poland / . . . good job Mr. Pietrzak."[51] A radio reporter for the regional station out of Szczecin complained on air about its presence as park-bench graffiti in the winter of 1982 as she tried to avoid taking a political stand. The real heroes in her eyes were local business operators, doing their best to obtain consumer goods. "No one has ever created prosperity with mere slogans—we've learned that from experience. I don't know what traitors the writer of that graffiti had in mind."[52]

In the twenty-first century, the sound bites of Solidarity's decade have increasingly been hurled to effect the violence of "excitable speech," particularly at ever more frequent rallies for the far right and across polarized media platforms.[53] In October 2016, the literary theorist Maria Janion mourned the work of shouting and the focus on Polishness, as in Pietrzak's anthem, when she offered guiding words to the hundreds of cultural organizers and political activists gathered at the Congress of Culture in Warsaw. Thirty-five years earlier, at the Congress of Polish Culture in December 1981, she had celebrated the vernacular poetry and songs of street protests and had urged the leaders of the opposition to take this creative energy seriously.[54] I heard Janion's open letter, in which she alluded to her past utilitarian optimism, read from the stage by Kazimiera Szczuka at the 2016 event:

> Thirty-six years have passed, and the vicious circle of Polishness comes full circle. . . . The culture of the state and church—and, let us add, of the military and hunters—draws on the opposition's little national songs of the 1980s. . . . The outcry, "This is Poland," honestly, I'm sick of it. I trust it will not be shouted today.[55]

---

51 "Polka z Polską o Polsce . . . bardzo dobrze panie Janku" in "Song at the Bus Stop" ("Na Przystanku PKS-u").

52 Paweł Szulc, ed., *Fikcja czy rzeczywistość?: Wybór audycji Polskiego Radia Szczecin z lat 1946–1989* (Szczecin: IPN, 2016), 457.

53 Judith Butler, *Excitable Speech: A Politics of the Performative* (New York: Routledge, 1997).

54 See Maria Janion, "Słowo i symbol w miesiącach przełomu," in *Kongres Kultury Polskiej, 11–13 grudnia 1981*, edited by Władysław Masiulanis (Warsaw: Oficyna Wydawnictwa Volumen Instytut Kultury, 2000), 37–44.

55 "Mesjanizm to przekleństwo: List Marii Janion do Kongresu Kultury," *Gazeta Wyborcza*, October 10, 2016; http://wyborcza.pl/7,75410,20813344,mesjanizm-to-przeklenstwo-list-marii-janion-do-kongresu-kultury.html.

The crowd applauded; the affective release of Janion's clear frustration and hopeful request for decorum had been palpable through the auditorium as people nodded along and interrupted with stray claps and cheers. The 2016 Congress, a forum for cultural organization and educational reform, was their space to avoid the street theaters where verbal violence was a weapon of exclusion. Like Janion, those gathered were both weary of loud self-proclamation and aware that their present was brewed in the cultural politics of their recent—and glorified—past. Try as they might, however, the teachers, artists, curators, and journalists could not clear that weekend's political action of sonic cacophony, of the disagreement that Keff resounded in canon. On the final Sunday morning of the meeting, a conversation about feminism broke down when a pro-life activist grandstanded during the question-and-answer period. The audience booed and clapped, trying to drown him out. The actress Maja Komorowska, a voice heard in the church concerts of Chapter 2, stood up to face the room, "We must listen to him! We cannot avoid this Poland!" she implored. There is a persistent stubbornness to Solidarity's aural cultures—songs persist, myths collude the quotidian, powerful individuals speak over others. There are also moments of sublime hope, intimate voices preserved in personal memories, and radical breaks that release humor and play. I learn from the fine grain of collective work that comes from the close reading of multimodal archival materials and absences. The particularity of sounding politics likewise emerges through fieldwork—careful attention to stories and songs as I overhear them, seek them out, and even prompt them in my present.

From Sound to Chorus

Musical Solidarities confronts the canonic songs, scenes, and figures of Solidarity while also approaching key concepts in social movement studies. Each chapter brings case studies from across the decade to bear on one vector that connects music and politics. In lieu of a chronological approach to the decade, I shape the study through a focus on sound, silence, protest, voice, megaphone, and chorus. As chapters, these concepts frame the modes in which music intersected with, generated, and fractured the opposition's culture. *Musical Solidarities* traces several theoretical trajectories: from the abstract to the concrete, from the individual and ideal to the communal, from the material to the embodied. None of these is linear or exclusive: I do not position music as necessarily instrumental, or politics as a consistent or privileged impetus for musical performance. Rather, the chapters' themes keep in tension the individual and the collective as well as the populist and the powerful. As I write and listen to twenty-first-century reverberations of this pivotal decade, I keep in play street sounds, celebrated anthems, and commemorative symphonies, paying attention to their transnational resonances and remediations.

The story begins in Chapter 1, "Sound," which lays out the tension between ideas about music's political efficacy and the actual work that sound did for opposition. I work with—read and listen to closely—archival materials: one tape of Stefan Bratkowski's *Sound Gazette* (1983–88), the print run of the oppositional journal *Independent Culture* (*Kultura Niezależna*), and the paperwork of the Communist Party. These position the pervasive claim that music was "asemantic" as a shared assumption across state institutions and the so-called second circulation (*drugi obieg*), the unofficial print culture that was similar to *samizdat* in the Soviet context. *Musical Solidarities* makes the case for the rigorous inclusion of sound archives in music historical work: oral histories, cassette/radio archives, documentary footage, and, of course, commercially produced sound recording. This first chapter shapes a broad understanding of aural culture in Poland that is foundational to this methodology. Oppositional work in sound (which includes music) circumvented mechanisms of the censorship bureau and stumped secret police surveillance. Sound archives also reveal the work of sound to organize and perform solidarity. I focus here on the cassette culture of the second circulation (1982–90): its founders' interest in tape contra print, transnational distribution, and alternative economies. As sounding artifacts, its cassettes reveal diverse repertories and creative editing techniques that belie the assumption that music was politically impotent for the opposition.

Chapter 2, "Silence," ushers the reader into the horrors of December 13, 1981, the day on which martial law was imposed upon Poland by its prime minister. I offer a three-pronged approach to writing the history of this significant date, based on accounts from 1981 to 1984. The violent incursion on everyday life, which lasted two years, was designed to curb the efforts of the Solidarity movement. It defined everyday life in the 1980s and continued to arouse tremendous fear after its economic curtailments and military patrols had been lifted by the mid-1980s. The sudden and confusing nature of this event stimulated music making that confronted historiographic silence in three zones: public streets, church sanctuaries and private homes, and internment camps/prisons. Oral histories, captured by members of the opposition, and diaries offer the opportunity to rehear the interplay between singing and military sounds during protests against martial law. Experimental scores, concert programs, and observational songs played in domestic salons push against the frequent assumption that martial law effected a cultural hold—a metaphorical silence. Finally, I analyze the material culture of music in detainment to argue that song—religious hymns, ballads, and legion songs—provided internees and prisoners the opportunity to reclaim authorship over their own history. Recordings by prisoners upon their release, in dialogue with those by the SB, reveal singing rituals; the personal archive of musicologist Małgorzata Pietkiewicz offers insight to the paper and tape preservation then and now. One song family, with all of its variants, shows the pluralistic potential of song to write histories. Music, I argue, was a mode of civil resilience that was never inactive, and a crucial means of conveying information and writing histories from below.

Successful nonviolent protests are the celebrated theaters of musical politics; the same is true for the month of protests that brought about the legalization of the Solidarity union, the first independent trade union in the Eastern bloc. Chapter 3, "Protest," takes the reader into the important role that sound media played both in coordinating efforts on the ground and in narrating the August 1980 strikes' power to a broader public in Poland and abroad. I compare written and recorded accounts of the protest scenes to show sound's coordinating power and music's entertainment value for this weeks-long occupational strike. Stories about politics gained authority as objective accounts when they included sound to frame the protests as vital and inclusive. Performances by one of the opposition's most charismatic representatives, Lech Wałęsa, also integrate singing on the political stage. The chapter critiques romantic notions of music and protest, of heroic bards who rally publics behind a cause, to dwell on questions of authorship and agency. I follow the rise of the opposition's protest anthem, "Walls" (1978), by singer-songwriter Jacek Kaczmarski, and highlight several political histories within its music and history. The song itself is ambivalent: it tells the story of an artist rallying crowds to fight injustice, but its narrative is ultimately pessimistic about the power of song to make change. While Kaczmarski sang it for the opposition in the early 1980s and approved its use as a signal for a main underground radio station during martial law (Radio Solidarity), he ultimately composed a counter-ballad ("Walls '87, in the Courtyard," 1987) that critiqued the opposition's thirst for an artist willing to sacrifice all for dissent.

Chapter 4, "Voice," opens up the presence of the Roman Catholic Church across the opposition. The symbols and rituals of Polish Catholicism structured much of the opposition's work and discourse, and the Polish Pope, John Paul II, brought the world's attention to their plight. One cherished spiritual leader, Father Jerzy Popiełuszko, is the focus. During martial law his weekly services on patriotic themes ("Masses for the Fatherland") were the central site for the opposition in Warsaw and beyond to meet, reflect, and organize. These came under scrutiny because of their power to amass crowds and their critique of the government. When Popiełuszko was violently murdered by the SB in late 1984, he became a martyr for the opposition across religious differences. The chapter presents a media archaeology of his voice to suggest that the priest's power lies at the nexus of sound technology, sound theology, and sound musicology. I am sensitive to his intonation of Polish-language chant and seek out its resonance in musical commemorations of his death in compositions by Krzysztof Knittel, Andrzej Panufnik, and Bryn Jones (aka Muslimgauze). Through my own sonic analysis, I offer the reader the opportunity to listen to his sermons (distributed on cassette), eavesdrop on his masses through the captures of the SB, and hear intimate recollections of his person. I draw on conversations with members of Popiełuszko's parish to analyze the hymn written for him and unpack his 1984 burial through ethnographic encounter at the 2009 re-enactment of his funeral. The portrait sprawls and shows how the opposition, as a media assemblage, was concerned with bodily vulnerability.

Chapter 5, "Megaphone," expands upon Popiełuszko's charisma to frame the stages that the most heroic figures of the opposition enjoyed and to examine the sonic amplification of their leadership. To consider the scope of sound—its volume—I bring together (1) the prominence of speeches and ceremonies as public interfaces for solidarity and (2) the importance of dramatic retellings of a violently squelched protest from 1970 for galvanizing energy through the two decades that followed. A dramaturgical analysis of the December 1980 unveiling of the monument commemorating this protest serves as the core reference throughout. The playback of Krzysztof Penderecki's *Lacrimosa* (1980) over loudspeakers at this event grounds my analysis of the Party's conversations about and censorship of Penderecki. I analyze the composer's self-positioning as a champion of the Polish people in contrast. December 1970 also unfolds across interpretations of a ballad, "Janek Wiśniewski Fell," written immediately following the funeral of a young student murdered by the police at the 1970 demonstrations. This vernacular song opens up a discussion of trauma, memory, and place in counterpoint to the commemorative work done at the unveiling. Three recordings offer additional valences: one by an activist released on leftist labels worldwide, one for the soundtrack of Andrzej Wajda's *Man of Iron* (1981), and one manipulated by electronic-music composer Elżbieta Sikora (1984–85). The chapter concludes with a musical study of Solidarity's leading figure, Lech Wałęsa, in transnational contexts. His charisma invigorated the solidarity afforded the electrician-turned-labor organizer by Joan Baez, who wrote songs for him and traveled to Gdańsk to perform for the opposition.

The final chapter, "Chorus," takes a long historical view of musical solidarity in Poland to gesture toward the real power of imagined musical solidarity. The chapter presents the history of one patriotic and Catholic hymn, "God Save Poland" (1816), three times. First, as a list—almost without narrative—that obsessively tracks its prominence in the 1980s and in grassroots accounts of the Polish opposition (though it had almost no resonance in global social movement networks at the time). This catalog enacts the saturation of symbols that many have analyzed as the heart of Solidarity's nationalist enterprise, but positions them as driven by song. Second, the performance history of the song reveals its constant position on a threshold, both among the hymns of Polish Catholicism and as a galvanizing refrain at the secularized scenes of popular uprisings. The history of the hymn's chorus (also sung in chorus) shows that it mattered not just that the hymn was song but *how*: the song at times challenged Catholicism as normative for Polish identity. Finally, I take a forensic look at collective song's communicative power as it is worked for Krzysztof Meyer's *Polish Symphony* (1982), the composer's response to martial law. The symphony, like other art music examples across *Musical Solidarities*, suggests that, despite their vocal abnegation of political entanglement, composers, too, joined in the core musical strategies of the opposition.

Recall the forward momentum—the subjunctive tenses of musical solidarity—of the refrains within the two anthems in this chapter: "So that Poland will be Poland" and "Poland has not yet perished." These place music as initiator and engine. By avoiding a chronological narrative, this book works out of a different fundamental tone—sounding confusion, vulnerability, and a din of human utterances. This ethos is conjured well in Seyla Benhabib's description of 1989 as "noncontemporaneous contemporaneity." I suggest a way to theoretically engage with this unstable time of those past presents through sound and music.[56] In the language and register of Keff and Janion: fleeting and troubling, triumphant and distorted, the sounds of the opposition's 1980s mix and remix history. Solidarity's musics are inherent in that pluralizing gesture of musical solidarit*ies*.

---

[56] Seyla Benhabib, "The Strange Silence of Political Theory: Response," *Political Theory* 23, No. 4 (1995), 675.

1 | Sound

A rather unremarkable compact cassette landed in the special collections of Harvard University's Houghton Library in the late 1980s as the result of an initiative by Alicja Altenberger, a librarian who had fled Poland in 1981 for Cambridge, Massachusetts. Through the decade she was dedicated to building a repository of the material culture—posters, radio transcripts, pamphlets, underground print material, and cassette tapes—of the Polish opposition as it was gifted to the Boston area's Polish community. The black plastic tape is stored in a case without a liner; a dot-matrix printer had printed the album's title: *Gazeta Dźwiękowa* #16 (*Sound Gazette* No. 16).[1] Another copy of this album, a white tape with no label, is held by the Museum of Independence in Warsaw (see Figure 1.1). This recording is wrapped in a flimsy photocopy of a line-art cover that bears the title and depicts a newspaper, a gramophone, and a hand holding up two fingers in a victory sign. There are other copies, too, in archives and personal collections, each with their own minor material variations on the themes of these black and white copies. These are not mass-produced tapes, nor are they intimate mixtapes tailored to an individual. One copy of the album, seized from an activist during a raid of his home on the northern coast of Poland, even resides within the archive of state surveillance—the Security Service (Służba Bezpieczeństwa, SB). Having been digitized, it is inaccessible in original format.[2]

---

1 Stefan Bratkowski, *Gazeta Dźwiękowa* 16, Solidarity Bibliographic Center, Houghton Library, Harvard University, Cambridge, MA. Alicja Altenberger, "Solidarity Bibliographic Center at Harvard," *Harvard Librarian*, 18, no. 3. Bratkowski's newspaper was published at irregular intervals and was numbered consecutively. For clarity I have referred to these as "issues," though in his spoken text he uses a handful of terms indiscriminately to describe publication units.

2 IPN Gd 749/7, Oddziałowe Archiwum Instytutu Pamięci Narodowej w Gdańsku, Gdańsk, Poland. The collection inventory does contain a table of contents for the tape

FIGURE 1.1. One liner for Stefan Bratkowski's *Sound Gazette*.

Each tape is a unique record of its contents' circulation. These bootlegs have traces of their makers' care for the tapes. They reveal a particular route through the hands (and, presumably, ears) of members of and sympathizers with the Polish opposition to state socialism. At the same time, they are all quite similar. Tape collections like the dispersed archive of the *Sound Gazette* are typical, both obsolescent relics of the dominant audio format in Eastern Europe in the 1980s and evidence of the networks of exchange these cassettes' portability and recordability facilitated. Like their print analogs, the self-published periodicals of what in the Polish context was called the *drugi obieg* ("second circulation"), the unofficial recordings are resilient relics of a late

---

and lists the names—including the pseudonyms—mentioned. See also the People's Republic of Poland Collection, Museum of Independence, Warsaw, Poland. The cassette is also held in duplicate at the Archiv der Forschungsstelle Osteuropa an der Universität Bremen, Bremen, Germany.

Cold War political climate in which ideas, words, and sounds made people vulnerable to persecution, but long-standing organizations, discourses, and practices of dissent had been established.

These sounding periodicals, the opposition's print culture, and the top-down regulation of culture shaped the discourse on sound, the place of music, and the spaces of musical performance through the 1980s. But ignoble objects—like the sixteenth issue of Stefan Bratkowski's *Sound Gazette*—offer particular insight to the stakes of listening, too. On tape, Bratkowski crafts a relationship between sound and political action that took radical advantage of a historical media regime to thematize the vulnerability of speaking out. Let's listen to the newspaper's opening seconds ⓘ:

> Hello, my friend. I'll repeat what I always say: if a tape with this recording reaches your cassette player, remove or erase it. This is not for distribution. After a six-month break, the sixteenth *Sound Gazette* is, as always, one copy, made for my own pleasure and out of my own right. Because I cannot be silent when it is necessary to speak. And I speak, more or less, to a wall. "Hello, my wall, it's been long since we listened to one another. Listen to me, once again, with patience."

Each edition of the *Sound Gazette* (1983–88) begins with a variation on this tongue-in-cheek disclaimer by its author, journalist Stefan Bratkowski. These formulaic riffs set up an ironic tone for the audio newspaper that keeps the speaker's intentions a matter of interpretation and his report on current events a matter of opinion. The framing material pushes back at the storage function of magnetic tape—the affordance that ultimately lands it in archives—to emphasize the medium's inherent potential for impermanence ("erase it"). None of these tapes is the master. As we shall see, Bratkowski employs strategies that confront the Polish state and its attempt to control words and how they circulate. When he frames the wall as his conversant (as though the tape recorder is not also his witness), he translates the concept of "desk drawer literature" from written to spoken text. The *Sound Gazette* is, however, not a project for himself. Nor is it for later, as his facetious performance suggests at face value. But that dangling invitation remains: listen and pay careful attention to what follows.

The *Sound Gazette* positions listening as a means of participating in oppositional discourse, making things out of sound as a social project with political force. The tape is a remix of cutting critiques of contemporary politics. Bratkowski's gazettes are editorial monologues fashioned according to the sections of a newspaper: current events, culture, business, and local and international politics. Across each issue he speaks in different linguistic and vocal registers to conjure various journalistic styles. He is critical of actually existing socialism and analyzes strategies and cultures of political action. In other words, there is nothing much unusual about this newspaper's format beyond its release on tape, a feature that Bratkowski draws attention to and plays with across the *Gazette*'s six-year run.

The *Sound Gazette*'s content is instructive about the issues that mattered to Bratkowski and his listeners; his voice bears some witness to the tenor of the opposition. The performance on the *Sound Gazette* is confident: Bratkowski was at the helm of the Polish Journalists' Association (Stowarzyszenie Dziennikarzy Polskich) in 1980, when the independent trade union known as Solidarity (Solidarność) was legalized. He had been a key force in negotiating for greater freedom of the press and Communist Party reform in the late 1970s. When, in December 1981, martial law was declared, he was expelled from the Party and he continued to advocate for other journalists who had lost their employment from state-sponsored media.[3] The sixteenth issue, most likely from 1987, includes a playful ridicule of Gorbachev, curt attacks on the divide between workers and the intelligentsia in Poland, and a measured narration of book reviews.

As an aperture into sonic practice and culture within the communication network of the opposition, the *Sound Gazette* reveals the importance of listening, music, and sound. I begin here by paying careful attention to the tape's bricolage, hearing and reconstructing auditory culture out of Harvard's copy of Bratkowski's recording. This work necessarily precedes my attention to print material—an unofficial literary magazine and the paperwork of the Party—through the rest of this chapter. What music can be and what sound can do for the opposition emerges *first* from materials that did the work of organizing. These are in counterpoint with attempts to define and critique music, which, I argue, constrain the sonic and occlude the histories that unfold across this book. The *Sound Gazette*'s audio is dense, filled with cultural references, and the product of deft recording practices. Listening to it at temporal, geographical, and physical remove is hard historiographic work.

Listening to the Sound Gazette

To start: Bratkowski's delivery of the introductory remarks drips with an irony that matches the ambivalent text. He wants his voice to be heard and the world to respond—recasting the Polish-language idiom, "talking to you is like talking to a wall." Through most of the tape's A side, a swift cadence strummed loudly on the guitar gives the news an edge, bulleting each item and pulling wandering minds back into the dense spoken text. The journalist marks authorial control and awareness of this media format as he speaks.

---

3 Jack M. Bloom, *Seeing through the Eyes of the Polish Revolution: Solidarity and the Struggle against Communism in Poland* (Leiden: Brill, 2013), 241–47.

Perfunctory spoken notes indicate "the end of the first side" and the "beginning of the second." The signals bound his authorship, making clear that any material audible before or after them is not intentionally included ⏵. Longer musical excerpts complement Bratkowski's animated spoken performances. Across the 60- or 90-minute newspapers, refrains from the legendary Cracovian political cabaret, Cellar Under the Rams (Piwnica pod Baranami), and newly composed sung poetry (*poezja śpiewana*) frame "sections" of the gazette.

The sixteenth edition begins with a blistering downward chromatic run on a piano. "We Must Plant" ("Musimy siać") is a rallying cry to cultivate the earth despite a litany of obstacles (barren soil, broken equipment) that was set to music by the Cellar's resident composer (and filmmaker Krzysztof Kieślowski's collaborator of choice), Zbigniew Preisner.[4] The loud keyboard sets the martial pulse for the cabaret singer Tamara Kalinowska, Preisner's sister ⏵. She has described her early-career performance technique, emphasizing that she was self-taught and raw: "What I did on stage was yelling more than it was singing, though I trusted that one day I would be able to sing."[5] As the banging piano and almost overpowering slap of an acoustic guitar mark the square beat, the focused strain of her gut-driven vocalization sounds more like the pulsing fighting words of Patti Smith's *Horses* (1975) than the open release of Yoko Ono's howl. Bratkowski's disclaimer interrupts the bootleg cabaret recording, which fades back in after his invitation to listen. The song's unattributed text is easily heard as an allegory to rally the opposition. A riff on an old Polish scouting proverb, it sends a message about investing in renewal despite its obvious risk.[6] The music is at once a counterpoint to the demure disclaimer and an overture to the indignant program that follows. Across the tape, Bratkowski is concerned about the upcoming

---

4 The recording here was only commercially released after the end of state socialism. *Piwnica pod Baranami: Piosenki piwniczych kompozytorów*, volume 2. Warsaw: Pomaton, POM CD 039. On Preisner's musical biography, see Nicholas Reyland, *Zbigniew Preisner's Three Colors Trilogy: Blue, White, Red: A Film Score Guide* (Lanham, MD: Scarecrow Press, 2012). The bulk of the popular songs mentioned across this book are available on YouTube.

5 "O sobie"; http://www.tamara.hg.pl/o_sobie/index.html.

6 An editorial in an online Polish-language newspaper devoted to Israeli politics traced the term through Zionist scouting books ("Czy Piotr Skrzynecki czytywał syjonistyczne gazety? Tajemnica piosenki 'Musimy siać'"; http://izrael.org.il/kultura/4431-czy-piotr-skrzynecki-czytywal-syjonistyczne-gazety-tajemnica-piosenki-musimy-siac.html; the 2014 article is no longer online). A Catholic Priest noted its quotation across the Polish scouting tradition and frequent attribution to the poet Wincenty Pol; see Antoni Pacyfik Dydycz, *Homilie 1994–2000* (Drohiczyn: Drohiczyńskie Towarzystwo Naukowe and Kuria Diecezjalna w Drohiczynie, 2011), 7.

visit (June 8–14, 1987) of Pope John Paul II to his homeland, Poland. He warns that the Poles most invested in Christian salvation will look to His Holiness for guidance instead of to local, grassroots leaders who actually have the power to renew and re-energize. He ends one of the tape's editorials with a serene statement that "change must come from us," repeating "from us" (*od nas*) three times.

Following the news report, another song that speaks of popular power swells up out of a recorded silence. This time it is the light baritone and well-enunciated Polish of the most recognizable singer-songwriter of the 1980s, Jacek Kaczmarski (see chapter 3), who sings his own poem, "Litany" ("Litania"). Kaczmarski's voice flanks a ten-minute commentary on the Pope's visit, "Before the Pilgrimage," which just barely spans the tape's two sides (there are fifty seconds of leftovers at the start of the B side). Originally composed in 1981—a live recording of an acoustic version circulated through Polish communities across the globe after he performed it in Chicago—this poem links images of persecution and weakness with those of defiance and resilience in nine rhyming couplets.[7] "Sometimes those weaker than dust withstand the storm / to raise monuments to forgotten culture," he sings. The text is an elaborated axiom on the power of the powerless, to gesture toward Vaclav Havel's influential moral text, in a melancholic tone.[8] Its commentary on history, however, also allowed people to hear local resonances: the reference to monuments would have reminded some of the celebrated 1980 unveiling of the Monument for the Fallen Shipyard Workers (see chapter 5).[9]

The Kaczmarski track loops the *Sound Gazette* in a network of unofficial media beyond Poland's borders. Bratkowski most likely dubbed "Litany" from its illegal circulation beyond the state recording industry, in the cassette culture of the drugi obieg, which I will examine. On the *Sound Gazette* this verse of poezja śpiewana, the guitar poetry tradition local to Poland, is plugged-in.[10] The over-produced track would have sounded unusual for

---

7 Jacek Kaczmarski, *Antologia poezji* (Warsaw: Demart, 2011).

8 As Jonathan Bolton has written: "'The Power of the Powerless' presents dissent as maximally open—Havel is speaking to a world of strangers and asking them to step into the unknown. He is more concerned with the hope of transformation than with the scene of practical activity, more concerned with an inspiring call to action than with a description of what that action would look like." See Jonathan Bolton, *Worlds of Dissent: Charter 77, the Plastic People of the Universe, and Czech Culture under Communism* (Cambridge, MA: Harvard University Press, 2012), 220–30, at 228.

9 "Czasem słabsi od kurzu wstrzymujemy wichury / I stawiamy pomniki zapomnianej kultury."

10 I discuss this genre at greater length in chapter 3, but the most robust scholarly literature addresses its Russian relative, *avtorskaia pesnia*. See Gerald S. Smith, *Songs to Seven Strings: Russian Guitar Poetry and Soviet "Mass Song"* (Bloomington: Indiana University Press, 1984); Rachel S. Platonov, *Singing the Self: Guitar Poetry, Community, and Identity in*

Kaczmarski and foreign in its production value, because the so-called bard had mostly sung alone with his guitar since leaving Poland in 1981. When martial law was declared, Kaczmarski was on tour in France and remained abroad, hosting a radio show on the CIA-funded, but émigré-operated, Radio Wolnej Europy, the Polish-language Radio Free Europe station in Munich, West Germany ⏵.[11] Along with physical albums produced abroad and sent back to Poland, the radio station was the primary channel through which Polish audiences within the country's borders could have heard Kaczmarski's new compositions. He hosted a regular show, on which he performed new songs, played back old recordings, and discussed both his artistic practice and current Polish politics. It was, as Kaczmarski reflected in 1989, "the best way to keep in consistent contact with my country from the West."[12]

Bratkowski's *Sound Gazette* and Kaczmarski's guitar poetry are archetypal products of the opposition's cassette culture, a foundational archive for this cultural history. The sounds that Brakowski grabs amplify and nuance his own politics, weaving him in to a network of people writing and sounding against the state media monopoly. MIDI brass usher in a light loop crafted on a Yamaha drum machine by Peter Puk, a Polish-Australian studio musician. This amped-up take of "Litany" opened the twenty-third tape, an album titled *An Hour with Jacek Kaczmarski* (1987, see Figure 1.2), released in Poland by the unofficial label "CDN."[13] The CDN album reproduces in

---

the *Post-Soviet Period* (Evanston: Northwestern University Press, 2012). Rossen Djagalov sees singer-songwriters as localizations of the international left, writing, "In every culture in which [bards] appeared, they were deeply rooted in local poetic, musical, and performative traditions, yet everywhere their performance exhibited several fairly constant characteristics: a powerful potential to construct counterpublics; a critique of the state, whether of a state socialist or capitalist variety; and a tense relationship with the musical industries" in Rossen Djagalov, "Guitar Poetry, Democratic Socialism, and the Limits of 1960s Internationalism," in *The Socialist Sixties: Crossing Borders in the Second World*, edited by Anne E. Gorsuch and Diane P. Koenker (Bloomington and Indianapolis: Indiana University Press, 2013), 148.

11 Listener data for Radio Free Europe is notoriously difficult to analyze because the ideological drive to emphasize success or failure drove poll methodologies on both sides of the Iron Curtain; see Lechosław Gawlikowski with Yvette Neisser Moreno, "The Audience to Western Broadcasts to Poland during the Cold War," in *Cold War Broadcasting: Impact on the Soviet Union and Eastern Europe, A Collection of Studies and Documents*, edited by A. Ross Johnson and R. Eugene Parta (Budapest and New York: Central European University Press, 2010), 121–41.

12 "Najlepszy na zachodzie sposób na zachowanie stałego z kraju," "Rozmowa z Jackiem Kaczmarskim," *Aneks: Pismo NZS Uniwersytet Wrocławski* 3–4 (1989), 9.

13 *Godzina z Jackim Kaczmarskim,* CDN Oficyna Fonograficzna 23, 1987. Another copy of the tape with the same label, held by the Jacek Kaczmarski Foundation, dates that bootleg to 1988, suggesting further its popularity.

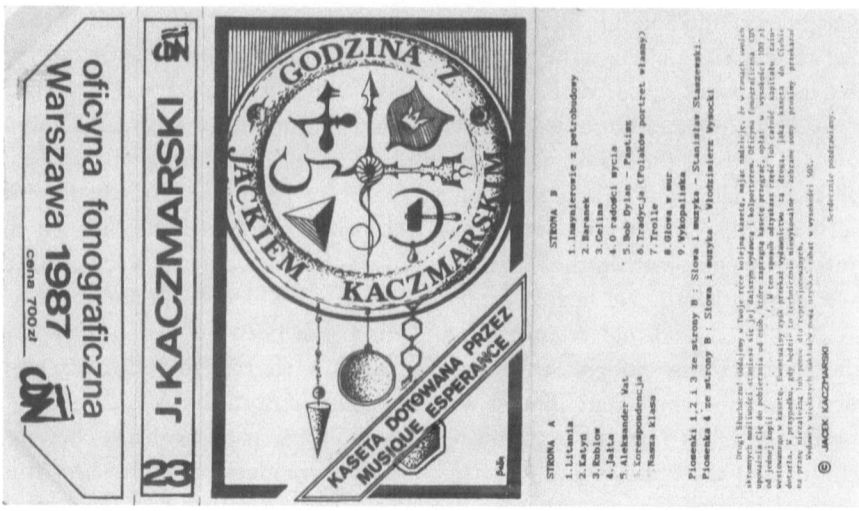

FIGURE 1.2. *An Hour with Jacek Kaczmarski* (1987), drugi obieg release.

its entirety the likely source for Bratkowski's track: an imported LP that captures the repertory from Kaczmarski's 1985 tour through Australia.[14] The tour was for and by musicians who could not return to their home countries in Eastern Europe. According to a note on its sleeve: "This album is the first product done in co-operation between various Polish and Czechoslovak exile organizations."

The *Sound Gazette*'s intimacy also lies in its media density: it tells the story of media networks (telephones, radios) but is also produced by their convergence (magnetic tape, vinyl). Near the beginning of the B side, as Bratkowski concludes the pilgrimage editorial, he snarls at his audience, addressing them with the informal second-person plural (*wy*). He slows down his reading pace and asks people to make demands of the Pope. "He will not renounce you," Bratkowski pointedly states. A cut of George Frideric Handel's "Halleluja" chorus that I hear as satire and respite at once punctuates the essay's conclusion. The excerpt is another transfer from vinyl: I can hear the pops and cracks of a needle tracing a groove. The phonographic effect, to use Mark Katz's term, is the audible evidence of the social practices (listening, dropping the needle, collecting the record) that relate Kaczmarski and Bratkowski as creators in sound.[15]

14 *Litania*, Saturn Recording Company, Iron Curtain Records 3, 1987.

15 Mark Katz, *Capturing Sound: How Technology Has Changed Music* (Berkeley: University of California Press, 2004), 1–6.

In another editorial, "Gorbachev's Russia," Bratkowski critiques *perestroika*, the restructuring program spearheaded by the then-General Secretary of the Soviet Communist Party. Bratkowski even acts out a dialogue with himself to highlight contradictory proposals for plans of action and their potential impact on Poland. The song that abuts the analysis of the Soviet Union's reforms on Poland comments on political oppression directly. Another bard, Tadeusz Sikora, speak-sings an uncomplicated verse over a simple chord progression:

Gdy w słuchawce przyciszony głos słyszysz,	When you hear a muted voice through your telephone receiver,
Że nie można szczerze nic przez telefon.	You know you can't trust anything over the phone.
To widomy masz tu znak, moje dziecko,	That's when it's obvious, my child,
Że nasz kraj się upodobnia Sowietom.	Our country is becoming like the Soviets'.

The song, "Sovieticization" ("Sowietyzacja"), diagnoses the situation in Poland with a list of symptoms. The first clue is audible for the song's narrator: the surveillance of communications media poignantly calls back to Bratkowski's opening remarks. Sikora's vocal declamation is unabashedly loud, though. It is rougher than Kaczmarski's, the verse less refined. The song's gritty observational poetics starkly contrast with the metaphorical language and unresolved tension of "Litany." Sikora is angry and direct. Most of the other tracks on *Straddling the Barricade* (*Okrakiem na barykadzie*, 1986), an album he recorded for the drugi obieg, tap the same aggressive spirit.[16] Even that album's cover suggests that he has reached some kind of limit of decorum. Front and center is an unarticulated four-letter word, "[_ _ _ _]," that listeners are to imagine for themselves.

The concluding sections of the newspaper continue to weave a portrait of everyday life in Poland in which text and sound, reading and listening, are intertwined. After the 30-second musical bridge, Bratkowski relates news from Warsaw—he says it's all "words, words, words" there—and again turns to Sikora. "Do not delay" ("Nie zwlekaj"), from the same tape, lines up a string of negative commands to underscore the spoken admonition that it is time for action. As he shouts, "The Party must leave!" ("*Partia musi odejść!*"), Bratkowski (or a collaborator) fades out the volume on the source sound. The manual dub—at least this is my sense—comes against the rhythmic energy of Sikora's performance. Finally, on the *Sound Gazette*'s so-called back page, the journalist gives out an award to an outstanding book. The commendation also acknowledges

---

16 Tadeusz Sikora, *Okrakiem na barykadzie*, CDN Oficyna Fonograficzna 20, 1986.

the drugi obieg, but this time it is print matter: a children's book that parodies René Goscinny and Jean-Jacques Sempé's series, Le petit Nicolas. He reads a section of Miłosz Kowalski's *Nicholas in School in the People's Republic* (*Mikołaj w szkole PRL*), adopting a nasal voice to take on the role of Nicholas, who is describing school under the military watch of martial law.[17] A final song fragment brings back Kaczmarski, this time from the stage of a 1980 concert in Gdańsk, playing alongside his Polish collaborators Przemysław Gintrowski, guitar and vocals, and Zbigniew Łapiński at the keyboard. In the evening's introductory remarks, captured in a live recording, Łapiński addresses audience members present and listening to bootlegs at home. He describes the program, *Paradise* (*Raj*), as a theatrical presentation that pairs songs and paintings.[18] The *Sound Gazette* outro, "Massacre of the Innocents" ("Rzeź niewiniątek"), is both a biblical retelling and a musical response to Peter Breughel the Elder's circa 1565–67 painting of the same name. The excerpt here is uncannily light and its major key is unsettling. The patter of piano arpeggiation plays with the soft consonants in Polish that keep the story and its allegorical potential haunting: "Children, children, come and play with the soldiers. . . ."

The sound labor of the opposition implicates tidy boundaries between music and sound. I have purposefully begun in the middle of *things*: unpacking one tape, sounding its author's performance, and taking seriously its peripheral musics. Its compositional gestures both counter and complement the private work of art music composers, the loud performances of rock musicians, and the monumental dramaturgy of protests and public commemoration—all examples of labor that will animate musical solidarities in the pages to come. The cassette culture of the Polish opposition affords attention to other musical work and other musical workers: making and listening to cassettes; their curators, recordists, and distributors. The musics of this unofficial culture are shaped by people thinking about listening and sound, but who are not necessarily "musicians." Even singers like Tamara Kalinowska, Jacek Kaczmarski, and Tadeusz Sikora were considered and identified themselves as actors or poets.

The sounds of Bratkowski's newspaper suggest the power of listening as a historical methodology, the importance of aurality for the expressive culture of the Polish opposition, and the presence—indeed, integration—of music in the political work of sound. Tape makers and consumers ignored borders inscribed between musical genres and figured music as politically efficient. This simple and single tape, through its incessant remediations of books, telephones, paintings, and records, lets music tell a story, comment on

---

17 Bratkowski awards the prize specifically to one imprint: Miłosz Kowalski, *Mikołaj w szkole PRL*, illustrated by Masław (Warsaw: Rytm, 1986). The two pseudonymous authors were a mother and her ten-year-old son.

18 *Raj*, unattributed cassette, Muzeum Niepodległości, People's Republic of Poland Collection, Warsaw, Poland.

politics, provide emotional catharsis, and continue traveling. The histories spooled onto tapes like the *Sound Gazette* thus—through their particularity—push back against the dominant narrative, spun by the movers and shakers of the Polish musical intelligentsia and maintained into the present, that music makers and music itself existed in a world apart from the opposition to state socialism. This unremarkable and uncelebrated inclusion of music across oppositional cassette culture exists in a world apart from the stagnant debates about music's political efficacy across Polish culture.

The drugi obieg

Cassettes like Stefan Bratkowski's involve music and invite musical listening; they position the aural as "a formation and a force" through the opposition that we can follow into its written culture and route through paths of distribution.[19] As the journalist relates his speech to writing and to music, he transforms held texts into heard stories. Interweaving aurality and literacy, he is aware of his media's affordances. Recall the preamble, in which Bratkowski played with the physical fate of the cassette and its contents. He varies his disclaimer across issues of the gazette: "Reuse it!" "Delete it!" "Ignore it!" "Destroy it!" "Copy it!" The self-made cassettes themselves signal distribution: made for playback on current technology, the recording does not happen by accident. It is made possible and audible by the drugi obieg, the Polish self-publishing culture under state socialism that defined itself—as "second circulation"—outside of official publishing.[20]

The diffuse unofficial media that circulated beyond Party censorship and outside the Polish state's economy make up the drugi obieg.[21] In a 1985 article published in the *Index on Censorship*, a magazine produced by the UK nonprofit of the same name to monitor global infringements on civil liberties,

---

19 Ana María Ochoa Gautier, *Aurality: Listening and Knowledge in Nineteenth-Century Colombia* (Durham, NC: Duke University Press, 2014), 5.

20 Peter J. Schmelz articulates the importance of the term "unofficial" for music studies, which has tended to valorize un-supported music and musicians as de facto dissident in the haze of Cold War ideologies. See Peter J. Schmelz, *Such Freedom, If Only Musical: Unofficial Soviet Music during the Thaw* (Berkeley: University of California Press, 2009), 14–21. On the tensions between national and transnational circulation, see Lars Fredrik Stöcker, "The Baltic Connection: Transnational Samizdat Networks between Émigrés in Sweden and the Democratic Opposition in Poland," in *Samizdat, Tamizdat, and Beyond: Transnational Media during and after Socialism*, edited by Friederike Kind-Kovács and Jesse Labov (Oxford and New York: Berghahn Books, 2013), 51–69.

21 Marek Jastrzębski and Ewa Krysiak, "Avoiding Censorship: The 'Second Circulation' of Books in Poland," *Journal of Reading* 36, no. 6 (1993), 470–73.

Bratkowski reported on the state of journalism in Poland. He described the importance of the opposition presses, which commissioned, printed, and distributed books, newspapers, and other print media—including alternative postage stamps and posters—as a crucial counterpoint to the government-controlled press.[22] The writing is animated, as was his tone on tape: "The mass media have come to a total impasse; pollsters have found that readers do not *ever* read certain parts of the daily papers' front pages carrying official news!" He counters that the dynamic network of independent presses and self-publishers: "the underground press is flourishing."

In 1976 the Workers' Defense Committee (Komitet Obrony Robotników, KOR) issued an *Information Bulletin* and a literary journal, considered the drugi obieg's first publications.[23] From the get go, the endeavor created shared culture, involved people, and communicated—the flip side of desk drawer literature. Leading off the first *Information Bulletin*, the editorial committee wrote, "The purpose of this bulletin is to break the state monopoly on information, made possible by the existence of censorship in this country. . . . Read it, copy it, and give it to others to read. . . . Remember—by destroying this bulletin you are sealing your own lips and those of others."[24] Aside from setting an obvious precedent for the commands that characterize Bratkowski's tapes, the instructions lay out a clear moral imperative. The individual who halts the bulletin's reach censors themselves and others.

The drugi obieg was structured as an alternative economy—thus the name, "second circulation"—and was anchored by traditional news formats like the newspaper (e.g., *Tygodnik Mazowsze*) and literary journal (e.g., *Zapis*).[25] In other words, it built on the discourse of the socialist public sphere while claiming moral authority by rejecting its structures. Serguei Alex. Oushakine describes this interface—his study is concerned with the "self-published" *samizdat* of the Soviet Union—as "terrifying mimicry."[26] He

---

22 Kristi S. Evans, "The Argument of Images: Historical Representation in Solidarity Underground Postage, 1981–87," *American Ethnologist* 19, no. 4 (1992), 749–67.

23 John M. Bates, "From State Monopoly to a Free Market of Ideas? Censorship in Poland, 1976–1989," in *Censorship and Cultural Regulation in the Modern Age*, edited by Beate Müller. Critical Studies 22 (Amsterdam: Rodopi, 2004), 145.

24 Translated for and published in the *Index on Censorship* 6 (1977), 54.

25 Malgorzata Mazurek and Matthew Hilton, "Consumerism, Solidarity and Communism: Consumer Protection and the Consumer Movement," *Journal of Contemporary History* 42, no. 2 (2007), 315–43.

26 Serguei Alex. Oushakine, "The Terrifying Mimicry of Samizdat," *Public Culture* 12, no. 2 (2001), 191–214. Literally "self-published" in Russian, *samizdat* refers specifically to the illegal or unofficial publishing activities in Eastern-bloc countries during the Cold War. A 2008 issue of *Poetics Today* brings together articles examining the practice from different disciplinary perspectives; Peter Steiner provides an overview of the complex legacy of the practice and its historiography in his introductory piece, "On Samizdat,

suggests that the unofficial presses of the Cold War always must be read in relation to official publications and the paperwork of the state because they always built on or critiqued its forms, institutions, and conventions: "The oppositional discourse in a sense shared the symbolic field with the dominant discourse: it echoed and amplified the rhetoric of the regime, rather than positioning itself outside of or underneath it."[27] Other scholars, for example Jesse Labov and Friederike Kind-Kovács, emphasize that homemade publications, often duplicated on tabletop mimeographs, and illegal imprints, made after hours in sympathetic publishing houses, were in dialogue with writing by émigré communities, so-called *tamizdat* ("published there," see Figure 1.3).[28] The looming exemplar for the Polish intelligentsia by the 1980s would have been the preeminent émigré journal in Paris (*Kultura*), founded in 1947 by Jerzy Giedroyc.[29] The left-leaning literary publication, frequently smuggled into Poland on microfilm and in print, consistently provided a platform for Polish-language debates on politics and nation, as well as a literary outlet for prolific writers in exile, such as Czesław Miłosz and Witold Gombrowicz.[30] The observations by scholars of unofficial print culture about referentiality hold for non-written material, as in the case of the *Sound Gazette*, which parodies official language and depends on listeners' familiarity with daily news formats and radiophonic conventions.

The drugi obieg shaped community across its audiences. It also depended on community for (re)production and distribution. Many of the presses and cassette labels advertised for each other and shared material ("Copy it!"). The

---

Tamizdat, Magnitizdat, and Other Strange Words That Are Difficult to Pronounce," *Poetics Today* 29, no. 4 (2008), 613–28.

27 Serguei Alex. Oushakine, "The Terrifying Mimicry of Samizdat," *Public Culture* 12, no. 2 (2001), 192.

28 Friederike Kind-Kovács and Jesse Labov, editors, *Samizdat, Tamizdat, and Beyond: Transnational Media during and after Socialism* (Oxford and New York: Berghahn Books, 2013). Figure 1.3 reproduces the inside back cover of *Kontakt* 33, no. 1 (1985); University Libraries, University of North Carolina at Chapel Hill, United States.

29 Włodzimierz Bolecki describes the ambition of the émigré writers with respect to the intellectual elite in the People's Republic: "*Kultura*'s aim was to effect change in the communist camp by intellectual means. This is why Giedroyc reacted to events in Poland by including articles that dealt with current affairs; his ambition was to shape the opinion of the Polish intelligentsia under communist rule, which, exposed to primitive Party propaganda, was deprived of information, democratic models, and a freedom to exchange thoughts"; in Włodzimierz Bolecki, "*Kultura* (1946–2000)," in *The Exile and Return of Writers from East-Central Europe: A Compendium*, edited by John Neubauer and Borbála Zsuzsanna Török (Berlin: Walter de Gruyter, 2009), 155.

30 Timothy Snyder examines the politics of Giedroyc's periodical in *The Reconstruction of Nations: Poland, Ukraine, Lithuania, Belarus, 1569–1999* (New Haven, CT: Yale University Press, 2003), 218–31.

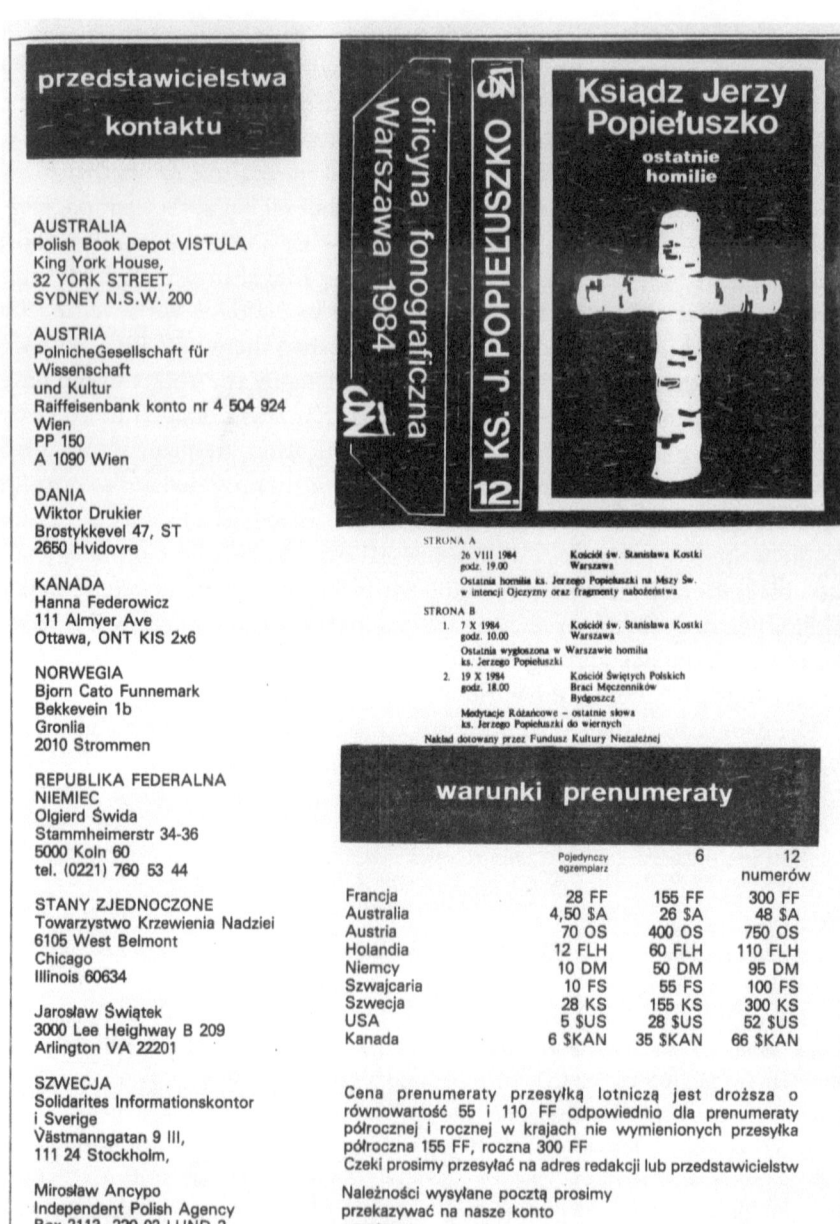

FIGURE 1.3. Advertisements for the Parisian *tamizdat* journal, *Kontakt*, and a cassette with global distribution details.

FIGURE 1.4. "Song of the Pamphlet Distributor" in *Tygodnik Mazowsze*.

labor behind self-publishing was, at times, celebrated more than the work of its authors. The "Song of the Pamphlet Distributor" ("Piosenka kolportera bibuły," see Figure 1.4), which was circulated in drugi obieg literary anthologies and newsletters, even used the metaphor of the freedom fighter to champion the intermediaries and incite people to work for the cause.[31] The poem's reproduction just beneath the masthead of *Tygodnik Mazowsze* served as a gesture of open gratitude to the messengers' political courage.[32] The newsletter's editors dedicated the anonymous verse to their printers and distributors, emphasizing the decentralized nature of the network. Bratkowski's message echoes again in the refrain ("Read them. Copy them."). The artifact also provides instructive meta-commentary, outlining the process of circulation. As the conduit for "words of truth" with which these pamphlets are burdened, the courier works for posterity and makes history. Elsewhere in the

---

31 For example, it was collected in the typescript *Antologia poezji ulotnej*, which had 2,000 copies in its original print run, available for purchase for 50 złoty (Gdańsk: REDAKCJA Terytorialno-Związkowego Komitetu Samoobrony Społeczno SOLIDARNOŚĆ, 1982). National Commission of the Independent and Self-Governing Trade Union "Solidarity," Gdańsk, Poland.

32 *Tygodnik Mazowsze* (March 31, 1982), 1.

drugi obieg the moral imperative was heralded more brazenly, as one press printed all caps in an advertisement: "We alone are responsible for the fate of the free word in Poland!"[33]

Piosenka kolportera bibuły	The Song of the Pamphlet Distributor
Słowo prawdy na wagę złota,	A word of truth weighed as carefully as gold,
Myśl prawdziwa na wagę pamięci.	A true thought weighted as carefully as memory.
Gdy kolporter wyrusza z bibuła,	When the distributor sets out with his pamphlets,
Trzymaj kciuki, nich mu się poszczęsci.	Keep your fingers crossed, may he fare well.
Na wolność to wkrótce wymienisz.	You'll soon convert them to freedom.
Przeczytaj. Przepisz. Nie niszcz.	Read them. Copy them. Don't destroy them.
Z dużą torbą wyrusza na miasto,	He sets out for the town with his big bag,
Gdzieś za sobą zostawił drukarnię.	Leaving the printing press behind somewhere.
Nie oglądaj się, nie spiesz, patrz: patrol.	Don't look back, don't hurry, watch out—a patrol.
Jeśli skrewisz, drukarnia też wypadnie.	If you mess up, the press will be done for, too.
Na wolność to wkrótce wymienisz.	You'll soon convert them to freedom.
Przeczytaj. Przepisz. Nie niszcz.	Read them. Copy them. Don't destroy them.
Kiedy idzie z bibułą na punkt	When he carries his pamphlets with a goal in mind,
Jak bombowiec, odwrotu już nie ma.	Like a bomber, there's no turning back.
Co za ulga, otwiera ktoś drzwi,	What a relief, someone opens the door,
Hasło, odzew, bibułę odbiera.	A cue, a password, they receive the pamphlets.
Na wolność to wkrótce wymienisz.	You'll soon convert them to freedom.
Przeczytaj. Przepisz. Nie niszcz.	Read them. Copy them. Don't destroy them.
UBe sceżnie i ZOMO zaginie,	The UB will go belly up, ZOMO will flatline,
Generałów przegonią do koszar,	The generals will go running to their barracks,
Do historii zaś wejdzie na zawsze	But the illegal newspaper and the wartime underground press
Bibuła i wojenny kolportaż.	Will go down in history forever.
Na wolność to wkrótce wymienisz.	You'll soon convert them to freedom.
Przeczytaj. Przepisz. Nie niszcz.	Read them. Copy them. Don't destroy them.

While print culture always dominated the drugi obieg, the power of the cassette for its work in the 1980s was a result of both historical circumstances and possibility of magnetic tape. The Communist Party's embargo on paper during martial law spurred the drugi obieg to use a greater range of media for their messages: radio, microfilm, tape, and eventually videocassettes. The cassette format's fungibility and plurality made it not only a convenient conduit for discussion, but also confirmed tape as a medium that—in form and substance—modeled the importance of revision in political discourse. Tape had other affordances, too. As

---

33 Advertisement for NOWa, 1985. Back cover of Stefan Bratkowski, *Trzy teatry* (Warsaw: Rytm, 1987). Copy held in Houghton Library, Harvard University.

one album art designer put it, "A tape could fit more information than a compact volume of the 'underground' press."[34] Some made their own tapes; others formed cassette labels. Recordists embraced the vulnerable materiality of these objects, which could not be traced to their makers, since the SB did not have the technology to link a disembodied voice back to an individual. And, a strong magnet could swiftly erase any confidential or vulnerable messages.

Within the drugi obieg, the tapes collectively represent what Peter Manuel has labeled a "cassette culture": a sphere of cultural activity that is contingent upon the cassette tape from an economic and substantive perspective.[35] Projects like the *Sound Gazette* emerged from traditions of unofficial recording in the People's Republic (elsewhere in this study, for example, concert bootlegs will constitute sound archives), but mark an institutionalization and monetization of the practice that is specific to the final years of the Cold War and the social networks of the drugi obieg. The singer Jan Krzysztof Kelus situated his recordings as such as he made his financial stakes and personal risk clear on the liner notes to his *Songs from an Old Cassette* (*Piosenki ze starej kasety*, 1984):

> As an independent artist working outside the State Entertainment Monopoly, I claim ownership of copyright on the texts and melodies on this tape. I grant permission for the tape to be reproduced for a royalty fee of 100 złoty (or 10 abroad) per copy. Persons who believe it is currently appropriate to make use of the postal service—and who, at the same time, are unable to hand the royalty fees over to me directly or through our mutual acquaintances—are asked to donate the equivalent for the support of repressed individuals.
>
> Any large-scale reproduction requires separate permission.
>
> In the case of my longer-term absence, I transfer the ownership of copyright to my wife, Urszula Sikorska.[36]

Kelus makes a veiled reference to the possibility of arrest (I tell the story of his actual imprisonment at this chapter's conclusion) and lays out terms and conditions for the tape. Though his ownership claims directly counter the logic of Bratkowski's cassette disclaimer, both individuals are responding to the alternative economy's terms and conditions.

---

34 "Był ten materiał obszerniejszy, na taśmie mieściło się więcej informacji, niż w niewielkiej objętościowo 'podziemnej' prasie," Jan Bokiewicz, email communication with author, September 27, 2013.

35 Peter Manuel's cassette culture is specifically musical. He writes of North Indian *ghazal* in the 1980s: "Their form, content, and meanings are strongly conditioned by and inseparable from the advent cassettes, and hence they must be holistically understood in that perspective"; Peter Manuel, *Cassette Culture: Popular Music and Technology in North India* (Chicago: University of Chicago Press, 1993), 17.

36 *Piosenki ze starej kasety*, Oficyna Fonograficzna CDN 01, 1984.

To manage content and facilitate collaboration, the cassette labels worked in tandem with print publishers. Founded in 1977, the Independent Publishing House—NOWa (Niezależna Oficyna Wydawnicza)—is typical of the larger-scale recording operations. In 1982, five years after it had been founded to publish literary journals, poetry, and monographs, Marek Chimiak, a production coordinator for print, initiated a series of cassettes, "NowaKaseta." NOWa's series benefited from the efforts of at least two hundred individuals, and by the mid-1980s they could invest in at least 1,000 copies for the initial production runs. Through 1990, the label produced 39 cassette albums, each of which has some musical content. In some cases the non-spoken content is reduced to the radio signals that function as intros and outros. Other albums are re-releases of popular guitar poetry albums by performers with sympathetic politics. These were issued with the hope that people could purchase them without funding the state. The NOWa tapes accomplish much that "print did not," to borrow a phrase from an actor who was responsible for cassette recovery and recycling in Wrocław.[37] As I hear them, they fall into four general categories: music album (9), audiobook (10), theatrical production (7), and documentary montage (13). Represented in comparable proportion, the categories mark diverse creative responses to the potential of editing sound. Music had a radically different presence across the publisher's books. Of the 230 books and 48 plays and poetry collections, only four present or discuss music explicitly: *Street and Domestic Songbook* (*Śpiewnik uliczny i domowy*, 1978); *Agitator's Songbook* (*Śpiewnik Warchoła*, 1979); Dmitri Shostakovich, *Testimony* (1987); and Karel Kryl, *Songs* (*Piosenki*, 1986).

In an extended conversation I had with Chimiak, he impressed upon me the ease with which the culture's success emerged out of established practices: "Were the tapes popular? People were already listening all the time: I imagine that even the SB would keep our tapes after they confiscated them and listen."[38] Music's ability to shape intimacy for the drugi obieg emerges in some of the stories I have heard while sitting with research associates in an effort to learn more about tape production.[39] It also resounds in close listening—as in my opening work with the *Sound Gazette*. I have also had exchanges, however, that push back against my presumption that music did work. "These cassettes have nothing to do with music," one couple responsible for their transport across Warsaw explained to me.[40] Such claims indicate the delimited definition of music among the Polish intelligentsia. The same activists who rejected the tapes' musicality recalled

---

37 Maciej Orłoś, email correspondence with author, September 28, 2013.

38 Marek Chimiak, Skype conversation with author, October 8, 2013.

39 Andrea F. Bohlman, "Making Tapes in Poland," *Twentieth-Century Music* 14, no. 1 (2017), 119–34.

40 Anonymous email communication with author, September 26, 2013.

cherishing an album of songs by Czech singer-songwriter Karel Kryl sung in Polish translation: they would urge their three-year-old daughter to sleep while singing along to the recording.[41] This is the one tape they still have ▶.

Music in Independent Culture

Across the opposition, artists allied the promise of state sovereignty, personal freedom, and artistic independence, which they conflated in the concept of "independent culture" (*kultura niezależna*).[42] The project grew out of the civilizing ethos of nineteenth-century German *Kultur*, and the managing structures for "culture and the arts" established across Eastern Europe's socialist governments after the Second World War.[43] It was crucial to what Lisa Jakelski has called Witold Lutosławski's "ethics of abstraction," which cast artistic interiority as a social and political move to keep creative work beyond analysis and the subjective.[44] It was also a bridge that kept the artistic community in the fervent discussions of civil society and its relation to or rejection of the undemocratic state.[45] Mirosław Chojecki, the founder of NOWa, underscored the concept in his oral testimony about the drugi obieg: "independence—not only in publishing but also and above all—in thinking and social action."[46] The labor of independent culture (performing, printing, debating), opposition leader Jacek Kuroń had provocatively suggested in 1974, was itself political opposition and could function as a model for the (re)organization of the Polish public sphere.[47]

---

41 Antonina Krzysztoń and Andrzej Michalski, *Piosenki Karela Kryla,* NOWa Kaseta 033 (1986); Translations first published in "Karel Kryl: Piosenki," *Kultura Niezależna* 11–12 (1985), 19–24.

42 Dietrich Beyrau and Wolfgang Eichwede, eds., *Auf der Suche nach Autonomie: Kultur und Gesellschaft in Osteuropa* (Bremen: Donat & Temmen, 1987).

43 I discuss the structures of the Polish United Workers' Party (PZPR) later. For an elaboration of governmentality and the idea of culture in Eastern Europe, see Nicholas Tochka, *Audible States: Socialist Politics and Popular Music in Albania* (Oxford: Oxford University Press, 2016), 13–16.

44 Lisa Jakelski, "Witold Lutosławski and the Ethics of Abstraction," *Twentieth-Century Music,* Vol. 10, no. 2 (2013), 169–202.

45 Michael D. Kennedy, *Professionals, Power, and Solidarity in Poland: A Critical Sociology of Soviet-Type Society* (Cambridge: Cambridge University Press, 1990), 161–95.

46 Wiesława Grochola, "Słowo jak dynamit: Rzecz o niezależnej oficynie," unpublished typescript, Polish Independent Periodicals Collection, Hoover Archives, Stanford, CA.

47 Jacek Kuroń, "Polityczna opozycja w Polsce," *Kultura* no. 326 (1974), 11. See also p. 6 in the same text for his description of artists as political workers.

The drugi obieg's primary literary journal, *Independent Culture* (*Kultura Niezależna*, 1984–91), served as the central forum for writing on culture and politics. The first issue of the Warsaw-based monthly periodical appeared in August 1984 through the sponsorship of Solidarity, then illegal. The editorial board explicitly incorporated the ideals and successes of the Solidarity movement on its cover, through its personnel, and by awarding the noteworthy "Solidarity" Prize to artistic works that supported its cause (see Figure 1.5).[48] The monthly publication was shaped as a literary journal contra contemporary society, presenting otherwise-censored poems and short stories, translations of banned foreign texts, cultural reviews, editorials on artistic agendas, and a rigorous cultural calendar that highlighted oppositional activities. To understand music's place in the debates about the meaning of culture for politics and the meaning of state socialism for culture, I read the journal's fifty-five issues through the end of 1989—with an eye toward moments when music mattered.

The Polish language distinguishes between state independence (*niepodległość*) and an individual's autonomy (*niezależność*), and activists deployed both, along with the concept of "freedom" (*wolność*). *Niepodległość* concerns collective sovereignty. In contrast, the *niezależność* flagged in the journal's title referred to individual autonomy, a core foundation of the opposition's model of civil society.[49] The journal's editorial board set its agenda as the "societalization of culture," an almost Attali-esque prophetic imaginary that the social and economic systems of the arts model and even herald revolution.[50] Rather than devoting themselves to publishing works banned by the state, the journal's editors looked forward: How could they realize

---

48 For a summary of the various projects associated with it, see Tadeusz Ruzikowski, "Kultura niezależna," in *NSZZ Solidarność 1980–89, tom 2: Ruch społeczny*, edited by Łukasz Kamiński and Grzegorz Waligóra (Warsaw: Instytut Pamięci Narodu, 2010), 315–85. Historian Sheila Fitzpatrick understands such closed communications loops as products of the system of patronage effected by Soviet state socialism. See Sheila Fitzpatrick, "Intelligentsia and Power: Client-Patron Relations in Stalin's Russia," in *Stalinismus vor dem Zweiten Weltkrieg: Neue Wege der Forschung*, edited by Manfred Hildermeier (Munich: R. Oldenbourg Verlag, 1998), 35–53.

49 Aleksander Wojciechowski, *Czas smutku, czas nadziei* (Warsaw: Wydawnictwo Artystyczne i Filmowe, 1992), 8.

50 Jan Krajowiec [Andrzej Jarecki], "Dzień trzeci," *Kultura Niezależna* 1 (1984), 10. My main source for pseudonyms is the Warsaw Institute of Literary Research's reference volume, *Kto był kim w drugim obiegu: Słownik pseudonimów pisarzy i dziennikarzy 1976–89*, edited by Dobrosława Świerczyńska, Cecylia Gajkowska, Joanna Król, and Irena Stemplowska (Warsaw: Instytut Badań Literackich, 1995). While I refer to the authors by their name in print in *Independent Culture*, when possible I provide their legal name in parentheses at first mention and when subsequently relevant.

FIGURE 1.5. The cover design of *Independent Culture*.

independent culture already, despite the restrictive state? Instead of taking a reactionary stance to the policies of the government, *Independent Culture* planned a future for art worlds protected from regulation and control. While, as we shall see, musicians were less active in the opposition broadly—and indeed rarely wrote for the journal—music and song aided and challenged debates in the journal's pages about the political expediency of the arts.

In 1980, Varsovian critics had formed a cultural commission within Solidarity, which, for example, took responsibility for the Week of Christian Culture, a festival devoted to the sacred in literature, music, and theater. The commission circulated the *Cultural Brochure* (*Informator Kulturalny*), a pamphlet that announced cultural events in support of and supported by Solidarity during the Union's legal interval. They formed the Committee on Independent Culture (Komitet Kultury Niezależnej) in December 1981. Many of these organizers served on the editorial board of *Independent Culture*, and the committee was responsible for the "Solidarity Prizes"—the first was given to Witold Lutosławski for his Third Symphony (see Tables 1.1 and 1.2).[51] The awards—presumably also examples of successfully independent culture—lent the journal's utopian project concrete examples, while simultaneously tapping eminent artists as supporters of their cause. Among the music awardees were not only distinguished composers, but also some of the cultural organizers who will emerge as central characters in this book (such as Tadeusz Kaczyński), and, in Zygmunt Mycielski, a composer best known at the time for his meticulous and critical editorials on Polish politics.

The first four volumes of *Independent Culture* in 1984 were devoted to debates on two themes: a functional definition of "independent culture" and its current status. An editorial call to action in the first issue opened the discussion:

> The journal *Independent Culture* should help give a voice to those who want to speak about what is going on and what will happen in contemporary Polish culture. We would like for *Independent Culture*, as a monthly publication, to respond quickly to events; so that readers should be able to find as much up-to-date information and as many reviews as possible. Whether we will be able to realize these ambitions . . . we shall see. We invite you to collaborate.[52]

The invitation stimulated a flow of communication that consistently placed *Independent Culture* in relation to the vast materials and expansive networks of the drugi obieg. Consider, as an example of the journal's broad scope, the journal's eighth issue (see Table 1.3).[53] The final "events" section fills the

---

51 While some—especially Western audiences during the Cold War—might hear or have heard the award's epithet as a rejoinder to the renowned Stalin Prize, the Soviet awards had relatively little notoriety in the People's Republic of Poland, in which prize culture—from the Composers' Union, the Ministry of Arts and Culture, and the Communist Party—was robust and far from stigmatized, as I shall discuss. On the Stalin Prize, see Marina Frolova-Walker, *Stalin's Music Prize: Soviet Culture and Politics* (New Haven, CT, and London: Yale University Press, 2016).

52 Krajowiec, "Dzień trzeci," 8.

53 The shifting currents of the SB's attitude toward underground print culture is beyond the scope of the present study, but one simple barometer of the stakes of publishing might be a survey of the number of authors writing under pseudonyms versus legal names. In *Independent Culture*, the practice of publishing under a name recognizable to the authorities began in 1986 and was standard by 1988, but was not to be taken for granted until summer 1990.

TABLE 1.1 Members of the Independent Culture Committee, Members of the Editorial Board of *Independent Culture*

Members of the Independent Culture Committee	Members of the Editorial Board of *Independent Culture*
Teresa Bogucka	**Marta Fik**
Kazimierz Dziewanowski	Andrezj Kaczyński
Marta Fik	**Małgorzata Łukasiewicz**
Kazimierz Kaczor	Zyta Orysyzn
Tadeusz Kaczyński	**Andrzej Osęka**
Krzysztof Knittel	Jerzy Slawiński
Małgorzata Łukasiewicz	Jan Walc
Andrzej Orłoś	
Andrzej Osęka	
Janusz Ściskalski	
Aleksander Wojciechowski	

***Bold** indicates a member of both committees

TABLE 1.2 Musicians Awarded "Solidarity" Prizes by the Committee for Independent Culture

1983: Witold Lutosławski, Third Symphony [awarded before *Independent Culture* was founded]
1984: Wiesław Wodyk, for vocal-electronic settings of contemporary poetry
1984: Tadeusz Kaczyński, for the organization of the Traugutt Philharmonic
1985: Krzysztof Knittel, String Quartet No. 2
1986: Zygmunt Mycielski, *Liturgia Sacra*
1987: Henryk Mikołaj Górecki, *Miserere*
1987: Waldemar Frydrych, as leader of the Orange Alternative happenings

bulk of the journal's pages with a potpourri of cultural happenings sourced from readers.

In the very first article, Piotr Suchocki (art critic Andrzej Osęka) analyzes the status quo with confident lucidity to make a case for independent culture. He sketches a terrain that is free of ideological intervention:

> Two things seem certain: among people, of course not among all, there is a great need for culture that is uncensored, unregulated, and uncontaminated by compromise. And there are also many artists who imagine their place to be precisely in this sphere. Certainly, independent culture will develop. Over the years it will accumulate books, exhibits, concerts, and cassette tapes with songs.[54]

---

54 Piotr Suchocki [Andrzej Osęka], "Po dwóch latach," *Kultura Niezależna* 1 (1984), 3.

TABLE 1.3 The Table of Contents for *Independent Culture* 8 (March 31, 1985)

(1) Editorial introduction
(2) "Witness" (an interview with interned poet Wiktor Woroszylski)
(3) Poetry (by Jerzy Harasymowicz and Bogusława Latawiec under pseudonyms)
(4) Reviews (for example of a poetry anthology published underground and Kurt Vonnegut's *Mother Night*)
(5) Feuilletons (including an editorial by a board member)
(6) Documents (announcements from various opposition groups and an account of the trial against Jerzy Popiełuszko's murderers)
(7) Letters (in response to previous articles)
(8) Events

Independent Culture encompassed a broad and dynamic definition of culture beyond text, as Suchocki's series of media and emphasis on growth suggests. Across the report, he hopes for a dynamic cultural life that enables performance alongside elite literary discourse. In his report, music is crucially and terrifyingly alive. The "forbidden singing of songs" can turn performance into resistance. When people embody music that is banned, he writes, they counteract the power of melodies to subordinate—that act of "singing happy little ditties on a master's command."[55]

Suchocki's provocations shaped the focus of a questionnaire circulated among the readership.[56] Many self-described "artists" chimed in anonymously or under coded pseudonyms with answers to the question, "What is independent culture?" that were published over the course of 1984. Contradictory visions emerged. Jan Biuletyn (Jan Walc) wrote with an aggressive call to Polish artists to fight for their independence: "If Polish culture is to achieve independence, it will have to establish itself as a forum of true discussion, collaboration, and confrontation in the name of values."[57] Another respondent suggested that it was the task of a "full" and "healthy" independent culture to "concentrate on the most important matters." Artists ought not, they contend, take part in the "tactics of the current political battle."[58]

The role that the state would play for an ideal and independent culture was a contentious subject. One anonymous contributor suggested that the whole endeavor of societal reform was steeped in paradox: culture writ large was inherently and integrally dependent on patronage, a receptive audience, and a clear relationship to history. The journal, they argued, should lay out strategies to extract cultural life from the *current* government, from "official forms

---

55 Suchocki, "Po dwóch latach," 3, 5.
56 See *Papierowa rewolucja: Z dziejów drugiego obiegu wydawniczego w Polsce 1976–1989/1990* (Warsaw: Instytut Pamięci Narodu, 2010), 91–101.
57 Jan Biuletyn, "Czy kultura może wybić się na niezależność?" *Kultura Niezależna* 3 (1984), 8–9.
58 "Co to znaczy 'kultura niezależna'? cz. 2," *Kultura Niezależna* 3 (1984), 11.

of organization in the Communist state."[59] Another contributor envisioned living in a society in which independent culture had a tripartite relationship to official culture: in parallel, as a complement, and with the ambition of ameliorating it.[60] Across the debate, the "human spirit" (*duch ludzki*), as well as the image of the arts "fighting," anchored definitions of culture in human society or as a symbolic system. One author creates a typology of culture in the People's Republic: there is "oppositional" culture (the drugi obieg), "apositional" culture (*kultura wysoka*, or high culture), and "positional" culture (socialist realism).[61] These categories, the anonymous writer explained, emphasized that the Party tolerated and monitored religious culture but scrutinized alternative and émigré culture: the government assessed people, not works of art.[62]

These debates referenced music at remove. Many made the distinction between music for the stage (*estrada*) and music for music's sake—a distinction also made by the Party, as we shall see. For example, Jan Krajowiec (Andrzej Jarecki) described cabaret as the counterculture to state-funded song festivals—referencing Jan Pietrzak's "So That Poland Will Be Poland," discussed in the Introduction. But even though—or perhaps because—Krajowiec was a professional songwriter whose lyrics Pietrzak himself sang, he considered this theater, not music.[63] As far as music—classical music—was concerned, Krajowiec asked, "Is musical life's weak pulse a result of the crisis [i.e., martial law]?"[64] He held that the low production value of musical media (radio, television, and film), poor concerts, and a paucity of recordings were all symptoms of a fundamental problem: the emigration of performers and composers as a result of poor economic conditions.[65] An update in a subsequent issue reported that as many as five hundred musicians had moved abroad since 1981.[66]

---

59 "Co to znaczy 'kultura niezależna'?," 13.

60 "Co to znaczy 'kultura niezależna'?," 15.

61 "Co to znaczy 'kultura niezależna'?, cz. 3," *Kultura Niezależna* 5 (1985), 66.

62 Leon Bober [Andrzej Kaczyński], "Polityka kulturalna real-socjalizmu," *Kultura Niezależna* 16 (1986), 88.

63 Jan Krajowiec [Andrzej Jarecki], "Stan kultury polskiej w 1983 roku," *Kultura Niezależna* 1 (1984), 15.

64 Krajowiec, "Stan kultury polskiej w 1983 roku," 23.

65 Composer Krzysztof Knittel explained to me that emigration was a recurring topic for the Committee on Independent Culture: "I took part in a discussion with, among others, Tomek Jastrun, . . . in which each of us had a different vision of the future, of what would happen. . . . I remember that Jan Walc said that many people would leave Poland (I think it was him, but I'm not sure). And that's what happened"; in interview with author, April 26, 2010; quotation confirmed June 6, 2012.

66 *Kultura Niezależna* 5 (1985), 91–92.

In a brief opinion piece, "107 Minutes in a Year," an anonymous individual lamented that the recording industry was anemic and increasingly commercial.[67] They asserted: "Music is apolitical, even though musicians are frequently politicians," perhaps gesturing toward the celebrated pianist, champion of Polish independence, and interwar Premier Ignacy Jan Paderewski.[68] Teodor Ursyn (Jacek Bocheński) went so far as to dismiss music on the grounds of its meager political potential: "So, if journalism, literature, the fine arts, and some humanities research can function underground and can truly perform a great function there, theater is less successful in this regard. Cinema is even less suitable. And what of music and much scholarly research—it seems nearly, though not completely, unnecessary."[69] More anecdotal writings—in particular, the news items—resist the essayists' abstraction. In an effusive review of Miloš Forman's *Amadeus* (1984), one documentary filmmaker interprets the film as a plea for artistic freedom, a rejection of patronage systems, and an attack on censorship. Tomasz Werny (Andrzej Titkow) recognizes Mozart as a rebellious peer passing through one of musical Warsaw's transnational contact zones: "Playing Mozart, Tom Hulce, whose general expression, notably, is particularly close to that of the pianist Ivo Pogorelic—the *enfant terrible* of Warsaw's last Chopin Competition—gives the composer an utterly contemporary air."[70]

Across the periodical's run, music and sound are rarely the quilting points of independent culture. But when they are present, they shed light on the mechanisms of the *drugi obieg* and its power to facilitate conversations impossible in the monitored meetings of the Party, but also not shielded from the public by closed doors and private networks. For example, concealing authors' identities, pseudonyms allowed individuals to speak out in *samizdat* across the Eastern Bloc. They shielded authors from the state and, to some extent, from each other. In *Independent Culture*, the protection made space for controversy. One of the few rebukes of composer Krzysztof Penderecki's iconoclastic self-image as maverick appears in an anonymous letter in its pages.[71] Its author, "M.," outright rejects comments the composer

---

67 The observation is apt: the Party did increasingly understand that rock music could earn it money that could be funneled into other sectors. See Raymond Patton, "The Communist Culture Industry: The Music Business in 1980s Poland," *Journal of Contemporary History* 47, no. 2 (2012), 427–49.

68 "107 minut za rok," *Kultura Niezależna* 3 (1984), 85.

69 "Co to znaczy 'kultura niezależna'? cz. 2," 71.

70 See Tomasz Werny, "Amadeusz—ktoś bliski," *Kultura Niezależna* 11–12 (1985), 53.

71 M., "Pomówienie czy intryga?," *Kultura Niezależna* 10 (1985), 96. Another ad hominem attack, this time about censored lyrics and partisan song, is made in A. L. K., "Moskali usunięci, Litwa też," *Kultura Niezależna* 6 (1985), 47–49. It is a review of *"Bywaj dziewczę zdrowe": Śpiewnik na głos i gitarę*, edited by Janusz Jędrzejczak (Cracow: Polskie

of *Threnody for the Victims of Hiroshima* had made in an interview in a Polish-language UK weekly. The article, they write, makes a hero of Penderecki by giving the impression that he was the lone courageous composer willing to put his name behind Solidarity with the performance of *Lacrimosa* at the anniversary ceremony of December 1970 (discussed at length in Chapter 5). "M." counters: one need not compose music in order to express one's political position as an artist.

Some—but far from a comprehensive register—of the opposition's formal musical activity was advertised in the events listings. These spotlighted concerts outside state channels, such as the celebration of the University of Lviv's 325th anniversary October 4–5, 1985, which the correspondent noted was not officially recognized by the government's calendar.[72] The editors also called out the dismissal of musicologist Józef Patkowski from Polish Radio's Experimental Studio, an ambiguous reaction to Patkowski's outspoken frustration as president of the Polish Composer's Union during martial law. The report includes a list of those willing to put their legal names behind an open letter in solidarity with him.[73]

Ultimately, music surfaces in the journal's pages when the writing in *Independent Culture* captures assembled publics. For example, an intriguing concert description clarifies the kinship between the Independent Culture Committee and Witold Lutosławski, as expressed in his receipt of the "Solidarity" Prize.[74] At the fourth anniversary of the trade union's establishment, the committee hosted a week of festivities that climaxed in a concert, written up in the periodical, at St. Bridget's Church in Gdańsk, Lech Wałęsa's home parish.[75] Musicians performed at cultural events throughout the anniversary celebrations: rock bands (Duval, Pomorzanie), singer-songwriters (Piotr Szczepański, Wiesław Wodyk, and Antonina Krzysztoń), soprano Stefania Woytowicz—in a concert of contemporary and early religious music—with organist Michał Dąbrowski, and the Independent Electroacoustic Music Studio ▶. At the concert, satirical actor Jacek Fedorowicz led the assembled crowd—which included Zbigniew Herbert

---

Wydawnictwo Muzyczne, 1984). A letter to the editor resolves the issue in B. C., "Kto usunął moskali?," *Kultura Niezależna* 9 (1985), 95.

72 *Kultura Niezależna* 26 (1986), 135.

73 See "Dekompozycja," *Kultura Niezależna* 10 (1985), 78.

74 I elaborate on this concert elsewhere and also argue that Lutosławski was a mentor—on an interpersonal level—for many on the Committee on Independent Culture. See Andrea F. Bohlman, "Lutosławski's Refrains," in *Lutosławski's Worlds*, edited by Lisa Jakelski and Nicholas Reyland (Woodbridge, UK: Boydell and Brewer, 2018), 273–300.

75 *Kultura Niezależna* 2 (1984), 60.

alongside activists Wojciech Onyszkiewicz and Adam Michnik—in song and introduced Wałęsa to a standing ovation. The crowd's loud enthusiasm convinced Wałęsa to read the historic twenty-one demands made by the strikers in the shipyards aloud in the sacred space. Numerous actors and actresses, such as KOR member Halina Mikołajska, read texts, and, to open the sanctuary to a mass service, Woytowicz sang an "Ave Maria" setting by film composer Andrzej Kurylewicz.

Witold Lutosławski headlined the festivities. Lech Wałęsa mentioned the esteemed composer's presence when he offered formal thanks at the celebrations:

> A few weeks ago, on the anniversary of the dissolution of the Association of Polish Artists and Designers, I appealed to artistic circles for proud participation in the August anniversary of the Gdańsk Agreement. Today we are witnesses to and participants in the opening of an exhibit of visual artists from the coastal region and a meeting with the excellent world-class composer Witold Lutosławski, laureate of the "Solidarity" Prize.[76]

The composer gave prefatory remarks to his Third Symphony before its playback on tape. This was its second public "performance" in Poland: the previous tape playback occurred at a musicological conference.[77] The composer's live presence appealed to the assembled crowd, even if they did not witness a live musical performance. Lutosławski was a frequent presence at oppositional events as a concerned citizen: notably he stood vigil at Popiełuszko's graveside (Chapter 4) and spoke at the Congress of Polish Culture in 1981 (Chapter 2). But this is the one occasion I have heard or read of when his music was performed or discussed in an official political gathering. How striking, then, that the performance is made possible through sound reproduction, casting attention, again, on the instrumental significance of magnetic tape for the musical work of the opposition. Having traced the music from tape to print and back to tape again, I turn to ask about the place of music in the institutional structure that the Independent Culture Committee was trying to circumvent: the paperwork of the Communist Party.

The Party's Music

Professional makers of destiny
Specialists in songs and masses.

—Lady Pank, "Less than Nothing" ("Mniej niż zero," 1983 ▶)

---

[76] "Lipcowy apel Lecha Wałęsy," *Kultura Niezależna* 2 (1984), 95.
[77] Bohlman, "Lutosławski's Political Refrains," 294.

The 1980s were a decade of swift transformation. Anthropologist Alexei Yurchak captures the ethos in the Soviet Union with the phrase, "Everything was forever, until it was no more."[78] Cold War institutions and structures permitted Solidarity to rise in 1980, adapting censorship policies and redirecting resources, and they orchestrated the military rule of martial law in 1981. From 1984 onward they worked toward so-called normalization, a socioeconomic project aimed at re-energizing institutions as well as the everyday, and they negotiated the end of state socialism in conversation with the opposition at the iconic "round table" discussions in 1989. To borrow the language of my research associates, "the most powerful and feeble" of these state institutions was the Polish United Workers' Party (Polska Zjednoczona Partia Robonicza, PZPR), the governing communist party.[79]

Where was music in this stagnant state? How did the ideas about what music could do change as the political status quo came undone and a new one was imagined? Burrowing into the Party's inner workings over the course of this decade lays bare the tension that Raymond Patton describes as "reform versus retrenchment, ideology versus practical necessity, and the need for change versus the inertia of the immense bureaucracy."[80] The power of the PZPR over culture was in the media network of their administrative practice: paper, paper, and paper.

PZPR committees, bureaucrats, and directors communicated rules, made complaints, and riffed on ideas at their typewriters—very occasionally by hand. This is paperwork as Ben Kafka has defined it: "documents produced in response to a demand—real or imagined—by the state."[81] The memos, speech drafts, censorship reports, and accounting tables produced by the Party are recognizable as bureaucratic records that have become the Party files—the archive of its activity.[82] The Party considered the place and stakes of music in its cloistered offices on an abstract and organizational level. Current events seldomly informed their fantasies and programs for music's political efficacy, even while music journalists complained openly about cultural stagnation and financial frustrations.[83]

---

78 Alexei Yurchak, *Everything Was Forever until It Was No More: The Last Soviet Generation* (Princeton, NJ: Princeton University Press, 2005).

79 Interview by author with Dorota, May 21, 2010; interview by author with Agnieszka, June 22, 2010.

80 Patton, "The Communist Culture Industry," 430.

81 Ben Kafka, *The Demon of Writing* (New York: Zone Books, 2012), 10.

82 Cornelia Vissmann, *Files: Law and Media Technology*, translated by Geoffrey Winthrop Young (Stanford, CA: Stanford University Press, 2008), xi–xiii.

83 The perennially sensational critic Jerzy Waldorff complained about musical stagnation in his "Jedynie możliwe . . .," *Polityka* 41 (1984), reprinted in *Warszawska Jesień w zwierciadle polskiej krytyki muzycznej: Antologia tekstów z lat 1956–2006* (Warsaw: Polish Music Information Center, 2006), 237–39.

The history of the Party and the officials who sought top-down control of Polish society has been an important reference point for political histories of the People's Republic of Poland—subsuming "Poland under Communism," to quote A. Kemp-Welch. On one hand, the activity of the Party's Central Committee had a monolithic presence, emphasized by the colossal socialist-realist building that housed it in central Warsaw. On the other, Party politics were fashioned by bureaucrats whose proof of labor was a bounty of documents, most of which were what Lisa Gitelman calls "no show" documents—designed to be stored and ignored.[84] The reams of paper produced by the Party's many committees, councils, and departments aimed to micromanage activity in Poland—from industrial production to school curricula to words in print. This encompassed a range of musical activity, too.[85] In the People's Republic, the greatest ideological tensions for music had been under stalinism. The structures set in place during before 1956, and their relationship to organizations like the Polish Composers' Union (Związek Kompozytorów Polskich, ZKP), defined the institutional history of music under communism, even after the aesthetic imposition of socialist realism had been tabled.[86] The Departments of Culture (primarily), Learning and Education, and Television and Media all administered musical matters (see Table 1.4). The Culture Department was just one of the Central

---

84 Gitelman writes, "Documents help define and are mutually defined by the know-show function, since documenting is an epistemic practice: the kind of knowing that is all wrapped up with showing, and showing wrapped with knowing. Documents are epistemic objects; they are the recognizable sites and subjects of interpretation across the disciplines and beyond, evidential structures in the long human history of clues. Closely related to the know-show function of documents is the work of no show, since sometimes documents are documents merely by dint of their potential to show: they are flagged and filed away for the future, just in case." See Lisa Gitelman, *Paper Knowledge: Toward a Media History of Documents* (Durham, NC: Duke University Press, 2014), 1–2.

85 Numerous other music studies follow the programs and practices of modern governments on musical culture. See, for example, Emily Abrams Ansari, "Aaron Copland and the Politics of Cultural Diplomacy," *Journal of the Society for American Music* 5, no. 3 (2011), 335–64; Jane Fulcher, *French Cultural Politics and Music: From the Dreyfus Affair to the First World War* (Oxford and New York: Oxford University Press, 1999); Michael H. Kater, *The Twisted Muse: Musicians and Their Music in the Third Reich* (New York: Oxford University Press, 1997); Simon Morrison, *The People's Artist: Prokofiev's Soviet Years* (Oxford and New York: Oxford University Press, 2009), particularly 295–341; Nicholas Tochka, *Audible States*; and Kiril Tomoff, *Creative Union: The Professional Organization of Soviet Composers, 1939–53* (Ithaca, NY: Cornell University Press, 2006).

86 David G. Tompkins, *Composing the Party Line: Music and Politics in Early Cold War Poland and West Germany* (West Lafayette, IN: Purdue University Press, 2013).

TABLE 1.4 The Organizational Hierarchy of the Central Committee of the Polish United Workers' Party, 1981–85

Central Committee Politburo (and SB) Secretariat	
Office of the Secretariat	Bureau of the Central Party Control Commission
Bureau of Letters and Inspection	
General Department	Bureau of the Central Auditing Commission
Central Archive of the Central Committee	Department for Ideological-Educational Work
Bureau of Parliamentary Matters	Press, Radio, and Television Department
Department of Organization	Department of Learning and Education
Personnel Department	Culture Department
Department of Administration	Department of Agricultural and Food Economy
Socio-Professional Department	Department of Industry, Construction, and Transport
Department of Public Organization, Sport, and Tourism	Department of Trade and Finance
Foreign Sector	Institute for Basic Problems of Marxism-Leninism (from 1984 known as the Academy of Social Sciences)

Committee's subdivisions, but its leaders operated in tandem with the other units (see Table 1.4).[87]

The Party did not write off music. Frequent communiques ensured contact across the wide range of bureaus. In the documents of the Culture Department, classical music (referred to as "serious music," or *muzyka poważna*) and music for the stage (*estrada*) both consistently attracted bureaucrats' attention. Breadth was essential to the Party's understanding of music as an art form: music appeals broadly and circulates widely, qualities that were instrumental for the top-down constructive and restrictive policies of the 1980s.[88] The directors and secretaries kept tabs on wide-ranging musical domains—hard rock, cabaret, contemporary music, "old" Polish music, folk music, punk, singer-songwriters, and more—revealing the expanse of

---

87 For detailed attention to the organization of the apparatus, see Krzysztof Dąbek, *PZPR—Retrospektyuwny portret własny* (Warsaw: Wydawnictwo TRIO, 2006), 45. Translations of Party bureaus and divisions are based, when possible, on Paul G. Lewis, *Political Authority and Party Secretaries in Poland, 1975–1986*, (Cambridge: Cambridge University Press, 1989), xviii–xix.

88 One position statement proposed the development of an new periodical to promote classical music to a "broad audience"; see "Stanowisko uczestników krajowego spotkania muzyków w węzłowych sprawach rozwoju polskiej kultury muzycznej," LVI-1735; Wydział Kultury, Komitet Centralny, Polskie Zjdenoczona Partia Robotnicza, Archiwum Akt Nowych, Warsaw, Poland (hereafter WK KC PZPR, AAN). One 1987 outline for entertainment reform notes the range of musics "broadly understood" as entertainment as a strength; see "Główne kierunki zmian organizacyjnych i programowych w Polskiej sztuce estradowej i przemyśle rozrywki," LVI-1747, WK KC PZPR, AAN.

their musical investment in and regulation of music, even if not all musics had equal value or expediency, as we shall see. Genre and other bearers of cultural capital were relevant for the Department's policies and projects. The paperwork reflects a haphazard logic of inclusivity over scrutiny, as though music making is growing beyond the Party's understanding or bureaucrats' comprehension.

There are limits to the glimpse of music provided by paper. The memos, reports, transcribed speeches, and letters are a fraction of the government's inner workings; they are only the written, still-accessible traces of the intricate tap dance of Soviet-socialist politics. Indeed, reconstructing bureaucratic practices is possible because of a simple reality: the Culture Department's archives maintain the collected materials as they were originally filed away for bureaucratic reference. Folders present the paper trail as it was organized (or not) in the 1980s. Extra photocopies, fragmentary telephone messages, and the occasional doodle bring the secretarial desks to life, even if the bulk of the Department's archive preserves an office culture of circulated documents, of communication without its ephemeral conversation. Many missives note their desk of origin rather than their author, official correspondence specifies the other eyes that will read the briefs, and clear headings frequently summarize the function of a report.[89] In the seven years that I have been consulting the archives, documents have been added and folders have disappeared as other scholars troll for their own stories to tell. The Central Committee continues to have a life of its own.

Over the course of Solidarity's decade, the Culture Department discussed the role of music during the process of post-martial law "normalization," a term wielded somewhat imprecisely—but frequently—to justify policy changes and distract from the energy of the opposition by initiating new projects.[90] With the 1984 normalization, the Culture Department briefly established a Subcommittee on Music (Departament Muzyki). It would be

---

89 In the Culture Department of the PZPR in the 1980s there are few full transcriptions of meetings. Studies of earlier Cold War archival trails have been able to make clear distinctions between Communist Party plans for action, verbal debates, and public-sphere outcomes. See, for example, Rachel Beckles Willson's attention to adjudication boards at the Hungarian Composers' Union in *Ligeti, Kurtág, and Hungarian Music in the Cold War* (Cambridge: Cambridge University Press, 2007), 34–42; and Joy H. Calico's discussion of the fabrication of censorship in the German Democratic Republic in "The Trial, the Condemnation, the Cover-up: Behind the Scenes of Brecht/Dessau's *Lucullus* Opera(s)," *Cambridge Opera Journal* 14, no. 3 (2002), 313–42.

90 Padraic Kenney, *A Carnival of Revolution: Central Europe 1989* (Princeton, NJ: Princeton University Press, 2003), 26. See also Paul G. Lewis, *Political Authority and Party Secretaries in Poland 1975–1986*, 218–52, for reforms within the Party. As David Ost writes, "The period from 1982 to 1986 was marked by an effort to win *some* support from *some* sections of civil society"; see David Ost, *Solidarity and the Politics of Anti-Politics* (Philadelphia: Temple University Press, 1990), 155.

disbanded by the second normalization efforts in 1987, which focused on so-called *rozrywka,* or entertainment, about which more in this chapter. Like the authors for *Independent Culture*, the Music Subcommittee's director, luthier Włodzimierz Kamiński, had to define his task. He deployed Polish music's strength of identity as a bait and switch in his assessment of the state and needs of music in Poland, the most extended written examination of music by the Party in the 1980s. "Poland's musical society is too strong to allow a general collapse of musical arts," he claimed.[91] Kamiński further suggested that music's exceptionalism had also left it untended by the Party:

> In terms of cultural political interests, music has always had an inferior position as compared to other artistic genres [*gatunki*]. This does not mean that it is completely neglected; in official declarations one speaks with pride of its international successes, of its historical traditions. In concrete administrative divisions, music escapes purview as a less urgent problem, of minor importance in the shaping of the cultural image of our society: it is neglected as an instrument of cultural politics. One can find the source of such attitudes in the popular belief that, as an asemantic art, it can only influence the shaping of society's beliefs to a small degree in contrast to literature, film, theater, and, possibly, sculpture. Only the latter are considered effective mediators of ideas—political, national, societal [*społeczny*], patriotic—and as a result, only they are credited with shaping the desired cultural model of our society.

He draws attention to the contradiction that it is successful despite the state's neglect or lack of clear vision.

Throughout the time of Solidarity, the Party's cultural organizers and bureaucrats planned and reviewed specific cultural events in conversation with the Ministry of Arts and Sciences. With the numerous state-sponsored artists' organizations in Table 1.5 in consistent competition for financial attention and a less-watchful Party eye (which could result from good behavior), the desk of the Culture Department was often the last stop a set of regulations made before approval.[92] One need only glance through the

---

91 Włodzimierz Kamiński, "Polska kultura muzyczna: Stan i potrzeby," LVI-210, WK KC PZPR, AAN.

92 Information in Table 1.5 was culled from the Culture Department's report in 1983 (536 897/88, WK KC PZPR, AAN). For example, a summary of jazz's growth in Poland until 1985 details the financial stability of the major festival, the Jazz Jamboree; see "Stan aktualny i perspektywy rozwoju ruchu jazzowego w Polsce: Wyprowadzenie do dyskusji," 1185 930/9, WK KC PZPR, AAN.

TABLE 1.5 Musical Associations Receiving Funds from the PZPR in 1983, with Membership Estimate When Available

---

Wieniawski Musical Society of Poznań (Towarzystwo Muzyczne im. H. Wieniawskiego w Poznaniu), 273 members
Polish Jazz Clubs (Polskie Stowarzyszenie Jazzowe), 236 members
Polish Association of Contemporary Music (Polskie Towarzystwo Muzyki Współczesnej), 60 members
Authors' Guild, or Union of Authors and Composers for the Stage (Stowarzyszenie Autorów "ZAIKS"), 3,951 members
Association of Polish Musician-Artists (Stowarzyszenie Polskich Artystów Muzyków), 4,132 members
Association of Polish Musical Youth (Stowarzyszenie Polskiej Młodzieży Muzycznej), 1,755 members
Frédéric Chopin Society (Towarzystwo im. F. Chopina), 819 members
Szymanowski Musical Society in Zakopane (Towarzystwo Muzyczne im. Szymanowskiego w Zakopanem), 229 members
Polish Composers' Union (Związek Kompozytorów Polskich, ZKP), 288 members
Union of Polish Rozrywka Authors and Composers (Związek Polskich Autorów i Kompozytorów Utworów Rozrywkowych, ZAKR), 314 members
Union of Polish Luthiers (Związek Polskich Artystów Lutników), 96 members
Polish Branch of the International Society for Music Education (Stow. Wychowania Muzycznego ISME)
Folk Institute of Music (Ludowy Instytut Muzyczny)
Polish Union of Choirs and Orchestras (Polskich Związek Chór i Orkiestr)

---

diverse constituencies represented—luthiers, jazz musicians, Chopin enthusiasts, and more—to understand the sprawling scope of musical concerns the Culture Department faced.

The PZPR favored festivals and concerts that promoted Polish music, in addition to the transnational festivals like the Warsaw Autumn Festival for Contemporary Music and the Intervision Song Festival in Sopot.[93] Maria Fołtyn, an opera singer turned dramaturg, repeated the Party line as she sought support for a summer music festival devoted to the nineteenth-century composer Stanisław Moniuszko in 1985. "I was encouraged to hear that during the meeting of the Central Committee, the role of music in society was recognized as an important element in educating [*wychowanie*] the nation; its problems should not be overlooked in cultural politics."[94] Fołtyn tapped Moniuszko as a Polish cultural "diplomat," ignoring his significance

---

93 For an extended analysis of music festivals and international history, see Andrea F. Bohlman, "'Where I Cannot Roam, My Song Will Take Wing': Polish Cultural Promotion in Belarus, 1988," in *Music and International History*, edited by Jessica C. E. Gienow-Hecht (New York and Oxford: Berghahn Books, 2015), 226–55.

94 Letter dated April 4, 1985, LVI-1735, WK KC PZPR, AAN.

across the multiethnic landscape of nineteenth-century Eastern Europe.[95] For her, his two celebrated operas *Halka* (1847) and *The Haunted Manor* (*Straszny Dwór*, 1861–64) on Polish themes and built of regional dances proved the inherent value of the festival. She had built her own career as a soprano on Moniuszko's music ▶. When she founded the festival in 1962 along with a partner song competition (in Warsaw) to "propagate his music through the whole world" she positioned it as what Lisa Jakelski, with respect to the Warsaw Autumn Festival, has called a "contact zone."[96]

Culture, the PZPR set out in a series of theses, "provides an interpretation of social values."[97] Its artifacts, the document suggests, could be used for specific and practical political, economic, and social goals, just as Fołtyn hoped for Moniuszko:

> The Polish United Workers' Party considers progressive humanism and interdisciplinary heritage to be the greatest value in Polish culture. At the same time, it strives to assimilate the cultural heritage and ideas of other nations—especially those building a new order through socialism or the struggle for freedom—into contemporary culture. [It also strives] to spread the achievements of Polish culture broadly among other nations.[98]

Notably absent across both Kamiński's assessment and the program articulated here is any reference to the uses of music in the social formations of protest (Chapter 3), counter-memorial projects (Chapter 5), or in alternative economies such as the drugi obieg. Polish culture remained not only distinct and distinctive, but also defined as heritage groomed by the nation-state.

Włodzimierz Kamiński turned to Chopin-based specifics to link the national and the universal in his 1984 report.[99] Chopin served as the thread

---

95 Rüdiger Ritter, "Polnisch, litauisch oder weißrussisch? Stanisław Moniuszko und das Problem der nationalen Musik," in *Nationale Musik im 20. Jahrhundert: Kompositorische und soziokulturelle Aspekte der Musikgeschichte zwischen Ost- und Westeuropa*, edited by Helmut Loos and Stefan Keym (Leipzig: Schröder Verlag: 2004), 182–204.

96 Ewa Solińska, *W salonie muzycznym: Wywiady* (Bydgoszcz: Pomorze, 1986), 267. Jakelski, *Making New Music in Cold War Poland*, 163.

97 "Tezy do dyskusji nad polityką kulturalną Partii," LIV-1413, WK KC PZPR, AAN.

98 "Tezy do dyskusji nad polityką kulturalną Partii", LIV-1413, WK KC PZPR, AAN.

99 During the Cold War, writers found the roots of the composer's universal appeal in undeniably Polish detail: the vegetation surrounding his birthplace, the "Polish" dance styles in which he composed, and his ties to Polish émigrés upon his arrival in Paris. Jim Samson discusses the museology of the Chopin residence in Żelazowa Wola as representative of the "Chopin cult's" obsession with the composer's Polishness in the 1970s, in *Chopin* (New York: Schirmer, 1996), 2. See, for example, the coffee table book published for tourists to Warsaw, *Żelazowa Wola*, edited by Irena Lange (Warsaw: Wydawnictwo "Sport i Turystyka," 1970).

through his brief history of music and oppression from the time of the French Revolution through the end of the Second World War:

> Music, like a mirror, reflects all of the most important historical events. As in the case of literature, Poles sought national identity in music during the time of partition. Musical societies were at that time beyond a doubt safe and were the most important means of creating continuity in national culture. Furthermore, as Schumann wrote to Chopin about music: there are weapons hidden in the flowers. Not without reason [Poles] remember those Nazi [*hitlerowcy*] weapons that strictly forbade the performance of Polish music during the Nazi occupation—above all Chopin. Music accompanied movements for freedom: it was at the barricades of revolution. It accompanied the French people and the Polish, German, and Russian workers, in the same manner, remaining the most universal and transnational carrier of political ideas.[100]

For Kamiński, music's consistent presence and capacity to both reflect and enact political ideology was evidenced in both Polish and European history. The text reads peculiarly, however, given the more recent occupational strikes and public unrest of the Polish opposition during the Cold War—whether in 1956, 1968, 1970, or in the examples about which I write in the chapters that follow. Kamiński's selective examples of songs as nonviolent weapons underscore the disconnect between cultural policymaking and undeniably loud and present political singing in their contemporary world.

There were national quotas and language requirements that kept official music making marked as Polish, especially in the case of popular song.[101] When Johnny Cash performed at the Sopot Song Festival in 1987, his American act was flanked by a battalion of Polish stars ▶.[102] For the "Country Picnic" Festival, the Department insisted that the performers' language be Polish and country of origin be Poland, even if their songs came from abroad.[103] At the Intervision Festival in Sopot, the Soviet

---

100 Kamiński, "Polska kultura muzyczna: Stan i potrzeby," LVI-210, WK KC PZPR, AAN.

101 Fifty years earlier, Stalin had famously outlined the function of socialist realism for socialist republics: "The development of cultures national in form and socialist in content is necessary for the purpose of their ultimate fusion into one General Culture, socialist as to form and content, and expressed in one general language." Quoted in Marina Frolova-Walker, "'National in Form, Socialist in Content': Musical Nation-Building in the Soviet Republics," *Journal of the American Musicological Society* 51, no. 2 (1998), 331.

102 LVI-1750, WK KC PZPR, AAN.

103 LVI-1738, WK KC PZPR, AAN.

broadcasting network's counterpart to the Eurovision Song Contest, foreign representatives were required to include a song in Polish in their musical arsenal. When GDR Schlager superstar Frank Schöbel performed his "Ich geh' vom Nordpol zum Südpol zu Fuss" ("I Travel from the North Pole to the South Pole on Foot," 1973) at the 1975 competition, he had to sing it in Polish with a new refrain for this sentimental love song: "Po pocałunek" ("For a kiss"). Schöbel's "Polish music" was released on an LP devoted to the GDR in advance by the state recording label, Polskie Nagrania.[104] Live performance, unvetted by the Party, articulated the limits of the project of Polonization. In the simple and alliterative text, some phrases full of a range of consonants pass as over-accented Polish. Others are made of smaller, repeated units. As Schöbel tries again and again to pin down vowel nasalizations, the foreignness (and probable incomprehensibility) of these sounds to his tongue feels audible.

Music as Entertainment

The Party understood the diplomatic potential of Moniuszko's *krakowiak*s and Schöbel's Polish-adaption of Schlager to *szlagier* on the axis of nationalist ideology. But they did not consider both music. Popular song for the stage instead was rozrywka, perhaps the most inclusive sphere of the arts within the Polish culture and the PZPR's Culture Department. As a discursive construct, rozrywka served to distinguish between those artistic activities that the Party could confidently refer to as music, literature, or visual art. It was the popular other that confirmed the high-brow status of the intelligentsia's arts. Translated variously as entertainment, recreation, amusement, pastime, and diversion, the term referred and refers to an ever-expanding group of cultural activities. The sincerity of the drugi obieg—and its distance from commercial markets—keeps the term from being relevant for or in use by people like Bratkowski, but rozrywka's flexibility as a label recalls the capaciousness of the musics excerpted as incidental, influential, and informational on the *Sound Gazette*.

With each wave of normalization, the Culture Department updated its understanding of rozrywka.[105] In 1988 the operating definition for rozrywka confirmed its widespread influence and low-brow aura:

---

104 *Przeboje z Niemieckiej Republiki Demokratycznej*, Polskie Nagrania, SXL 1167 (1974).

105 Houses of Culture, where rozrywka was performed, were also re-evaluated. See Anne White, *De-Stalinization and the House of Culture*, 69–78.

Rozrywka is a broad concept. It includes: stage arts, music, the circus, cabaret, variety shows, amusement parks, and even that so-called 'gastronomic rozrywka,' in addition to media for transmission and dissemination such as records and video.

In such a large field of activity it is unusually important to penetrate the cultural domain, to formulate its political judgements, and to delineate its tasks. Especially, since it is rozrywka—mass culture—that has a very large influence on the patterns of life, relaxation, and the preference of particular ideas and values.

In Warsaw, as in the whole country, there has never been a fully developed definition of popular and mass culture. Rozrywka was always used for art of a lower quality and treated as thus by both policy makers and art criticism.[106]

"Mass culture," a critical concept for any Culture Department under Soviet state socialism, had power. Though rozrywka could be fleeting and thrilling, it was still influential and popular—to be taken seriously. For example, the profits from the Party's bouquet of popular song festivals were frequently rerouted to fund art music.[107]

During normalization, the Subcommittee on Rozrywka and the Stage hosted a conversation about mass culture, technology, and artistic value parallel to Kamiński's assessment of music and the hand wringing at the foundation of *Independent Culture*. Many of its documents drip with an idealism that rozrywka can and does effect unity across society, profession, age, religious heritage, and nation. One missive outlined almost breathlessly: "Emphasis on events not only for youth, but also for the middle as well as older generations. Rehabilitation of sensational rozrywka (melodic songs, literary cabaret, musical spectacle!). Rozrywka of social value and engagement."[108] The PZPR also understood American popular music as a tool: by crafting rozrywka "near to the Anglosaxon style" they strategized that the Party could cater to generations that enjoyed the "primitive or apparent non-conformism or demonstrative ambivalence toward everything."[109] The Party's consistent investment in dissemination and education (*upowszechnienie*) in the 1950s set the tone for its reinvestment in popular music and youth culture in the 1980s.[110]

---

106 "Ocena stanu rozrywki w Warszawie, 1988," LVI-1750, WK KC PZPR, AAN.

107 Patton, "The Communist Culture Industry," 435.

108 "Program SBIA na lata 1986/89 (skrót—też programowych)," LVI-1748, WK KC PZPR, AAN.

109 "Czym jest SBiA na dziś?," LVI-1748, WK KC PZPR, AAN.

110 Lisa Cooper Vest, "Educating Audiences, Educating Composers: The Polish Composers' Union and *Upowszechnienie*," *Musicology Today* 7 (2010), 226–42.

On Warsaw's stages the government-affiliated Capital City Bureau of Artistic Events organized rozrywka.[111] Zbigniew Adrjański, its director, boasted of the breadth of its offerings. He took credit for the following: the formation of experimental avant-garde theater; three cabaret artists' employment; what he called "political and parapolitical" concerts of historical and patriotic popular song; and other parties that involved music. The Bureau supported the seasons of two chamber orchestras, a big band orchestra, a ballet ensemble, and two series of light classical music. Rock and punk musicians performed under the organization's wings; Adrjański sponsored the seasons of three Polish bands. A number of internationally famous touring heavy metal and punk bands (including Iron Maiden), as well as prominent Polish punk bands (Dezerter, TSA, and Kult), put on concerts in Warsaw ▶.

Writing on music in the People's Republic of Poland, whether within the reams of Party communiqués or in the press, made a clear distinction between those who hear (*słuchaczy*) and those who "receive," or watch (*odbiorcy*). As the Party understood it, rozrywka was directed at the latter. A 1984 summarizing diagram reflects this emphasis on the "receivers": they are placed in a large square that dominates the right side of a landscape A4 page.[112] Arrows labeled video, television, radio, press, and publishers—all distribution media—point to the box. Performance modes that made "immediate confrontation possible" also flow toward it: concerts, festivals, competitions, trade fairs, variety shows, and workshops. These live performances also reached "receivers" on air and in print. In moments of financial crisis during the 1980s, the Polish People's Republic sought out "new forms of spectacle" precisely *because* they combined song and scene. These realized the ideal of Soviet *estrada*: urban-oriented, cabaret-influenced songs that were sentimental and nostalgic.[113] When the "controversial singer and cabaret actor" Andrzej Rosiewicz, for example, fell under scrutiny for his mocking texts and financial ambition, it was his humor's legibility on the stage that his defenders offered as evidence of his "good programs."[114]

---

111 "Czym jest SBiA na dziś?", LVI-1748, WK KC PZPR, AAN.

112 "Proces promocyjno-przemysłowy w muzyce rozrywkowej," AAN, KC PZPR, WK LVI-1746.

113 On the Soviet tradition, see David MacFadyen, *Estrada?!: Grand Narratives and the Philosophy of the Russian Popular Song since Perestroika* (Montreal: McGill-Queen's University Press, 2005), 175.

114 Letter from Witold Tadeusz Łojkowski to Witold Nawrocki, January 26, 1985, 1185 930/9, WK KC PZPR, AAN.

Party-funded events that were understood to have failed audiences generated the most detailed paperwork: consider the file reporting on the public concert to celebrate the 40th anniversary of Warsaw's liberation.[115] The evening was designed as an ode to the city's recent history in full *estrada* glory. As the review in the Party's newspaper described:

> A journey back into the past—this is, in a nutshell, how we could describe the [concert's] peculiar mystery. It consists of snippets from archives, documentary films interlaced with songs performed by well-known theatre and music performers from Warsaw. Melodies and images of the capital as it is today illustrated specific moments in the lives of Varsovians and their city.[116]

The final assessment must reconcile these objectives while explicitly acknowledging that there were "clear mistakes." Perhaps this is a reference to other, uncited complaints about the event from within the Party. In another report, Adam Kaczmarek, working for the Culture Committee, critiqued the final song, Agnieszka Osiecka's "Susanna" ("Zuzanna," 1985), performed by Maryla Rodowicz. The lyrics' sparkling adoration of disco, Cadillacs, and African Americans was, for Kaczmarek, too positive a sketch of Western commerce.[117]

The anonymous report summarizes the care that went into the concert's organization. Its team—a scenic designer, theater director, and a filmmaker—had previous experience with anniversary concerts. The document defends creative decisions with reference to extensive conversations between the City Bureau, the City of Warsaw, and the Culture Department. All had agreed that the event should foreground Polish singers performing current hits from radio and television. They would play back films that show the friendship with the Soviet Union, since "formulating a political position is difficult to accomplish in the context of rozrywka." With this backstory in mind, the author reports that the stage design, list of performers, film, and "particularly the texts" had all been approved. The officials in attendance at the dress rehearsal are named. The Party is wrestling with its failure: some critics found it hard to hear or excessive. The report even acknowledges the hostile climate engendered by the ideological persecution of actors during martial law over the course of 1982 (see Chapter 2).

---

115 "Notatka w sprawie koncertu z okazji 40 rocznicy wyzwolenia Warszawy," 1185 930/9, WK KC PZPR, AAN.

116 "Notatka w sprawie koncertu z okazji 40 rocznicy wyzwolenia Warszawy," 1185 930/9, WK KC PZPR, AAN.

117 "Notatka informacyjna nt. koncertu z okazji 40-lecia wyzwolenia Warszawy," 1185 930/9, WK KC PZPR, AAN.

Ultimately, the Party formulaically concedes one dramaturgical problem before delivering a final assessment: success. The problem:

> The premise was that the finale would be a "contemporary frame that held the spectacle together." Following the film that showed the devastated city of Warsaw, a reflective poem, the little song, "Dove of Peace," the composition, "Susanna"—a popular hit with children participating—was supposed to show the joy of the young generation and its hopefulness.
>
> We had already realized at the rehearsal that this effect had not been achieved. That is why the decision was made to bring out the flower basket earlier, and to have the final song performed outside of the concert, as it were: "as an encore." That intervention, it turned out, was not enough. The negative impression was aggravated by the full-on lighting in the auditorium and the overly expressive, "forceful" performance of the piece on the part of the orchestra as well as by Maryla Rodowicz.[118]

The rip-roaring chest voice of Rodowicz, a supreme belter of the pop industry in Poland, undermined the event's reach when the audience refused to sing along or felt themselves literally under the spotlight ▶.

The Culture Department functioned as much as an institution to whom other administrators reported—a mediator that regulated—as it did as a watchdog or menacing financier. This entailed processing letters of complaint by rozrywka darlings. In December 1985 the jazz crooner and three-time winner of the Opole Festival, Andrzej Dąbrowski, learned that Polish Radio had canceled a scheduled appearance and banned his songs from its airwaves. He was given a clear reason: there were rumors he had "participated in performances organized by churches."[119] The implication was that he furtively supported the opposition. (The summary of this incident contains no evidence or suggestion that he did.) Dąbrowski submitted an official refutation of this accusation in a letter sent to the Party and Polish Radio and Television on December 31. He listed a handful of recent concerts at official venues: at limestone quarries, the anniversary of an iron foundry, and other performances for workers. He also spoke with pride of the success of his most recent single, "*Szał* by night" ("Nighttime frenzy"), on air ▶. He concluded with a sense that the mythical power of the Party bureaucracy might also be its Achilles heel. If there was so much paperwork, some, surely, must go wrong: "I could list many more such examples

---

[118] "Notatka w sprawie koncertu z okazji 40 rocznicy wyzwolenia Warszawy," 1185 930/9, WK KC PZPR, AAN.

[119] Letter to the Cultural Committee from Andrzej Dąbrowski, December 31, 1985, 1185 930/9, WK KC PZPR, AAN.

of my actual activities, and I am happy to do so should the need arise. More than twenty years as a stage performer—that is too great an artistic achievement to be lost suddenly due to an irresponsible bureaucrat's unfortunate mistake." Whoever processed this request likely did so away from the written record: we know it was taken seriously because it was kept (very few such letters remain) and because the resumé he attached bears evidence that it was read carefully. The state's recognition of his artistic merit (Zasłużony Działacz Kultury) was underlined.

Wending our way through the logic and log jams of the Culture Department, the Party's consistent ambition—if often unfulfilled—materializes. The PZPR managed events and institutions more than people. In order to track, promote, and celebrate music, the Department broke it down into its smallest unit: songs. One Party memo succinctly described the appeal of these small units: "It's a short dramatic form, easy to display. The dramaturgy is contractually regulated, and the methods of presentation are extremely easy and tread on stereotypes."[120] Songs could be reduced to lyrics. The Censorship Bureau piled song lyrics up for scrutiny; festivals were made of detailed programs with songs that were vetted and celebrated.[121] Songs, too, suited the rather porous generic categories of rozrywka and also enable people like Kamiński to construct a conceptual bridge to high culture. There are rock songs, cabaret songs, chansons, art songs, protest songs, religious songs, and the list proliferates.

As bounded units, songs fostered close reading by the Party, particularly songs by the performers on Bratkowski's tapes: poezja śpiewana authors like Kaczmarski or cabaret artists from the Cellar Beneath the Rams.[122] But the Culture Department always treated songs as texts. On one rare—perhaps single—occasion, they scrutinized a cassette tape; the files leave no record of listening to the drugi obieg. The tape that landed on a bureaucrat's desk was by an unknown author and contained two songs about the premier, General Wojciech Jaruzelski. The aesthetic object fared poorly. Stanisław Stęcik signed a scathing report in which he commented explicitly on fidelity and performance:

> The quality of the recording is very poor. The sung melody is unrecognizable. Very few expressive phrases in a singular, vague sound. Everything is unsettled rhythmically and with respect to verse.

---

120 "Uwagi do programów rozrywkowych TVP," LVI-1745, WK KC PZPR, AAN.
121 "Wyjaśnienie dotyczące występu Jana Pietrzaka 18.08.88 r. w drugim dniu MFP Sopot 88," LVI-1749, WK KC PZPR, AAN.
122 Jolanta Drużyńska and Stanisław M. Jankowski, *Kolacja z konfidentem: Piwnica pod Baranami w dokumentach Służby Bezpieczeństwa* (Cracow: Przedsięwzięcie Galicja, 2006).

Neither the text nor the wailing singing contain any artistic value. Primitive thoughts and "Częstochowa" rhymes.[123] You can sense the author's intentions are good, but the result is embarrassing and disgraceful. There are two works (naïve and truly laughable) about General Jaruzelski, but the rest of the songs belong in the category of "humorous" folk chatter or pastoral songs.

The whole cassette is the a cappella singing of a single woman whose voice is reminiscent of the wails of women in a Rosary Prayer group.[124]

The bureaucrat concludes that there is no reason to circulate the tape further or pursue action. Paperwork, it seems, and tapes did not mix.

Songs from an Old Cassette

A final cassette story positions tape as an opening once more—this time not into the sound world of the opposition or as a counterpoint to the Party's obsession with text, but as a reminder of the range of channels the state used to control. For though it was the Culture Department that *managed* expressive culture, including music, the SB used sound to incriminate. They swiped whole tape collections when they raided apartments: though these sounds remain inaccessible beyond official publications by the Institute of National Memory in 2018, their records are catalogued. In addition to the drugi obieg cassettes like Bratkowski's, the SB agents kept tapes of domestic and international rock, children's stories, classical music, and many, many unlabeled others. But making moves based on what they heard—taking legal action on the basis of musical sound—was a challenge for the agents. Attribution issues, like those flagged by Bratkowski in his disclaimer, prevented persecution, as in the case of Jan Krzysztof Kelus, a singer I have already mentioned, who founded one Warsaw-based drugi obieg cassette label, CDN.

When Radio Solidarity, an underground station founded in April 1982, aired its first broadcast, the agents working for the Ministry of Internal Affairs (Ministerstwo Spraw Wewnętrznych) struggled to trace its signal as they worked to arrest its operators and halt its transmission. But someone recognized Kelus's voice, singing with guitar. In the singer's own words: "That wild recording . . . for them it was clear, that

---

123 "Częstochowa," a snobbish reference to a city in Poland, refers to common, predictable, and tired rhyme patterns that denote an anthem's narrow literary range.

124 "Notatka w sprawie opinii o nagraniach na załączonej taśmie," LVI-1734, WK KC PZPR, AAN.

that was me—my voice was instantly identifiable."[125] Indeed, the broadcast begins with a quick signal played on recorder from the song "Axe, Hammer" ("Siekiera, Motyka"), part of the urban folklore of resistance in Nazi-occupied Warsaw ▶. Two hosts—a man and a woman—then introduce the station, which they call their "experiment." Those at home are invited to listen in, to tape the broadcast and disseminate it, to keep the work of Solidarity going during martial law. After three minutes of commentary, they play back an entire track by Kelus from tape: his December 1981 setting of Jakub Broniec's "Last Shift at the Piast Mine" ("Ostatnia szychta na KWK Piast").[126]

Kelus was immediately imprisoned and put under investigation. After four months, however, he was found innocent. Even though the SB was confident that this was Kelus's voice, the SB could not pin him to the illegal radio operation. His official release notes the disjuncture between what is heard on the radio and who makes that sound. "A recording of his performance was broadcast on the program on April, 12 1982. There was no evidence in the course of conducting investigative work to indicate clearly that J. Kelus was directly involved in the development or operation of an illegal radio station."[127] Another report notes that his voice is not "legal evidence that would make it possible to charge him."[128] Though Kelus's tape was a dead end for the SB's investigation, it also gestures toward the defining moment of the cultural history of 1980s Poland: the declaration of martial law on December 13, 1981.

---

125 In interview with Krzysztof Gajda, *Poza państwowem monopolem—Jan Krzysztof Kelus* (Poznań: Wydawnictwo WiS, 1998), xxxix.

126 The first eight minutes of broadcast are available online at Polish Radio: http://www.polskieradio.pl/5/3/Artykul/495729,Radio-najwazniejsze-medium-stanu-wojennego.

127 "Wniosek o uchylenia internowania wobec Jana Krzysztofa Kelusa," IPN BU 0787/477, Institute of National Memory, Warsaw, Poland.

128 IPN BU 01326/1755 (3956/3), Institute of National Memory, Warsaw, Poland.

2 | Silence

W grudniu nad ranem straśna {sic} wieść
  gruchła
W noc mroźną dnia trzynastego,
Że u nas w Polsce wojna wybuchła
I to tak sobie z niczego.

One morning in December terrible
  news struck
During the frosty night of the 13th,
Here in Poland war had erupted,
Just like that, out of nothing.

—*"Files of Plebian Verses: Martial Law"*

Sunday, early morning, the thirteenth of December 1981: General Jaruzelski declares a state of martial law with the goal of curbing threats to the stability of the Communist Party in Poland. The Security Service (Śłużba Bezpieczeństwa, SB) and militia take to the streets in tanks and with guns, where they enforce a new curfew and are empowered to search citizens at will. The military pounds at activists' doors and seizes leading dissidents, loading them into transport vehicles that deposit them in internment camps across Poland over the following days. Overnight, the independent trade union known as Solidarity, the first lawful trade union in the Eastern Bloc, is made illegal. Sunday, the thirteenth of December 1981, would become an indelible date in any history of Poland.[1]

---

1 My account of martial law follows the political history as presented by A. Kemp-Welch in *Poland under Communism: A Cold War History* (Cambridge: Cambridge University Press, 2008), 302–32; and by Tadeusz Razukowski in *Stan wojenny w Warszawie i województwie stołecznym 1981–83* (Warsaw: Instytut Pamięci Narodu, 2009), but evokes the experience of the first days of martial law based upon my own interviews (Piotr Wierzbicki, June 30, 2010; Małgorzata Pietkiewicz, July 2, 2010). Numerous oral histories of the

Musical Solidarities. Andrea F. Bohlman, Oxford University Press (2020). © Oxford University Press.
DOI: 10.1093/oso/9780190938284.001.0001

This chapter is the music history of that day and its impact on the culture of martial law: the sounds that charged its affective atmospheres, the efforts to respond to its devastation through music, and the everyday work that singing did to keep its reality from becoming normalized oppression. Jaruzelski's drastic measures were designed to prevent public assembly, to keep workers from striking and the opposition from demonstrating. The implementation of martial law targeted gatherings organized by the opposition, but its imposition of a nightly curfew, license to search private citizens in public spaces, and dispersion of military police and tanks on city streets had ramifications for every person living in Poland. Martial law affected everyone, across geography, class, and generation. The all-encompassing and acute nature of this state intervention explains its continued resonance as the most terrifying moment in postwar Polish history: its modulation from acute military force into a social metaphor of silence in public memory. Theater critic Marek Miller eventually wrote of an "aesthetics of silence" that emerged from this standstill.[2] In social memory, the cold winter of 1981–82 is elided with a freeze on everyday life that extended to musical culture, which had otherwise been funded and celebrated across genre by the Party. Composer Paweł Szymański, in a program note considered too provocative for publication by the Censorship Bureau, described his disinterest in working on the commission request from his friend, the critic Andrzej Chłopecki, that would become his Sonata for Strings and Percussion (1982) ▶. As he recalled their early 1982 meeting to discuss a piece by the early twentieth-century composer Karol Szymanowski that was meant to be the inspiration for his new work: "Szymanowski's mazurka was not at the center of my consciousness. We were sitting then—with Andrzej—for a weak coffee in a decrepit cafe in central Warsaw. People were stooped over the stables talking in hushed voices."[3] Such allusions to muted or altered social and creative conditions evoke the weighted omnipresence of martial law.

---

weeks following martial law's declaration further substantiate the memorable nature of this period of Polish history: Jan Kulas, *Stan wojenny: Wspomnienia i oceny* (Gdańsk: Pepliń "Bernardinium," 1999); Janina Jankowska, *Portrety niedokończone: Rozmowy z twórcami "Solidarności" 1980–81* (Warsaw: Biblioteka "Więzi," 2003). The epigraph's story of December 13 is that from an anonymous typescript, III/20K.1, Opposition Archive, Karta Organization, Warsaw, Poland.

2 Quoted in Kathleen Cioffi, *Alternative Theatre in Poland, 1954–1989* (London: Routledge, 1996), 155.

3 Quoted in the program for *Festiwal Muzyki Pawła Szymańskiego*, November 24–December 1, 2006, Witold Lutosławski Studio of the Polish Radio, 111. The composer comments that this text was submitted to the Warsaw Autumn Festival program book as a note (from the December 15, 1982 premiere). However, it was rejected by internal censorship.

Despite the many ways in which Jaruzelski's government designed martial law to silence the Polish opposition to state socialism, cultural activity proved a crucial means of reclaiming agency in response to the intrusion upon personal freedom. Artistic collaboration and production allowed people to keep their knowledge of recent events up to date in the absence of direct communication. I locate several sites of musical action through the initial, most severe months of martial law, approximately until July 1982, by which time the harshest restrictions had been lifted. In this local—and acute—political context, musical action refers to moments in which citizens turned to music to express themselves at once politically and imaginatively. But this is not political protest or organized opposition. Instead, I suggest, it is the crafting of an everyday life infused with sonic thinking and being to keep Jaruzelski's intervention from becoming normal.[4]

December 13 configured new "worlds of dissent" across the spaces in which social activity was still permitted: the barren street, the safeguarded church, and the surveilled prison. In Jonathan Bolton's theoretical engagement with the dissidence crafted in late 1960s Prague, he evokes dissent "as a world, a form of experience and behavior. Dissent was a philosophy, but it was also a common set of situations and experiences closely tied to daily life—experiences that had little to do with politics, theory, or Western reception."[5] Across the examples here, citizens assert individual agency through musical articulation; they reclaim their voices as modern subjects.[6] Musical action can take its impetus from sound—the boundary between sound and music during martial law was frequently heard as fluid, as I shall show. Listening as historians to martial law allows us to relocate the agency that drives the cultural work to understand, remember, and reclaim the state's "invasion."

It has been assumed that martial law halted music making, that it effected literal silence.[7] The internationally renowned Warsaw Autumn Festival

---

4 As one activist in the opposition described martial law, "The most serious threat was that Solidarity would dissolve into this normalcy." Quoted in Shana Penn, *Solidarity's Secret: The Women Who Defeated Communism in Poland* (Ann Arbor: University of Michigan Press, 2005), 167.

5 Jonathan Bolton, *Worlds of Dissent: Charter 77, the Plastic People of the Universe, and Czech Culture under Communism* (Cambridge, MA: Harvard University Press, 2012), 13.

6 Ana María Ochoa Gautier, "Silence," in *Keywords in Sound*, edited by David Novak and Matt Sakakeeny (Durham, NC: Duke University Press, 2015), 183–92.

7 Cindy Bylander focuses on censorship and restriction at the Polish Composers' Union in the immediate aftermath of its declamation in an article that otherwise frames martial law as the impetus for post-1983 concert life for classical musicians. See Cindy Bylander, "Responses to Martial Law: Glimpses of Poland's Musical Life in the 1980s," *Musicology Today* (2010), 176–77.

was canceled, several music periodicals ceased publication, and prominent popular musicians on tour—like Solidarity's bard, Jacek Kaczmarski (see Chapter 3)—elected to stay abroad. Beyond official culture, however, there was a rich musical network that involved prisoners', amateurs', and professional musicians' communal music making. Song, performance, and communities of participation linked activity across the presumably discrete spaces and united displaced political activists. The story of martial law that follows is at its base about navigating the inconsistent archives of late-twentieth-century cultural history—personal and fallible oral histories, mixtapes, diaries, and scrapbooks. Music's presence and precariousness shaped its role in enabling individuals to take action.

I hear music across the geographic spaces delineated by military control, beginning with those accessible to nearly anyone—public soundscapes—and moving toward the smallest micromanaged area, the prison cell. Drawing on their experiences in empty, angry, and/or tank-lined streets, people used sound to depict their cold alienation from others while in those public spaces. Music was also present in private homes, artist's studios, and clandestine sanctuaries of churches—heard there by some.[8] The intimacy of these concerts crucially brought music to the foreground of citizens' (not necessarily musicians') stories about martial law. Even when the sources contain no music, historical subjects emphasize silence to attract attention. Considered together, martial law's musical action challenges the diametric opposition of specific geographies (public and private) with particular forms of experience (shared and individual) that decenters a narrative of silent suffering. Rather than retreating, then, citizens grappled with threats to their bodies and personhood by singing and composing music. Experimental and contingent, communal and participatory: these artistic practices became trusted models of musical action for the opposition. In the years that followed, they functioned as the foundation of Solidarity's cultural canon.

---

8 One Polish political scientist, then working in the United States, interpreted this domestic and "private" retreat on specifically Habermasian terms already in 1985. See Bronisław Misztal, "Social Movements against the State: Theoretical Legacy of the Welfare State," in *Poland after Solidarity: Social Movements versus the State*, edited by Bronisław Misztal (New Brunswick, NJ: Transaction Books, 1985), 147. Here I understand space both as physical scaffolding and social/discursive fabric, bringing the privacy of closed walls into contact with the public interface of the organizers, actors and musicians, and priests who worked in them. See, for example, the critique of Habermas in the context of social movements in Byron A. Miller, *Geography and Social Movements: Comparing Antinuclear Activism in the Boston Area* (Minneapolis: University of Minnesota Press, 2000), 43–47.

Media and the City

Only when, a few hours later, they drive you in the direction of Białołęka . . . will you hear on the prison van's radio, as your teeth chatter from the cold (these circumstances will later be called "humane conditions"), that war has been declared on your nation. It was declared by people who on behalf of this nation govern, proclaim, sign international agreements—the same people who publicly held out a conciliatory hand while secretly issuing orders to hunt us in the night.

—Adam Michnik, writing from internment in Białołęka

For leaders, organizers, and key observers of the opposition, the evening of December 12th, a Saturday night, shocked and frightened.[9] Activists, church leaders, and journalists were seized by the militia, or they learned of the abduction of their friends and family.[10] Most citizens learned of martial law from a prerecorded announcement by Jaruzelski, broadcast on Polish Radio and Television Sunday morning at 6 a.m. Others heard via word of mouth. Or, they spotted the notices hung on doors and walls in public spaces.

Jaruzelski's declaration of martial law can be read as a dramatic performance in its own right ⏵. Having exchanged his characteristic darkened glasses for a pair with clear lenses that diminished the barriers between himself and his audience, the General read an address to the citizens of the People's Republic in monotone, conveying the gravity of the resolution in the face of significant national instability. The televised tableau communicated his allegiance to Poland (see Figure 2.1). Further national symbols sounded: his speech was flanked by the national anthem (see Chapter 3 for an extended discussion of the anthem). An orchestral (and text-free) recording of the verse and refrain introduced the official address.[11] And at the conclusion of the declaration, Jaruzelski attempted to palliate potential alarm. Instead of reiterating his intentions to act in the best interest of the nation, he supplied the text for the first lines of the anthem, absent in the earlier orchestral introduction, "Poland has not yet perished as long as we remain alive."

---

9 Epigraph from Adam Michnik, *Letters from Prison and Other Essays*, translated by Maya Latynski (Berkeley: University of California Press, 1985), 5.

10 For the relation of these events from the perspective of two prominent intellectual leaders of Solidarity, see Adam Michnik, *Letters from Prison*, 3–10, and Władysław Bartoszewski, *Dziennik z internowania: Jaworze 15.12.1981–19.04.1982* (Warsaw: Świat Książki, 2006), 18–19.

11 Numerous accounts of the television broadcast highlight the charade of patriotism; for example, A. Kemp-Welch, *Poland under Communism: A Cold War History* (Cambridge: Cambridge University Press, 2008), 327; or Jan Mur (Andrzej Drzycimski), *A Prisoner of Martial Law: Poland 1981–82*, translated by Lillian Vallee (San Diego, CA: Hancourt Brace Javanovich, 1984), 13.

FIGURE 2.1. General Jaruzelski reading the declaration of martial law on Polish State Television.

Stories about this sudden intrusion—and the fright and loss it caused—thematize sound. Some storytellers assert vitality by insisting on themselves as hearing subjects, as did Adam Michnik in his diary. Other singing storytellers use music's intimacies to tell a "true" history of December 13. In "December Elegy" ("Elegia Grudniowa," 1982), singer-songwriter Jan Krzysztof Kelus, stunned by the predictability and simplicity of martial law's action, crafts the moment as trauma ⏵. The song works toward what Amy Lynn Wlodarski calls "musical witness." She emphasizes that composed music, as always mediating, necessarily has distance from a traumatic moment. Performances unfold in audiences' real time: musical witness therefore transforms and translates historical events. Its aesthetics therefore necessarily privilege disjuncture and discomfort.[12] Kelus, as both an observer (he lived in Warsaw at the time) and survivor (he was not interned until April 1982, after he wrote the song), dwells in this complex affective project in his story (see Example 2.1). The work taps into the atmosphere of insecurity: the strumming pattern before

---

12 Amy Lynn Wlodarski, *Musical Witness and Holocaust Representation* (Cambridge: Cambridge University Press, 2015), 2–7.

EXAMPLE 2.1. Jan Krzysztof Kelus, "December Elegy" (1982). From *Piosenki prawie zebrane* (London Fundacja Kulturalna, 1985), 1.

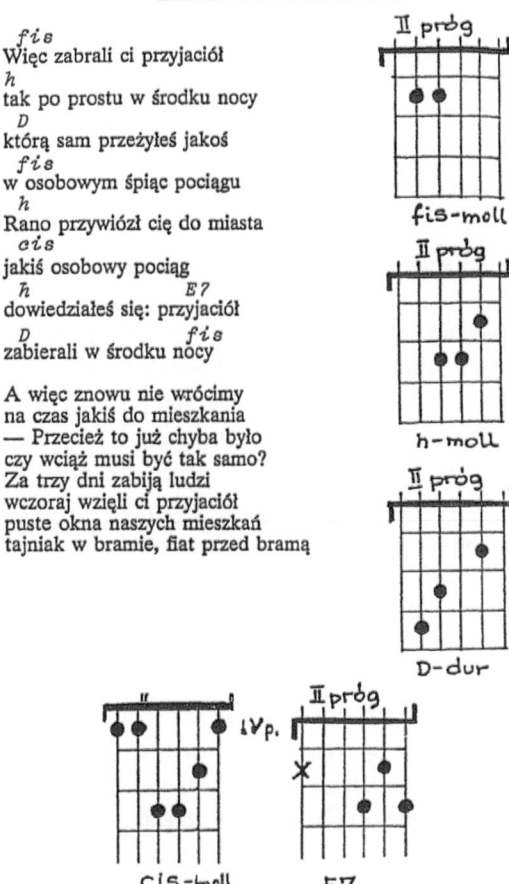

he begins singing suggests real waiting, but its irregular timing and patterning imply psychological instability. Perhaps this is the sound of the bleak and deficient realities of what Przemysław Czapliński has called "anti-socialist realism."[13] Kelus's fragile tenor voice and despondent melancholy details a harsh testimony of the night of the 12th to lead off the song: "So they took away your friends / just like that in the middle of the night, / which you

---

13 Przemysław Czapliński, "O realizmie antysocjalistycznym," *Teksty Drugie* 1 (1995): 31–48.

survived somehow."[14] In the lyrics Kelus chews over the basic facts of the declaration: each of the eight lines that make up the verses is allotted a single harmony. Only the final two lines, which cycle back to the opening sentiment ("you heard: your friends / they'd come to get them in the middle of the night")[15] use full, swiped chords to sound harmonic progress. The song's oscillation—Kelus contains tension through dialectics—continues. Past violence serves as the harbinger of impending murders. As much as the genre suggested by the song's title might anticipate a mournful, resigned conclusion, the musical and textual repetition leave things undone: his audience, the Polish intelligentsia, is still within the haunts of December. In the final verse Jaruzelski's television announcement is the ultimate use of mass media to disempower witnesses: "Will people look again / at the glass screen with a glassy gaze?"[16]

Martial law was harsh. Through its first months people survived on food rations and Western humanitarian aid; they despaired that Solidarity was forever defeated. This moment dictated the structure of feelings through the final decade of the Cold War.[17] It was a confusing shift from the free-flowing news media—radio stations, newspapers, open meetings—of the fourteen months during which Solidarity had been legal. Poles were left in the dark with regard to the location of their interned acquaintances and the long-term ramifications of the military presence in everyday life. Martial law's initial days were characterized by frustrated ignorance, and, in compensation, historians' efforts have focused upon detailing a play-by-play of December 1981.[18]

Martial law targeted the growing Polish opposition by forcing it into the clandestine spaces (like the living room) it had inhabited before August 1980, the legalization of Solidarity. Tanks filled streets and enforced restricted hours of permissible travel. In order to squelch the over fifty strikes that revolted against martial law in December 1981, the militia employed 80,000 soldiers, 1,600 tanks, and 1,500 armored vehicles.[19] While concrete violence

---

14 "Więc zabrali ci przyjaciół / tak po prostu w środku nocy / którą sam przeżyłeś jakoś . . . " This is the beginning (and end) of the first verse.

15 "dowiedziałeś się: przyjaciół / zabierali w środku nocy . . ."

16 "czy znów ludzie będą patrzeć / w szklany ekran szklanym wzrokiem . . ."

17 The narrative abroad was already one of drastic victimhood, as in the 1982 photo album *Polska 13 grudnia 1981: Wojna z narodem/Poland December 13th 1981: The War against the Nation* (Lund, Sweden: Stödkommitten för Solidaritet with Nowa, Krąg, and CDN in Poland, 1982).

18 Day-by-day accounts of martial law include: *Poland under Martial Law: A Chronology of Events 13 December 1981–30 December 1982*, edited by Roman Stefanowski (New York: Radio Free Europe Research, 1983); and *From Solidarity to Martial Law: The Polish Crisis of 1980–1981; A Documentary History*, edited by Andrzej Paczkowski and Malcolm Byrne (Budapest: Central European University Press, 2007), xxvii–xlvii.

19 Paczkowski and Byrne, *From Solidarity to Martial Law*, xlvi.

against and violation of citizens during the twenty months of martial law amounted to few deaths, Poles experienced vivid fear at its outset.[20] General Jaruzelski had abused his power as premier to turn the government of Poland against its citizens, reinscribing a binary opposition, a version of the "us versus them" paradigm so characteristic of Cold War culture. Philosopher Leszek Kołakowski felt the shockwaves in Oxford, writing: "The gap between real society and the imaginary country depicted in the official jargon of communism has never been so grotesquely wide in the history of Poland."[21]

Grzegorz Michalski, music critic and cultural organizer, remembers where he was when he learned of martial law.[22] Walking up the steps of Warsaw's towering monument to Soviet power—the Palace of Culture and Science—on Sunday morning, he and a group of colleagues were delayed at the entrance to the Congress Hall.[23] The flyer, similar in form to Figure 2.2, announced that the final day of the most prominent and public gathering of artists, the Congress of Polish Culture, had been canceled because of the state of martial law.[24] The Congress, held five times in the postwar era, has provided the arts a space for shared discourse about aesthetics, history, and Polish cultural identity during moments of historical significance, such as the celebration of the Millennium of Polish Christianity (1966) and, as in its 1981 iteration, the formation of the Solidarity Labor Union. Perhaps the prominent composer Witold Lutosławski was among those in Michalski's group, for he had given an address the day before that embraced music's apoliticality.[25] A gift

---

20 Historian Norman Davies captures the resonance of fear on the ground in Poland in his strongly essayistic description of martial law, *God's Playground: 1795 to the Present*, vol. 2 (New York: Columbia University Press, 2005), 491–93.

21 In Marek Nowakowski, *The Canary and Other Tales of Martial Law*, translated by Krystyna Bronkowska (London: Harvill Press, 1983), 7.

22 Interview with author, October 28, 2009.

23 The drugi obieg picked up on the Lutheran overtones of General Jaruzelski's manner of proclamation. The Swedish Stödkommitten för Solidaritet published one such single-page broadsheet in their photo-journal of martial law (*Polska 13 grudnia 1981/ Poland 13 December 1981: The War against the Nation*, page unnumbered). For a description of the building's symbolic importance, see David Crowley, "People's Warsaw/Popular Warsaw," *Journal of Design History* vol. 10, no. 2 (1997), 212–14.

24 See *Kongres Kultury Polskiej: 11–13 grudnia 1981*, edited by Władysław Masiulanis (Warsaw: VOLUMEN, 2000). Some of the lectures planned for the final day of the Congress were given in the aftermath of the declaration, for example in internment camps (Władysław Bartoszewski, *Dziennik z internowania*, 27). "Zawieszenie i wznowienie działalności ZKP w okresie stanu wojennego, 1981–82," Folder 44/12, Archive of the Polish Composers' Union, Warsaw, Poland.

25 Reprinted in *50 lat Związku Kompozytorów Polskich*, edited by Ludwik Erhardt (Warsaw: Polish Composers' Union, 1995), 139–42.

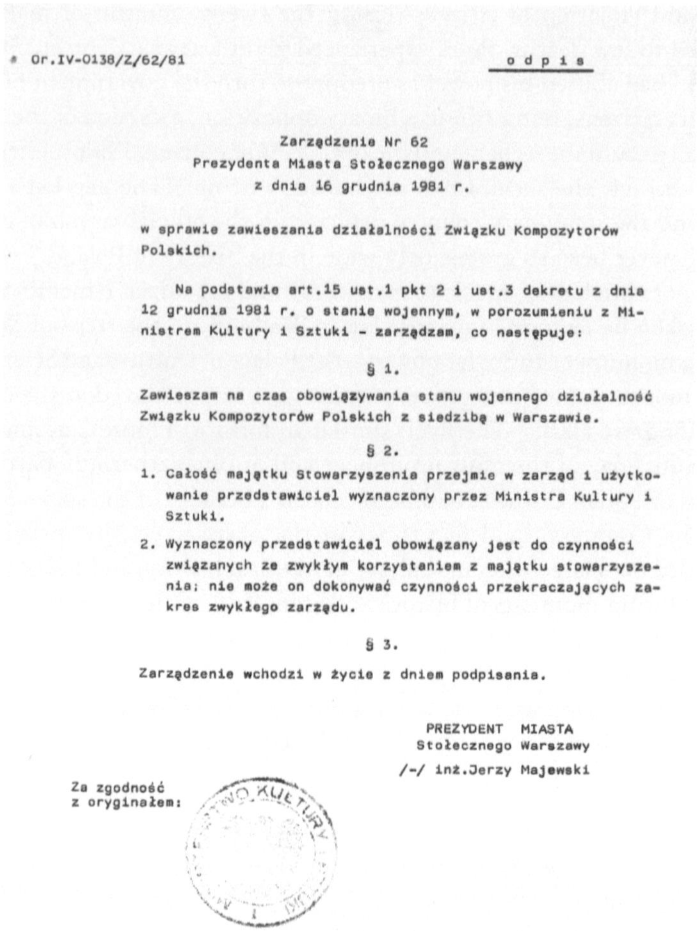

* Or.IV-0138/Z/62/81 odpis

Zarządzenie Nr 62
Prezydenta Miasta Stołecznego Warszawy
z dnia 16 grudnia 1981 r.

w sprawie zawieszania działalności Związku Kompozytorów Polskich.

Na podstawie art.15 ust.1 pkt 2 i ust.3 dekretu z dnia 12 grudnia 1981 r. o stanie wojennym, w porozumieniu z Ministrem Kultury i Sztuki - zarządzam, co następuje:

§ 1.

Zawieszam na czas obowiązywania stanu wojennego działalność Związku Kompozytorów Polskich z siedzibą w Warszawie.

§ 2.

1. Całość majątku Stowarzyszenia przejmie w zarząd i użytkowanie przedstawiciel wyznaczony przez Ministra Kultury i Sztuki.
2. Wyznaczony przedstawiciel obowiązany jest do czynności związanych ze zwykłym korzystaniem z majątku stowarzyszenia; nie może on dokonywać czynności przekraczających zakres zwykłego zarządu.

§ 3.

Zarządzenie wchodzi w życie z dniem podpisania.

PREZYDENT MIASTA
Stołecznego Warszawy
/-/ inż.Jerzy Majewski

Za zgodność
z oryginałem:

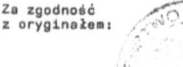

FIGURE 2.2. The martial law memo through which Warsaw's mayor ordered the suspension of organizational activity, as glued on the doors of the Polish Composers' Union (December 16, 1982). In translation the document title reads: "Ordinance No. 62 from the President of the capital city of Warsaw, 16 December 1981. On the matter of the suspension of activity at the Polish Composers' Union."

from Stalin completed in 1955, the Palace, a colossal multifunctional building, hosted cultural and governmental institutions side by side throughout the People's Republic—and continues to do so. In 2016 another Congress of Culture—discussed in the Introduction—was held in the building by choice. In conversation, Michalski recalled the perverse feelings of exclusion he felt that morning. Prohibition from entering Stalin's "birthday cake," one of the sardonic nicknames given to the Palace, brought some sense of emancipation from the architectural symbol. But he also remembers that the ominous implications of the declaration's "state of war" (*stan wojenny*), as he translated martial law to me, were confusing.

At the Polish Composers' Union, martial law's consequences were clearer. As was the case at the Palace of Culture and Science, a leaflet announced the new status quo (see Figure 2.2). It was a photocopy of the capital city's ordinance, tailored to the Union and glued to the doors of the organization's offices above a restaurant. The ordinance addressed all independent associations across the city, disbanding them temporarily.[26] In the wake of ceased publications, postponed meetings, and stalled concert seasons, musicians were unable to work. Restrictions on public assembly implicated a range of workplaces where "public" and "private" were always intersecting.

Workers demonstrated illegally in the streets during the week that followed December 13; the deadliest interventions by the Motorized Reserves of the Citizens' Militia (Zmotoryzowane Odwody Milicji Obywatelskiej, abbreviated in song texts as ZOMO) occurred in these high-stakes environments. Marian Terlecki described a performance of the Polish national anthem at the Gdańsk Shipyards, where workers were striking on December 15:

> Some guy shouted through the roar of the motors [of tanks and trucks]. "People don't be afraid. The soldiers are not going to shoot at us. If you hear a shout, it's just to terrify us, blindly. So, don't be afraid now, don't run away." The guy intoned: "Poland has not yet perished . . ." and people joined, overpowering the motors' roar and the terror had subsided.[27]

Military technology orchestrated a heightened listening environment for Terlecki in which all signals became noise. The industrial complex where he worked (the setting I analyze in Chapter 3) became a stage that he and his colleagues could reclaim not with shouts, but through song. Across witnesses' recollections, embodying—staging—songs is framed as a principal technique of being loud and vital.

Performances of the national anthem, which bears a long history of nationalist inspiration at times of oppression, drew attention from the militia.[28]

---

26 While cultural activities were suspended simultaneously, organizations were reactivated discretely over time; see Tadeusz Ruzikowski, *Stan wojenny w Warszawie*, 471.

27 Quoted in *Stan wojenny: Ostatni atak systemu*, edited by Agnieszka Dębska (Warsaw: Karta, 2006), 44.

28 See Halina Goldberg, "'Remembering That Tale of Grief': The Prophetic Voice in Chopin's Music," in *The Age of Chopin: Interdisciplinary Inquiries*, edited by Halina Goldberg (Bloomington: Indiana University Press, 2004), 64. See Chapter 3 for an extended discussion of this eighteenth-century legion song.

They listened to the text. A member of the reserve forces, Tadeusz Kruk, participated in efforts to pacify striking communications manufacturers. In his journal he noted the strength of the opposition: "We were stationed near the plant.... Mighty singing was to be heard: 'Poland has not yet perished....' Tanks stood around the factory."[29] Émigré dissidents in Paris organized action at a safe distance, but borrowed the opposition's strategies to embody nation in rhythm. In his recollection of one such gathering, Seweryn Blumsztajn let music structure geography:

> On the fourteenth of December there was a great demonstration.... Around one thousand people took part; all of Paris was ours.... It happened that through the course of our journey, we came across a Polish folk music band from Lille that the [Parisian] leftists did not find at all engaging. At our destination, there were Poles. Yeah, so these Poles danced for a while—this mazurka and that *oberek*—and the demonstration came to an end.[30]

Just one week earlier, at the Congress of Polish Culture, Maria Janion had underscored the value of performances' social work for political mobilization: "not just to bolster their confidence, but to reassure themselves that their actions made sense, and to find out what to do next."[31] Oral histories of martial law center the aural through stories that hinge on a romantic—but powerful—notion of song and singing as resisting and reconstituting political order.[32]

In other mediations of martial law's first days, the sound of silence proved just as capable of taking on "truth-bearing significance" as the musical *communitas* people remembered.[33] Marek Nowakowski's brief story, "The State of War" (1982), the first of the anecdotal scenes the writer published in *The Canary and Other Tales of Martial Law*, uses sound to write, through fiction,

---

29 Quoted in Dębska, *Stan wojenny*, 48.

30 Quoted in Dębska, *Stan wojenny*, 38.

31 See Maria Janion, "Słowo i symbol w miesiącach przełomu," in *Kongres Kultury Polskiej, 11–13 grudnia 1981*, edited by Władysław Masiulanis (Warsaw: Oficyna Wydawnictwa Volumen Instytut Kultury, 2000), 42.

32 For an extended discussion of song as magnetic agent of empowerment at the scene of protest, see Chapter 3. The scene here resounds with Attali's prophetic hopes for music, imagined poetically in revolutionary contexts: "Rumblings of revolution. Sounds of competing powers. Clashing noises, of which the musician is the mysterious, strange, and ambiguous forerunner—after having been long emprisoned, a captive of power." See Jacques Attali, *Noise: The Political Economy of Music*, translated by Brian Massumi (Minneapolis: University of Minnesota Press, 1986), 12.

33 Ron Eyerman and Andrew Jamison, *Music and Social Movements: Mobilizing Traditions in the Twentieth-Century* (Cambridge: Cambridge University Press, 1998), 24.

"actions as they occurred in Poland."[34] In the fictional vignette, written on January 1, 1982, he draws readers' attention to the desolate soundscapes of patrol.[35] Nowakowski narrates the three-page snapshot from the perspective of a soldier whose task is to monitor the streets of an Everytown in January 1982. He sets the scene near an unknown factory: "The only sound was a metallic clanking from the black fortress-like mass of the steelworks."[36] Descriptions of the streets spin out this frigid aural loneliness. A family walks by; members of militia check cars' registration documents. The routines hardly interrupt the oppressive silence of the barren cold, as Nowakowski has it. After one taxi drives away, following an inspection of its trunk, the writer delivers the audience the frosty soundscape in further detail:

> The silence was now complete. The armoured vehicles had stopped their clanking. For quite a time no-one came into view. When the clatter of footsteps came it sounded unduly loud. Someone was shuffling along slowly and heavily. An ungainly hunchback figure loomed dimly in the gateway, hobbled towards the brazier. . . . A siren sounded from the steelworks. Tore up the frozen silence. The sentries in the roadway moved uneasily. The young soldier looked up. The old woman didn't stir. She seemed more dead than alive.[37]

Nowakowski's listener has an unstable relationship with the environment. Silence and uncanny absence are synonymous, but so are sound and unwanted presence, whether that of the older woman who hobbles slowly and is "more dead than alive," or of the tearing siren from the factory. Instead, Nowakowski focuses on the abrasive sound effect, a far cry from emboldening collective rallies and protests. The "clatter" draws disproportionate attention to her, emphasizing the winter. The cultural freeze of martial law is audible.

The crackdown on the film industry kept cameras from documenting or dramatizing the streets in early 1982.[38] Portraits like Nowakowski's echoed in nonfiction reports of the streets. As a Canadian journalist commented one year after martial law's declaration, on Christmas 1982:

---

34 Antoni Libera, "Marek Nowakowski: Everyday Life under Communism," *Modern Drama* 27, no. 1 (1984), 61. For a theoretical engagement with the sound in literature as real auditory echo and listening didactic, see John M. Picker, *Victorian Soundscapes* (Oxford: Oxford University Press, 2003).

35 The English translation gives much stronger indication that Nowakowski's book is fictional. The Polish title, translated as *Report on Martial Law* [*Raport o stanie wojennym*] (Paris: Instytut Literacki, 1982), suggests a closer relationship to historical document.

36 Nowakowski, *The Canary and Other Tales of Martial Law*, 9.

37 Nowakowski, *The Canary and Other Tales of Martial Law*, 10.

38 Mark Haltof, *Polish National Cinema* (New York and Oxford: Berghahn Books, 2002), 164–69.

The city was strangely quiet and serene. . . . A heavy snowfall was one reason: even tanks and guns look less threatening when they are draped in a canopy of white. And there was no traffic on the streets. Even in the people there was a silence. On a crowded bus there was no idle chatter, no gossiping or banter. Just the occasional nervous whisper or crying child, and silence.[39]

Foreboding descriptions of everyday reality on the streets were, however, only one locus of the sonic significance of martial law as life went on, though changed. The composer Krzysztof Knittel recalled his own reaction to the sudden declaration as somewhat practical—even logical. "I . . . said, somewhat naively, that people would meet up in private homes and that there would even be private concerts. Just like it had been in private homes in times long past, and I remember that we put on many such concerts, above all in churches."[40] Martial law cast his imagination into Polish history. Musical life under the censorship of nineteenth-century partition and the occupation following Nazi invasion set historical precedents for Knittel's present.[41]

Sanctuary Spaces

Without the possibility of cultural gatherings hosted by state-funded musical ensembles or theaters, people made do behind closed doors. In the near absence of official culture, which had otherwise sponsored jazz, new music, rock, opera, and more, professional musicians worked in the home and the church.[42] Music accented religious, literary, and political meetings dependent

---

39 Mark Lukasiewicz, "Passion Fades, Life in Poland Back to Normal," *Globe and Mail* (December 24, 1982). Newspaper clippings in IV/209, Opposition Archive, Karta Organization, Warsaw, Poland.

40 In interview with author, April 26, 2010; quotation confirmed June 6, 2012.

41 Katarzyna Naliwajek-Mazurek, "The Racialization and Ghettoization of Music in the General Government," in *Twentieth-Century Music and Politics*, edited by Pauline Fairclough (Aldershot: Ashgate, 2012), 191–210, especially 204–6.

42 An important genre that is the exception to the story I tell here is punk/rock, which has received substantial scholarly attention. One of the most championed aspects of youth culture during the People's Republic is that it reveled in performing against authorities in front of their eyes at the Jarocin Festival. The Party's targeted investment in and surveillance of this annual event began in 1982. On this festival's function and (contested) political impact, see Tom Junes, "Facing the Music: How the Foundations of Socialism Were Rocked in Communist Poland," in *Youth and Rock in the Soviet Bloc: Youth Cultures, Music and the State in Russia and Eastern Europe*, edited by William Jay Risch (Lanham, MD: Lexington Books, 2015), 229–54; and Krzysztof Lesiakowski, Paweł

on walls for safety but still paranoid of surveillance. After state-funded concert life resumed in the summer of 1982, music making in unofficial spaces continued and even shaped a common culture across the rooms.[43] The government treated musical activity with the same disdain that other private spaces, notably the salon, had been subject to through continental European music history.[44] Though the SB sent informants (when they could) to track attendance and political discourse, they assumed the repertories and musical organizing behind closed doors was so insignificant that they did not track it. Instead, they tapped musicians in major ensembles.[45]

In private dwellings, dinner parties turned into cultural events. During the 1970s, poets had spearheaded the activities of the cultural underground. The cabaret texts of the Salon of Independents (Salon Niezależnych) and Jan Krzysztof Kelus's lamenting observational songs had complemented the realist poetry of the so-called New Wave (Nowa Fala) ▶.[46] After December 1981, domestic gatherings took up the task of perpetuating unofficial culture's commitment to poetry, particularly the politically engaged texts of Stanisław Barańczak, Juliusz Kornhauser, Ryszard Krynicki, and Adam Zagajewski.[47] At readings, pamphlets of banned verses circulated. Pocket-sized and homemade, the volumes occasionally included songs and give us a sense of the repertory with currency. Out of these evenings, the *drugi obieg*

Perzyna, and Tomasz Toborek, *Jarocin w obiektywie bezpieki* (Warsaw: Instytut Pamięci Narodu, 2001).

43 Trever Hagen and Tia Denora track a similar movement of music between in a similar (but not analogous) historical context. See Trever Hagen with Tia Denora, "From Listening to Distribution in Hungary and Czechoslovakia from the 1960s to the 1980s," in *The Oxford Handbook to Sound Studies*, edited by Trevor Pinch and Karin Bijsterveld (Oxford: Oxford University Press, 2012), 440–58.

44 Jeanice Brooks, "Nadia Boulanger and the Salon of the Princesse De Polignac," *Journal of the American Musicological Society* 46, no. 3 (1993), 415–68.

45 IPN BU 0258/69, Institute for National Memory, Warsaw, Poland.

46 Katarzyna Przyborska and Marta Markowska, *Salon Niezależni w "świetlicy" Anny Erdman i Tadeusza Walendowskiego 1976–79* (Warsaw: Karta, 2016). Kleyff remembered that it was through these friendships that he was housed and supported in the first months of martial law. Jacek Kleyff with Kazimierz Malinowskia, *Rozmowa* (Warsaw: Wydawnictwo Czarne, 2012).

47 Kelus was collected along with these poets; see *Wszystkie seanse zarezerwowane*, Archive of the Solidarity National Commission. Evidence that this collection of song and verse was a guide for performance is in Joanna Krakowska-Narożniak, Wojciech Miszczuk, and Marta Fik, *Teatr drugiego obiegu: Materiały do kroniki teatru stanu wojennego 13 XII 1981–15 XI 1989* (Warsaw: Oficyna Wydawnicza Errata, 2000), 20. A "Domestic Theater" performance based on this program from Warsaw's Teatr Powszechny occurred in the home of Ewa Dałkowska, beginning November 1, 1982, with further performances in private homes in the weeks that followed.

press "CDN" anthologized the most popular as "forbidden songs," fixing the performances as subversive and calling out a film by the same title (discussed below) that told the story of Warsaw under Nazi occupation.[48] The homemade aesthetic would continue to characterize these materials' legacy. At the time of her death in 2013, Małgorzata Pietkiewicz was preparing a musicological edition of martial law songs, which she titled the "Home Songbook" after a collection of poetry set to piano accompaniment (1842–72) by Stanisław Moniuszko.

Participatory events recalled gatherings in times of political stability and relative wealth. The literary salon, upon which many such concerts were modeled, dated to the time of Prussian partition and Parisian influence at the beginning of the nineteenth century.[49] Hosts arranged programs of mixed performance: theatrical scenes, poetry recitations, songs, choruses in which the audience joined in song, prose readings. Unemployed actors took center stage, along with those who retreated from public performance to boycott the state. Table 2.1 flags just some of the musico-dramatic offerings recollected by dissident actors and their patrons to theater scholar Marta Fik: many of these are musical potpourris.[50] The programs often weave together the musical registers that frame the rest of this book—voice, song, chorus, and protest. The major themes of political action and music converge in the heightened intensity of this moment of Cold War history.

The patriotic domestic programs resonated with—mirrored, referenced, and inspired—analogous traditions in internment camps that artists heard about from internees upon their release or in letters. In his diary, historian Władysław Bartoszewski described an evening at the camp in Jaworze. The program of new poetry and nineteenth-century legion songs framed his spiritual hope:

24 January, Tuesday:
Visit by the Canon Wojnicki from Drawsko. Donations: coffee, tea, soap, detergent, shoes. I received the book by Roman Brandstaetter, *The Biblical and Franciscan Circle*. At 17:00: Evening celebration of the 119th anniversary of the January Uprising (1863–1982). To start, a verse by Woroszylski,[51] then Konopnicka's "Reveille" (in

---

48 *Zakazane piosenki* (Warsaw: CDN, 1983). See Chapter 1 for a discussion of the drugi obieg ("second circulation").

49 Halina Goldberg gives an extensive overview of the Parisian influence upon Varsovian salons' emergence in the nineteenth century in *Music in Chopin's Warsaw* (New York: Oxford University Press), 147–76.

50 Based on the concert information from Krakowska-Narożniak, Miszczuk, and Fik, *Teatr drugiego obiegu*, 13–52.

51 It is very likely that the poetry came from his collection of internment poetry, published as *Lustro: Dziennik internowania* (Cracow: Oficyna Literacka, 1983).

TABLE 2.1 Trends in Salon, Museum, and Church Concerts during Martial Law

Select Program Titles	We Ask God for Such Strength Our Likeness "Mother of Poland" Is the Song of My Fathers The Works of Rabindranath Tagore Would That You Believed Closer to God through Suffering and Prayer The Nighttime Conversations of Poles: The Poetry of Adam Mickiewicz with Piano . . . That You Guard the Luminous Częstochowa
Formats	History of Polish uprisings told through poetry with musical accompaniment and a selection from the hymn "Mother of God" (Bogurodzica) Concert of poetry and song associated with the anniversary of the constitution of May 3, 1791 Evening of poetry and songs of Polish national uprisings The poetry of Cyprian Kamil Norwid with the music of Frédéric Chopin and Johann Sebastian Bach A theatrical production of poetry with newly composed music Theatrical evening with the music of Chopin and contemporary Polish composers Wojciech Kilar, Aleksander Lasoń, Irena Gielowa, and Zenon Kowalowski
Performing forces	Voice and guitar Voice and piano Choir Solo piano Organ, cello, and voice Local choirs Organ with chamber ensemble

song). Rayzacher recites "Captivity" by Konopnicka, a lecture by Jurek Jedlicki, the choir sings "Hey, snipers, together," Norwid's, "To the enemy." Komorowski[52] read fragments from the memoirs of Stanisław Krzyżanowski, a 15-year-old participant in the January Uprising. [Then] Kornel Ujejski: "Final verse"; Zygmunt Krasiński: "Whatever will be, whatever will happen." To conclude my words on the moral meaning and the psychological fruits of rebellion.[53]

The nineteenth-century texts would have been known to members of the intelligentsia from school. Literary performances prompted discussion of historical events' relevance for the current political situation. Products of a

---

52 The president of Poland, 2010–15.
53 Bartoszewski, *Dziennik z internowania*, 38.

shared cultural heritage, these were "concerts" in the political, collaborative, and artistic sense.

The politically engaged song offers another peak into the ephemeral gatherings of martial law's first months. Amateur musicians like Jan Krzysztof Kelus—more generally, bards of the 1970s—were important touchstones for these ad hoc performances. A sociologist by training, Kelus had participated in literary salons since taking part in 1968 student protests in Warsaw. A self-taught musician and poet who has kept bees in Warsaw's suburbs since the 1990s, he self-consciously addressed the intellectual circle to which he belonged through literary citation. As "December Elegy" recounts, he was away from Warsaw when martial law was declared. The song's elusive narrator does not say why, but Kelus had been invited to organize with students compelled by his songs in Białystok.[54] Upon his return he first wanted to "sleep through" the new state of affairs. Instead, he and his wife fled the city. They eventually returned, and he set to work making songs and tapes. These clearly had an audience: he later claimed that the initial run of a cassette for his label (CDN) increased from 1,000 to 6,000 copies over 1982. As I discuss in Chapter 1, the broadcast of one of these recordings on the illegal station, Radio Solidarity, led to his internment from April to July in Białołęka, where he continued to compose.[55]

Kelus's dark musical material and subtle manipulation of rhythm underscore his despondent commentary. His new works thematized the new pessimism of martial law and the splintering of political discussions effected by the clampdown. His cynical texts were passed around in the concerts' pamphletry. One presumes they were performed, though when I pressed my research associates, no one could recall specifics. One song from that time, "Pathetic Song" ("Piosenka patetyczna"), reads of the activist movement's future ▶:[56]

---

54 For Kelus's later account of December 1981 through autumn 1982, see Krzysztof Gajda, *Poza państwowem monopolem—Jan Krzysztof Kelus* (Poznań: Wydawnictwo WiS, 1998), 30–33; xxxxiv–v.

55 The songs recorded before April and in internment are released without clear chronology on Jan Krzysztof Kelus, *Z nie skończoną wciąż piosenką: lata 1980–83* (Warsaw: CDN, 1984).

56 Thanks to Barbara Milewski for assistance with this translation. Kelus attributes the song's internal textual quote to Michał Tarkowski in an interview quoted online (http://www.kelus.art.pl/piosenka/piosenka-patetyczna; accessed May 20, 2012: this website is no longer online). For a discussion of Kelus's relationship to the sarcasm of the Salon of Independents, see *Był raz dobry świat*, interview with Wojciech Staszewski (Warsaw: Prószyński i S-ka, 1999), 105–6.

Dostaliśmy od historii	From history we received,
i oddamy komuś w spadku	and to someone we'll bequeath,
czas wystąpień i protestów,	a time to join, and [a time] for protests,
czas wydarzeń i wypadków,	a time of happenings, and [a time] for incidents.
Czekaliśmy przez lat dziesięć	We waited for ten years
by znów przyszedł do nas w gości	so that it would arrive again to us as a guest.
jak to śpiewał mój przyjaciel,	As my friend used to sing,
"Czas rozliczeń i szczerości."	"The time of reckoning and sincerity."

The song is deeply ambivalent: neither a salve to treat the victimhood of the Polish nation nor a pointed condemnation of Jaruzelski—both "overkill" refrains.[57] Speaking with the authority of a "we" entangled in battles against an oppressor, Kelus begins trapped inside predetermined history. I hear in his performance the energy that fellow Varsovian "68-er" Zygmunt Bauman ascribed to ambivalence: "The struggle against ambivalence is, therefore, both self-destructive and self-propelling."[58] The simple musical cycle over which the bard aligns a loosely metrical recitative delivers stability as he hesitates—literally pauses—in reflection upon the failures of the opposition (see Example 2.2). Kelus's language conveys the weight of the repetitive descending bass line; the sincerity of historical assessment halts progressive momentum.

Writing about and documenting the urban salons was perceived as a risk—one reason my work reads the oblique evidence offered by Bartoszewski and Kelus. The primary contemporary accounts of the cultural salons remain international journalists' descriptions. Mark Lukasiewicz of Toronto's *Globe and Mail* talked his way into the country even when its borders were closed to non-nationals—he had abundant family in Warsaw—and observed domestic gatherings. Lukasiewicz was compelled by the cultural response to martial law, coming dangerously close to suggesting that control and censorship inspired passionate artistic responses. He collected stories from clandestine performance events, considering them together in an article devoted to the "seething" artists, published in April 1983.[59]

---

57 He used the English word when expounding on his opaque prose. See Kelus, *Poza państwowem monopolem*, 31.

58 Zygmunt Bauman, *Modernity and Ambivalence* (Ithaca, NY: Cornell University Press, 1991), 3.

59 Mark Lukasiewicz, "Repressed Arts Seethe with Life behind Curtains," *The Globe and Mail* (April 4, 1983), IV/209, Opposition Archive, Karta Organization, Warsaw, Poland.

EXAMPLE 2.2. Jan Krzysztof Kelus, "Pathetic Song," bass ostinato. Fermata indicates pause for recitation; meter refers to solo instrumental passages.

Lukasiewicz reports that private performances usually consisted of banned, censored, and vulnerable works. Artists themselves might appear anonymously, constantly on guard against members of the SB. The performances were "geared toward their audiences," which varied depending on organizers' trusted network of friends. The intimate settings provided space for scenes with four or five actors, poetry, and songs. Organization was of the utmost concern, according to the journalist, since people perceived themselves to be under close surveillance. Guests were asked to stagger their arrivals, and apartments with thick walls were ideal. Lukasiewicz describes a variety of creative responses—cabaret productions that imitated television announcers, communal singing, and poetry readings. His narrative evocation for the Canadian press provides a window into his experience: "The actors [in the wake of few props] are inventive. One 'internment camp' scene is played in the dark; the only light is from the tip of a lit cigarette passed among the characters, occasionally illuminating a face as one of them inhales. A guitar provides not only music but sound effects, such as galloping horses, military drums and a dripping faucet."

Members of the fringes of the visual and musical avant-gardes—the self-proclaimed "independent" artists—worked in studios and clubs throughout Warsaw before martial law, practicing a kind of "anti-politics" by working outside of the public eye in what Klara Kemp-Welch describes as "a non-coercive sphere for engaged citizens with a sense of common purpose."[60] One musical collective in this tradition started performing concerts in churches to restore the possibility of artistic exchange and to do charitable work through music: the Independent Electroacoustic Music Studio (Niezależne Studio Muzyki Elektroakustyczne), founded by composers Krzysztof Knittel and Paweł Szymański.[61] Music critic Tadeusz Kaczyński explained: "Despite initial individual successes, both of these composers did not lock themselves away in their own studios in order to further build their own personal careers, but instead desired to work together with other musicians."[62] The "Studio" was always a

---

60 Klara Kemp-Welch, *Antipolitics in Central European Art: Reticence as Dissidence under Post-Totalitarian Rule, 1956–1989* (London: I. B. Tauris, 2014), 3. See Chapter 1 for a discussion of "independence" (*niezależność*).

61 "Zima wasza (1982–3)," Krzysztof Knittel, Private Collection.

62 Unpublished draft from the Tadeusz Kaczyński Papers, Archive of Musical Sources, Special Collections, University of Warsaw Library, Warsaw, Poland.

group in progress, functioning as a workshop for its performers, musicians, and public alike. Knittel and Szymański were the nucleus of the ensemble, which grew with the addition of performance artist and composer Andrzej Bieżan, fellow composer Stanisław Krupowicz, sitarist Mieczysław Litwiński, jazz vocalist Andrzej Mitan, and electronic musician Tadeusz Sudnik.

The Studio's musicians, trained in the prominent music schools of Warsaw, represented a branch of Polish musicians engaged in the Cagean buzz of New York performance art. Unified by an interest in the "experimental" and an insistence on the ephemeral, this group positioned its aesthetic world at the threshold between composition and improvisation, electronic and environmental sounds. A recent CD re-release of a 1985 improvisation by Mitan and Litwiński to a recitation of the Book of Job offers a taste of one evening's music. The expansive use of sustained electronic devices and sparse, tonally inflected sound effects as a backdrop for punctuated improvisation and booming vocal recitation were common techniques to effect atmosphere for the performers ▶.[63]

Kaczyński, a music critic active among oppositional circles in Warsaw, promoted the group because of its relationship with audiences, which he understood on ethical terms. Performances, according to Kaczyński, tended toward the "metaphysical." He writes,

> Among [the members of the group] the most important thing is this: mutual trust, respect for others (even contradictory aesthetic tendencies) and especially solidarity.[64] The latter manifests itself equally in the relationships between certain musicians of the group, as well as toward listeners, who are not treated here as "recipients" of art, but rather as co-creators. . . . This "co-creation" is not of a "physical" nature, but of a spiritual one, since it does not depend on the public connecting to the concert through musical, acoustic, or any other means—though nothing here is out of the question—but rather on the co-creation of an atmosphere.[65]

This is not audience participation in the traditional sense: the audience does not join in according to script. The score of Knittel's electroacoustic *Black Water, White Water, Old Stream* (*Czarna woda, Biała woda, Stary strumień*), performed in August 1983, indicates that the group might ask children in the audience to take part (see Example 2.3).[66] The most insistent component of

---

63 *Księga Hioba*, Galeria 2b/Stowarzyszenie STEP, 2007, TR 020.

64 This reference to solidarity is similar to that throughout the periodical *Kultura Niezależna*, the primary publication of the similarly named coalition of artists against the party. It casually but obviously uses the concept to refer to the movement; see Chapter 1.

65 Unpublished draft from the Tadeusz Kaczyński Papers, Archive of Musical Sources, Special Collections, University of Warsaw Library, Warsaw, Poland.

66 Interview with author, April 26, 2010.

EXAMPLE 2.3. Krzysztof Knittel, *Black Water, White Water, Old Stream*, excerpt. The note "and listen" (*i słuchaj*) serves as a directive to musicians and audiences alike.

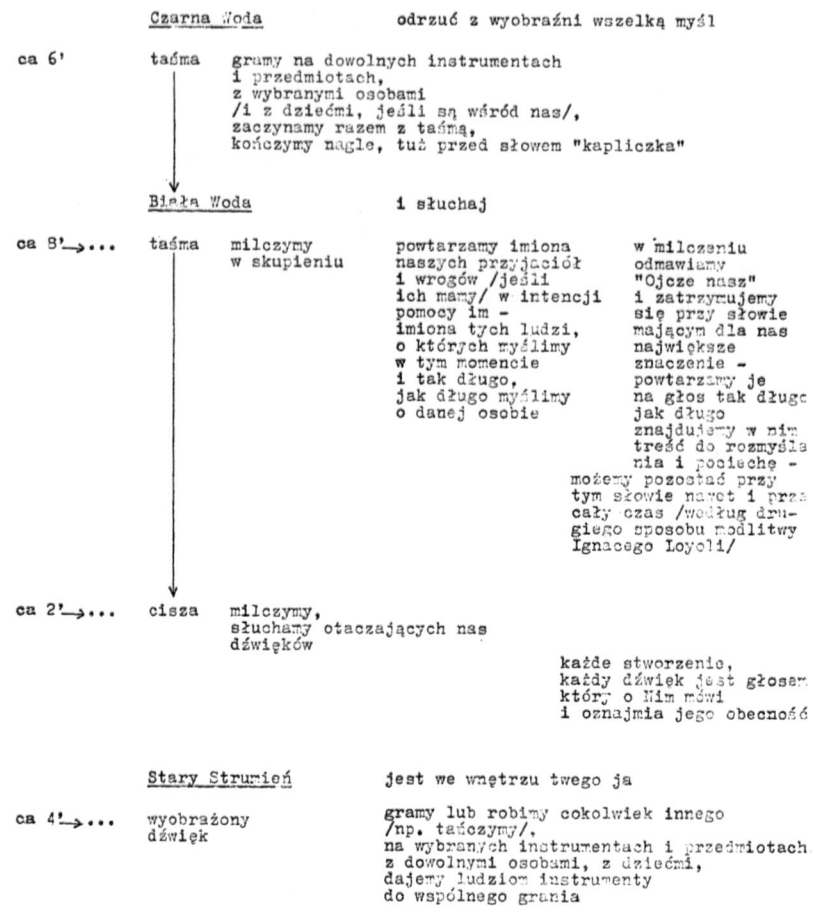

this cue guide is a list of suggestions for how the artists might explore the audience's attention. The movement "White Water" begins with the command "and listen"—a simple call to stop action, its meaning for the ensemble obviously contingent on live performance and trust. The performers conceive of their audience members as feeling, critical, and creative beings. The Studio crafted musical works, but the performances' success lies in their creation of a communal and contingent interdependence. Musical call and spiritual response generate the "atmosphere," a world that sounds somewhere between the meditative collaborations of Pauline Oliveros and Stuart Dempster and the amateur audience-inclusive improvisations of Musica Elettronica Viva.

The cultural work invested in sanctuary was also founded upon the link between the Polish Roman Catholic Church and the opposition.[67] The Polish Pope, John Paul II, brought a concern for the Soviet Union as a political power to his position at the helm of St. Peter's after his election in 1978. Following Solidarity's legalization in 1980, masses were increasingly politicized. Communal musical performances had served as weekly refrains during the year of Solidarity's legal presence in Poland. At the conclusion of Sunday masses, congregations at churches would sing "God Save Poland" (the hymn I discuss in Chapter 6), directing their hands, clenched in a "V" for "victory," to church ceilings. By 1981, mass offered physical safety and emotional support to worshippers. In other words, churches were confirmed as cultural sanctuaries, especially under the auspices of Father Wiesław Al. Niewęgłowski, who shepherded a parish that served actors and musicians specifically and organized their involvement in a range of humanitarian aid programs.[68] As he proclaimed, "Culture was a place of meeting."[69] His parish's physical sanctuary, near the National Theater in Warsaw, hosted performances and plays in addition to organizing political action. The soprano Stefania Woytowicz was one of five women artists who took a leading role with the Primate's Committee to Help the Families of Prisoners and Internees, organizing food and clothing delivery across greater Warsaw. Beginning in November 1982, these informal gatherings turned into concerts. She sang Bach, the early music ensemble Bornus Consort performed, and the cabaret composer Wojciech Młynarski took to the mic ▶. Krzysztof Knittel brought the Studio into this network, too. They offered a concert of free improvisation beneath the recitation of selected biblical Psalms in Czesław Miłosz's celebrated translation into Polish ▶.[70]

---

67 Sylvia P. Ramet, *Nihil Obstat: Religion, Politics, and Social Change in East-Central Europe and Russia* (Durham, NC: Duke University Press, 1998), 90–120.

68 Katarzyna Iwanicka and Małgorzata Romańska, *25 lat Duszpasterstwa Środowisk Twórczych: Księga jubileuszowa* (Izabelin: Rosikon Press, 2004). For the parish archive's catalogue of meetings, conferences, and concerts in 1982; see pp. 76–79.

69 Ks. Wiesław Al. Niewęgłowski, *Kościół i kultura w dialogu* (Warsaw: Oficyna Wydawniczo-poligraficzna "Adam": 2008), 51–60.

70 Krakowska-Narożniak, Miszczuk, and Fik, *Teatr drugiego obiegu*, 23.

The Traugutt Philharmonic and Musical Politics

One group associated with Niewęgłowski had an instrumental role to play in the historiography of martial law's "silence." In a detailed 1983 review for the unofficial journal *Independent Culture* (*Kultura Niezależna*, discussed in Chapter 1), Rafał Bracki announced the first church gathering devoted to music—a concert by an ensemble that came to be known as the Traugutt Philharmonic (Filharmonia imienia Tragutta).[71] The ensemble's January 1983 concert at the Dominican Church in Warsaw's Old Town commemorated the one-hundred-twentieth anniversary of the January Uprising, an Uprising of the Polish-Lithuanian Commonwealth against the Russian Empire. The rebellion, led by Romuald Traugutt, the hero in whose name the Philharmonic took its own title, failed, as did the November Uprising of 1830–31, the Kościuszko Uprising in 1793, and the Warsaw Uprising in 1944. The Philharmonic devoted a program to each of these Uprisings that was structured around songs historically or thematically linked with insurrection. After the declaration of martial law, the legacy of Solidarity as success or failure remained unclear. Recall Kelus's "Pathetic Song": the Philharmonic likewise expressed anxiety about a predestined cycle of tragedy for Polish history by lining up moments of resistance but also reminding of loss and sacrifice. Organized by Tadeusz Kaczyński, the music critic who wrote in praise of the Independent Electroacoustic Music Studio, the Philharmonic specifically framed its project as a compensatory response to a double absence: musicians' lack of political engagement and the opposition's assumption that music was politically impotent and insignificant. While there had been music at oppositional gatherings, Kaczyński explained in 1993, he was critical that music was ancillary.[72]

Over the course of the first evening concert in January 1983, actors and singers retold history using skits, letters, and political writings to give the spoken portion of the program a dramatic dimension (see Table 2.2 for the Philharmonic's first concert, "God Save Poland").[73] The variety of the program showcased young musicians' skills. Students from Warsaw's Music Academy performed instrumental music and sang patriotic songs. Some music, such as Henryk Wieniawski's *Legend* (1859), illustrated the vitality and historical significance of music in the Russian partition. Songs sung

---

71 Rafał Bracki, "Filharmonia imienia Tragutta," *Kultura Niezależna* 3 (1984), 55–58. Cindy Bylander builds on her own experiences of the Traugutt Philharmonic in concert to reflect on the musicians' "courage and . . . sense of moral imperative" ("Responses to Martial Law," 176).

72 Program for the 10th anniversary concert, reprinted in Tadeusz Kaczyński, *Ze ściśniętym gardłem . . . : 10 lat Filharmonii im. Traugutta* (Warsaw, 1993), xix.

73 *Będziemy dalej uprawiać ten ogród: 25 lat Filharmonii im. Romualda Traugutta 1983–2008*, edited by Krzysztof Kur (Warsaw: Traugutt Philharmonic, 2008), 73.

TABLE 2.2 The Traugutt Philharmonic's First Program, "God Save Poland"

Legend (1859) ~ Henryk Wieniawski
Mierosławski's March (1848) ~ Ludwik Mierosław, text; from *Lucia di Lammermoor,* Gaetano Donizetti
Song of the Langewicz Branch (1863) ~ anonymous
Song of Freedom (1863?) ~ anonymous
March of the Zouaves Regiment (1863) ~ Włodzimierz Wolski, text; music attributed to Stanisław Moniuszko
Hey, Pole, Hey Fellow Pole (1863) ~ Stanisław Hernisz
Anna's Song (ca. 1864) ~ Józef Kościelski, text; Stanisław Moniuszko, music
March of the Sniper (1862) ~ Władysław Ludwik Anczyc
Uprising Carol (1863) ~ Mieczysław Romanowski, text; traditional tune
Reveille (1863) ~ Wincenty Pol, text; Alfred Bojarski, music
Soldier's Song (1863) ~ Mieczysław Romanowski, text; Stanisław Duniecki, music
Little Black Cross (ca. 1860) ~ Bruno Bielawski, text; Stanisław Moniuszko, music
The Last Partisan (1863) ~ Maria Konopnicka; folk melody
The Uprising's Sentry (1981) ~ Jacek Kaczmarski, Przemysław Gintrowski, Zbigniew Łapiński
The Poisoned Well (1981) ~ Kaczmarski, Gintrowski, Łapiński
The Students' Exile (1981) ~ Kaczmarski, Gintrowski, Łapiński
Christmas Eve in Siberia (1981) ~ Kaczmarski, Gintrowski, Łapiński
The Cell (1943) ~ Beata Obertyńska, text; Adam Sławiński, music (1986)
Largo (1832) ~ Frédéric Chopin
God Save Poland (1816) ~ Alojzy Felisński, text; music anonymous (1828)

---

during the Uprising positioned the performers as themselves soldiers; poetic texts memorialized the lives lost in this unsuccessful rebellion ▶. Four pieces of *poezja śpiewana* (sung poetry) by Jacek Kaczmarski from his album *Muzeum* (Museum, 1981) were performed in arrangement by guitarist Przemysław Gintrowski and pianist Zbigniew Łapiński.[74] These described turn-of-the-century oil paintings depicting Polish legions in battle, Siberian prisons, and exile. One song, "Christmas Eve in Siberia" ("Wigilia na Syberii," 1980), based on the 1892 Jacek Malczewski painting with the same title, anthologizes Polish resistance in song: it quotes a Warsaw Uprising song "Michael's Small Palace" ("Pałacyk Michła," 1944), as well as "Do Hush, Little Jesus" ("Lulajże Jezuniu"), the lullaby that many hear in the middle of Frédéric Chopin's Scherzo, Opus 20 ▶.[75]

---

74 See Chapter 3 for a discussion of poezja śpiewana and resistance.

75 In the words of Jim Samson, it is a "delicate realisation," for Mieczysław Tomaszewski it is "at the limit of audibility," and for Jeffrey Kallberg, the quotation just simply doesn't hold: it "dissolves when one compares the whole tune in the trio with contemporary transcriptions of the entire Christmas melody." See Jim Samson, *The Music of Chopin* (Oxford: Clarendon, 1985), 162; Mieczysław Tomaszewski, *Frederic Chopin und seine Zeit*, translated by Małgorzata Kozlowska (Laaber: Laaber Verlag, 1999), 155; Jeffrey Kallberg, *Chopin at the Boundaries: Sex, History, and Musical Genre* (Cambridge, MA: Harvard University Press, 1998), n34, 235.

Through the program, the ensemble insisted that music was integral to the multimodal cultural fabric that had nurtured political debate, stimulated fighting stamina, and mourned traumatic loss in Polish history. Like Krzysztof Knittel before him, Kaczyński invited active participation during the musical event, but only after Chopin's Funeral March brought the conventional portion of this first concert to a close. After a few measures of the church hymn quoted in the concert's title on the organ, the audience began to sing "God Save Poland" with the Philharmonic. The concert concluded in a climactic chorus that performed opposition: this was a hymn that explicitly linked this concert with Solidarity's masses and protest scenes (see Chapter 6).

The concert's organist remembered Kaczyński's efforts as dramaturg hinged on the successful choreography of collective singing. In 2008, Krzysztof Bilica described the logistics:

> Before the concert, Tadeusz handed out to the public the full ten-stanza text of "God Save Poland," and asked me to accompany on the organ. . . . He only warned that I should not repeat the refrain, because that would have significantly extended the time of the concert. I was to intone the hymn at the conclusion of the concert. Immediately after the refrain—in agreement with Tadeusz's request—I began to play the next verse, but the people, accustomed to repetition, didn't take this into consideration and repeated the refrain with the then manifestly sung plea, "Return a free Fatherland to us, Lord!" . . . No one of those gathered thought to leave the church early![76]

A clear story of the ensemble's origins is hard to find, and many of the individuals involved with the group to this day repeat the accepted narrative, which celebrates Kaczyński's commitment to music, his homeland, and the community so robustly portrayed in Bilica's memory. Tenor Krzysztof Kur, then the artistic director and a longtime member, clarified the group's name to me at the ensemble's Christmas party in 2009: "A real philharmonic. That is, a group of people who love harmony. In other words, friends of music."[77] Bracki, the group's first reviewer, played with authenticity and etymology, too, writing, "that's what the group is calling itself, half-jokingly."[78]

---

76 Krzysztof Bilica, "Wspomnienie o Tadeuszu Kaczyńskim," *Ruch Muzyczny* 53, no. 18 (September 6, 2009), 36–7.

77 Interview with author, December 15, 2009.

78 Bracki, "Filharmonia imienia Traugutta," 58.

The ensemble's staunch agenda for reviving music within oppositional culture suggests a historical lack where there was none. We have already seen a loud presence of communal song at poetry readings, biblical recitation, and with the spontaneous singing of national anthems: the Traugutt Philharmonic hardly represents a departure from these unofficial activities. Kaczyński's idea, to revive nineteenth-century hymns as a means of stitching Polish history back together, also has precedents in popular singer-songwriter ballads in the 1970s, which, like "Christmas Eve in Siberia" in the Philharmonic's very first concert, often quote lullabies, carols, and patriotic songs in their instrumental bridges. Why, then, was Rafał Bracki, the Philharmonic's first reviewer, so excited about the ensemble's role as the *first* to contribute to what he calls a "manifestation" (*manifest*) taken in response to martial law? Bracki suggests that artists who make a "full conscious choice" (*w pełni świadomego wyboru*) to work with the church's underground ultimately have an ethical relationship with their artistic activity. He applauds them.

In fact, Bracki's claims for the ensemble take on new significance in light of a critical detail. "Rafał Bracki" was one of Tadeusz Kaczyński's pseudonyms in the drugi obieg press.[79] The first review of the Traugutt Philharmonic, then, is less a review than a mission statement and advertisement for the ensemble, written by its founder. The historical understanding of martial law's musical productivity is at stake in the control Kaczyński exerted when he invented his ensemble as the first of its kind and as the rebirth of concert culture.[80] He participates in obscuring a music history of martial law, of sidelining his compatriots and colleagues. Kaczyński links his self-proclaimed "cultural participation" (*kulturalna działalność*) to a clear concept of what art must mean in dire times that is exclusionary to the point of implying (and condemning) silence. Prescriptive definitions of music serve to promote the organizational actions of the musicologist and inscribe his action as the "original" and most significant response. By limiting music's ontologies, by claiming to understand *what* music means and *why* people love it, Kaczyński plays a part in keeping martial law's clandestine musical activity exceptional, contained behind doors, and more muted than actually was the case during the twelve months that followed December 13, 1981.

---

79 *Kto był kim w drugim obiegu: Słownik pseudonimów pisarzy i dziennikarzy 1976–1989*, introduction by Andrzej Friszke, edited by Dobrosława Świerczyńska, Cecylia Gajkowska, Joanna Król, and Irena Stemplowska (Warsaw: Institut Badań Literackich, 1995), 42.

80 He uses "first" a number of times with reference to the ensemble, for example as "the first musico-poetic program, prepared completely 'on the occasion' of martial law." In Bracki, "Filharmonia imienia Traugutta," 56.

Music in Detention

Today someone threw us a sheet of paper with a song written on it. Many songs are being composed in camp.

—Jan Mur (Andrzej Drzycimski)

The internment camps and prisons that housed political organizers and oppositional journalists hosted a rich musical life in near isolation from street demonstrations and with little contact from the private musical sphere.[81] Detainment put the opposition's activity on hold; it did not condemn dissidents. Though I have reproduced the scary presence of tanks in this account of martial law, Jaruzelski rarely silenced individuals through assassination—important and symbolic exceptions were the massacre of nine miners at protests at the Wujek Coal Mine in Katowice on December 16, 1981, and the murder of Father Jerzy Popiełuszko, which I discuss in Chapter 4. It is crucial to distinguish between the more common situation, internment, and the less frequent, graver intrusion: arrest and imprisonment.[82] Internees were charged with the potential to commit a crime against the state versus being charged with having done so, as was the case with prisoners. They had more rights, ranging from permission to organize cultural and political activities behind walls to greater contact with family and friends through the mail and visitation. At internment camps, inmates were subject to a routine that they assumed would shape their lives indeterminately. As communities united by a political debate, they developed a social order, cultural life, and coping mechanisms to mark the passing of time. Jan Mur journaled in January, for example: "Last week we returned to our forgotten habit of singing during walks."[83] Even at prisons the restricted gathering hours allowed discussions, lectures, and activities. As sociologist Marek Kamiński wrote of his own imprisonment in the 1980s: "unstructured time is abundant."[84]

---

81 Epigraph from Jan Mur, *A Prisoner of Martial Law: Poland 1981–82*, translated by Lillian Vallee (San Diego, CA: Hancourt Brace Javanovich, 1984), 44.

82 David Ost, *Solidarity and the Politics of Anti-Politics* (Philadelphia: Temple University Press, 1990), 154.

83 He went on, "In the meantime, thanks to the singing talents of our older colleagues, our repertoire has been exploded. We added the insurrectionary hymn, 'O Lord, who art in Heaven . . . ,' which has now become the camp hymn"; see Mur, *A Prisoner of Martial Law*, 87. Later in the same entry he references the "ironclad repertoire" of the camp.

84 Marek M. Kamiński, *Games Prisoners Play: The Tragicomic Worlds of Polish Prison* (Princeton, NJ: Princeton University Press, 2004), 33. Kamiński's sociological study does not focus on the special situation of martial law, but does contextualize it in broader prison cultures in Poland in the 1980s.

Attempts at continuity were political and intellectual. Historian Władysław Bartoszewski, for example, organized a lecture series for intellectuals at Jaworze, a small camp outside Cracow. Andrzej Tyszka delivered the address he had originally intended for presentation at the Congress of Polish Culture on December 13 before Jaruzelski's declaration had truncated the conference.[85] The public forum provided one means of continued engagement in the opposition's politics, even if the dissemination of these ideas depended on the release of individuals from captivity or the transmission of coded messages per post. In conversation with me, Małgorzata Pietkiewicz explained that she delivered musicological lectures at Gołdap, an internment camp for women on the border with the Kaliningrad Oblast, to keep her academic work active.[86]

Song had a central role to play. As Tadeusz Mazowiecki, who would later become Poland's first non-communist prime minister, wrote in his essay on internment,

> This singing was really our only form of protection. It was the only form of protest and the only form of communal strength. Internal freedom—that is what always remains for the individual. But a group that is persecuted as a collective, as a part of a larger community, must have its own ways of preserving identity. And that was by singing.[87]

At most camps, storage rooms were converted to stand-in chapels for daily mass, where hymns marked liturgical time within the prison, as in Catholic churches outside the camps. Prisoners also sang together in cells and at various gatherings within the prisons' walls, from lectures to strikes.[88] Well-known songs offered the prisoners creative opportunities, the results of which are accessible in an archive of penciled song texts noted on the paper of unwrapped cigarettes (known as *bibuły*, after the tissue paper most commonly used; see Figure 2.3).

Evidence of this moment of music's social and political function in detention is both voluminous and idiosyncratic. Internment music's oral culture resides in diverse historical media: cassette tape recordings by opposition members and the SB, diaries, songbooks, and oral histories.[89] The written

---

85 Władysław Bartoszewski, *Dziennik z internowania*, 27.
86 Interview with author, June 28, 2010.
87 Quoted in the front matter for *Śpiewnik ekstremisty, czyli zakazane piosenki* (Cracow: Quarter II, 1986).
88 Władysław Bartoszewski, *Dziennik z internowania*, 31.
89 Published journals, in addition to Bartoszewski's, from internment camps include Andrzej Jóźwiakowski, *Internowanie we Włodawie i w Lublinie: 13 grudnia 1981–30*

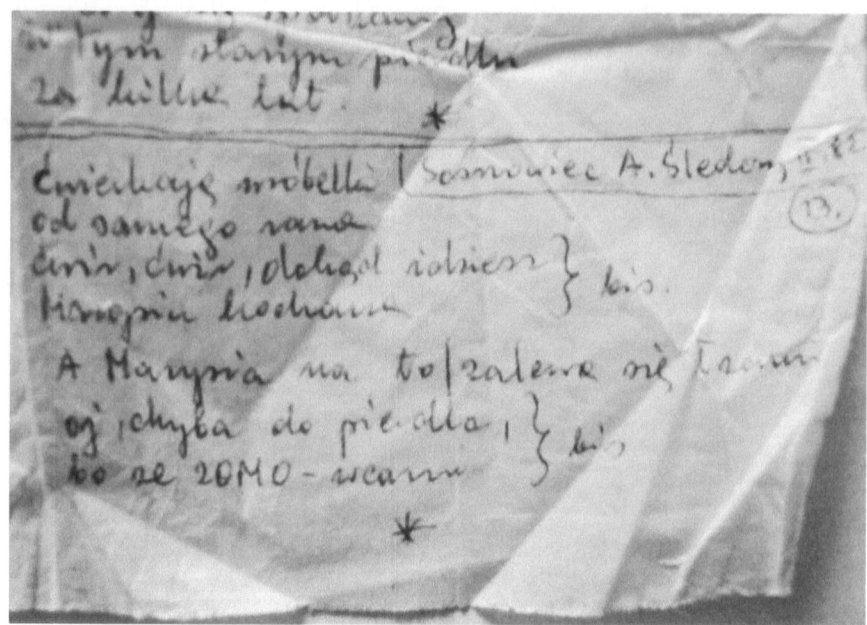

FIGURE 2.3. A *bibuła* with a martial law interpretation of "The Little Sparrows Twitter" ("Ćwierkają wróbelki").
Collected by Małgorzata Pietkiewicz in February 1982 from a person detained in Sosnowiec.

record of this music—song texts—already circulated in private collections and unofficial pamphlets in the 1980s.[90] Projects to resound this history in its immediate aftermath, as on one cassette recorded and produced by Pietkiewicz, reassembled released prisoners from men's and women's camps to revive their songs and capture their voices ▶.[91] Few recordings of internees singing during martial law exist; some visitors—mothers, priests—managed

---

kwietnia 1982 roku (Lublin: "EL-Press," 2004); Roman Górski, *Dziennik z internowania 1981–1982: Krasnystaw—Włodawa—Kwidzyń* (Boston: Roman Górski, 1991). Two drugi obieg presses published poetry by internees conceived under the rubric of a diary: Lothar Herbst, *Polska więzienna: Dziennik liryczny pisany od 16 lutego do 6 czerwca 1982 r. w Strzelcach Opolskich, Nysie, we Wrocławiu* (Warsaw: AD SUM, 1983) and Wiktor Woroszylski, *Lustro*.

90 For example, *Więzienne tango, śpiewnik internowanego: Opole, Kamienna Góra, Nysa, Zaborze, Głogów, Grodków* (Uherce: Wolna Drukarnia im. Józefa Piłsudskiego, 1982). See the pamphlet collections discussed in the following, as well as the bountiful holdings in the National Commission of the Independent and Self-Governing Trade Union "Solidarity," Gdańsk, Poland.

91 *Zielona wrona czyli obozowe piosenki z Łupkowa i Gołdapi*, NOWa 001, 1982.

to smuggle handheld mini-recorders into the camps.[92] The SB and prison guards occasionally recorded singing for internees' files surreptitiously.[93] A Sunday mass recorded by agents of the SB at the prison in Głogów, for example, details a sequence of chant alternating with hymns. These performances provide access to the prisoners' embodiment of song, often "not falling into musical meter," as one anthology would have it.[94] Though handwritten songbooks from the internment camps occasionally contain transcriptions of hymn texts, on recordings the congregations sound as though they sing from memory: occasionally two different verses are sung simultaneously.[95]

Through the first month of internment, the Christmas holidays and the weekly mass cycle provided prisoners with opportunities to sing seasonal repertory: carols (*kolędy*), a staple of Advent within and outside services. Maciej Zembaty, the prolific singer-songwriter responsible for translating Leonard Cohen into Polish, adapted many of their texts to the situation of internment ▶.[96] In diaries, holiday rituals brought with them the first notation of songs. In his account, published in the drugi obieg in the 1980s, Jan Mur took down the memories of prisoners from Wierzchowo when they joined him at Strzebielinek in April 1982:

> Christmas Eve was a very moving time for us. Everyone gathered in the corridors and sang Christmas carols. We shared bread and the Christmas wafer at supper, and we talked about the past and the future. . . . Bishop Kazimierz Majdański came to visit us, among others. The mass was solemn, patriotic and very moving. The hymn, ["The Oath"], ["God Save Poland"], "The Song of the Confederacy," and others.[97]

---

[92] Joanna Wierzbicka-Rusiecka, ed., *Głosy zza muru: wiersze i piosenki z obozów dla internowanych (grudzień '81–listopada '82)*, 4 volumes (Warsaw: "W," 1984). An digital edition, no longer online, on the occasion of this volume's 30th anniversary explained that Wierzbicka-Rusiecka was inspired to collect songs and recordings through visits to camps after visiting her son, who was involved with KOR. http://j_uhma.republika.pl/glosy6.html; last accessed August 1, 2017.

[93] *Stan wojenny w Małopolsce: Relacje i dokumenty* (Cracow: Księgarnia Akacemicka, 2005), accompanying CD.

[94] Introduction, *Głosy zza muru*, Volume 3.

[95] As is the case with "O Panie, który jesteś w niebie" ("Oh Lord, Who Art in Heaven"), which was released in 1983 on a cassette of songs, *Piosenki z obozu Głogów*, private collection, Małgorzata Pietkiewicz.

[96] As in one of the most frequently reproduced, the "Internment Carol," an adaptation of *"Bóg się rodzi."*

[97] Mur, *A Prisoner of Martial Law*, 230.

Where communal space did not exist, it was found. At Wierzchowo, the prisoners gathered in the hallway; elsewhere the prisoners sang in courtyards, or when they were permitted on brief walks around the grounds. In Mur's description of Strzebielinek, rituals abound. The Christmas wafer ritual (*opłatek*) offers Polish Catholics the opportunity to share well-wishes and prayers with friends and colleagues as well as family members. The anonymous Wierzchowo prisoners do not embellish their description of carol singing with detail. Naming songs is a means of detail-oriented cataloguing shared cultural references—and, one assumes, nurturing spirituality at the camps.

Tunes appear and reappear across accounts. (Note that each of these hymns was sung on the Traugutt Philharmonic's first concert.) Consider again Władysław Bartoszewski's account of life at Jaworze. His diary moves beyond the opaque descriptors Mur's subjects use (e.g., "very moving"). Bartoszewski, who had also been an inmate in Auschwitz during the Second World War and in the Mokotów prison in the early years of the People's Republic, compares the Christmas of 1981 to those of his past political incarcerations:

> We make a Christmas Eve supper of canned fish, and since I obtained permission from the Commandant for extended visitation with the female prisoners, at 9 p.m. we celebrate Christmas Eve together on the first floor, first in the hall, then afterward in our rooms. In the hall we sing the hymn, "God Save Poland": afterward, carols in our rooms. I pass well-wishes in all of our names to all of them, placed in the hand of [actress] Halina Mikołajska, with whom I break the blessed wafer in the name of the community and myself. The theme of my wishes: I am observing the ninth Christmas of my life in prison already. It is painful, but to be endured. The most important thing is not *how long* one sits, but *how* one accepts it, what motivations accompany the person, and what sort of sense one makes out of one's own activity.[98]

The historian, too, describes a Christmas made unremarkable by the repetition of tradition. The typical fish dinner invites celebration as well as religious reflection as a modest vegetarian feast in anticipation of Christ's birth.

Is there a political dimension to these two experiences of Christmas Eve, beyond the fact that their witnesses are political prisoners? Routine and ritual made space not only for religious observance, but also for many of the symbolic performances that had punctuated the months of Solidarity's legal existence. For example, Bartoszewski and the Wierzchowo prisoners report singing "God Save Poland," the nineteenth-century religious hymn sung at

---

98 Bartoszewski, *Dziennik z internowania*, 29; emphasis in the original.

the end of mass as an anthem of Solidarity that called for a free fatherland (see Chapter 6). Shared texts and customs, however, were also important sites of revision at which inmates reflected on their disrupted lives and political visions. In other words, alongside ritual stability, the possibility of adapting tradition—what Catherine Bell calls "ritual change"—drove the songs' dynamic presence for the prisoners.[99]

Firsthand accounts of internment emphasize cooperation and community similar to the collectivity Mazowiecki located in song. With the invocation of a "we" in their Christmas stories, diarists speak on behalf of their colleagues. Memoirs testify to a group's shared experience, rather than the individual author's fate. Transcriptions of private conversations or interactions stand in for a coherent collective, as when Bartoszewski imbues his shared wafer with communal significance. The social value of unity and optimism, not the arbitrariness of diarists' suffering, is foregrounded across singing stories. At Jan Mur's Christmas Eve, prisoners sang a shared repertory and revised song texts, writing their own experiences into the celebrated Christmas story.

> Here, too, within these prison walls, we felt the profundity of the carols. We sang all the ones we knew, and then we reached for the children's prayer books written by Father Tymoteusz that we received today from the chaplain. . . . One of the Christmas carols was rewritten. Now it is about us, that is how the birth of Jesus got mixed up with our imprisonment. We listened to the primate shout at Herod and bless the united shepherds.[100]

Mur refers to a number of practices that influenced the internees' daily existence: visits from local priests, recourse to any and all literature at hand, and the sense of a shared knowledge base that was instrumental for unity. Of particular interest here is the suggestion that musical revision enabled the internees to write stories about themselves. A new interpretation of the Christmas story that translated the villainous Herod into Jaruzelski emphasized the "profundity" of the religious observance, while inspiring "unity," the value at the heart of community and the social movement, Solidarity.

Music's volume in particular drew attention from patrol. A journalist standing outside the prison nearest Warsaw reported hearing inmates singing Christmas carols.[101] Patrol was also on alert, not least because they recognized the tunes that colored sing-alongs. Guards and commandants had the power to halt activity at any moment through isolation and punishment. The guards listened to the internees and prisoners: they did not, as far as

---

99 Catherine Bell, *Ritual: Perspectives and Dimensions*, revised edition (Oxford: Oxford University Press, 2009), 210–52.

100 Mur, *A Prisoner of Martial Law*, 59.

101 IV/209, Opposition Archive, Karta Organization, Warsaw, Poland.

I have been able to discern, regulate sonic activity, or use sound to regulate or discipline imprisoned bodies. (I did not succeed in arranging conversations with former prison guards.) One agent, Captain Zbigniew Zioro, was tasked with providing evidence of their "revolutionary and anti-national" songs.[102] He notes silence at regular time stamps on his muffled recordings. When he captures a song in full, he occasionally pinpoints the loudest voice or instigator by name ⏵. But his task is primarily that of the collector, depositing the tapes with his superiors, who report further up the hierarchical ladder that they have ten cassettes worth of recordings.[103] The recordings were absorbed into banks of evidence that might have been mobilized to incriminate at any point—but were not.

The guards—"functionaries"—were not always perceived as hostile: for prisoners, music had the potential to reveal their oppressors' humanity. The internees saw the guards as both sympathetic and antagonistic. According to Pietkiewicz, SB agents dwelled on the insurrectionary politics of song texts and the strength in numbers that communal singing displayed. She remembered the experience of music making at Gołdap in the introduction to her songbook:

> We saw the effect the songs had on our guards. Some of them (those with so-called human faces), frequently asked for the transcriptions of texts for themselves; others (primarily the functionaries of the SB), called us in for questioning, threatened us with arrest and the initiation of trial proceedings, performance, and circulation of works with anti-government, anti-socialist, and any other "anti-" contents. Oh, this unsettled them greatly![104]

The internment experience, along with the confidence that music not only had sustained her and her colleagues but had also made the guards' life at the prison better, shaped Pietkiewicz's musicological (and music journalism) career after her release. She published cassettes through NOWa, collaborated with the Traugutt Philharmonic on their concerts in the early 1990s, and maintained a personal archive until her death from cancer in 2013 (see Figure 2.3). When I spoke with her in 2010 we poured over her tapes and papers. She had only recently begun revisiting them for the *Home Songbook*—a twenty-first-century edition of martial law repertory—that she was preparing. Over our time together, I witnessed her forceful hope for music's power to generate resistance. For Pietkiewicz, singing and talking—activities she understood to have been the core of political participation during martial law—were

---

102 Remit reproduced in *Stan wojenny w Małopolsce*, 196–97.
103 Report reproduced in *Stan wojenny w Małopolsce*, 308.
104 Pietkiewicz, *Śpiewnik domowy*, 1.

necessarily active: forms of breathing (*oddech*) and thinking (*pomyślenie*).[105] They prevent terminal stagnance: "That is how it is with people. After a certain amount of time [without agency] people get bored. And the communists, they knew this, that you could tire out a nation, you know?"[106]

Jan Mur, on the other hand, imagined that when patrol units listened, they scrutinized and strategically intimidated. He writes of musical performance as political risk, a political act:

> When it was our turn to take a walk, we gathered in a circle, and opening our circle we unfurled the flag and stood in a row facing the pavilions, from which our friends watched. After a minute of silence, we sang the national anthem and the hymn, "God [Save] Poland," together with our fellow prisoners from both pavilions. The [militia] and guards reacted in a variety of ways. Some of them moved discretely aside, others smoked cigarettes and did not react to the words of the anthem but simply stared at us menacingly. We felt strong, stronger with each line of those songs, and they knew it.[107]

Mur's guards at Strzebielinek may have uncannily turned the other cheek, but at other camps there were repercussions, albeit nonviolent ones intended to restrict internees' behavior more than physically restrain or punish performers. A group of Toruń detainees for whom Mur served as a scribe recounted:

> The singing drove the prison authorities to blind fury. They worried about the effect we would have on the regular inmates. They looked for the instigators, and watched the cells. Especially determined was the camp warden, Captain Wysocki, a psychopath devoid of all scruples. For a while the punishment for singing the hymn was a dark isolation cell. We responded to this by making a racket. After a while they stopped the repression but we did not stop our singing.[108]

"On the Thirteenth of December in the Year We Remember..."

For people in detention, internment song culture was a means of reclaiming place. Songs were reinvented locally as contrafacts; their texts, especially as transcribed by internees after their release, often named the source

---

105 Interview with author, June 28 and July 12, 2010. See Chapter 1 on tape-making in the opposition.
106 Interview with author, June 28, 2010.
107 Mur, *A Prisoner of Martial Law*, 28–29.
108 Mur, *A Prisoner of Martial Law*, 146.

camp.[109] Some internees wrote down aural culture—poems, too—in lieu of a diary, as did Wojciech Sobolewski, whose collection I explore here. These songbooks are multi-authored, unbounded works, but they are not haphazard. Jan Mur described the scrutiny of written documents by inmates: "Today someone threw us a sheet of paper with a song written on it. Many songs are being composed in camp. We didn't like this one. Somebody said, 'Listen, we have to be straightforward about this, this isn't a text under which I would want to sign my name.'"[110] To conclude this history of musical activity during martial law, I investigate this material culture in social context by turning to a single family with remarkable historical significance and a pervasive presence across the broadsides of produced in detention. The corpus positions contingent amateur singing as the powerful engine that transmitted—and transmits—memories of December 13.[111] There was never silence, never a moment in which songs were not historical vessels.

Five extant songbooks without musical notation collected by Wojciech Sobolewski from two camps register music's presence and invest in its power (and stakes). As artifacts they offer a window into the process of reinvention undertaken by the inmates.[112] Across the volumes, advisory notes indicate tunes to which texts are to be sung or describe particular performance conditions ("a cackling voice"). They contain multiples: contrafacts and covers. Some are slight modifications of patriotic, religious, and legion songs circulated in songbooks throughout the eighteenth and nineteenth centuries, anthologies which themselves bear witness to the vital song culture of the Second World War and earlier moments of national repression and struggle.[113] The process of covering commercial song personalizes melodies from further afield: it creates difference from sameness.[114] Adaptations emphasize Polish themes and make explicit political agendas. Yet other annotations

---

109 I/038, Opposition Archive, Karta Organization, Warsaw, Poland.

110 Mur, *Prisoner of Martial Law*, 44.

111 Jan Assman, "Communicative and Cultural Memory," in *Cultural Memory Studies: An International and Interdisciplinary Handbook*, edited by Astrid Erll and Ansgar Nünning (Berlin: de Gruyter, 2008), 109–18.

112 These belonged to Wojciech Sobolewski, who collected texts. Handwriting comparison suggests that he was often, but not always, the scribe of the songs in these notebooks and folders (III/24K, Opposition Archive, Karta Organization, Warsaw, Poland).

113 One of the most widely circulated in the 1970s and 1980s was also the most authoritative in terms of inclusion and commentary: Tadeusz Szewera, ed., *Niech wiatr ją poniesie: Antologia pieśni z lat 1939–45*, 2nd edition (Łódź: Wydawnictwo Łódzkie, 1972).

114 See Charles Seeger, "Versions and Variants of Barbara Allen," in *Studies in Musicology, 1935–1975* (Berkeley: University of California Press, 1977), 273–321.

invite covers of popular tunes of diverse origin: "Auld Lang Syne," "Silent Night," and interwar tango hits.

The musical activity in Sobolewski's notebooks figures song as a dynamic expressive art form, weaving together the formation of political opinion, an active practice of remembering, and the creative process. I focus on a particular song family to recapture the experience of December 13 as trauma. The collection is a meticulous—if barely legible—record across which repetition combats silence and preempts historiographic silence. These songs are also self-conscious attempts by dissidents to control the historical legacy of the government's aggression by supplying revisions of Jaruzelski's declaration and clarifications of their experiences. They share the incipit, "On the thirteenth of December in the year we remember . . ." They assert this date remain unforgotten and that its story must always be told. What is that story? Wojciech Sobolewski's song collection has four legible answers, all untitled:

- "On the thirteenth of December in the year we remember, the worker understood, that Poland was not his . . ."
- "On the thirteenth of December in the year we remember, the enemy had to flee the country . . ."
- "On the thirteenth of December in the year we remember, a bitch came to my door . . ."
- "On the thirteenth of December in the year we remember, WRON attacked Poland, from a neighboring country . . ."[115]

The repertory constantly returns to the beginning of martial law. When considered beyond exact repetition, the corpus extends to thirty-plus songs in his collection. The recurring incipit's distribution across scores of songs suggests not multiple verses of the same song, but multiple variants: each iteration has at least three verses. A musical ancestor lurks as the progenitor of these untitled stories. Indeed, one version indicates, "to the melody of 'On the first day of September in the year we remember . . .'"[116]

The popular song, still played on the streets of Warsaw's tourist districts, describes the outbreak of the Second World War in a manner easily glossed to describe martial law ▶.[117]

---

115 III/24K, Opposition Archive, Karta Organization, Warsaw, Poland.
116 IV/56.8, Opposition Archive, Karta Organization, Warsaw, Poland.
117 The internal rhymes, as well the analogous cadence of September and December, do not exist in the Polish, which might serve as an important reminder of the amateur craftsmanship here.

EXAMPLE 2.4. The melody of "On the First Day of September. . . ."
From Tadeusz Szewera, *Niech wiatr ją poniesie: Antologia pieśni z lat 1939–45*, p.187.

Dnia pierwszego września roku pamiętnego,	On the first day of September in the year we remember,
Wróg napadł na Polskę z kraju niemieckiego [sąsiedniego].	The enemy attacked Poland from the German [neighboring] lands.
Najgorzej się zawziął na naszą Warszawę, Warszawo kochana, tyś jest miasto krwawe.	They took the most from Warsaw. Warsaw, my dear, you're a bloody city.

Calling out this original verse aligns December 13 with another overnight catastrophe in Polish history. Anonymous in origin, the song circulated widely in the pamphletry of the Home Army (Armia Krajowa), the underground resistance to the Nazi occupation of Warsaw. Robert A. Rothstein has located the first brochure containing the text, from April 1943.[118] This version contains an introductory stanza, occasionally present in later songbooks, that draws attention to the currency of the story's content. Casting himself as a news agent, the singer begins, "Listen, people, to my tale; / What I'm singing for you here boggles the mind."[119] A straightforward musical lament structures each simple four-line stanza, so that the structure of the ballad invites cumulative detail (see Example 2.4). In the original broadside ballad, which falls into the Polish tradition of *pieśni nowiniarskie* (songs about news events), the singer details Poland's retribution as Germany suffers under the wrath of God.[120] It concludes with a stanza inciting listeners to rebuild Poland together from the mountains to the sea, a message that emphasizes the complete destruction Warsaw experienced during the war. The call to action with which the singer closes also offers a clue for the song's enduring significance in the postwar decades.

---

118 Robert A. Rothstein, *Two Words to the Wise: Reflections on Polish Language, Literature, and Folklore* (Bloomington, IN: Slavica, 2008), 167.

119 Translated by Rothstein in *Two Words to the Wise*, 167.

120 "The songs called by these various names represented a kind of tabloid journalism in rhyme, providing the public with accounts of murders and other sensational events," Rothstein writes of the Polish context for this genre in *Two Words to the Wise*, 167.

EXAMPLE 2.5. A new melody for "On the Thirteenth of December. . . ."

One of the first films released in the People's Republic threaded political songs from the Second World War into a historical account of the underground's struggle. In *Forbidden Songs* (*Zakazane piosenki*, 1946), the verses of "On the First of September" string together recollections of the German attack by citizens across society. A ranging catalog of characters sings each one: beggars on the street, a pianist in his home, children at the playground, a peasant from the country, and more. When the woman peasant calls for the rebuilding of Poland in the final verse, she describes postwar viewers' contemporary Warsaw: the fervent reconstruction of the Old Town and the monumental socialist realist project underway on Marszałkowska Street.[121] And so the song was always about spreading the latest news—a conduit for truth telling. The simple lament made its way from the Home Army's covert missives to the first blockbuster of the Polish People's Republic and accumulated nationalist and popular relevance along the way.

The song family's pre–December 13 heritage enables further reimagination of singing in prisons. An anonymous street song about the German army begets a whole catalog of anonymous prison songs that tell individuals' experiences, through a mediating witness, as had Kelus ⓦ. The straightforward repetition of a four-bar melody that rises and falls to convey despondence makes the tune easily learned and remembered. In particular, the timely return to the first scale degree, when compounded with the tune's brevity, invites ad hoc invention of supplementary verses. But the musical connection between shared history, text, and music is not as stable as the "December Thirteenth" family would suggest. A drugi obieg cassette tape contains a variant that is musically unrecognizable as part of the family, even though the prisoners sing the incipit I have reiterated time and again (see Example 2.5). The tune's levity counters the sorrow of "On the first day of September . . ."

---

121 Annamaria Orla-Bukowska, "New Threads on an Old Loom: National Memory and Social Identity in Postwar and Postcommunist Poland," in *The Politics of Memory in Postwar Europe*, edited by Richard Ned Lebow, Wulf Jansteiner, and Claudio Fogu (Durham, NC: Duke University Press, 2006), 183.

and suggests that internees freely dis- and reassembled commercial, folk, and scout songs and texts, covers and contrafacts.

A final example of the "December Thirteenth" song text reiterates music's insistence on the political moment and song's capacity to loopback and spin out the history of December 13. In another prison songbook, the incipit signals the television announcement: "The thirteenth of December is just a few days before the holidays, but the address of the General changed history before the flag. . . ."[122] The text that follows is angry, calling out international disregard for Poland's distress. The incipit is a call, then, to fight the presumption that when we do not hear distress, it is not there—that silence is absence. It asks us to hear Jaruzelski's speech act again and to pair the national anthem with the national flag. We, too, can then remember that music was always there and that attention matters. It is, perhaps, a monumental history because of its clutter of national symbols and sounds that, as we shall see, time and again narrate Polish twentieth-century history.

---

122 III/24K, Opposition Archive, Karta Organization, Warsaw, Poland.

3 | Protest

The refrain of guitar poet Jacek Kaczmarski's song, "Walls" ("Mury") (Jacek

Wyrwij murom zęby krat!	*Tear out those fang-like bars from the walls!*
Zerwij kajdany, połam bat!	*Break your shackles; shatter the whip!*
A mury runą, runą, runą,	*And the walls will fall, fall, fall,*
I pogrzebią stary świat!	*Burying the old world!*

Kaczmarski, "Walls" (1978), refrain), draws listeners into the climax of a political protest ▶. He and his fellow musicians, guitarist Przemysław Gintrowski and pianist Zbigniew Łapiński, tear into fury as they sing a text laced with imperatives. Their rendition of the refrain verges on pitchless shouting, and their aggressive strumming drives the physicality of the performers' snarled rolled *r*'s (*wyrwij, mury, runą*) and percussive hard consonants (*połam bat!*).[1] This Polish singer-songwriter anthem,

---

[1] Although my analysis draws upon the widely circulated 1980 recording, the trio's performance practice was consistent, even amplified, as the song gained popularity. The original audio was rereleased on CD (*Mury*, Wifon audiocassette [1981], remastered Pomaton EMI CD 7243 522839 2 7 [1999]), and a DVD set chronicles Kaczmarski's performances through his career (*Scena to dziwna . . . 1981–2001*, Metal Mind Productions MMP5DVDBOX001 DVD [2008]).

Musical Solidarities. Andrea F. Bohlman, Oxford University Press (2020). © Oxford University Press.
DOI: 10.1093/oso/9780190938284.001.0001

composed in 1978, tells the story of a nameless artist trapped with compatriots behind placeless walls. The musician-protagonist teaches the masses to rebel against their oppressors by leading a musical outcry—the refrain. This song within a song brings walls tumbling down. Its rallying cry demolishes the introspective tone of the song's opening, its sparse arpeggiations and narrative of artistic solitude.

In many respects, this refrain contains key elements of a protest anthem, the least of which is that both lyrics and music invite participation. Melodies and words repeat, as does the entire chorus, and when the trio sings in unison, one can easily imagine joining in without being singled out. The chorus does the work: this feature of the song still holds power in Poland. In a video of a 2016 protest, for example, journalist Marcin Rola captured members of the press and of oppositional parties reading verses from their smartphones, but looking up and growing in number and volume during the refrain.[2] The opening lyrics also articulate confidence: "He was inspired and young, they countless many. / Giving them strength through song, he sang of a nearing dawn" ▶. The message that art can make political change endows "Walls" with a didactic sensibility that complements its lack of historical specificity. Like "We Shall Overcome," the song, taken on its own, harbors potential for use at any public manifestation of dissent, presumably because it performs an affirmative vision of collectivity.[3] "Walls" is itself an adaptation of a Catalan resistance ballad by Luís Llach, a reinterpretation from one rhetoric of protest into another.[4] When the song's refrain was mobilized as the rallying cry for the Solidarity movement in Poland through the 1980s, the citizens and activists who sang it at concerts, shouted it in the streets, and quoted it on posters and pamphlets responded to the anthem's ambiguity and at the same time transformed it into an icon of tremendous national import that was specific to the Polish opposition to state socialism.

Polish audiences listening to Kaczmarski's first performances of the song at private concerts in 1978 might have heard the falling walls as those of Jericho, or might have hoped that the song predicted the fate of Berlin's

---

2 He disseminated the video, which he referenced in a story for the online outlet wRealu24.pl, on his Twitter account and YouTube channel; https://www.youtube.com/watch?v=S2kyKfhFvDw.

3 For a survey of the performance possibilities and rituals of "We Shall Overcome" as the song connects social movements, see Ron Eyerman and Andrew Jamison, *Music and Social Movements: Mobilizing Traditions in the Twentieth Century* (Cambridge: Cambridge University Press, 1998), 2–4.

4 He substantially modified Llach's 1968 Catalan song, "L'Estaca" (The Stake), explicitly directed at Francisco Franco. The Polish text shares the symbolic "fall" with the original Catalan lyrics, but "walls" is the Polish singer-songwriter's addition.

dividing barrier.⁵ Kaczmarski's refrain was the title of one songbook of internment songs, for example.⁶ But people also heard the song as distinctly Polish, not just because of its language, but also because of its generic context, that of *poezja śpiewana* (sung poetry), a nationally marked singer-songwriter tradition linked with university youth culture. The genre encompasses anthems like "Walls" and the quiet and ironic verses sung by Jan Krzysztof Kelus discussed in Chapters 1 and 2. Kaczmarski was a singer for the intelligentsia, taking seriously the task of influencing society with his words and deeds.⁷ The film director Andrzej Wajda excitedly reported on hearing Kaczmarski for the first time in a 1979 letter to his friend, the writer Jarosław Iwaszkiewicz: "It has been a long time since I heard someone take this kind of singing so seriously."⁸

By the early 1980s, the local also resounded loudly in this refrain's symbolic focus. The song became about August 1980, when within the walls of the Lenin Shipyards in Gdańsk, occupying strikes and ensuing negotiations successfully fought for the legalization of the first independent trade union in the Eastern Bloc, known as Solidarity. The Solidarity trade union later became the victorious Solidarity Party at the first democratic elections in Poland on June 4, 1989. The collective oppositional action in Poland is the crucial sparkplug in what historian Tony Judt critically termed the "conventional narrative of Communism's final collapse."⁹ This teleological narrative locates the beginning of successful popular protest at the scene of Solidarity's formation, follows popular dissent's increasing presence across Eastern Europe in the late 1980s, and posits the culmination of this corrective revolution at the crumbling Berlin Wall of November 9, 1989.¹⁰ The crucial contributions of Poland to the carnivalesque politics of the 1980s—first in Gdańsk in 1980

---

5 For a detailed analysis of the wall as a motive in Kaczmarski's repertory, see Piotr Wiroński, *Wbrew, pomimo i dlatego: Analiza twórczości Jacka Kaczmarskiego* (Cracow: Księgarnia Akademicka, 2011), 127–34.

6 Zygmunt Stępiński, *A mury runą, runą, runą . . . : Pamiętki internowanych* (Warsaw: Wydawnictwo CDN, 1983).

7 Katherine Verdery, "Theorizing Socialism: A Prologue to the 'Transition,'" *American Ethnologist* 18, no. 34 (1991), 28–33.

8 Andrzej Wajda and Jarosław Iwaszkiewicz, *Korespondencja*, edited by Jan Strzałka (Warsaw: Zeszyty Literackie, 2013), 51.

9 Tony Judt, *Postwar: A History of Europe since 1945* (New York: Penguin, 2005), 585. See also his profile of give-and-take between the Polish opposition and the United Workers' Party over the course of the decade, 585–608.

10 Susan Peace has termed the legacy of this public history in cultural memory as the pressure to "perform firstness"; see Susan C. Peace, "Who Owns a Movement's Memory: The Case of Poland's Solidarity," in *Cultural Memories of Nonviolent Struggle: Powerful Times*, edited by Anna Reading and Tamar Katriel (New York: Palgrave Macmillan, 2015), 172.

and then with the anticipatory democratic elections—heralded Solidarity as a paradigm for political engagement from below.[11] In this context, music's triumph in "Walls" accumulated a new resonance. After 1989 the song could narrate the end of the Cold War and thereby rally Polish nationalism: one protest brought down all the walls. Indeed, Central European memory culture has conflated the toppled partitions: a section of the wall from the Lenin Shipyards (scaled by strike leader Lech Wałęsa) now flanks the German Bundestag and commemoratively decorates the former no man's land of the Berlin Wall.

Into the twenty-first century, "Walls" retains a place as Solidarity's song in public memory and performance, in part because of its refrain's consonance with the "conventional narrative" and the song's capacity to celebrate the 1980 protests. As early as 1984, the union mobilized the refrain as an identifying sound bite when it was one of the signals for Radio Solidarity ⏵. It is crucial to what Ron Eyerman and Andrew Jamison term the "mobilization of tradition" in their sociological study of the Civil Rights Movement.[12] In the Polish context, "Walls" links younger generations to politics of the past through cultural—particularly musical—revival in the present. When the international electronic music personality Jean Michel Jarre headlined a concert celebrating the trade union's twenty-fifth anniversary in 2005, for example, Kaczmarski's refrain echoed between each number, and the evening culminated in a multimedia spectacle devoted to the anthem.[13] In performance, the chorus sings a successful and unison legacy for the popular opposition to state socialism in Poland and celebrates the politically engaged artist. The song has been empowered to tell one story of Gdańsk through August 1980. Here I challenge its representative capacity. Through this

---

11 Padraic Kenney, *A Carnival of Revolution: Central Europe 1989* (Princeton, NJ: Princeton University Press, 2002), for example, situates Polish actors at the center of a regional success story of raucous political engagement rooted in cultural performance, even if he does not elevate the Polish case as exceptional. While the failures of Solidarity, especially in its negotiations with Communist authorities in the 1989 roundtable, have been increasingly debated in the context of twenty-first-century Polish politics, it is important to keep in mind Poland's pride of place in the early studies of transition and celebrations of Western "victory" over communism. Compare Dariusz Aleksandrowicz, Stefani Sonntag, and Jan Wielgohs, editors, *The Polish Solidarity Movement in Retrospect: A Story of Failure or Success?* (Berlin: Gesellschaft für sozialwissenschaftliche Forschung und Publizistik, 2009), and Roman Laba, *The Roots of Solidarity: A Political Sociology of Poland's Working-Class Democratization* (Princeton, NJ: Princeton University Press, 1991).

12 For the theoretical backdrop for their study of the US context, see Eyerman and Jamison, *Music and Social Movements*, 26–47.

13 The concert's music later became the soundtrack of Völker Schlöndorff's dramatic film *Strajk* (2007), which is loosely based on the events of August 1980.

chapter, I compare the histories of Gdańsk across the "first-person" accounts linked with Solidarity's grassroots ethos. How, I ask, do sound and music participate in the celebration of protest as the paradigmatic scene of political performance, participation, and progress?

Kaczmarski has come to stand in for the heroic singer activist at the heart of his song, as a kind of musical double for the worker-turned-union-leader Lech Wałęsa, who spearheaded Solidarity and is one of the protagonists of Chapter 5. In a December 2013 commendation, President Bronisław Komorowski transmuted the song's motto to describe the singer's influence, "Today I think about Jacek Kaczmarski as someone who had his own prominent part to play in building our hope and our determination to fight, so that the walls would fall and Poland would be a free country."[14] Such conflations of political symbol and political change permeate reflections on Solidarity and social movements more broadly.

Yet what is it about "Walls" that made it appealing as an anthem? And what is it about Kaczmarski that made him an ideal voice for the Polish workers' movement? Through the ten years I have done fieldwork in Poland, activists and musicians have repeatedly drawn attention to the guitar ballad explicitly as a hymn of Solidarity. In the summer of 2014, I told an older porter at the University of Warsaw library what I was researching—"politics and music in the 1980s"—and was treated to a full voice performance of the song's refrain in an otherwise silent reading room. It would be difficult to exaggerate the transcendent power and historical agency still ascribed to Kaczmarski's song. It conveys—even celebrates—Polish history, at the same time restaging Solidarity as a moment of historic and historical unity and hope.

Capturing Protest

The protest story contained in "Walls" and strung along its forty-year reception prompts my search for other modes of capturing protest and of using affect (especially shouting) to propel protest action. Does the history written in "Walls" match up with the Polish context? What music did protesters hear, sing, and perform in the Lenin Shipyards? How did music fit into the broader sonic environment and artistic atmosphere of the strikes? Following the theoretical work of Marié Abe, how did music and sound constitute and reconstitute the communities and socialities of these protests?[15] The Polish

---

14 Quoted in "Jacek Kaczmarski: 25 lat Wolności," supplement to *Gazeta Wyborcza*, May 31, 2014, 1.
15 Marié Abe, *Resonances of* Chindon-ya: *Sounding Space and Sociality in Contemporary Japan* (Middletown, CT: Wesleyan University Press, 2018).

guitarist frames sound as a crucial element to cohering collective action. The narrative's singer-crusader provides "strength through song," but ultimately "silently listens." This chapter argues against the assumption that that protest scenes are necessarily shaped communally and driven affectively by defiant music.[16] At the same time, I demonstrate the importance of the frequently ambiguous and ambivalent relationship to music and sound held by political activists on the ground in Poland: the irreducibility of the sonic—to use the language of sociologist Alberto Melucci—positions it as a crucial component in histories of this protest by those protesting.[17] Like "Walls," these histories turn to the authenticity ascribed to hearing to project confidence into this pivotal triumph for the Polish opposition.

The stories from Gdańsk's archive reveal musical stakes that engage the cacophony of crowds, amateur artistic creativity, moments of ritual and repose, the orchestrations of communication media, and thunderous nationalist celebration at the scene of dissent. Sound casts the protests as dynamic, vibrant, and "irredeemably plural," to recall Homi Bhabha's analysis of the "heterogenous histories of contending peoples."[18] Working toward an eventual return to "Walls," I unpack and cast the stories of two sound documents: an almanac (*The Polish August of 1980*) and a radio reportage (Janina Jankowska's *Polish August*). The interaction of sound, political action, and history within the context of Solidarity provides a model for studying and placing music and collective action in constant dynamic tension—that is, I present culture as a site that resists the reduction of protest to binary opposition.

The first historical accounts of August 1980 were written by the strikes' participants, political actors. Audio and visual recording, too, was a kind of writing, understood as inscription.[19] As they taped, filmed, transcribed, and

---

16 For a compendium of politically charged songs that register defiance and determination in Poland during the postwar period, see Marek Payerhin, "Singing Out of Pain: Protest Songs and Social Mobilization," *Polish Review* 37 (2012), 5–31. Defiance also plays out in high profile in the music historiography of the Black Freedom movement, with the evaluation of violence and nonviolence in the balance, as carefully analyzed in Tammy L. Kernodle, "'I Wish I Knew How It Would Feel to Be Free': Nina Simone and the Redefining of the Freedom Song of the 1960s," *Journal of the Society for American Music* Vol. 2, no. 3 (2008), 295–317.

17 Alberto Melucci, *Challenging Codes: Collective Action in the Information Age* (Cambridge: Cambridge University, 1996), 10.

18 Homi K. Bhabha, *The Location of Culture* (London and New York: Routledge, 1994), 147–48. Thanks to an anonymous reader for Oxford University Press for drawing my attention to this connection.

19 For a critique of the pervasive equation of sound recording with inscription, see Andrea F. Bohlman and Peter McMurray, "Tape: Or, Rewinding the Phonographic Regime," *Twentieth-Century Music* 14, no. 1 (2017), 3–24.

journaled, and as they collected slogans and drew posters, they lent their documentary efforts authenticity and authority through sound, in sound, and with sound—taken by the notion that multimodal "recording" could reproduce or at least echo their own proximity to the events.[20] They bear a certain similarity to the breadth of cultural ephemera at other central European scenes of protest, such as May 1968 in Paris or Leipzig's "Monday demonstrations" in the fall of 1989.[21] As Eric Drott writes of Paris, "Creative expression possessed a more profound function, that of nourishing the movement's utopian aspirations."[22]

In Poland, the "opera-ready" protests, to borrow from sociologist Elżbieta Matynia, functioned as an imperative to record on film, tape, and in print.[23] Western journalists at the scene played their own role in amplifying the events and bringing a global audience to witness the protest, too.[24] The heavily mediated protest was, in a sense, already unfolding as representation and in representations. The details of these stories shape a vital role for sound quite distinct from the inspirational and spiritual ones that dominate social movement literature.[25] The accounts of the strikes and negotiations capture patriotic shouting, pattering laughter in response to satirical cabaret, and the wavering of voices as they burgeon in devotional hymn singing—all of these

---

20 They thus participate in the inclusive fantasy of the soundscape, what Martin Daughtry critiques as "both presuming and *erasing* the listener," in J. Martin Daughtry, *Listening to War: Sound, Music, Trauma, and Survival in Wartime Iraq* (New York: Oxford University Press, 2015), 122.

21 Eric Drott, *Music and the Elusive Revolution: Cultural Politics and Politics of Culture in France, 1968–81* (Berkeley: University of California Press, 2011); and Wolfgang Schneider, ed., *Leipziger Demontagebuch: Demo, Montag, Tagebuch, Demontage* (Leipzig and Weimar: Gustav Kiepenheuer Verlag, 1990). Many of these protesters would have kept the model of the 1789 French Revolution in mind. For articles examining its mixed media, see Robert Darnton and Daniel Roche, eds., *Revolution in Print: The Press in France 1775–1800* (Berkeley: University of California Press, 1989), 141–289.

22 Drott, *Music and the Elusive Revolution*, 25.

23 Elżbieta Matynia, *Performative Democracy* (Boulder, CO: Paradigm, 2009), 50.

24 The part of witness-historian, author of "the history of the present," was played most notably by journalist Timothy Garton Ash, whom I discuss in the following. See George Kennan, "Witness," *New York Review of Books*, March 1, 1990, 3–6.

25 Focusing on anthems, for example, T. V. Reed writes of the Civil Rights Movement in the United States, "Songs, especially as embedded in a rich church culture and later in Black pop music, formed the communication network of the movement, and they also expressed the 'soul' of the movement, linking its spirit to centuries of resistance to slavery and opposition." T. V. Reed, *The Art of Protest: Culture and Activism from the Civil Rights Movement to the Streets of Seattle* (Minneapolis: University of Minnesota Press, 2005), 2.

resounded at Solidarity's nascent moment. Activist filmmakers, pamphleteers, scribes, and radio engineers attended to the ubiquity of songs, giving the brief musical narratives prominent positions in the union's first histories. A reconsideration of social movements' cultural history includes both the iconic songs of protest and the music histories that emerge from the acoustic experiences of those at the scene.

Gdańsk: August 1980

The power of August 1980—and the power of the opposition—was to amass people: to strike within the Lenin Shipyards and to generate political participation across Poland. The work stoppage successfully provoked the Central Committee of the Communist Party to negotiate with a committee of workers, the Inter-Factory Strike Committee (Międzyzakładowy Komitet Strajkowy), on site. From August 14 through 31, civilians, clergy, and workers intermingled across the grounds until the Gdańsk Agreement was signed, paving the way for the union's legalization that November. By December 1981, Solidarity had ten million members. Like May 1968 in Paris, August 1980 has come to index the field of political dissent in Poland in the 1980s.

Physical presence manifests allegiance.[26] At the gates of the Lenin Shipyards in 1980, workers and strike organizers distributed pamphlets and posted demands to recruit for their cause. The protesters filled the open spaces of the shipyards, where they slept on styrofoam mattresses to claim their turf, debated their goals and expectations, and shared food. Sound media united the masses: the loudspeakers of the complex broadcast the strike negotiations across the gathered crowds.[27]

A quotidian scene in Andrzej Chodakowski and Andrzej Zajaczkowski's 1981 documentary film about the Gdańsk strikes, *Workers '80 (Robotnicy '80)* provides a glimpse into the heart of the activity: at a series of long tables at the front of a large hall, a group of men speak into microphones. They are animated, but they take their turn. The enclosed space is full. Some of the people assembled wear suits, others are dressed in slacks or skirts and

---

26 On the highly emotional tenor of Solidarity's scene, see Colin Barker, "Fear, Laughter, and Collective Power: The Making of Solidarity at the Lenin Shipyards in Gdansk, Poland, August 1980," in *Passionate Politics: Emotions and Social Movements*, edited by Jeff Goodwin, James M. Jasper, and Francesca Polletta (Chicago: University of Chicago Press, 2001), 180–85.

27 Timothy Garton Ash, *The Polish Revolution: Solidarity*, 3rd ed. (New Haven, CT: Yale University Press, 2002), 43.

button-down shirts. They are sitting in folding chairs, standing in the aisles with tape recorders, and milling about, smoking and chatting all the while ▶. Inside this meeting hall, journalists from abroad and across Poland stood for hours among the activists, who took turns addressing the crowd and negotiating with Party officials. The overflow spilled into the surrounding streets, halting public transportation and commerce.[28] The disruptive value of this protest was in its place: the strike was not on the move.[29]

Little formal music making occurred. One exceptional concert was explicitly framed as a musical event. It presented performances of Frédéric Chopin and Stanisław Moniuszko as Polish composers by members of local professional ensembles.[30] Otherwise, amateurs performed on site. Singer-songwriters—of the same generation as Kaczmarski—brought their guitars and sang soldiers' songs, cabaret tunes, and simple laments that played to their audience's enthusiasm for strophic songs with first-person narratives. The mysterious minimal presence of live art music did not go unnoticed: a radio broadcast on August 20 prompted a minor debate about music's relevance and *esprit de corps*. One activist noted the conversation:

> The workers comment on the specific selection of music on the local radio. There they broadcast classical music all the time. With the passage of time its character changes and it becomes, in the opinion of those who listen, funereal: this does not bode well. However, our command is steadfast: persevere.[31]

Protesters were invested in what music they heard and whether it expressed the emotional tenor of the political moment.

---

28 The film *Robotnicy '80* (dir. Andrzej Chodakowski and Andrzej Zajaczkowski, 1981) and Erazm Ciołek's photographs provide visual evidence of music making and crowd convocation; see Erazm Ciołek, *Sierpień Solidarności* (Warsaw: Centrum Sztuki Współczesnej, 2010).

29 Writing in 1990, David Ost used the language that would form the mantras of the 2011–12 Occupy Movement to explain Polish protest tactics. David Ost, *Solidarity and the Politics of Anti-Politics* (Philadelphia: Temple University Press, 1990), 150.

30 Two singers from the Baltic Opera and a pianist from the Baltic Philharmonic performed songs by Polish composers to an audience of one thousand. This is mentioned in "Strajkowy Biuletyn Informacyjny Solidarność," August 27, 1980. See also Adam Orchowski, "Przebieg strajku okupacyjnego w Stoczni Gdańskiej im. Lenina w dniach 14–31 sierpnia 1980 roku," in *Polski Sierpień 1980: Reedycja Almanachu Gdańskich Środowisk Twórczych "Punkt" nr 12/80* (New York: Biblioteka Pomostu, 1981), 27.

31 Orchowski, "Przebieg strajku okupacyjnego," 18.

Though they mark the crest of Polish dissent, the 1980 strikes were not the first high-profile public protests in the People's Republic. Numerous precursors in cities across the country—Poznań (June 1956), Warsaw (March 1968), Gdańsk (1970), and Radom (1976)—took on historiographical import.[32] But from the litany of mythologized protests, one stands out as a figurative premonition of what was to come: December 1970. When riots across the tri-city region of Gdańsk, Sopot, and Gdynia halted local industrial plants, the police responded with violence, killing hundreds of workers. The government left these murders unacknowledged, and the event remained an open wound through the 1970s. The living memory of December 1970 became a touchstone in August 1980, central to the amalgam of grievance and critique in cultures of resistance. One of the first demands to which the government conceded was the construction of a memorial in honor of those fallen.[33] The protesters in Gdańsk officially demanded that the workers who had been fired because of their participation be re-employed; Lech Wałęsa consistently referenced the murders to strengthen the emotional pull of the negotiations. The shared geography of 1970 and 1980, which I analyze further in Chapter 5, also meant that the protests involved experienced actors with tactical knowledge of the tri-city police, media, and other institutions.

As a new series of general strikes swept Poland beginning in June 1980 in Lublin, attention shifted toward the active ports and shipyards on the Baltic coast.[34] In 1980 the termination of Anna Walentynowicz, a crane operator at the Lenin Shipyards, on August 7 for participating in an illegal trade union catalyzed organized action. The crowd of workers that approached the second gate of the shipyards on the morning of August 14, 1980, was certainly aware of the brutal violence that had occurred in that place almost ten years earlier. Just moments before, the workers' leader, Wałęsa, had heralded action: "We

---

32 For a discussion of the influence of local protests on regional political mobilization, see Padraic Kenney, "Opposition Networks and Transnational Diffusion," in *Transnational Moments of Change: Europe 1945, 1968, 1989*, edited by Gerd-Rainer Horn and Padraic Kenney (Lanham, MD: Rowman & Littlefield, 2004), 207–23.

33 Borrowing from Pierre Nora, Matthias Riess has argued that objects derived from protest marches rearticulate the political and sociocultural work such protests undertake. See Matthias Reiss, ed., *The Street as Stage: Protest Marches and Public Rallies since the Nineteenth Century* (Oxford: Oxford University Press, 2007), 9. On popular critique and protest in the People's Republic, see Paweł Machcewicz, *Rebellious Satellite: Poland, 1956*, translated by Maya Latyński (Stanford, CA: Stanford University Press, 2009).

34 For accounts of the late 1970s consolidation of the opposition and its foundational role for Gdańsk in 1980, see A. Kemp-Welch, *Poland under Communism: A Cold War History* (Cambridge: Cambridge University Press, 2008), 203–68; and Barbara J. Falk, *Dilemmas of Dissidence in East-Central Europe* (Budapest: Central European Press, 2003), 27–43.

are taking on an occupational strike." Though permitted, striking remained a form of resistance, and shouting the word empowered Poles as an articulation of free speech. As Lech Wałęsa recalled, "It was repeated loudly and thousands of times: Strike! Strike! Strike!—a taboo word, a word that they tried to suppress all too unsuccessfully."[35] The crowd's endorsement was a loud "Hurra!" An anonymous worker, interviewed on August 31, describes the workers' coordination: "We approached the gate, where we commemorated those who died in 1970 with a moment of silence, and, after, we sang the national anthem."[36] The sonic arch, from coordinating shout through the secularized ritual of political quiet to the nation-state affirming chorus, moves through a range of performative and acoustic registers, establishing the energetic and performative tone of the strikes as, per Hannah Arendt, "initiatory action."[37] The poetics of this choreography shaped it as canonic: it recurs in oral histories of the strikes and anchors the workers' actions in those previously taken at the peripheries of Gdańsk's factories. This historiographic repetition signals a punctuating role for Wałęsa and the national anthem, one that echoes the transformative power of the leader and the chorus in "Walls." Silent commemoration deflected attention to the emotional from what would become a discourse on labor union policy. When the government acknowledged these strikes (initially reported at 16,000 workers), Solidarity grew loud and visible as Poland and its national anthem reached the global stage.[38]

Audio material recorded on handheld mini-cassette recorders perhaps most thoroughly captured sounds in the shipyards over the following weeks (Figure 3.1).[39] The constantly flowing tape tracked all of the formal

---

35 See Lech Wałęsa, afterword to Józef Tischner, *The Spirit of Solidarity*, translated by Marek B. Zaleski and Benjamin Fiore (San Francisco: Harper and Row, 1984), 106.

36 See "Wywiady: Jak rozpoczął się strajk," in "Strajkowy builetyn informacyjny Solidarność," reproduced in *Zapis wydarzeń: Gdańsk-Sierpień 1980; dokumenty*, edited by Andrzej Drzycimski and Tadeusz Skutnik (Warsaw: Niezależna Oficyjna Wydawnicza NOWA, 1999), 8.

37 Dana R. Villa, *Politics, Philosophy, Terror: Essays on the Thought of Hannah Arendt* (Princeton, NJ: Princeton University Press, 2009), 124–27; Georgina Born, "Introduction," in *Music, Sound and Space: Transformations of Public and Private Experience*, edited by Georgina Born (Cambridge: Cambridge University Press, 2013), 39–40; and Karsten Lichau, "'The Moving, Awe-Inspiring Silence': Zum 'emotionalen Potential' der Schweigeminute," in *Performing Emotions: Interdisziplinäre Perspektiven auf das Verhältnis von Politik und Emotion in der Frühen Neuzeit und in der Moderne*, edited by Claudia Jarzebowski and Anne Kwaschik (Göttingen: V&R unipress, 2013), 69–72.

38 Anthony Barbieri, Jr., "Polish Government Discloses Walkout at Site of Bloody 1970 Workers' Riots," *The Sun*, August 15, 1980, A1.

39 I refer here to the extensive collection of recordings at the National Commission of the Independent and Self-Governing Trade Union "Solidarity," Gdańsk, Poland. In conversation with me, Małgorzata Pietkiewicz spoke of the devices she used to record

FIGURE 3.1. Recording at the Lenin Shipyards in August 1980. Witold Górka and Zbigniew Trybek, Ośrodek Karta.

negotiations—the material has been collected and cared for by the Solidarity trade union's archive as such. It comes closest to "contain[ing] everything to which the ear was exposed in a given sonic setting," to invoke the representational capacity implied by the notion of a soundscape.[40] The constant rearticulation of the protestors' specific goals colored the atmosphere at the shipyards as collaborative and provided forward momentum to the conversation. Accordingly, the activists thirsted for stirring and inspiring music that predicted a positive resolution for what they understood to be the negotiations' realistic demands. The ebullient birthday song "One Hundred Years" ("Sto lat") served such a role, with its affirmative message and simple musical profile (see Chapter 5). The song welcomed the focus on progress and the future: the call, "one more time," rebounds with a simplicity that is anything but fatalist. Furthermore, recordings of the song—whether excerpted for documentary purposes, or archived as reference material—represent the clearest, most unified, and loudest singing of August captured on tape ▶.[41]

---

professionally as a journalist, as well as surreptitiously for the opposition (Małgorzata Pietkiewicz, July 2, 2010).

40 David W. Samuels, Louise Meintjes, Ana María Ochoa, and Thomas Porcello, "Soundscapes: Toward a Sounded Anthropology," *Annual Review of Anthropology* 39 (2010), 329–45, at 330.

41 The beginning of Solidarity's first documentary film, *Robotnicy '80*, features representative performances. Hear also the song's presence on Jan Gall's audio-biography of the leader for further evidence of its close association with Wałęsa: *Wałęsa* (Warsaw: NOWA

Timothy Garton Ash's account of the scene, collected in 1983 in the international bestseller *The Polish Revolution*, participates in the positivist spirit of documenting the spoken deliberations in every detail, heightening the drama of negotiation.[42] The historian and journalist privileged the role of sound as communication and *communitas*. He listens carefully and evokes a cacophonous sensorium, projecting himself as earwitness.[43] Standing among the crowds at the shipyards, the reporter writes as one of the captivated participants. The first one hundred pages of his history of Solidarity focus on the minute-to-minute waves of tension and release as Wałęsa, the voice of the workers at the head of the Inter-Factory Strike Committee, and various missionaries from the Polish United Workers' Party engage in heated conversation.[44] At one point Garton Ash even conjures up a musical duel that stands in for the political *tête-à-tête* underway in Gdańsk. The Party's most important annual plenary in Warsaw was broadcast on television:

> Many of the strikers watch the end of the [Central Committee's] Plenum on television. When the Party men on the screen rise to sing "The Internationale," the delegates stand up, as if at an inaudible command, to answer them with the national anthem. "Arise ye prisoners of want" pipes the box; "Poland is not yet lost," thunders the hall.[45]

He relocates friction between the Party and opposition in cultural performance, using cacophony (or at least loudness) to underscore the nonviolence of August 1980. Agitated group performances frequently drowned out

---

Oficyjna Wydawnicwa, NOWa audiocassette 013 [1983]) at the Solidarity Collection, Houghton Library, Harvard University, Cambridge, MA.

42 The book gathers writings from the *Spectator, The Times*, and *Der Spiegel* (Garton Ash, *The Polish Revolution*, ix).

43 In his influential treatise on the soundscape, R. Murray Schafer promoted the earwitness's authority as chief conduit for historical soundscapes. R. Murray Schafer, *The Soundscape: Our Sonic Environment and the Tuning of the World* (Rochester, VT: Destiny Books, 1977), 8–9.

44 Recently scholars of protest have drawn attention to the impact of media presence on popular resistance as theater. William Marotti, "Japan 1968: The Performance of Violence and the Theater of Protest," *The American Historical Review* 114 (2009), 97–135. In Gdańsk, journalists represented activist constituencies, the Party, the state-subsidized Polish Radio and Television, and international news sources from the East and West. The semi-fictional film *Człowiek z żelaza* (1981) by Andrzej Wajda portrays the fervent energy of journalists in Gdańsk as contributing to a sense of witnessing history.

45 While the "Internationale" had frequently been mobilized by workers in protest over the course of the twentieth century, at the 1980 strikes, the song was firmly in the grips of the Party, since its performance was a ritual part of the Central Committee's proceedings. Garton Ash, *The Polish Revolution*, 60.

individual voices—at least as I heard them on the taped record of these negotiations ⏵. This one, however, is more than just a song or slogan snowballing across assembled protesters. When Garton Ash locates performative resilience in sonic power, he offers evidence of the cultural fabric that connects the workers.

A generous reading of this passage's political action might dwell on that magnetic suggestion that the musical articulation was spurred by an "inaudible command." Singing, the sounding response to this silent impulse, proves the coherence of the opposition and by extension its organization. Reimagining scenes like this one, the workers are a hopeful flicker of what Michael Hardt and Antoni Negri have called the multitude, the collaborative political organization from below that anchors their theory of global protest. Hardt and Negri write against the fantasy of improvised action and individual freedom as the counterpoint to top-down control: "Like the formation of habits, or performativity or the development of languages, this production of the common is neither directed by some central point of command and intelligence nor is the result of a spontaneous harmony among individuals, but rather it emerges in the space *between*, in the social space of communication."[46] The leaderless performance of the national anthem is anything but anarchic or spontaneous; it is directed not at the Party, but across the scene of protest—after hours—among peers. The repertory flags the demand of the social movement, and song shapes a register at which it can communicate and build energy against state-monopolized media.

The journalist's chronicle of life at the shipyards is also laced with musical references that reinvest in romantic notions of political rebellion from below. Garton Ash uses music to highlight his position as a spectator, as when he interpolates the texts that workers sing to pass the time. He latches on to songs as symbols and as evidence of that alluring spontaneous vernacular expression deemed particular to late twentieth-century social movements. Like protests themselves, songs' power lies in their ability to "pop up from nowhere."[47] Garton Ash introduces the texts as though they are haphazardly improvised: "As one striker puts it, in the doggerel verse with which they while away the hours of waiting. . . ."[48]

---

46 Michael Hardt and Antoni Negri, *Multitude: War and Democracy in the Age of Empire* (New York: Penguin Books, 2004), 222.

47 Beate Kutschke, "In Lieu of an Introduction," in *Music and Protest in 1968*, edited by Beate Kutschke and Barley Norton (Cambridge: Cambridge University Press, 2013), 2. Kutschke describes the lateral organization—what she calls "self-dynamic action"—of 1968 protests to make a case that protesters are autonomous subjects. This cultural-historical take stands in striking contrast to the analysis of these—largely transnational—student movements by political theorists. See Michael Hardt and Antonio Negri, *Assembly* (New York and Oxford: Oxford University Press, 2017), 3–14.

48 The translation is Garton Ash's original (Garton Ash, *The Polish Revolution*, 59).

Już od lat są te metody	The tricks have been known for years,
Zna je stary, zna je młody	both old and young know them:
Dużo słów, a sensu brak	lots of words but no meaning—
Ogłupienia wierny znak.	a clear sign of brainwashing.

This is, however, no impromptu riff. The original song—for the Gdańsk version is a cover of a signature tune of the State Folk Song and Dance Ensemble "Śląsk" (Silesia)—poked fun at the rather mundane existence of a retired man ⏵. At the shipyards it was adapted to criticize the Party's propagandistic techniques.[49] The sing-song rhyme of the text, including its pseudo-alliterative rhyme between *"metody"* (methods) and *"je młody"* (young), contributed to the song's air of folk authenticity for Garton Ash. But the song is also not an ephemeral contrafact in the spirit of the "December Thirteen" family described in Chapter 2. A studio recording made by activists in the months after August circulated transnationally.[50] A singer whose presence at the shipyards will become important later, Maciej Pietrzyk, theatrically modulated his otherwise well-enunciated Polish into comedic parody of a town drunkard's fumbled rambling on his cover of the stable, new text.[51]

One of the first self-conscious histories of Solidarity by its members suggests both the instrumental nature of sound on the scene and its instrumentality in initial attempts to preserve the strikes' reality. The almanac, *The Polish August of 1980* (*Polski Sierpień 1980*), is itself a celebration of the free speech made possible by Solidarity's legalization, published in the final months of 1980 by Gdańsk-based independent publishers, but with the approval of the government (and hence legal).[52] To a certain extent, the volume indicates the primary-source documents that Solidarity's members deemed most significant for the negotiations and most representative of August.[53] The materials emphasize Solidarity's legitimacy by foregrounding text and word, but the dynamic range of the documents also draws attention to the moments when written discourse fails. The activists packaged the documents as broadsides, building on centuries-old traditions of immediate print news circulation. The highly edited collection contains brief essays and recollections, bolstered by posters, pamphlets, poetry, transcriptions, and legal documents. These source materials are framed as artifacts, prefaced with introductory captions and judiciously truncated, explained, or summarized

---

49 The original track appeared on Śląsk's first album, Muza SX 182 (nd).
50 *Solidarity! Postulat 22*, Smithsonian Folkways (1981) FSS 37251
51 *Sierpień 80*, Wifon LP 163 (1989).
52 *Polski Sierpień 1980*.
53 Roy Palmer emphasizes print documentation's relationship to orality in his *The Sound of History: Songs and Social Comment* (Oxford: Oxford University Press, 1988), 1.

to make them simultaneously recognizable to those who had lived at the Shipyards in August and those just learning of the strikes.

The almanac's editors also struggled to balance the objective and subjective throughout the volume, explicitly dividing the evidence into three categories to organize recent history: documentation, reconstruction, and interpretation. Each bears the additional qualification of the scrapbooking effort as an attempt (*próba*), an exploratory contextualization of the wealth of documentary evidence that anticipates revisions of this recent event's legacy. Calling their fledgling historical work "attempts," in the sense of *Versuche*, the activists rejected absolute empiricism, inferring the documents' stability in contrast to the fallibility and instability of historians' work.

Two entries that exhibit the sheen of objectivity also reveal this historiographic anxiety. The almanac begins with a skeletal narrative of August: a timeline.[54] Adam Orchowski reconstructed August in detail, presenting an overview of key days indexed by time stamps. Yet Orchowski's interpretive style is discernible in the bare bones history. He occasionally zooms in with minute-by-minute transcriptions of dialogue from the negotiations, and complements the policy focus with descriptions of events elsewhere at the shipyards; for example, when Catholic mass is held. In a second ostensibly empirical document, Stanisław Rosiek aggregated transcriptions of what he called the "tape player's account" (*zapis magnetofonowy*) from the opposition's repository of recordings.[55] Rosiek necessarily truncates, but rarely editorializes, giving his interpretive hand a subtle presence through the document.

The Polish August of 1980 is peppered with sonic traces (Table 3.1). Orchowski has a proclivity for the atmospheric and the cultural. Over the course of his list of events, the presence and the significance of communications and sound media emerge: they become means for creating support for the strikes locally, nationally, and internationally. In addition to tracking the steady increase in journalists at the scene, he notes when strike organizers began using radio communication, when workers brought television sets to watch state newscasts, and when speakers required megaphones to communicate with the amassed crowds.[56]

In Rosiek's efforts, parenthetical references to applause draw attention to persuasive comments and resounding arguments; even an intermittent "Bravo!" or laugh is documented.[57] Occasionally, his stenographers note

---

54 Orchowski, "Przebieg strajku okupacyjnego," 9–44.

55 Stanisław Rosiek, ed., "Zapis magnetofonowy przebiegu obrad plenum Międzyzakładowego Komitetu Strajkowego w Stoczni Gdańskiej," in *Polski Sierpień 1980*, 55–120.

56 Orchowski, "Przebieg strajku okupacyjnego," 13, 21.

57 The transcriptions' incorporation of general responses from the room follows the format established by the Central Committee of the United Workers' Party.

TABLE 3.1 Sonic Traces in *The Polish August of 1980*

Print documentation	Stenographic transcriptions of the events document applause, spontaneous choruses, and shouts Collected "verses" include many song texts
Interpretation and reflection	Orchowski's everyday history of August Bieńkowski's and Skutnik's brief introductions to the poetry of the Gdańsk shipyards
"Preliminary reconstruction" of the events (Adam Orchowski)	Singing: of the national anthem, usually under the direction of Lech Wałęsa (9 times) Singing: of "One Hundred Years," usually in celebration of Wałęsa (3 times) Singing: of "God Save Poland" outside liturgical context Efforts made to record the proceedings Debate among workers over local radio stations' music programming Listening to the radio or watching television together Gratitude expressed in official remarks toward intoned liturgy of masses held at the shipyards Concert by artists from the Baltic Opera and Philharmonic in the cafeteria Interviews by documentary filmmakers Formal registration of concern as to who can listen to the proceedings, within Poland, across the globe Broadcast of music across the radio transmitter Concern that the microphone is not properly amplified Warning to monitor your conversations because all microphones are live Transcription of chanting by the assembled crowd (e.g., "Leszek, Leszek," in honor of Wałęsa)

voices' sources beyond the political protagonists who utter them; for example, announcements through the factory's loudspeakers or transmissions on walkie-talkies. A word-for-word negotiation transcript provides documentary precision, and only rarely does a scribe indicate foregoing transcription because of a comment's lack of clarity. The three notes on performances of song thus momentarily pause the policy-driven account of events. Twice, the crowd's adoration of Wałęsa is transformed from chants of praise into the singing of "One Hundred Years."[58] With a frantic shout that the day is over, Wałęsa interrupts an opponent, and only when the governmental representative formally closes the meeting does music—the national anthem—become woven into the events of the negotiation. In Wałęsa's words, "Wait a second! I suggest that, with permission, we sing 'Poland has not yet perished.' "[59]

58 Rosiek, ed., "Zapis magnetofonowy," 93, 107.
59 In Rosiek, ed., "Zapis magnetofonowy," 120.

The National Anthem as Resistance

Jeszcze Polska nie zginęła,	Poland has not yet perished,
Kiedy my żyjemy.	So long as we still live.
Co nam obca przemoc wzięła	What the foreign force has taken from us,
Sablą odbierzemy.	We shall retrieve by sword.
Marsz, marsz, Dąbrowski,	March, march Dąbrowski,
Z ziemi włoskiej do Polski.	From Italian soil to Poland.
Za twoim przewodem	Under your command
Złączym się z narodem.	We shall rejoin the nation.

—"Dąbrowski March," Józef Wybicki (1797)

At moments of great tension or resolution, Wałęsa rallied the crowds to sing the Polish national anthem ▶.[60] His emphatic performance of this forceful patriotic song conferred might upon the Solidarity movement that buoyed Wałęsa's heroic image through the 1980s.[61] The scenario almost always unfolded in the same manner. His gravelly tenor intoned the verse's first words in rhythm but without pitch, and the assembled crowd would fall in line to affirm that Poland "has not yet perished" (*jeszcze nie zginęła*). Hovering in the fifth beneath C4, men and women sang at opposite extremes of their registers. As chorus, it dispelled conversations and cleared the air of clatter. It cut off, for example, Anna Walentynowicz as she stood in front of the camera giving an interview to the directors of *Robotnicy '80* ▶. In Orchowski's chronicle, Wałęsa's association with the national anthem emerges forcefully: it is integrated into the account of the negotiations at nine points, many times under his direction. Numerous firsthand accounts are scattered with notes that conflate singing the anthem with confidence: "For the concluding 'Jeszcze Polska' we were strong and tight-knit."[62]

The anthem's refrain, "Poland has not yet perished," had affirmed Polish identity in the nineteenth century, when the nation was under partition.

---

60 Janina Jankowska's award-winning radio montage contains a number of sound clips from the scene. Janina Jankowska, *Polski Sierpień*, NOWa audiocassette 006 (1981), analyzed later in the chapter.

61 Maja Trochimczyk, "Sacred/Secular Constructs of National Identity: A Convoluted History of Polish Anthems," in *After Chopin: Studies in Polish Music*, edited by Maja Trochimczyk (Los Angeles: Polish Music Center at the University of Southern California, 2000), 263–94.

62 "Na zakończenie *Jeszcze Polska* byśmy byli silni i zwarci." In Orchowski, "Przebieg strajku okupacyjnego," 32. Orchowski also notes, for example, standing ovations held at the conclusion of the anthem, 43.

"Dąbrowski's March," or "Dąbrowski's Mazurka," was written in 1797 as military music to accompany the Polish troops serving under Napoleon. The text's author, Józef Wybicki, had accompanied the Polish Legions to Spain and Italy as a general. Though the march alluded to by its sometimes-title describes the textual narrative rather than the musical topic, the anthem is first and foremost military music that was imagined to unite Poles fighting in proxy battles on behalf of their partitioned nation. Sung across Europe from Paris to Crimea, from Rome to London—and even in the US Civil War—it was an instrument of resistance within the confines of modern warfare.[63]

In the late eighteenth century, the song that would become the national anthem—in many ways it is a song in search of a nation—became inextricably linked with the modernity of independent Poland from the signing of the Polish Constitution on May 3, 1791, until the Third Partition in 1794.[64] The patriotic significance of the ratification snowballed through the nineteenth century as Poland remained partitioned.[65] In Adam Mickiewicz's 1834 pastoral epic, *Pan Tadeusz*, a boisterous performance of the national anthem marks the insurrectionist hopes of a reveling crowd: "That march of triumph: *Poland is not dead! / Dąbrowski, march to Poland!* With one accord / They clapped their hands, and 'March Dąbrowski!' roared [*okrzyknęli*]."[66] By 1980 the mazurka's status as national anthem had been official since its constitutional provision in 1926. The state remained invested in the song's continued relevance: the Polish Composers' Union was called upon to update the official orchestral and military band arrangements following the 1977 revision of the Constitution.[67]

---

63 On instrumental uses of music for resistance, see Eric Drott, "Resistance and Social Movements," in *The Routledge Reader on the Sociology of Music*, edited by John Shepherd and Kyle Devine (New York: Routledge, 2015), 171–74. On the politics of place and Polish military music, see Andrea F. Bohlman, "Orienting the Martial: Polish Legion Songs on the Map," in *Hearing Crimea*, edited by Gavin Williams (New York: Oxford University Press, 2019), 105–28.

64 Maja Trochimczyk, "National Anthems of Poland," essay for Polish Music Center, University of Southern California; https://polishmusic.usc.edu/research/national-anthems/.

65 Patrice M. Dabrowski, *Commemorations and the Shaping of Modern Poland* (Bloomington: Indiana University Press, 2004), 102.

66 "Uderzenie tak sztuczne, tak było potężne, / że struny zadzwoniły jak trąby posiężne / I z trąb znana piosenka ku niebu wionęła, / Marsz tryumfalny: *Jeszcze Polska nie zginęła! . . . / Marsz Dąbrowski do Polski!*—I wszyscy klasnęli, / I wszyscy: 'Marsz Dąbrowski!' chórem okrzyknęli!" See Adam Mickiewicz, *Pan Tadeusz*, translated by Kenneth R. Mackenzie (New York: Hippocrene Books, 1986), 568–69.

67 Letter from Józef Patkowski to the membership, Archive of the Polish Composers' Union, Folder 33/3 (1977), Polish Music Information Centre, Warsaw, Poland.

EXAMPLE 3.1. 1978 piano-vocal arrangement of the Polish national anthem. *Polski hymn narodowy.*
Polskie Wydawnictwo Muzyczne, 1978.

The anthem's history as a song accompanying nineteenth-century campaigns for independence and its status as the official national anthem make its resonance at the shipyards coherent. Its musical and textual content also confirm that this patriotic song could be a protest song (Example 3.1). The upbeat and celebratory nature of the anthem grows out of its musical material, which satisfies many of the conventions that we have come to expect of the songs modern nations select to represent their peoples.[68] The melody lends itself to contrafacts, and its sectional form is based on the alternation of verse and refrain.[69] As a mazurka, the anonymously composed music resists being heard as ambiguous with respect to nation in Poland.[70]

68 Philip V. Bohlman, *The Music of European Nationalism* (Santa Barbara, CA: ABC-CLIO, 2004), 155.

69 Contrafacts span the local and national. At the Lenin Shipyards, protestors sang "March, march Wałęsa!" Its version as the pan-Slavic anthem, "Hey Slovane" (1834), was further altered to be the Yugoslav national anthem (1943–91), witnessing further polysemic potential.

70 The tune itself emerged from the nationalist project that was the fervent composition of patriotic mazurkas and polonaises. See Barbara Milewski, "Chopin and the Myth of the Folk," *19th-Century Music* 23 (1999), 113–35; and Halina Goldberg, *Music in Chopin's Warsaw* (New York: Oxford University Press, 2008), 62–77.

Wałęsa's memoir from the mid-1980s explains his perspective on the anthem's link with the ongoing struggle for liberation.[71] He identifies with the insurrectionists of the nineteenth century, explaining, "I sometimes feel as if I belong to a past age, the age which is . . . evoked in our national anthem, 'Poland has not perished.' The conditions in which this anthem saw the light of day are much the same as those we live under today, and the same can be said of the hopes and values it expresses: courage, defiance, pride." Wałęsa writes as the figurehead of the opposition, rallying from within Solidarity as much as he is reflecting upon Solidarity. His orchestration of spontaneous performances of the national anthem at the scene of negotiation perpetuated this stable meaning.

Garton Ash latches onto the national anthem's presence during negotiations, noting its communal performance on August 14, 24, 27, 30, and 31. His documentation indulges in a transformative vision of the anthem and politics, one in which music leveled conflict and magnified elation. Garton Ash's careful notes on sound add dimension to the inkling of heroic charisma with which Wałęsa credited himself.[72] In *The Polish Revolution*, the workers' representative receives acknowledgment for the aura at the negotiations as much as he does for their measured progress. Garton Ash conjures up a mighty image of the Polish electrician-turned-political leader:

> I notice how skillfully Wałęsa manages this unruly assembly. Whenever the arguments become furious and voices from the floor are raised in anger he summons up the ghosts of General Dąbrowski's Polish legions, whose splendid marching song is now the national anthem.
>
> "Poland is not yet lost so long as we live . . ." he intones, and all controversy is stilled as everyone rises to their feet, "March, march Dąbrowski, From Italian soil to Poland . . ." and the roof nearly lifts off, all dissension swept away in this never-failing catharsis, "Under thy command, we rejoin the nation . . ." and is it of Wałęsa or Dąbrowski that they sing? It is pure Polish magic. You know that magician has turned it on deliberately, almost cynically. Yet as he sings he is transformed: no longer is he the feisty little electrician in ill-fitting trousers. The sharp talker with many human weaknesses; no longer does his authority derive merely from his patter and repartee; now he stands

---

71 Lech Wałęsa, Andrzej Drzyciński, and Adam Kinaszewski, *A Path of Hope* (London: Collins Harvill, 1987), 310–11.

72 Wałęsa's charisma emanates as a decisive factor in the role he played for Solidarity. It is no coincidence that when the events of 1989 came to pass, it was Wałęsa to whom people dedicated songs. See "Wiersze poświęcone Lechowi Wałęsie," National Commission of the Independent and Self-Governing Trade Union "Solidarity," Gdańsk, Poland.

up straight, head thrown back, arms to his sides, strangely rigid and pink in the face, like a wooden figure by one of the naive sculptors from the Land of Dobrzyn where he was born.[73]

Garton Ash's impressions of the national anthem—that it is "never-failing" in rousing the entire crowd to their feet, or that it diffuses debate and inspires—preface an amalgamation of Wałęsa-as-leader-in-song with Wałęsa-as-leader-of-Solidarity that glows with praise. It is through music that the Western journalist can see and feel Polishness, linked with the timeless practice of rural folk art that stands in for purity. Garton Ash's description decodes Wałęsa's appeal for international readers. More waffling caricature than political profile, the significance of the journalist's evaluation lies not in its substance but in the mode in which Garton Ash tells the story: through performance analysis. Wałęsa's musical charisma becomes bound up with national symbols, planting the seed for an anthem like "Walls" to tell Solidarity's story. For Garton Ash, it is song that creates the hero, musical charisma that conscripts phantom Polish paragons, and the act of singing that gives Wałęsa's voice political power.

Hearing Solidarity in Stereo

Across the factory grounds, wires connected televisions and microphones to speakers, and activists and reporters held recording devices and megaphones. It was radio's potential to receive and transmit that established it as the preferred communication media for Solidarity. The low-tech media connected constituencies across the grounds and bridged the strikers and the world.[74] In the months following August, Solidarity's radio stations routinely

---

73 Garton Ash, *The Polish Revolution*, 64. Wałęsa's powerful position during the 1980s has made him the target of much scrutiny: see, for example, the examination of his files collected by the SB (Służba Bezpieczeństwa) in Sławomir Cenckiewicz and Piotr Gontarczyk, *SB a Lech Wałęsa: Przyczynek do biografii* (Warsaw: Instytut Pamięci Narodu, 2008). The debates about his complicity and negotiation with the SB continue through August 2019.

74 By the time of the 1989 revolutions, news broadcasts on television notably inspired participation in street demonstrations. Andrei Ujica and Harun Farocki's documentary film *Videograms of a Revolution* (1992) thematizes the role of Romanian television in that national context. See also David Culbert, "Memories of 1945 and 1963: American Television Coverage of the End of the Berlin Wall, November 9, 1989," in *Television Histories: Shaping Collective Memory in the Media Age*, edited by Gary R. Edgerton and Peter C. Rollins (Lexington: University of Kentucky Press, 2001), 230–43; and Joshua Clover, *1989: Bob Dylan Didn't Have This to Sing About* (Berkeley: University of California Press, 2009), 113–40.

re-broadcast recordings of the proceedings in Gdańsk so that citizens could record the proceedings for themselves. Practically speaking, these broadcasts modeled negotiations for regional unions. On an emotional level, however, they also kept August's impetus for political change vital through sound. In private tape collections, homemade recordings of radio broadcasts, whether the BBC, Voice of America, or the hardly coded "Radio 'S,'" abound ⊙. Like the rampant publication of documentary material from the scene in print, radio transmission was driven by an impulse to archive the prolific extant evidence of successful organizing.

As she abridged source material in the process of preparing a one-hour special on the birth of Solidarity in early 1981, radio journalist Janina Jankowska navigated a vast sound repository. Her radio program, *Polish August (Polski Sierpień)*, was devoted to capturing the essence of the strikes through the montage of documentary footage she and other journalists from the state media conglomerate, Polish Radio and Television, had accumulated.[75] Jankowska's project overcame any potential deficiencies of sound media that excluded the visual.[76] In 1980s Poland, the unofficial publishing networks—called the *drugi obieg* (second circulation)—nurtured a thriving cassette culture.[77] Cassette tapes' portability, reproducibility, and low cost were essential to *Polish August*'s continued dissemination through the decade (Figure 3.2). Jankowska's program became an important documentation of Solidarity at home and abroad: broadcast on Polish Radio and Radio Solidarity, it was awarded the 1981 Prix Italia for radio documentaries and circulated through Polish communities around the world on cassette tape.[78]

---

75 In a twenty-first-century interview, Jankowska elaborates on the compositional process, noting that she returned from Gdańsk with "so much material, so many recordings," http://sierpien1980.pl/portal/s80/952/7372/Janina_Jankowska.html.

76 For a discussion of the tension between the audio and visual in documentary practices, see Virginia Madsen, "'Your Ears Are a Portal to Another World': The New Radio Documentary Imagination and the Digital Domain," in *Radio's New Wave: Global Sound in the Digital Era*, edited by Jason Loviglio and Michele Hilmes (New York: Routledge, 2013), 126–44.

77 See Chapter 1 for a discussion of the opposition's cassette culture. One anonymous member of the opposition wrote: "Cassettes played a major role during the time of the August strikes; recordings of the MKS at the shipyards and the negotiations with the state commission were remarkable instruments of information and built solidarity" ("Video," *Kultura Niezależna* 11–12 (1985), 125–27, at 127). Peter Manuel's observation of the "democratic restructuring of media control and content" in North Indian popular music is also relevant in the Polish context; see Peter Manuel, *Cassette Culture: Popular Music and Technology in North India* (Chicago: University of Chicago Press, 1993), xv.

78 Janina Jankowska, *Polski Sierpień*. Witness the tape's presence in Houghton Library's Solidarity Collection at Harvard University, a repository of private

FIGURE 3.2. The cover of the drugi obieg edition of Janina Jankowska's *Polish August*, 1983.

Partly a window into journalists' reporting practices, partly a monumental *laudatio* to Solidarity's singularity, the sound documentary offers a fresh history of Gdańsk nurtured by the radio.

Divided into three parts (Strike, Waiting, Dialogue), Jankowska's reportage is a dramatization of the stepwise negotiation and an evocation of the shipyard atmosphere. *Polish August* is a montage of sonic documents that give the negotiations an immediate local context. Jankowska employs a range of editorial techniques that highlight her heterogeneous material and the multitude of voices that sound. A third-party narrator reads historical summaries that punctuate Jankowska's manipulation of varied source sounds: prayer at the shipyards, strike negotiations, and announcements across the factories' loudspeakers. Sometimes one hears the messages' mediators: record buttons click as journalists depress them. The very diversity of the sounds' origins, statuses, and curations on the program lends sound an ethos of power in the story of Gdańsk's August. Enticing "sonic layers" discernible in Jankowska's final program are not merely an

---

collections from the Boston-area Polish-American community. Though I have not been able to establish the initial broadcast date, Jankowska remembers that the program was broadcast without censorship on the state network in 1981 (Bogumił Łoziński, "Bez etosu," December 31, 2015; http://spotkania.wiara.pl/doc/2297458. Bez-etosu).

TABLE 3.2 Sonic Layers of *Polish August*

December 1970	Historical recordings of shooting and sirens Recollections by eyewitnesses in interview with Jankowska
December 1980: 10-year anniversary	Public address Daniel Olbrychski Excerpts from a studio recording of Krzysztof Penderecki's *Lacrimosa*, played back live at the ceremony Moment of silence
Day-by-day accounts of August 1980	A narration read by a male actor Recollections on key events (e.g., assembly on August 14, Lech Wałęsa's leap over the wall) by workers present Excerpts from negotiations, both addresses and discussions Fragments of Polish Television's reports on the events Interviews by Jankowska with participants and observers of the general strike as well as other civilians in the tri-city region Weather forecasts from Polish Radio Recordings of the soundscape of waiting, frequently featuring religious prayer Documentary recordings of loudspeaker announcements Newspaper articles and press releases read by a male actor (from *Trybuna Ludu*, *The Washington Post*) Reflections by Jerzy Kołodziejski, governor of Gdańsk and signatory of the Gdańsk Accord

indulgence in sound's dialogic complexity (Table 3.2). The radio montage effected through combination, distortion, and decay reveals Jankowska's investment in a cacophonous historiography.[79] Furthermore, the complex layers had an additional practical function: to transform mono source material from the mini-cassette recorders into stereo.[80]

Music is never just one kind of sound. Jankowska gives it many formal roles in the framing of this history, highlighting the diverse functions and presences music had at the shipyards. And with it, Jankowska begins (▶

---

79 Radio Solidarity recordings bear witness to the influence of Janina Jankowska's editing style and content. *Nowa Huta '82–'84* (Nowohucka Oficyjna Fonograficzna audiocassette 002 [1986]), for example, includes Jankowska's mix of crowd exaltation from Gdańsk while complementing it with new footage from the artificial milltown outside Cracow.

80 Interview hosted on sierpien80.pl. Studies of the recording studio frequently credit engineers with artistic craft; radio engineers similarly refract and shape the sounds we hear. See René T. A. Lysloff, "Mozart in Mirrorshades: Ethnomusicology, Technology, and the Politics of Representation," *Ethnomusicology* 41 (1997), 206–19, at 216, and Eliot Bates, "Mixing for *Parlak* and Bowing for a *Büyük Ses*: The Aesthetics of Arranged Traditional Music in Turkey," *Ethnomusicology* 54 (2010), 81–105.

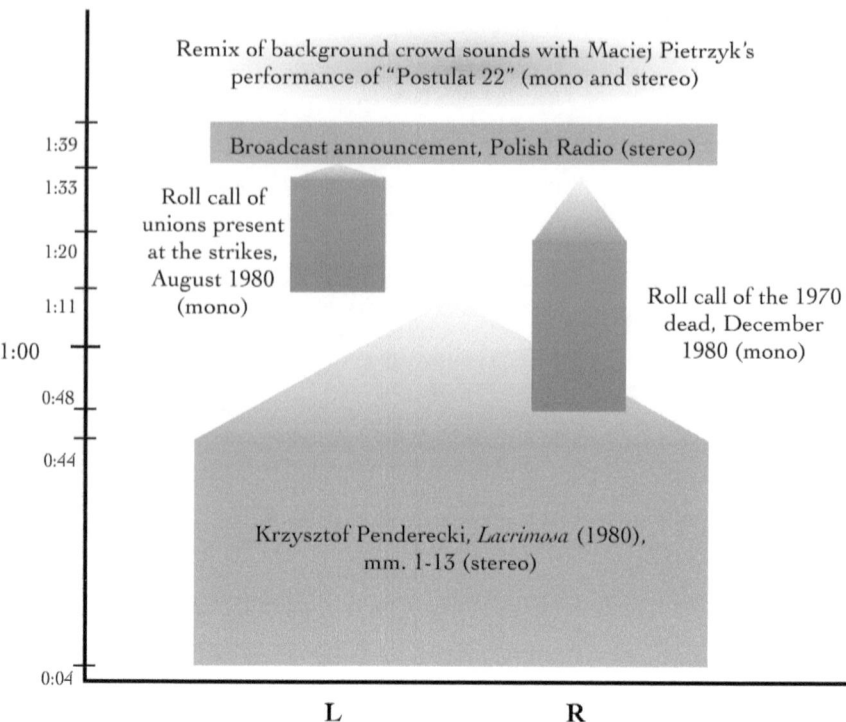

FIGURE 3.3. Transcription of the first two minutes of *Polish August*, as distributed across left and right channels.

Figure 3.3). Without verbal cue, listeners first hear double-basses and cellos performing the sighing three-note motive that drives the sorrowful lament of Krzysztof Penderecki's *Lacrimosa*, a work dedicated to the victims of the 1970 shootings in Gdańsk and premiered at their memorial in December 1980 (discussed at greater length in Chapter 5).[81] Jankowska has always credited her team of collaborators at the radio station with the inspiration to frame

---

81 Penderecki's composition squarely belongs to the neo-romantic strand of late twentieth-century Polish concert music, and the Polish opposition was otherwise invested in the nineteenth-century symphonic sound. Radio Solidarity marks the transition between news items with fragments of the finale from Antonín Dvořák's Symphony No. 9, "From the New World," between news items, for example in the broadcast of November 27, 1981, reissued on the CD accompanying Szczepan Rudka, *Radio "Solidarność" Wrocław 1981: Rozgłośnie wrocławskiej opozycji* (Wrocław: Muzeum Miejskie Wrocławia, 2005). Voice of America frequently interpolated Chopin's G minor Ballade (*Pielgrzym trudnych chwil: Odzyskać godność*, Solidarity Collection, Houghton Library, Harvard University, Cambridge, MA).

the project with a large symphonic work, and music journalists at the radio station still remember agitating to include the prominent composer's new piece.[82] The symphonic excerpt invites mournful reflection: Penderecki sets a swelling sob into motion as instrument upon instrument and voice upon voice intone the three-note motive of a rising diminished sixth and falling minor second. As the unrest becomes clamorous, Jankowska ushers the music to the background, and the naming of those killed in 1970 introduces the roll call from the Lenin Shipyards in 1980.[83]

Through *Polish August* we hear how, across the shipyards, people waited and watched, occasionally passing the time singing.[84] Among the crowds of observers, music helped pass the time and offered a means of manifesting subcultures at the scene, whether church parishioners offering Marian songs to icons or students enjoying the guitar-strumming banter of campfire culture. The tunes crucially give her portrait of August 1980 multiple subjectivities: Jankowska gives voice to the amateur musicians on the scene. The stagnation of time, the interruption of everyday life, and a concern for the end of history infuse the aesthetics and poetics of many amateurs' songs. In Maciej Pietrzyk's "Song for My Daughter" ("Piosenka dla córki") an activist-narrator pleads with his daughter to understand that he has left her so that she might have a better future ▶.[85]

Nie mam teraz czasu dla Ciebie.	Right now I don't have time for you.
Nie widziała Cię długo matka.	Your mother hasn't seen you for a long time.
Jeszcze trochę poczekaj dorośnij,	Wait a little bit longer to grow up,
Opowiemy Ci o tych wypadkach.	And we'll tell you about these circumstances.
O tych dniach pełnych nadziei,	About these days filled with dreams,
Pełnych rozmów i sporów gorących.	Filled with discussions and heated debate.
O tych nocach kiepsko przespanych,	About these nights poorly slept through,
Naszych sercach mocno bijących.	[And] of our strongly beating hearts.

82 Małgorzata Pietkiewicz, interview with author, July 2, 2010. Their journalistic collaboration across radio departments exemplifies the collaborative production spirit explored in Albin Zak, *The Poetics of Rock: Cutting Tracks, Making Records* (Berkeley: University of California Press, 2001), 163–82.

83 Jan Kubik describes the music during his own attendance at the December 1980 commemoration in *The Power of Symbols against the Symbols of Power*, 200–02.

84 *Dźwiękowa kronika strajku w Stoczni Gdańskiej im. Lenina*, Part 1; CD 352, National Commission of the Independent and Self-Governing Trade Union "Solidarity," Gdańsk, Poland.

85 Brief footage is available at http://sierpien1980.pl/portal/s80/973/Filmy.html.

This song was composed for the strikes, and he would later sing it around the country. Pietrzyk, whose parody recording of the waiting song I have already discussed, also released this song on his LP of strike music.[86] That recording had long legs—it was the background track for a 1980 news coverage of the strikes on public television in the United States.[87] Joan Baez learned to sing it on her 1985 visit to Gdańsk, more about which in Chapter 5, and sang it in the summer of 1989 in Bratislava to celebrate the arrival of democracy in Poland.[88]

A far cry from the ambition of communal anthems, the song takes the form of first-person direct address and, like Kaczmarski's "Walls," is an example of sung poetry. (As in singer-songwriter traditions elsewhere, in Poland both amateurs and professionals performed sung poetry in formal concert settings and everyday places.[89]) In Gdańsk, Pietrzyk performed simplistically, employing basic strumming as accompaniment, repeating transitional passages, and humming to encourage only muted participation. Jankowska interpolates multiple excerpts of Pietrzyk's performances to accompany human interest stories. "Where do you sleep?" she asks a female activist at the conclusion of the program's first half, the cassette's A side.[90] "Well, where I'm sitting!" the protester retorts. She proceeds to redirect Jankowska's inquiries about the practicalities of life in the shipyards and in the process introduces the singer-songwriter's verse:

> That text, that one I heard a recording of yesterday. The one that man wrote while he was waiting. Yes, some kind of ballad. That text begins so uniquely . . . well, because they are simple lyrics: "Right now I don't have time for you."

The protester goes on to recite—at a quick pace hardly reminiscent of Pietrzyk's deliberately sung declamation—the song's entire text by memory, and Pietrzyk's humming fades in.

---

86 Pietrzyk recorded rock versions of his own music and other songs under the direction of Maciej Zembaty on *Sierpień 80*, Wifon LP 163 (1989).

87 "Poland's Solidarity Movement, 1980," Films Media Group, 1980; fod.infobase.com/PortalPlaylists.aspx?wID=102632&xtid=46881.

88 The televised recording of this performance is accessible at https://www.youtube.com/watch?v=AgYDf-1N238.

89 Sylwia D. Ejmont, "The Troubadour Takes the Tram: Experience in Polish Poetry and Music" (Ph.D. dissertation, University of Michigan, 2008), 133–68.

90 Using the practical break between sides as a formal device for audio documentaries is a common practice; see Neil V. Rosenberg, "Documentary Sound Recordings," 348.

Solidarity's Songs in Print and On the Stage

As we have seen, song and sound receive careful attention throughout Solidarity's immediate histories. They are integral to the possibility of protest culture. They set actors in relation to one another to structure what Naomi Waltham-Smith astutely describes as a "simultaneous sharing and spacing" made possible through listening.[91] With time, the historiographic projects of Solidarity's activists shifted focus from the evocative atmospheres of these sound documents to song collections that fixed the cultural legacy of the autumn's labor unrest. The ontological status of songs changed in the process, even if compositions like Pietrzyk's could circulate both within Jankowska's framework as documents and in new arrangements on record. Rather than evidence of performances of patriotic unison, songs became objects to preserve, bound as relics or framed as brief stories that retold the lessons of Solidarity.[92] Print culture anthologized songs, and cassette culture's albums and mixtapes codified playlists. Taking their cue from street music's traditional form of circulation—pamphlets and broadsides—Solidarity's cultural organizers transformed music into discrete units, an archival impetus that set into motion the iconic singularity of "Walls" and a divorce of text from sound. Paradoxically, in extracting the songs from their originating political scene, the activists integrated music with the politically contested literary practice of poetry. On tape, songs frequently punctuated spoken text and poetry. In print, songs were most often collected among "verses" (*wiersze*) without musical notation. When literary scholar Maria Janion described the coastal activity in August 1980 as a "poetry microclimate," she evoked and lauded the spontaneous creativity of those gathered while muting the performative and, by extension, musicality of the strike culture.[93]

---

91 Naomi Waltham-Smith, *Music and Belonging Between Revolution and Restoration* (New York: Oxford University Press, 2017), 25–27, at 27. Her understanding of music's "condition of possibility in conventionality" builds on reading, together, Jean-Luc Nancy, *The Inoperative Community*, translated by Peter Connor, Lisa Garbus, Michael Holland, and Simona Sawhney (Mineapolis and Oxford: University of Minnesota Press, 1990) and Jean-Luc Nancy, *Listening*, translated by Charlotte Mandell (New York: Fordham University Press, 2007).

92 In compiling the most recent edition of *The Big Red Songbook*, Archie Green mused on the function of anthologizing the "songlore" of a labor movement in print: "What is a Wobbly song? Is it any piece printed in an IWW songbook, or just those that reflect IWW [Industrial Workers of the World, or Wobbly] philosophy?" In Archie Green, "Preface," *The Big Red Songbook*, edited by Archie Green, David Roediger, Franklin Rosemont, and Salvatore Solerno (Chicago: Charles H. Kerr, 2007), 7.

93 Maria Janion, "Słowo i symbol w miesiącach przełomu," in *Kongres Kultury Polskiej, 11–13 Grudnia 1981*, edited by Władysław Masiulanis (Warsaw: Volumen, 2000), 38.

Familiarity unlocked contrafacts' musical status for readers, as did the Brechtian titles that signaled musical form: ballad, song, couplet, and hymn. Very occasionally the incipit of a popular tune flagged a song to which a radically altered text could be sung. Marek Bieńkowski, the poet and Gdańsk native who was responsible for the poetry collected in *The Polish August of 1980*, saw great significance in culture's presence at the scene and advocated for the texts as authentic, almost Herderian, creativity on the part of the workers: "One of the documents that registered the strike's feeling is the poetry that emerged from 14 to 31 August. This type [*typ*] of authentic workers' composition is something new in the cultural landscape of the Polish People's Republic, as had been the spontaneous appearance of the phenomenon of Solidarity, which called them to life."[94] Poetry's energy is interpreted as analogous to that of Solidarity and immediately—confidently—inscribed as communal.

The legacy of Solidarity's music, however, contrasts strikingly with the sound on the ground at the shipyards. When an assortment of songs, many of them composed in the late 1970s, were programmed at the first Review of Authentic Song (Przegląd Piosenki Prawdziwej) on the first anniversary of August 1980, they became canonized as Solidarity's songs. The prominence of these "authentic" songs forestalled the documents from Gdańsk's sensorium from sounding Solidarity's music history.[95] Eighteen thousand workers, students, and journalists were in attendance for the three-day festival, which was recorded, rebroadcast on Solidarity's radio stations across Poland, and released on cassette in abridged and unabridged forms.[96]

The festival's prominence and close association with the trade union—it had Wałęsa's blessing, too—obscured the fact that few songs on its program originated at the scene of Solidarity's inception.[97] The credibility and quantity of the more than fifty performers who took to the stage, as well as their allegiance with the opposition, were crucial to the mission of the Review: the

---

94 "Jednym z dokumentów rejestrujących strajkowe nastroje jest powstająca od 14 do 31 sierpnia poezja. Tego typu autentyczna twórczość robotnicza jest czymś nowym w krajobrazie kulturowym Polski Ludowej, tak samo zresztą jak zjawisko spontanicznych wystąpień solidarnościowych, które powołały ją do życia" (Marek Bieńkowski, "Dialog czyli 'Gdański Janko Krytykant': kilka uwag o poezji strajkowej," in *Polski Sierpień 1980*, 126). He also uses phrases like "street poetry" and "city folklore" that allude to the voice of the folk as the voice of the oppositional, authentic nation.

95 The archival materials for this festival, a one-time occurrence, are housed at the archives of the National Commission of the Independent and Self-Governing Trade Union "Solidarity," Gdańsk, Poland.

96 Data concerning the original cost and attendance of the 1981 festival are available in Przemysław Ćwikliński, "Zembaty za kraty," *Nie* 37 (2001), 3.

97 Wałęsa's name appeared as the "honorary patron" of the event on the Solidarity-issued program and news bulletin for members of the press.

event's description alluded to the strong moral character of its participants.[98] The plan of organizer Maciej Zembaty, himself a cabaret artist, was to stage a festival of "forbidden songs" (*zakazane piosenki*), songs that could have been censored for commenting upon the political opposition, for incorporating nationalist symbols, or for satirizing the Party.[99] A crucial distinction must be made here in order not to sensationalize censorship: the festival itself was not banned or forced underground; its subtitle merely alluded to its oppositional tone.[100] After the event, the drugi obieg commodified its program, further perpetuating the implicit musical ties between the review, the Solidarity Union, and Gdańsk (see Figure 3.4). A one-tape abridgment of the festival by the Solidarity Radio Agency in Gdańsk (Radiowa Agencja "Solidarność") was circulated among union members, for example.[101]

The claim to authenticity for these songs lay in their candid and truthful depictions of society (*prawdziwy* is derived from *prawda*, or truth), which were buoyed by a direct and intimate musical language. We might think of this as an authenticity predicated on affect rather than on documentary evidence and thus a break from the impulse to capture August 1980 through source materials. Over time, however, many of the Review's songs have developed a resilient, though fictitious, link to the shipyard scene in public consciousness precisely because of the exalted ideal of truth. Of these songs, Kaczmarski's sweeping anthem remains most firmly linked with Gdańsk 1980 in public history, perhaps even especially since his death in 2004: think again of the importance of this song for the 2016 protests in Warsaw. A June 2014 poster in Warsaw used Kaczmarski to advertise a concert musical celebration of the twenty-fifth anniversary of the first free elections in Poland (see Figure 3.5). To ultimately explain the substitution of artistic authenticity for sound

---

98 The festival's organizers offered the following on the first page of the daily bulletin: "Everything that constitutes the Review of Authentic Song is the result of goodwill and social needs of everyone engaged with this project"; "Zamiast wstępu . . . i fanfar," *Biuletyn Przeglądu Prawdziwej Piosenki* 1 [1981], 1; National Commission of the Independent and Self-Governing Trade Union "Solidarity," Gdańsk, Poland.

99 *Biuletyn Przeglądu Prawdziwej Piosenki* 1, 1.

100 The Ministry for Internal Affairs collected the festival's programs and song texts but did not intervene. See IPN BU 024/179 and IPN BU 024/180, Institute of National Memory, Warsaw, Poland; LVI-1400, KC PZPR, Archiwum Akt Nowych, Warsaw, Poland.

101 A double LP published on the ECHO label in the United States (*Piosenki Solidarności—Songs of Solidarity*, E LP 901-2 [1981]) advertises the festival as *the* repertory of the union. Multiple-tape sets were made for journalists by the festival's organizers (*Biuletyn Przeglądu Prawdziwej Piosenki* 3 [1981]: 3).

FIGURE 3.4. "Twenty-five Years Later: A Concert for the Festival of Freedom," Warsaw, June 2014.
Photograph by the author.

documentation, and the metonymic shift from Wałęsa to Kaczmarski, I turn to examine "Walls" more closely and to understand the place that nation and nationalism have had in constructing the soloist of "Walls" as the musical champion of the people.

Solidarity's Bard

At the Review of Authentic Song, Kaczmarski was no new kid on the block. As the rising star of poezja śpiewana in the late 1970s, his performances and new compositions had become legendary in their own right. When the Review's emcee introduced the singer to the crowd, he traded on familiarity, saying: "Once, some years ago, some friends invited me to this small loft

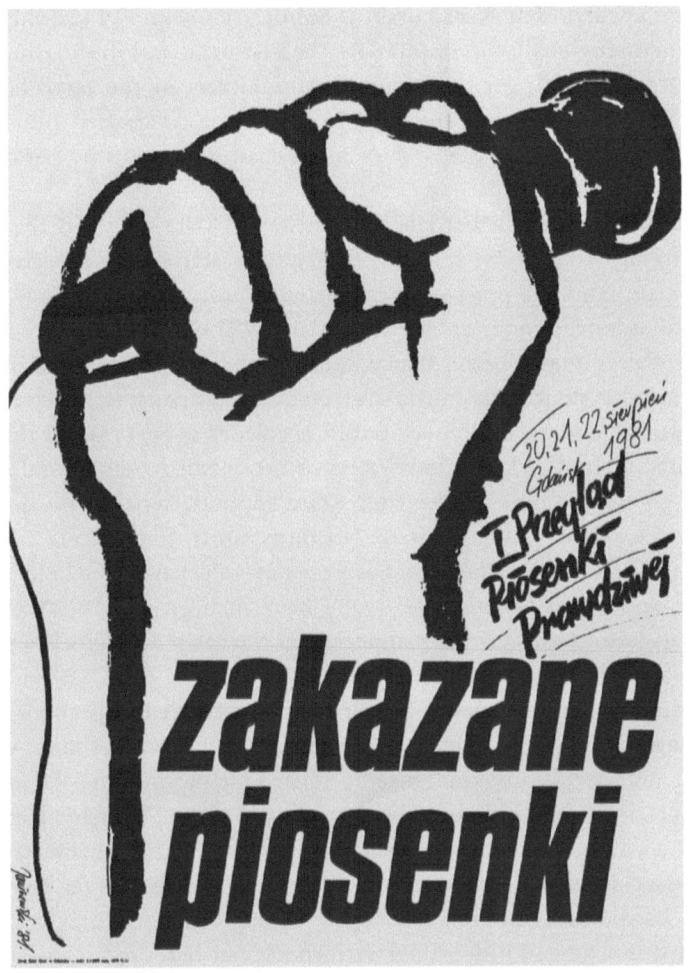

FIGURE 3.5. Poster advertising the Review of Authentic Song (1981) by Jerzy Janiszewski.
ECS/T/ASP/205, European Solidarity Centre collections.

apartment in Warsaw's center, where its owner played his poems over the course of a couple hours. He sang with a sensibility, strength, zeal, anger, and rebellion similar to my favorite Russian bards. The owner of this apartment was the (at that time still very young) Jacek Kaczmarski."[102] The prominence of "Walls" has as much to do with its singer as it does with the song, as much to do with symbolism as with Solidarity. Though Kaczmarski sings as a member of a trio, his voice, compositions, and subjectivity constitute

---

102 See "Caryca," *Zakazane piosenki: I Przegląd Piosenki Prawdziwej 20–22 08*, Biuro Organizacyjne PPP and AKWENDRUK, 2001.

the protest anthem. For Kaczmarski is Solidarity's *bard*.[103] I use this literary term quite intentionally; it emphasizes the historical and international reference points for the singer-songwriter, whose victory at the 1978 Festival of Student Song in Cracow at the age of twenty-one catapulted him into the national spotlight. "Walls" is one of more than 200 songs he performed in the late 1970s.

To call Kaczmarski a bard is to position his work within the legacies of two literary traditions: that of the Byronic artist who powered Polish Romanticism, and the practice of unofficial music making in Soviet Russia referred to as bardic song (*avtorskaia pesnia*).[104] The Polish practice of poezja śpiewana shares many performance conventions with the latter, in which artists compose their own music and texts, accompany themselves on the acoustic guitar, and generally seek public accolades as poets rather than musicians. During the Cold War, Soviet bards established their moral credibility through their independence from state support, writing music that, as J. Martin Daughtry has suggested, "encompass[es] dissidence . . . but also exceeds it."[105] In Poland, the great Soviet bards—Alexander Galich, Vladimir Vysotsky, and Bulat Okudzhava—were held in high esteem, and the first Polish translations of their work appeared in the early 1980s as Kaczmarski's fame blossomed.[106]

Kaczmarski attracted praise from critics as a result of his connections to Soviet song. "Here we have our Polish Vysotsky. . . . A bard of song, who took his young and demanding audience by storm. He has become the idol of his contemporaries," one critic extolled excitedly.[107] Like Vysotsky, Kaczmarski expresses a vitriolic frustration with the present. In this review, the Polish singer's association with the opposition to state socialism is far less relevant than his bardic authenticity, developed through the gesture to the great Soviet bard. Kaczmarski identified with the Soviet bard, mourning his death

---

103 Karolina Sykulska collates nearly seventy references to Kaczmarski as a bard in "Jacek Kaczmarski: Szkic do portretu," in *Bardowie*, edited by Jadwiga Sawicka and Ewa Paczoska (Łódź: Ibidem, 2001), 123–25.

104 See Gerald S. Smith, *Songs to Seven Strings: Russian Guitar Poetry and Soviet "Mass Song"* (Bloomington: Indiana University Press, 1984); and J. Martin Daughtry, "The Intonation of Intimacy: Ethics, Emotion, Metaphor, and Dialogue among Contemporary Russian Bards" (Ph.D. dissertation, University of California, Los Angeles, 2006).

105 J. Martin Daughtry, "'Sonic Samizdat': Situating Unofficial Recording in the Post-Stalinist Soviet Union," *Poetics Today* 30 (2009), 27–65, at 39.

106 An issue of the literary journal *Poezja* devoted to troubadours printed bilingual editions of Vysotsky and Okudzhava (volume 8, August 1982).

107 Wiesława Czapińska, "Budujcie arkę przed potopem—czyli Jacek Kaczmarski," *Ekran* 26 (1981), 10–11, at 10.

by telling his story in the 1980 song "Epitaph for Vysotsky" ("Epitaphium dla Wysockiego") ▶.

Being a *Polish* bard placed Kaczmarski in the lineage of nineteenth-century Romantic poet-heroes. In her sketch of the literary scene at the end of the Cold War, Joanna Niżyńska underscores the legacy of the nineteenth century: "The Romantic perception of literature as the fusion of word and deed, as a force capable of shaping history and morality, privileged the writer as the spokesperson for the community."[108] Kaczmarski was poised for a reception that confused his own politics with those of the poet in his song. When he transformed "Walls" from its Catalan origins into Polish poezja śpiewana, the anthem became specific and nationalist for Poland, despite the song's transnational history and broad ideals. Musically, the song accomplishes a sleight of hand with symbols similar to the sleight of hand that Solidarity realized with its own name. In reappropriating the principle of socialist collective action as its label for the opposition, the union disguised the long fight ahead with a concise brand name, complete with identifying font and color (see Figure 3.5). The excision of the "Walls" refrain from the tale Kaczmarski weaves likewise obscures a complex and cynical meta-commentary within the performance. Fragmentation eliminates a level of commentary: instead of singing about a bard, Kaczmarski sings about himself.

In his 2009 Kaczmarski biography, Krzysztof Gajda begins the section devoted to the singer's relationship to Solidarity with a simple statement: "Kaczmarski was not there at the time."[109] The need explicitly to draw attention to his absence indicates what might have been expected: that the bard was a participant in history's triumphs. It was through Kaczmarski's performance at the Review of Authentic Song that his voice became not only able to represent, but to validate Solidarity's history. Such small details may best serve the historian who delights in precision. But in the case of this story built on the thirst for source material from the scene, they also reveal the fault lines that, under a bit of pressure, have the capacity to open a conversation about the shortcomings of the conventional narrative of state socialism's collapse in Poland.

The status of August 1980 as the kernel of Solidarity's truth in the twenty-first century is anything but coherent and triumphant.[110] No longer is this

---

108 Joanna Niżyńska, "The Impossibility of Shrugging One's Shoulders: O'Harists, O'Hara, and Post-1989 Polish Poetry," *Slavic Review* 66 (2007), 463–83, at 465.

109 Krzysztof Gajda, *To moja droga* (Wrocław: Wydawnictwo Dolnośląskie, 2009), 125.

110 The anniversary of the first democratic elections in June 2014, for example, spurred a critique of the Polish state from all sides that focused on shortcomings in the 25 years since the end of state socialism. See Igor Stokfiszewski, "Should Poland Celebrate a Quarter Century of Democracy?" http://www.aljazeera.com/indepth/opinion/2014/06/should-poland-celebrate-quarter-201463105444559928.html.

the protest that initiated the triumphant march toward an undivided Europe or a Poland in which citizens live without the fear of censored media or a ban on public demonstrations.[111] Despite the "explosion of memory culture" in East Central Europe, the symbols around which it coheres are often contradictory or, at the very least, fractured.[112] The 1944 Warsaw Uprising looms so large that on August 1, 2017, its commemorative moment of silence rang out across Poland, while the signing of the Gdańsk accords was noted with a small academic conference debating the legacy of Solidarity on August 31.[113] Many have questioned their own euphoric celebration of the August strikes, as well as the stories out of that month that they clung to through martial law. One former activist commented on the false objectivity promised by documentary techniques: "[In] contrast with the tight control over television news exercised by the Communist regime, the documentaries of Solidarity really represented to us the truth. But all these years later, I can also say that they represent a series of myths, . . . which we experienced at the time as reality."[114]

Within "Walls"—or really, as the singer's voice trails off in the last rendition of the refrain—Kaczmarski warned of this fate. Not as a hazard particular to Polish history, along the lines of the fear laid out in the national anthem, but as a meditation on the dangerous power of the many to abandon and trample the individual. The reductive mantra at the heart of "Walls," in many ways, captures the thrust of Solidarity's legacy, the Polish opposition's hope that walls will fall (*mury runą*). Recall, again, its currency on the streets in contemporary Warsaw. Let the story play out, listen longer to Kaczmarski ▶. By the final refrain, the narrative of revolt has turned sour:

> Finally they saw how many they were,
> They came to feel the strength and the time,
> And with a sound about the nearing dawn
> They traversed the city streets,

---

111 Aleksandrowicz, Sonntag, and Wielgohs, eds., *The Polish Solidarity Movement in Retrospect*.

112 Michael Bernhard and Jan Kubik, eds. *Twenty Years after Communism: The Politics of Memory and Commemoration* (New York and Oxford: Oxford University Press, 2014), 1.

113 Joanna Wiśniowska, "Koniec sporu o obchody rocznicy Sierpnia '80. Lech Wałęsa: 'Bo mądrzejszy ustępuje głupszemu,'" *Gazeta Wyborcza*, August 25, 2017; http://trojmiasto.wyborcza.pl/trojmiasto/7,35612,22278381,koniec-sporu-o-obchody-sierpnia-80-lech-walesa-madrzejszy.html.

114 Film scholar Wiesław Godzić, as quoted in Michael Chanan, *The Politics of Documentary* (London: British Film Institute, 2007), 21. Chanan even coins the phrase "Solidarity syndrome" to refer to the historical distance between a documentary film and its audience.

They toppled monuments and tore out the cobblestone—
He's with us! He's against us!
He who alone is our greatest enemy!
But the singer, too, was alone.

He watched the regular march of the crowds,
He silently listened to their thunderous steps,
And the walls grow, grow, grow,
The chains sway at their legs.

Perhaps failure was intrinsic to Solidarity's iconic protests, imbued with a power to transcend everyday difference. We—both historians and political actors ourselves—hear the loud rallying cries of change more easily than mixed messages and disinterest. "Is the silent majority a chorus?" an anarchist in Warsaw asked in the years after August 1980.[115] Even if multiplicities are inherent in social movements, they depend on the illusion of unity in order to act collectively.[116]

Kaczmarski wrestled with the celebration of "Walls," for example, as it was used to ring out the end of the evening news on Radio Solidarity 1982–86. He benefited from singing for Solidarity, touring the globe to sing for Polish émigrés that heard, through him, a channel to Gdańsk. From his perch in Munich at Radio Free Europe at the microphone, he tried to explain and contextualize this song, to emphasize other political songs that call out anti-Semitism in Poland or critique the symbols of nationalism, and to push back against the pressure that music is an instrument for change. These were strategies to eschew authorship over Solidarity, to avoid becoming a hero, and to emphasize his distance from Gdańsk. The attraction people felt to sing the refrain of "Walls," he said, felt like a "prank" (*psikus*) on him as its lonely bard.[117] Exasperated, he suggests that Poles have to "do, progress, and win," not sing about it. Ultimately, however, he turned to song to offer the final pushback. In the second version of "Walls," subtitled "In a Courtyard '87" ("Podwórko '87"), he slowed down and respun the charged melody of the refrain: one version as verse, another as chorus. This time, Kaczmarski is alone again, sitting in a courtyard, in search of a song and in search of a reason to sing. Walls surround him, but this time, they are muddy, old, and dilapidated—ruins built by people long dead. The song is observational and pessimistic.

115 "Odezwa Międzymiastówki Anarchistycznej," IV/203.1, Archive of the Opposition, Karta Organization, Warsaw, Poland.
116 See Melucci, *Challenging Codes*, 20–32.
117 Interview with X. Woksal, "Jam po prostu jest rusofil-antykomunista," *Indeks* 9, no. 25 (1987), 2.

Solidarity does not haunt him, it is absent. "Here's what remains of the great river / Of thoughts, voices, colors," he mourns, highlighting the corpses of larvae and centuries' old bullet scars. Walls and graves outlast the history, the stories, and the storytellers he seems to suggest: "it's all gone . . ." (*nie ma już . . .*).

4 | Voice

Jerzy—you martyr
of the Polish nation
Can you hear it? The knelling of the bells
Of your church.

May these church bells,
Through your death,
Soon launch into a peal,
A sounding freedom.
—anonymous verse, Warsaw, November 2, 1984

As Father Jerzy spoke, his soft voice became the most powerful they had ever heard.
—John Fox, "Do You Hear the Bells, Father Jerzy?"

Solidarity's iconic strikes spurred vigilant attention to—sometimes celebration of—Poland by international news media and its global audiences.[1] The opposition's success and subsequent collapse made a recuperation of Central Europe and the end of the Cold War imaginable until, under martial law, they were not.[2] The nation attracted buzz abroad, manifest most visibly in the two Nobel Prizes awarded its prominent dissident voices: the Berkeley-based poet Czesław Miłosz, whose essays and poetry shaped the *New York*

---

1 Epigraphs taken from "FSO-2-003 Flugschriften, Flugblätter, Dokumente aus dem poln. zweiten Umlauf," Archiv der Forschungsstelle Osteuropa an der Universität Bremen, Bremen, Germany; John Fox, "Murder of a Polish Priest," *Reader's Digest*, December 1985, 217.

2 Tony Judt, "The Rediscovery of Central Europe," *Daedalus* 119, no. 1 (1990), 23–54.

Review of Books, with the award in literature in 1980, and Lech Wałęsa with the award for peace in 1983. Among the worlds of dissent behind the Iron Curtain, Poland was treated as a thread to pull so that the fabric of communism might unravel.

The murder of Jerzy Popiełuszko (1947–84), a Catholic priest openly sympathetic to the opposition, by the Security Service (Służba Bezpieczeństwa, SB) was decisive in maintaining the events in Poland as transnational media events. The priest, who has since been beatified, disappeared on the evening of October 19, 1984 while traveling home by car from holding mass. On October 30 his body was found in the Vistula River with stones tied to his angles. Over the next months, renegade members of the SB were accused, tried, and acquitted of the murder. Telling the priest's story, Western news outlets reconfirmed allegiance against communism in the affective register. While he was alive, Popiełuszko, the central personality around whom the activity of this chapter coheres, rallied the Polish opposition through nationalist sermons. These underscored the strength of spirit, culture, and morals that undergirded the ongoing struggle for freedom. His "Masses for the Fatherland" at a parish in northern Warsaw were some of the most visible activity in the name of the Church during martial law. They were amplified by loudspeakers, radio broadcasts, and cassette recordings, in addition to printed transcripts and extensive discussion in the Catholic press of the opposition's unofficial print culture, the *drugi obieg*.[3] His charity work and outspoken critique of General Jaruzelski's oppressive government ultimately even caused tensions within the Catholic Church; he was reprimanded by the Polish Primate, Józef Glemp. On October 19, 1984, Popiełuszko was kidnapped and murdered by three SB agents. Across the Polish opposition, the spiritual guidance he had offered, combined with the physical beating and traumatic drowning he endured at the hands of government agents, confirmed him as one of the most visible and mourned martyrs through the 1980s.

The agents' public trial and conviction (December 27, 1984–February 7, 1985) made the hostility of the SB visible. Through this moment of tension at home, Poland took on importance in the global Cold War. Pundits and strategists from abroad lavished attention on it in order to "manufacture consent," in the words of Noam Chomsky and Edward S. Herman.[4] In other words, while the incarceration of his murderers provided some hope in Poland that the

---

3 See Chapter 1 for a discussion of the drugi obieg (second circulation), the opposition's network of independent presses and self-publishers that circumvented censorship.

4 Noam Chomsky and Edward S. Herman, *Manufacturing Consent: The Political Economy of the Mass Media* (New York: Pantheon Books, 1988), 37–44. They compare the disproportionate coverage of this murder with the near silence on the murders of Latin American priests in US client states.

communist regime might be broken down by due process, in a transnational context the plain villainy of Popiełuszko's assassination lent further emotional charge to the division of the world into two parts—good and evil—in the 1980s. As Chomsky and Herman analyzed, by "generat[ing] the maximum emotional impact," the Polish priest could become intensely human and thus a "worthy victim" around whom Western publics and politicians could rally in support.[5] This claim, I suggest with the examples that follow, has musical relevance in transnational contexts and the Polish national circuit. How does Popiełuszko's affective labor charge—in the sense of loading energy—the opposition with coherence? I consider this question, extending it through the analysis of commemorative concert music composed by Andrzej Panufnik and Krzysztof Kniettel that explicitly work to reconstitute the priest's political action in sound. This chapter explores the winding and consistent presence of Popiełuszko's voice—as sound, metaphor, and referent—through the media that cast his profile larger than life before and after his death.

The front pages of Western newspapers offer a clear focus on Popiełuszko's voice as a technology of resistance. They focus on the police brutality laced through the witness account of the priest's driver and the murderers' confessions in court. In the *Los Angeles Times*, the driver is cast as a listener when the SB pull over the civilian car under the pretense that they have been caught speeding. The driver's testimony is quoted verbatim in the news item:

> Popieluszko told me to slow down, and the car overtook us and forced me to stop, Popieluszko was ordered out of the car. . . . I heard Popieluszko saying, "Gentlemen, what do you think you are doing?" Then I heard a noise like a sack full of flour being hit with a club and I realized they were beating him senseless. I heard his body being dumped in the trunk of their car.[6]

Formal address, in the driver's account, grounds the spoken text in an otherwise baffling—and increasingly muffled—encounter. What Popiełuszko says speaks back to physical violence gives him humanity.

The press latches onto the murderers' specific language, too, as they channel Popiełuszko posthumously.[7] The AP report in Toronto's *Globe and Mail* paints a picture of a scared victim, with the confessor presumably conveying

---

[5] Chomsky and Herman, *Manufacturing Consent*, 43.

[6] "Slain Polish Priest Was Clubbed 'Like a Sack Full of Flour,' His Driver Testifies," *Los Angeles Times*, January 18, 1985, B7.

[7] The Polish press and the drugi obieg transcribed the trials; non-governmental organizations watched to ensure due process. See "Proces morderców ks. Jerzego Popiełuszki," *Zeszyty Historyczne* 73 (1984), 80–108; Siegfried Lammich, *Der "Popiełuszko-Prozess": Sicherheitspolizei und katholische Kirche in Polen; Bericht und Dokumentation im Auftrag der Internationalen Gesellschaft für Menschenrechte* (Cologne: Wissenschaft und Politik, 1985).

remorse through a sense of the inhumane violence. The report on the trial leads: "Rev. Jerzy Popiełuszko pleaded in terror for his life under a rain of blows after being kidnapped by Polish security police, one of his confessed killers testified yesterday. Father Popiełuszko cried, 'Help, help. Spare my life, you people,' as he was being beaten unconscious with a club in a forest while trying to escape."[8] To others, the accounts provided raw contact with the scene of the crime and its bodily violation.

Homiletic Voices

In this chapter I hear Popiełuszko's cries with and against the writing and remembering of this looming figure. His utterances bind the diverse examples: many weep as they worship or work. They attend to speech as his gift to his congregation, the Polish people. Members of the opposition cling to—collect—his sermons *as said* in praise of the Lord and the Fatherland. These tokens constitute, on the one hand, his voice as object, as a "disturbance of aesthetic appreciation" that is insistently spiritual.[9] It can thus become present when it is not. In a censored account of Popiełuszko's funeral for the Catholic press, for example, Roman Graczyk described: "As the service began, another heavy silence fell; there was a slight echo of the chaplain's voice. A couple of thousand people heard themselves [*wsłuchuje się*] within his voice."[10] As Jeff Todd Titon lays out, preaching is a performance of devotion, as is the silent attention to it and the (in the Polish-Catholic context) serene and reserved responsory: "Amen." He writes of Baptist Appalachia that the "utterance [of language] constitutes an act or kind of commitment."[11]

Yet another community of Popiełuszko's devotees attends to the priest as performer: his mission for God and the mode in which he delivers—Gregorian chant—became the foundation of musical compositions. It is as speaker that Popiełuszko is projected as the charismatic leader, whether dead or alive. As Ed Harris, playing a scheming SB agent, says in Agnieszka Holland's fictionalized cinematic treatment of the priest (*To Kill a Priest*, 1988): "He's a very dangerous man. He's very charismatic. And all the people listen to him.

---

8 "Kidnapped Priest Pleaded for Life, Polish Court Told," *Globe and Mail*, December 29, 1984, 1.

9 Mladen Dolar, *A Voice and Nothing More* (Cambridge, MA: MIT Press, 2006), 4.

10 Roman Graczyk, "Pogrzeb Duszpasterza," reprinted following its censure at *Tygodnik Powszechny* in Szczepkowska, ed., *Ks. Jerzy Popiełuszko: Życie i śmierć; Dokumenty i wspomnienia* (Paris: Polemika, 1986), 114.

11 Jeff Todd Titon, *Powerhouse for God: Speech, Chant, and Song in an Appalachian Baptist Church* (Austin: University of Texas, 1988), 195.

TABLE 4.1 Cassette Portraits of Jerzy Popiełuszko at the Museum of Independence, Warsaw

Drugi obieg projects	
Words about Father Popiełuszko (Janina Jankowska)	Memorial documentary
Beginning of the Great Vigil	Funeral documentary
Father J. Popiełuszko's Final Sermon	Documentary
The Final Sermon of Father Jerzy Popiełuszko	Documentary
My Litany (Leszek Wójtowicz)	Musical dedication
Farewell: 3.XI.1984	Funeral documentary
Bootlegs	
"Ojczyzno Ma:" Sermons	Documentary compilation
Film about Father Jerzy	Audio bootleg
Father J. Popiełuszko	Radio Solidarity bootleg
"Ojczyzna Ks. J Popiełuszko"	Documentary compilation
The Truth about Father Jerzy Popiełuszko's Murder Trial	Unknown author/source

They're ready to follow him." Popiełuszko's assassination was experienced by many Polish Catholics as a condemnation of spirituality, an attack on the opposition, and a reproof of free Poland's legitimacy.[12] His death shaped the opposition as a community of mourners, who passed around, transmitted, recounted, and reheard Popiełuszko's voice on cassette (see Table 4.1).[13] The cassette makers crafted a sounding portrait of the priest out of this technology, a scaffolding through which he could continue to speak to them.[14] They rerecorded his sermons, captured their own memories of him, dubbed bootleg recordings of his funeral, and laid song tracks in his honor ⓘ.

Popiełuszko's voice, with its emergence out of one quiet and ultimately strangled throat, was absorbed into the orality of his sermons. It resonated across the echo chamber of one church, was captured and copied through magnetic recording, was and is recalled and reimagined in oral history, and has been conjured and lost in musical rewriting. We hear it today performed still and anew. It is the locus of Popiełuszko's posthumous politicized and emotional labor. Commemorative works, traumatized recollections, and

---

12 Interview with Jan Kossakowski, February 20, 2009.

13 The Museum of Independence does not have provenance information for the 102 cassettes held in its People's Republic of Poland Collection. One of its archivists, Emil Noiński, suggested that most of the objects were donations from the greater Warsaw area by several individuals (conversation July 14, 2010).

14 On the "infrastructure" of cassette sermons and their publics, see Charles Hirschkind, *The Ethical Soundscape: Cassette Sermons and Islamic Counterpublics* (New York: Columbia University Press, 2006), especially 56–63.

revival projects, then and now, refract the large, Gdańsk-oriented visions of Wałęsa and Penderecki into the particular "everywhere" and all-consuming work of faith. Technologies in search of the simple and soothing resonance (as in bells) and the direct communication of the human voice (speaking) do crucial historical—even historiographical—work. In recent years, music studies has turned to the voice as a means to foreground bodies and their bounds. "Vocality . . . is a social practice that is everywhere locally understood as an implicit index of authority, evidence, and experiential truth," write Steven Feld, Aaron A. Fox, Thomas Porcello, and David Samuels.[15] The Popiełuszko example, too, falls into step.

Across my analysis, news media—the dissemination of information—and the sound media of commemorative practice pull at the tension inherent in the notion of voice "everywhere locally." Other media (loud and electronic) play a crucial role, too. For example, sensational Western coverage provided the British electronic musician Bryn Jones a path into making anti-Soviet music in which Poland and Popiełuszko had a special place. Jones, who made music under the moniker Muslimgauze, snapped into political action during the 1982 Lebanon War. Through his career, until his death in 1999, he allied himself with any pro-Palestinian movement or broadly Islamist rhetoric through album names and song titles. In interviews across popular music journals and pamphlets, he proclaimed an agenda that had teeth in Europe, too, with its agitation against both Soviet interventionism and Israel as nation and aggressor.

In response to a question about his future plans in an interview published in 1984 in the zine *Elephant Quarterly*, Jones blasted out bullet points:

Ideas for the future are political
- freedom to Afghanistan from Soviet oppression
- unity of the two German lands, the destruction of the Berlin Wall
- freedom to Poland and all occupied lands by Russia, a total return to democracy
- the Gulf War to end

Well that's just a few.[16]

Muslimgauze was a project that constructed scores of tapes from synthesized sounds and samples found. The pulsing beats, distorted street clips, and

---

15 Steven Feld, Aaron A. Fox, Thomas Porcello, and David Samuels, "Vocal Anthropology: From the Music of Language to the Language of Song," in *A Companion to Linguistic Anthropology*, edited by Alessandro Duranti (Oxford: Blackwell Publishing, 2004), 341.

16 "Interview," *Elephant Weekly* 4 (1984); anthologized at his official posthumous website, http://www.muslimgauze.org/articles/elephantArticle.html.

heavily reverberated racket evoked a notion of the Middle East—to which Jones had never traveled. These sonic bricolages asked listeners to imagine a spirituality rooted in Islamic thought for his audiences. Fleeting voices and recognizable syllables provide Muslimgauze's output with occasional moments of what Jace Clayton has aptly described as "vague geopolitical verisimilitude."[17] Jones boasted that he made music with little technical help in austere studios from minimal equipment, a deliberate preference for the clean interface of technology that Timothy Taylor has discussed at length.[18] This streamlining—of production, of collaboration—extended to the artist's disinterest in text or in making his specific and volatile political message merge with the noisy aesthetics of his experimental electronica, driven by metallic timbres and clunky off-kilter loops. As he put it, "Well, there is a fine line between preaching and information. As soon as you start writing songs and lyrics you are preaching to people."[19]

How peculiar, then, is Jones's zoom into Poland. With "Under the Hand of Jaruzelski" (1984) he gestures toward the need, as in the "Thirteenth of December" songs of Chapter 2, to clarify that the unilateral declaration was totalitarian in nature ⏵. The track repeats an extract from the British television coverage of the Polish events without looping it. Jones varies the sample's speed to manipulate the English newscaster's voice. Each new beginning keeps us listening. The track in sum is a loud, if unsubtle, critique of martial law that is discernible for Jones's audiences because it is in a language many know (English). When Jones, as Muslimgauze, turns his craft toward the lesser-known priest, he casts an ambient response built from two untexted musical samples in tonal spaces ⏵. Titled "Homily to Popiełuszko" (1984), the project offers an emotional response on specifically spoken—even preachy—terms. Jones touches on the importance of this Solidarity chaplain's sermons with a memorial track—but without a text, and the mixer is not in exegetic mode.

The track is ambient, dark, and—to my ear—unresolved, composed of just a pedantic eight-second loop of low, synthesized strings oscillating through a harmonic ground. Sporadically injected jabs of violins reverberate. So one must know who Popiełuszko was, or take Jones's cue as an impetus to find out. Jones never explained "Homily to Popiełuszko," and it was not a track or an album (*Flajelata*, limited edition LP 1986) that circulated in

---

17 Jace Clayton, "Muslin Gaze: The Enigmatic Afterlives of Bryn Jones," *Bidoun* 11, Special Issue: Failure (2007), http://bidoun.org/articles/muslin-gaze. I am grateful to Wayne Marshall for drawing this essay to my attention.

18 Timothy Taylor, *Strange Sounds: Music, Technology, and Culture* (New York: Routledge, 2001), 144–48.

19 Interview in *Eskhatos Magazine* (1995), http://www.muslimgauze.org/articles/eskhatosArticle.html.

Poland in the 1980s. Like Agnieszka Holland's *To Kill a Priest*, it is a Western production that drew attention to the priest's terrible fate. But what if we hear the naming here as a kind of programmatic invitation issued by Jones? A hermeneutic reading might position the rhythm as an echo of the violent pummeling that the priest experienced at the hands of the SB. Or, more spuriously, the hazy ambience of the track as a musical trail of the mystery surrounding the circumstances of his abduction until the trial against his murderers. Jones's technoscientific imaginary could even be a translation of the materials—stones, metal, ropes, water—that robbed Popiełuszko of his breath. These are the media of extermination. This is a life snuffed out in darkness, a voice muffled and drowned.

Resounding Burial

On October 19, 2009, I find myself among pilgrims on foot, walking to a mass on the twenty-fifth anniversary of Popiełuszko's death.[20] Wandering the streets of Warsaw's Old Town earlier that afternoon, I had seen and heard small groups of pedestrians in song, beginning their journey toward mass at St. Stanisław Kostka Church in the bourgeois northern district of Żoliborz (see Figure 4.1a/b).[21] Bearing a cross constructed from recently fallen branches and singing Marian pilgrimage melodies, the elderly worshipers carefully processed through the cobblestone alleyways of Warsaw's medieval quarter in the freezing rain. In the evening, I walk ten minutes from the subway stop to the church's courtyard, the location of Popiełuszko's grave and the open-air mass.

A kind of reenactment is underway: it is as if I am among the vast crowds that attended his funeral. Some around me, I am sure, were. In 1984 the SB estimated that 100,000 attended the rite laying Popiełuszko

---

20 I attended the "Main Celebrations of the Twenty-Fifth Anniversary of the Martyrous Death in God's Service of Father Jerzy Popiełuszko" (the online program, formerly at www.popieluszko.net.pl/msze/rocznica/htm, is no longer available). The mass was the culmination of a week of events that included a vigil under the theme "Freedom-Unity-Love," an open-air exhibit, a theological symposium on the topic of canonization, a concert performance of Wojciech Kilar's *Missa pro pace* (1999–2000), an evening of theatrical scenes from the martial law underground I discussed in Chapter 2, and a poetry reading with musical accompaniment.

21 Ethnomusicologist Jacek Jackowski positions the renewal of Marian pilgrimage songs through textual and musical modification as a political act in rural Catholic communities (see "Folk Religious Songs Sung during the Peregrination of Virgin Mary's Icon: An Example of Traditional Polish Peasant Piety in Communist Times," *Musicology Today* 7 (2010), 182–211.

FIGURE 4.1A. Pilgrims singing to mourn Jerzy Popiełuszko, October 19, 2009.
Photograph by the author.

FIGURE 4.1B. Solidarity members on the road to St. Stanisław Kostka.
Photograph by the author.

to rest, but historians since have suggested that the real number was somewhere between 400,000 and 600,000.[22] The 1984 attendance is captured on a video that loops, echoing through the church's basement museum, which I had visited three days earlier (▶). Divisions of the Solidarity Trade Union walk alongside me bearing union, religious, and regional flags and wearing uniforms to designate their occupations (see Figure 4.1). On the corner, a woman, one of many vendors, offers to sell me flowers to place on his grave. When I finally reach the northeastern end of the church, I find myself one of many diverse pilgrims—civilians, workers, politicians, and church officials. One peddler offers me a slip of paper with a contrafact of "The Oath" ("Rota"). The patriotic anthem, composed before the First World War while Poland was under partition, has a new text, a critique of the European Union as an enemy of the Polish nation.

To ring in the hour, a recording of Pope John Paul II's favorite hymn, "The Barge" ("Barka"), is played over speakers adorning the church. Before the MIDI-rendition of the hymn comes to an end, an amplified organ introduces the last measures of the service's first congregational hymn from the bowels of the sanctuary (Reginald Herber's "Holy, Holy, Holy!" to an 1861 melody by John Bacchus Dykes). As the audience sings four verses of memorized text (I sing along), a third sonic signal commands us: the largest bell in the courtyard tolls, drawing our attention to the place of Popiełuszko's grave. The sounds from the bell tower prescribed and protected this space and time as sacred, to hear this moment with Alain Corbin.[23] After a brief pause, the presiding priest intones the Kyrie in Polish, "Panie, zmiłuj się nad nami. . . ."

At this beginning, the convergent musical, spoken, and sounded material drew attention to that funeral ritual's liminality "in and out of time."[24] Catholic and Polish mythologies competed with and conflated one another. We might hear the barrage of signals as what Charles Hirschkind calls the "acoustic flow of community"—sonic patterns that produce and regulate religious life through repetition.[25] Or, we might experience the range of

---

22 Ewa Czaczkowska and Tomasz Wiścicki, *Ksiądz Jerzy Popiełuszko* (Warsaw: Świat Książki, 2004), 57.

23 Alain Corbin, *Village Bells: Sound and Meaning in the Nineteenth-Century French Countryside*, translated by Martin Thom (New York: Columbia University Press, 1998), 95.

24 Victor Turner, "The Center Out There: Pilgrim's Goal," *History of Religions* 12, no. 3 (1973), 214.

25 Charles Hirschkind, "Religion," in *Keywords in Sound*, edited by David Novak and Matt Sakakeeny (Durham, NC: Duke University Press), 170–71.

historical references across the sensorium as "temporal compression" that manifests the abstract idea of the nation, to follow Geneviève Zubrzycki's study of Polish material culture.[26]

The 2009 representation of the event can also be understood as an affect-driven, public history projection of the past, consonant with other Polish reenactments. For example, during 2009–10, municipal, federal, and private funds like those behind the funeral update also funded other events I witnessed: scavenger hunts that help scouts to reimagine fighting with the underground resistance during the Warsaw Uprising of 1944, or the horse-riding pageants that remind participants of the Polish and Lithuanian victory over the Teutonic Knights in 1410, to name just two. In addition to its affective power the reenactment offered two historiographic critiques, to follow the call to take reenactments seriously as projects that affect historical knowledge by Vanessa Agnew.[27] In sound I heard ambivalent politics, on the one hand: anyone present that could "select one's own past" from the menu of sonic signifiers, each with a different path toward a relationship with worship, resistance, and history.[28] I also heard the exertion of control in its simultaneity, its cacophony of signals. The precarious—political and personal—uncertainty behind the pleas for Popiełuszko to listen from the grave from the 1980s were drowned out. With a command of its symbols, the organizers reaching toward his beatification made loud and clear that his death effected Poland's survival and even salvation.

The ceremonies incorporated elements of the togetherness Popiełuszko inspired while presiding over congregations during his "Masses for the Fatherland" and through the collective mourning following his death.[29] With the mass liturgy as its backbone and a political commendation by then-President Lech Kaczyński in person as its crowning point, the 2009 event told the story of Popiełuszko's life, from rural childhood to army service to commitment to God to martyrdom. His grave in the church's courtyard completes the story. It is surrounded by a circle of boulders chained together. The stones that dragged him to the bottom of the Vistula River honor him in death, his crown of thorns pushed into the earth as landscaping. The grass around his grave has been a terrain on which to stage one's political allegiance without public address, as did Margaret Thatcher when she laid a wreath

---

26 Geneviève Zubrzycki, "History and the National Sensorium: Making Sense of Polish Mythology," *Qual Sociol* 34 (2011), 21–57.

27 Vanessa Agnew, "What Is Reenactment?," *Criticism* 46, no. 3 (2004), 327–39.

28 Agnew, "What Is Reenactment?," 328.

29 The Polish government, through the Institute for National Memory (IPN), and the Catholic Church, through the Archdiocese of Warsaw, collaborated to organize the climactic service.

upon his gravestone in 1988.[30] Upon the first visit by Pope John Paul II, a crowd of a couple hundred gathered and sang, first "God Save Poland" ("Boże, coś Polskę") and then "My Fatherland" ("Ojczyzno ma," about which more later). The Pope kneeled, prayed, and kissed the grave in silence.

The iconic atmospheres of Solidarity—the bustle, creativity, and symbolic saturation of August 1980 and the solemnity, collective mourning, and symbolic saturation at the Gdańsk memorial just four months later—converged at the 2009 commemoration. Trade unions marched in formation and the broadside I received rearticulated the "folk poetry" practice of the Lenin Shipyards experience. The main touchstone for the reenactment of Solidarity's public assembly was Popiełuszko's funeral. His mother assumed the same position next to his grave that she had on November 3, 1984—a staging that received consistent commentary from the dignitaries who addressed those gathered. Over the loudspeakers, the hometowns of the pilgrim groups were announced, just as they had been in 1984. We sang "God Save Poland" as the mass came to an end; twenty-five years earlier, this hymn's collective performance had accompanied the lowering of the casket into the earth.[31] We were called on not just to watch and remember history, but to embody it. Scores of such details indexed the previous memorial service, which itself was built out of the patriotic and political discourses that flowed through the Fatherland Masses. These symbols have been maintained through the public history that casts the priest as a martyr for the nation: in 2009 I encountered videos, photography, and oral histories at countless street exhibitions across Poland and was pummeled by these throughout a commercial bio-pic released that autumn.[32]

A Portrait of Popiełuszko

Popiełuszko was not the only priest to hold services in support of the opposition; it is through his martyrdom symbolic power accrued to him. Following Solidarity's legalization, chaplains continued the shipyard tradition they had established of holding mass for the union's members as they organized and demonstrated. Through the services, patriotism and faith in the Catholic

---

30 Norman Davies, *God's Playground: A History of Poland*, Volume 2 (New York: Columbia University Press, 2005), 412.

31 Czaczkowska and Wiścicki, *Ksiądz Jerzy Popiełuszko*, 59.

32 An exhibit on a central boulevard, Krakowskie Przedmieście, accompanied his beatification ceremony in central Warsaw; his home parish, with the Institute of National Memory, houses a museum devoted to his life; and the film *Popiełuszko: Wolność jest w nas* (*Freedom Is within Us*) was released in theaters nationwide in the fall of 2009.

Church were threaded together. The sermons functioned as political addresses, rallying the workers to fight for their freedom. The thirty-four-year-old Father Jerzy Popiełuszko became connected with the steel mill "Warszawa" when workers there striked in spring of 1981. When martial law was declared, the masses' subversive power was increasingly realized: victims were mourned and named. This activity was obviously portable—Popiełuszko was traveling home from work when he was kidnapped. But most of the masses were held at his home parish, where he had been an assistant priest to Father Teofil Bogucki since May 1980. After the declaration of martial law, masses' exceptional and subversive nature was flagged with their designation ("for the Fatherland").[33]

Popiełuszko's spoken text and personality were intertwined with Solidarity's organizational structure and media. Within the confines of any Catholic mass, the priest speaks and he sings: worshiping with his sermons' exegesis became a crucial practice of the opposition, made possible by the fact that the Fatherland masses were broadcast on Solidarity's underground radio.[34] The historical specificity of his homily takes on even more significance through his sermons' wide circulation in print and on cassette tapes. The cassette collection at the Museum of Independence in Warsaw, for example, contains three homemade tapes, five drugi obieg tapes, and an album of sung poetry dedicated to the priest (see Table 4.1). Hearing Popiełuszko's voice prompted action, called for action, and inspired action. He sang, invited song, and—in death—motivated musical reflection. The singing crowd who shrouded his burial in communal song, for example, carried forth that day, November 3, 1984. Tens of thousands processed from the church in northern Warsaw to the city center, flanked by military patrol. At the busy intersection of Marszałkowska Street and Jerozolimskie Avenue, they sang "God Save Poland" one more time before dispersing.[35] Over the years that followed, musical compositions further amplified and supported collective mourning. These kept the close relationship between his sermonizing and leadership, vocal intonation and humanity, and hearing and singing together intertwined as they portrayed and remembered the chaplain.

Popiełuszko had been surveilled since martial law's imposition and was interrogated by the SB on numerous occasions. On the basis of tape recordings of his voice and transcripts of his sermons ("available for free" at his parish), the government formally accused him of purposefully undermining

---

33 Andrzej Paczkowski, *Revolution and Counterrevolution in Poland, 1980–1989*, translated by Christine Manetti (Rochester, NY: University of Rochester Press, 2015), 182.

34 Padraic Kenney, *A Carnival of Revolution: Central Europe 1989* (Princeton, NJ: Princeton University Press, 2002), 25.

35 Czaczkowska and Wiścicki, *Ksiądz Jerzy Popiełuszko*, 60.

the constitution and state: "Expert opinions were obtained on magnetic tape recordings of Father J. Popiełuszko's speeches. They indicated that the recordings are authentic or copies of authentic magnetic tape recordings. The recorded voice is the voice of Father J. Popiełuszko."[36] The Catholic Church intervened to protect him, but the Primate, Józef Glemp, urged him to tone down his addresses.[37] (After his murder, Glemp censured priests who "wish[ed] to voice their own teaching in their own way."[38]) The priest carried on; renegade members of the SB schemed to take matters into their own hands when the government seemed resistant to intervene.

Captain Grzegorz Piotrowski, Leszek Pękala, and Waldemar Chmielewski drowned Solidarity's chaplain while he was doing pastoral work in the name of a free Poland. He was intercepted on the road to Włocławek after holding mass in Bydgoszcz, two industrial cities in the Kuyawian-Pomeranian Province. After the driver pulled the car to the side of the road, he was gagged and left alone. Popiełuszko was pummeled with stones, gagged, and thrown in the trunk of the car. The perpetrators drove the car away from the crime scene. These SB officials harnessed the murder weapons to the priest's body, and the weight dragged him to the bottom of the Vistula River.

First Jerzy Popiełuszko was missing, then, when the driver bore witness, the case became a kidnapping. Vigils were held across the country, and the police searched for the missing folk hero. They combed the river bed and dragged out his bruised corpse; his wounds were described in gory detail by the priests who identified him. The very public trials of his murderers following the discovery of his body (December 27, 1984–February 7, 1985) brought the months of uncertainty to a close. These are the historical details that undergirded—though mostly unspoken—the 2009 reenactment at which I was a member of the congregation.

After Popiełuszko's passing, his services streamed through the lives of the faithful. At the 1984 General Conference of Polish Musicologists at the Catholic University in Lublin, an anonymous correspondent for the drugi obieg, "ais," relayed the powerful resonance of Catholic symbols throughout the discussion.[39] In this conference report they took note of scholars'

---

36 The legal case against him was reprinted in the drugi obieg. Quoted in "Akt oskarżenia przeciwko Jerzemu Aleksandrowi Popiełuszce," *Zeszyty Historyczne* 71 (1984), 64–78, here at 67.

37 Brian Porter-Szűcs, *Faith and Fatherland: Catholicism, Modernity, and Poland* (Oxford and New York: Oxford University Press, 2011), 260–61.

38 Bradley Graham, "Glemp Curbs Radical Priest: Polish Primate Targets Political Activism," *Washington Post*, December 2, 1984, A1.

39 "ais," "Obrady polskich muzykologów," *Kultura Niezależna* 5 (1985), 61. See Chapter 1 for an extended discussion of this journal.

"spiritual transformation and evolution," suggesting that it was a political phenomenon. The university transmitted recordings of Popiełuszko's voice through its classrooms through every day; "ais" observed, "History inscribed itself into our reflections. It did so in a very meaningful way, since the voice of [the priest], recorded on magnetic tape, sounded in our conference room while the discussion focused on the question of music, courage, and the interplay of these two aspects of our spirituality."[40] For the musicologists, the priest's voice functioned as an instrument of moral awakening and direction facilitated by coincidence (or consistency) and looping recording technology.

Hearing Popiełuszko, we learn about the relationship between the Catholic Church and the opposition, about cultural activity and political action in 1980s Poland. Through the forty-five years of the socialist state, the proportion of those living within Polish borders who identified as Catholic hovered around 90 percent.[41] Historian Brian Porter-Szűcs has convincingly argued that from the late 1940s onward, the normative Catholic-Polish identity nurtured connections with Western Europe and obscured the population losses and migrations that had precipitated the postwar Catholic majority. In the public mindset, Polish Catholicism functioned as an ideological counterpoint to the secular communist government, which was antagonistic toward Polish nationalism. When in the early 1950s anti-communist clergy were imprisoned for speaking out, the alignment between the opposition and the Church became explicit.

The Thaw in 1956 also allowed the Church to take on the role of a mediator in the public sphere. After the celebration of the Millennium of Polish Christianity in 1966, the election of Pope John Paul II in 1978, and the instrumental role the Church played in the organization of Solidarity in 1980, religious symbols, such as the image of the Black Madonna of Częstochowa, gained increased visibility.[42] The tenor of public political discourse shifted when the economy collapsed under Polish Premier Edward Gierek in the late 1970s, following the papal election and vital public strikes against price hikes. By 1980 religious symbols had been established as those of the Polish opposition—at the monument discussed in Chapter 5 crosses and anchors interface. When martial law was declared, the Church was given relative leeway compared to the banned Solidarity Trade Union.[43] In the power of Popiełuszko to cohere a public, we observe what might even be understood

---

40 "ais," "Obrady polskich muzykologów," 63.

41 Porter-Szűcs, *Faith and Fatherland*, 4.

42 Jan Kubik, *The Power of Symbols against the Symbols of Power: The Rise and the Fall of State Socialism in Poland* (University Park: Pennsylvania State University Press, 1994), 112. See also Jackowski, "Folk Religious Songs."

43 Paczkowski, *Revolution and Counterrevolution in Poland*, 225.

as an increased power for the Church to house oppositional activity and to support humanitarian work after the declaration of martial law—as in the case of Tadeusz Kaczyński's volunteer work for the Primate's Aid Committee.

Musical Politics in the Polish Catholic Church

The historian Adam Michnik, an activist whose parents were Jewish, framed the collaboration, confrontation, and conversation between members the clergy and the secular intelligentsia in his influential 1979 essay collection, *The Church and the Left*.[44] He reads pastoral letters and papal encyclicals carefully for signs of resistance and affinity. He analyzes how the Church protects itself, highlighting passages that coordinate political action against the secular state. For example, Michnik quotes from a letter circulated among the Polish bishops in the 1960s: "Do not sing their blasphemous and hate-filled songs and hymns, alien to the Christian spirit."[45] Michnik also critiques the allure of the Church by plucking questioning passages from the diaries of the modernist writer Witold Gombrowicz (1904–69), which were serialized in the toweringly influential émigré journal, *Kultura*, through the 1960s: "That is why we have we admire Christianity, which is a wisdom tailored to all minds, a song for all voices from the highest to the lowest, a wisdom that does not have to change itself into stupidity at any level of awareness."[46] Though laced with suspicion, this description puts the symbolic agency of voice into theological terms, as a site that might translate the egalitarianism of sacred song into a political reality.[47]

In the 1980s the Catholic Church was still wrestling with the expanded definition of religious music by the Second Vatican Council, which had, for example, expressly welcomed masses in the vernacular.[48] The 1962–65 Council redefined "sacred music" inclusively, directing awareness toward its

---

44 Adam Michnik, *The Church and the Left*, translated by David Ost (Chicago: University of Chicago Press, 1993).

45 *Konferencja Episkopatu Polski: Listy pasterskie Episkopatu Polski, 1945–1974* (Paris: Éditions du Dialogue, 1975), 75. Quoted in Michnik, *The Church and the Left*, 59. It was published in Polish as *Church—Left—Dialogue (Kościół, lewica, dialog)*.

46 Quoted in Michnik, *The Church and the Left*, 262.

47 Philip V. Bohlman and Jeffers Engelhardt, "Resounding Transcendence: An Introduction," in *Resounding Transcendence: Transitions in Music, Religion, and Ritual*, ed. Jeffers Engelhardt and Philip V. Bohlman (New York: Oxford University Press, 2016), 1–25.

48 Maria Bogusławska, ed., *Aktualna sytuacja muzyki religijnej i liturgicznej w Polsce* (Warsaw: Akademia Teologii Katolickiej, 1988).

popular significance: "The following come under the title of sacred music here: Gregorian chant, sacred polyphony in its various forms, both ancient and modern, sacred music for the organ and other approved instruments, and sacred popular music, be it liturgical or simply religious."[49] The provision made space for regionally specific musics and—as was the tendency in Poland—popular song to target youth.[50] In the late 1960s Katarzyna Gaertner composed a plugged-in "beat mass" (*msza beatowa*) for a leading rock band, the Czerwono-Czarni, and the jazz trumpeter Tomasz Stańko composed a "jazz mass" (*msza jazzowa*) ▶.[51] Both flanked traditional chant with musical jam sessions.[52] At Sacrosong, a festival of religious song in Cracow that had Karol Wojtyła (later Pope John Paul II) as its patron, youth groups sang Marian tunes while they strummed acoustic guitars, and rock bands' devotional ballads were judged by a jury.[53]

Theologians and scholars of religious music resisted the genre-inclusive spirit characteristic of global Catholicism. At academic conferences they discussed the musical and liturgical foundation of the mass as ritual: chant. The faith's constraint by and respect for structures and musical canons anchored the reevaluation of music, spirituality, and Christianity. Musicologist Bohdan Pociej argued, "The Bible is most important here. . . . The source of all poetry in Western culture is [the Book of Psalms]. They contain the primary motor of music, they hold enormous powers to generate melodies."[54] Indeed, according to Tadeusz Kaczyński, the Independent Experimental Studio's most popular work during martial law was an improvisation on Czesław Miłosz's translation of Psalm 23, which they angled to "current Polish

---

49 From the "Musicam Sacram," originally given March 5, 1967; http://www.vatican.va/archive/hist_councils/ii_vatican_council/documents/vat-ii_instr_19670305_musicam-sacram_en.html.

50 T. M. Scruggs, "(Re)Indigenization?: Post-Vatican II Catholic Ritual and 'Folk Masses' in Nicaragua," *The World of Music* 47, no. 1 (2005), 91–123.

51 These had none of the countercultural or politically critical resonance of the blues masses of the GDR discussed in Alison Furlong, "Politics, Faith, and the East German Blues," *Colloquia Germanica* 46, no. 4 (2013, available November 2016): 435–62.

52 Grażyna Wojczuk, "Sacrosong jako nowe zjawisko w polskiej kulturze religijnej ostatnich dziesięcioleci," in *Dramat i teatr sakralny*, edited by Irena Sławińska (Lublin: Redakcja Wydawnictw Katolickiego Uniwersytetu Lubelskiego, 1988), 209–16.

53 "Sacrosong '84," *Kultura Niezależna* 4 (1984), 83–84. This also occurred at Popiełuszko's services for youth. See Gabriel Bartoszewski, ed., *Bogosławiony Jerzy Popiełuszko: Zapiski, listy i wywiady ks. Jerzego Popiełuszki 1967–1984* (Warsaw: Oficyna Wydawniczo-Poligraficzna "adam," 2010), 101.

54 Bohdan Pociej, "Inspiracje biblijna w muzyce" in *Dialog Kościoła i Kultura: Materiały z IV i V Tygonii Kultury Chrześcijańskiej w Krakowie 1983, 1984*, Volume 1, edited by Stefan Misniec (Cracow: Kuria Metropolitalna, 1986), 209.

reality" (*dzisiejsze polskie rzeczywistości*).⁵⁵ Father Tadeusz Miazga argued that Polish churches should keep the aesthetics of Gregorian chant as the basis for new sacred music and turned to Pope Pius X's 1903 Motu Proprio, which claimed that chant's form and sound are fundamental to devotional power.⁵⁶ The priest prescribed effective chant intonation and scansion so that the sound would be good, holy, and balanced. He heard the liturgical music he approved as "breathing with the spirit of the church."⁵⁷ The challenges posed by the translation of chant into Polish after the Second Vatican Council were widely discussed among the clergy in the early 1970s. Popiełuszko's timid enunciation, which I discuss below, illustrates some of their fixations. The "difficult" sound of the language's soft consonants is hard to project: many suggested they should be avoided.⁵⁸ The close analog drawn between vocal inflection, on the one hand, and rising and falling pitches, on the other, in the Gregorian tradition nurtured at Solesmes was difficult to adapt to the customary emphasis on the penultimate syllable in Polish.⁵⁹

The interest in Popiełuszko's voice resonates with what the Jesuit theologian and media theorist Walter J. Ong prescribed as a "secondary orality," though Polish theologians made no reference to debates about religion and the sensorium on the other side of the Atlantic. Ong, convinced that listening and "the mystery of sound" are "closest to the divine," pushed for a reconsideration of the senses through the 1960s and 1970s.⁶⁰ He wrote against occularcentrism but not logocentrism: the Word of God was less present to believers when read. Heard, Ong suggested, begat "word-as-event," a potentially consciousness-altering mode of being. Read, Ong lamented, reduced the scripture's power, by bounding "word-as-thing."⁶¹

---

55 "Studio Independent de Varsovie," unpublished draft from the Tadeusz Kaczyński Papers, Archive of Musical Sources, Special Collections, University of Warsaw Library.

56 Tadeusz Miazga, *Z problematyki muzyki sakralnej w Polsce* (Graz: Akademische Druck- und Verlagsanstalt, 1986), 19.

57 Miazga, *Z problematyki muzyki sakralnej w Polsce*, 81.

58 Stanisław Ziemiański, "Ks. Józef Łaś SJ (1907–1990)—pizarz i kompozytor," in *Muzyka religijna między epokami i kulturami*, Volume 1, edited by Krystyna Turek i Bogumiła Mika (Katowice: Wydawnictwo Uniwersytetu Śląskiego, 2008), 120.

59 Katherine Bergeron contextualizes this characteristic "accentus" as a nineteenth-century historiography of neumes in Katherine Bergeron, *Decadent Enchantments: The Revival of Gregorian Chant at Solesmes* (Berkeley: University of California Press, 1998), 104–9. For engagement with the Solesmes notation and practice in the context of Polish accentuation, see Józef Łaś, "Rytmika polskich śpiewów liturgicznych," *Ruch Biblijny i Liturgiczny* 21(1968), 266–83.

60 Walter J. Ong, *The Presence of the Word: Some Prolegomena for Cultural and Religious History* (New Haven, CT: Yale University Press, 1967), 324.

61 Jonathan Sterne, "The Theology of Sound: A Critique of Orality," *Canadian Journal of Communication* 36 (2011), 215.

Solidarity's communities created a sound mysterium out of Popiełuszko through (1) broadcasts of his sermons on the radio, (2) the hymns that flanked his Masses, and (3) the overflow crowds at St. Stanisław Kostka. One of his fiercest advocates after his death—the author of a commentary that is still distributed to pilgrims who journey to his gravesite—wrote in line with Ong in his 1984 treatise on sermonizing after the Second Vatican Council: Father Antoni Lewek turned to St. Paul, whose claim that "faith cometh by hearing, and hearing by the word of God" (Romans 10:17) shaped his own assertion that the Word of God inspired faith best and most when heard.[62] Lewek insisted that sermons must be heard and that people must listen to them together. In his two-volume, 462-page treatise on Polish Catholicism after the Second Vatican Council, he devotes fifteen pages to hearing, which he understands as the crux of community and faith. He cites every instance of the call to *hear* the Word of God in the Old Testament.[63] He glosses Joseph Ratzinger's 1968 *Introduction to Christianity*, highlighting the auditory as a mode that facilitates unity. "It is the result of a dialogue," in Ratzinger's words, "the expression of a hearing, receiving, and answering that guides man through the exchanges of 'I' and 'You' to the 'We' of those who all believe in the same way."[64] Drawing on this influential text, Lewek urges that faith is collective and relational, not individual.

Because of Popiełuszko's death, the media problem of his voice is not only the technologizing of the word, but the need for a different voice object altogether. When activists listened to recordings of sermons, heard Popiełuszko's voice in their minds, and reconstituted his voice in compositions or performances, they practiced his work in the service of God and the nation. They focused not on his intercession, but puzzled and mourned over his fleshiness. It was not the voice of God that they strained for after his death, but the presence, the calm, and the address of their priest. Hanna Skarżanka's reverent memory—here the final sentences—conjures him as *Jerzy* and suggests he is in her mind's ear at all times: "I hear his voice very often; he speaks to me; I hear him all the time, whenever it is quiet. I hear him at home, in the street, at church, in the museum. I constantly hear him near me. That voice full of warmth, contentment, a little hoarse, cordial, intimate. I hear Jurek's voice without interruption" ▶.[65]

---

62 Antoni Lewek, *Funkcja kerygmatyczna Kościoła w świetle Vaticanum II: Istota i zadania*, Volume 1 (Warsaw: Akademia Teologii Katolickiej, 1984), 185.

63 Lewek, *Funkcja kerygmatyczna Kościoła w świetle Vaticanum II*, 189.

64 Joseph Ratzinger, *Introduction to Christianity*, translated by J. R. Foster (San Francisco: Ignatius Press, 2004), 90.

65 Szczepkowska, *Ks. Jerzy Popiełuszko*, 149.

Listening to Solidarity's Chaplain

The Masses for the Fatherland marked time. They measured distance from December 13, 1981: some were held purposefully on the thirteenth of every month, while Popiełuszko's were on the last Sunday of every month.[66] The clockwork regularity of the monthly services intervened in the drudgery of public life on standstill. Popiełuszko's homilies broke into the material concerns of the everyday and offered those in attendance messages of love and dignity. As Cardinal Józef Glemp remembered in the mass held on the fifth anniversary of his death, Popiełuszko "spoke peacefully and prudently about the ethical fundamental norms in social and civic life."[67] In this way, he built on the personalism associated with Pope John Paul II's papacy and a broader shift toward freedom and joy—away from the fear of damnation—across the Polish Episcopate after the Second Vatican Council.[68]

The masses reflected on history. The sermon on January 21, 1984, for example, used the story of the January 1863 Uprising against the Russian Empire as a story of sacrifice through which to illustrate the importance of "serv[ing] God, family, and Fatherland with all [one's] heart."[69] Popiełuszko tells of the faith and sacrifice of Romuald Traugutt, the commander of the uprising, who was executed by the Tsar's forces upon his arrest. In the sermon, Popiełuszko focuses on a moment of communal song: the public outcry following Traugutt's assassination. He describes how his countrymen reflect the transference of Traugutt's greater-than-life love for country: "His sacrifice was recognized by the people of Warsaw. Thousands thronged the place of his martyrdom, praying and singing, 'Święty Boże, Święty Mocny . . .' ('Holy God, Holy and Almighty')."[70]

Though historical, this could have been a scene right out of the early 1980s—or even a sonic premonition of Popiełuszko's own funeral just ten months later. Those hearing this text could not have helped but imagine these revolutionary Poles of the past as still alive in 1984: the sermon describes a practice of spontaneous performance of paraliturgical hymns that abutted every one of the Fatherland Masses (as they later would the memorial event in 2009). These pieces of homophonic counterpoint in staid common time were composed for performance with organ. Unlike in the more widely adapted

---

66 Paczkowski, *Revolution and Counterrevolution in Poland*, 182.

67 Quoted in Antoni Lewek, *Priester Jerzy Popiełuszko: Ein Symbol der Opfer des Kommunismus*, translator uncredited (Warsaw: Wydawnictwo Archidiecezji Warszawskiej, 1994), 22.

68 Porter-Szűcs, *Faith and Fatherland*, 71–73.

69 *The Price of Love: The Sermons of Fr. Jerzy Popiełuszko*, translated by Zygmunt Lawrynowicz (London: "Veritas," 1985), 20.

70 *The Price of Love*, 21.

tradition of four-part hymnody in the Protestant church, the congregation sings a single melody.⁷¹ They are thus not just tremendously accessible: they were portable as chants and morphable into unisonal anthems, as I discuss in Chapter 5. It was this identificatory power of music that Popiełuszko was playing on in his sermon on Traugutt.

In his homilies, Popiełuszko spoke often of cultural expediency. The poetry of the nineteenth-century Polish bards—in particular, Adam Mickiewicz—supplied him with messages of hope in their messianism and solace for pain in their treatments of martyrdom (see Chapter 3). He devoted one sermon, "Loyalty to Our National Culture," to the purpose of art in the world—a foundational ecology that he understood as a broad, constantly flowing "river" of a topic ⏵.⁷² Artists could catalyze change, he urged, while painting a sweeping picture of the moment in which poet-patriots had emerged under partition:

> Suddenly actors, journalists, writers, poets and painters understood. Their conscience woke up; the national conscience had, all along, been kept in suspended animation by the authorities. . . . The social, professional, economic, cultural and political conscience came to life again. As did the conscience of our creative community. From now on they spoke with their own voice. They decided to serve the truth with all their talent and ability. To serve the truth in the country of our grandfathers.⁷³

For Popiełuszko, cultural figures had a particular role to play in the present, reflected in the importance of the arts in the crucible of the Catholic opposition, the nineteenth century. Within the sermons, historical examples served to portray role models and to stage political engagement as moral and ethical imperative. Artists are intertwined across the domains that, for him, make up society and work toward the national consciousness that can lead to a fight for independence. The concision of these sermons—the recorded sermons last between ten and fifteen minutes—lends the catalog of heroic attributes and call to action heightened punctuation.

Popiełuszko envisioned song, poetry, and literature as a network that could unite the faithful, both among themselves and directly to God, through transcendental values, notably truth. He wove narratives in homiletic missives

---

71 Bolesław Bartkowski, "Polnische Kirchenlieder in der katholischen Liturgie," in *Kirchenmusikalisches Erbe und Liturgie*, edited by Karlheinz Schlager and Hubert Unverricht (Tutzing: Hans Schneider, 1995), 171–82.

72 Rereleased as track 12 on *Ksiądz Jerzy Popiełuszko: Zło dobrem zwyciężaj; Modlitwy, kazania, rozważania; Nagrania archiwalne z lat 1982–84*. CD 1 (Warsaw: 4BNB, 2010).

73 *The Price of Love*, 12.

and called upon members of the theater community—who were boycotting official stages—in the actual liturgy of the masses. He consulted with these groups of actors in meetings at the Żoliborz parish. The film and stage actress Hanna Skarżanka remembers the discussions as sites in which the very nature of culture's religious value and offering was formulated. She reflects on Popiełuszko's own understanding of liturgical dramaturgy:

> In our meetings, when we discussed our participation in the Masses for the Fatherland, we tried to learn the most important thing that he wanted to pass on, namely his understanding of what it means for an actor to participate in worship. We had to understand that we were rendering a rite—not showing off; this was prayer—not a performance; thanksgiving—not asking for applause. Whenever I'd come to church with a recitation I knew this, I recognized these ideas as obvious, and yet the many years as a stage performer often blurred the image, preventing me from fully understanding him.[74]

In this wistful recollection Skarżanka tells of what she has learned from reorienting her craft to a sacred setting. She speaks in deep appreciation of the call to participate, but with a clear awareness that speech (recitation, *recytacja*) from the nave has a different function than from the stage in a theater. Her observations suggest that Popiełuszko was both aware of the sound and affective power of the rite and emphasized its functional and modest nature.

Skarżanka's account, which she recorded for an audio-commemoration released on cassette, is an intensely personal one that provides particular insight into Popiełuszko's ideas about the arts and about the role of the voice.[75] It is also its own artful rendition of a portrait—not so different from the musical ones that conclude this chapter. Trained on the stages of Vilnius in the interwar period and made famous through the booming Polish film industry of the immediate postwar period, Skarżanka also enjoyed success as a chanteuse. These three registers ground not only how I read her comments on the priest's presence, but also how she reads this prepared text. The recording is edited; I can hear the splices, which correspond with shifts in declamatory and prose style. Through various takes, her energy shifts. Some of the discussions she recalls with Popiełuszko, in the middle of the text, she rattles off in almost systematic barrage. She smirks as she remembers meetings with students and disagreements—such as the Chopin performance I recount below.

The memorial commentary opens with a distinguished performance in which her cultivated Vilnius accent is prominent. By the 1980s (and certainly in the twenty-first century), her noble accent was an almost nostalgic

---

74 Sczczepkowska, *Ks. Jerzy Popiełuszko*, 142.
75 *Słowo o ks. Jerzym*, Arka, Cassette 023 (1985)

marker of a Polish cosmopolitain center of the distant past. In addition to its more tuneful contour and slower declamation, it is best captured by the mode of producing and displaying the letter ł—pronounced as a dark l (represented as [ł] by the International Phoenetic Alphabet, and most often shaped as a dental-alveolar consonant—one that requires the blade and tip of the tongue depressed across the front of the mouth). The speech pattern marks her age, geographical origin, and theatrical experience at once—it is a "melodiousness" that Longina Jakubowska has described as enchanting and seductive in her interviews of Polish nobility of the same generation.[76] She dwells on the soft plosives, too, in her portrait of Popiełuszko ▶. "It is hard for me to write about Jerzy," she begins. She starts by describing how these memories come to her: "I often hear his voice; I hear it very clearly. I listen deeply into this exceptional voice—hushed, delicate, somewhat flat, a little bit hoarse, saturated with warmth, with a smile. When he speaks to us, when he is attentive, even in a sermon, it has a warm, intimate timbre [*ton*]." She is not quite mimicking his voice. Even though at 67 her voice is no longer the steely alto it was in the 1950s, it still has a fortitude easily distinguishable from Popiełuszko's hoarse and gravelly baritone. Instead, she is sharing how she hears him—and that she hears his voice with intensity.

There was an everyman element of Popiełuszko's oratory that matched the folksiness in Wałęsa speech that Timothy Garton Ash described (see Chapter 2). Born in rural Poland, the priest did not enjoy the elite status of the Warsaw intelligentsia. His mother said of his school years, "He was always drawn to people; he wanted to speak with everyone."[77] He had a humble presence and familiar difference that was audible in his modesty. The parishioner "J. K." imaginatively and tenderly described his presence: "He wore the heavy cloak of human love, adorned with expressions made from words that are uttered rarely and very softly, just as lightly and smilingly as he wore his jeans and sheepwool sweater."[78] The parish pastor at St. Kostka remembered that when Popiełuszko was first called to service, his shy, even closed-off, personality meant that he "did not extend himself to preach, he avoided singing."[79] As he began to serve in explicitly political capacity in the summer of 1981, Popiełuszko encouraged and communicated with students and artists. When he offered a mass to open the 1981–82 academic year to

---

76 Longina Jakubowska, *Patrons of History: Nobility, Capital and Political Transitions in Poland* (New York and London: Routledge, 2012), 16–17.

77 Quoted in Lewek, *Priester Jerzy Popiełuszko*, 7.

78 Szczepkowska, *Ks. Jerzy Popiełuszko*, 105.

79 Quoted in Jakub Gołębiewski, Jolanta Mysiakowska, and Anna K. Piekarska, eds., *Aparat represji wobec księdza Jerzego Popiełuszki 1982–1984*, Volume I (Warsaw: Instytut Pamięci Narodu, 2009), 45.

medical students, they sang his favorite Marian song, along with a patriotic song calling for independence. "As the day ends," the first verse concludes, "I want to be singing."[80]

Despite the reserve attributed to him in early accounts, Popiełuszko sermonized slowly but with fortitude (and often into a microphone, a custom that continues today in large congregations). As he recited the responsory prayers in Polish-language chant, his voice wavered slightly. The importance of being present at his masses—hearing him live—crafts his voice as a site of vulnerability. Many informants to the SB prided themselves on the fact that they could not see Popiełuszko as he stood on the periphery of the congregation, but they could hear (and identify) his voice.[81] These records of surveillance have haunting echoes in the accounts of his murder as confessed by the SB agents whose hands extinguished his breath and as witnessed by fellow passenger Waldemar Chrostowski. As I have already suggested, the courtroom testimonies dwell in the muffled cries and attempts at reason through calm inquisition. Chrostowski conjured up the soundworld with precision, ears attuned to Popiełuszko: "I only heard the priest's voice: 'Gentlemen, what are you doing?' A thump—loud banging—as a heavy object was thrown into the car boot, and a bang as the lid was slammed shut. Two other men climbed into the back seat, one of them grabbed me by the neck and gagged me, 'So you don't yell on your last journey,' he told me."[82] Hearing—not seeing—he can verify that Popuełuszko was intentionally killed.

In a 1988 sermon held at St. Stanisław Kostka, one of Popiełuszko's colleagues told the story of his murder to teach lessons about attention and bearing aural witness, weaving the circumstances of his death together with the representative loss of his death:

> Those who kill a Prophet always make the same mistake. They want the pungent voice to be silent forever. But a murdered Prophet's voice can be heard much farther than that of a living prophet. The murdered prophet speaks much louder. And when that happens, it is undoubtedly a sign that the murdered person was indeed a Prophet of God.[83]

The notion of a universal voice (the voice of God) and the powerful metaphor of vocal agency shapes not only the activity inspired by hearing Popiełuszko. It was also the defining plot element in the final act of his chaplaincy for Solidarity.

---

80 Czaczkowska and Wiścicki, *Ksiądz Jerzy Popiełuszko*, 153.
81 Gołębiewski, Mysiakowska, and Piekarska, eds., *Aparat represji*, 175, 179.
82 Szczepkowska, *Ks. Jerzy Popiełuszko*, 54.
83 Homily delivered at St. Stanisław Kostka Church, October 19, 1988, by Father Kalinowski, quoted in Czaczkowska and Wiścicki, *Ksiądz Jerzy Popiełuszko*, 351.

The priest concluded what would be his final sermon, "Defeating Evil through Good," with a reflection on forced silence. Its specific resonance with his own death disturbed his audiences and would fix his own sacrifice as fate. "Everyone," he asserted as he wound up his commentary, "has the obligation to demand justice and to do justice. Because, as an ancient sage said, 'Times are bad when Justice has its mouth full of water and must remain silent.'"[84] These final words on the imperative to speak are amplified by the premonition of his aqueous suffocation, of the elemental danger of this natural medium. Popiełuszko's death is a real vocal silence, enacted by murder. His neck and mouth were the first targets of the attack. This physical violence is at the center of the traumatized journey of his voice; it is the focus of any historical treatment of the priest, whether in music, sound, and written text. It is the locus and the "force of vocal action," to follow Michelle Rosaldo.[85]

Popiełuszko's Music

At the Fatherland Masses in Żoliborz, the voices of Popiełuszko's congregations spilled out of the sanctuary and courtyard onto the streets. Other churches "remain[ed] silent and fail[ed] to fulfill their Christian duty," driving flocks of believers and secular activists to these services.[86] Sound effected community, as did banners and small, symbolic items. As the service ended, those gathered raised these crosses and rosaries or touched their radio resistors—small devices worn on lapels to identify Solidarity supporters. They would also raise their fingers in a "V," as has become customary since August 1980. As a matter of course, they broke out in song, cycling through a roster of at least three additional hymns semi-spontaneously after the final responsory prayer, most often "God Save Poland," "The Oath," and "My Fatherland." These three tunes have already moved in and out of the scenes and histories across this book. Popiełuszko is one impulse for this dynamic flow.

Though cast and heard as a leader, Popiełuszko also directed musical participation (see Figure 4.2). He encouraged the hymn-addendum routine by

---

84 Quoted—along with the entire sermon—in Lewek, *Priester Jerzy Popiełuszko*, 16. Thanks to the library staff of the Wissenschaftskolleg zu Berlin, Barbara Kowalzig, and Karen Rivers for plentiful brainstorming as to the source of this (still undocumented) aphorism.

85 Michelle Z. Rosaldo, "The Things We Do with Words: Ilongot Speech Acts and Speech Act Theory in Philosophy," *Language in Society* 11, no. 2 (1982), 213.

86 Letter from Krystyna J. to Popiełuszko, July 20, 1984. Reprinted in Szczepkowska, *Ks. Jerzy Popiełuszko*, 24.

FIGURE 4.2. "Popiełuszko sings a church song."
Author unknown, Ośrodek Karta.

calling out to those assembled to raise their crosses, not just their fingers in a "V," as they sang. Informants to the SB drew attention to this participation outside the bounds of the service, even describing the hymn as exit music (*pieśni 'na wyjście'*).[87] One observer, a professional church chorister who was asked to describe Popiełuszko's services as they diverged from those he had participated in over the course of his career "in every church in Warsaw," signed a testimony for the SB that described the performance of "The Oath" at this critical juncture.[88] He located the performance's transgression in the crowds' embrace of the priest's own transgressive politics: openly praising Solidarity and actively criticizing the government. Another informant, who had stayed in the parish's guesthouse, watched the Fatherland Masses "from outside." The agent also linked defiance with the congregation's musical performances—emphasizing their volume and vigor. "I observed, over the course of the mass, specifically when 'God Save Poland' was being sung, that those assembled held their hands high with crosses or fingers shaped in the letter 'V'. In the first verse of the hymn 'God Save Poland' the assembled

---

87 Gołębiewski, Mysiakowska, and Piekarska, eds., *Aparat represji*, 223.
88 Gołębiewski, Mysiakowska, and Piekarska, eds., *Aparat represji*, 108–9. The interrogation is listed as RSD S-51/83, carried out in Warsaw on October 15, 1983.

sang 'Return our free homeland to us, Oh Lord.'"[89] (The political significance of these lyrics is the focus of Chapter 6). The importance of such embodied responses in accusatory reports articulates a clear function for Popiełuszko as both voice for the people and provocateur of the people.

The priest stood among his congregation, too. One officer for the SB noted when he was in the audience for his colleagues' sermons: "At the end of the mass, while 'Oh, [Mary], Queen of Poland' was being sung, Father J[erzy] Popiełuszko joined the congregation in civilian dress. . . . Father Popiełuszko thanked those gathered making clear that he would not address them, since he did so only once a month."[90] This brief comment, made clear in the report, was also recorded and deposited along with the stenogram of the event. To the extent that such onlooker accounts are patently biased, they are crafted with attention to treacherous activity. They frequently triangulate Popiełuszko's presence as a leader, his congregation's singing, and his own sermons. The accounts carve out a resonant space for the sermons and also position the hymns as an extension—certainly a result—of the homily. The example of the priest *among* his flock of believers also reminds us that he sang with them in ways that were both heard (by his neighbors) and imagined (by those who could see, but not hear, him).

The privileged liminal space of music (as opposed to the prized ordinariness of chant) was by design. Hanna Skarżanka's memories of Popiełuszko shed light on the mission Popiełuszko had for music:

> When it came to music, especially, he had not the slightest clue. I remember how I was beside myself when, at the end of a particularly festive mass, the organist decided to butcher a piece of the Funeral March from Chopin's Piano Sonata in B-flat minor. Jurek [Popiełuszko] was enchanted, but I was furious. This was one of our earliest quarrels. He also hated the idea of voice soloists performing in the church—top-notch singers. He called it howling and wouldn't be persuaded otherwise. Too bad, we never managed to overcome that. . . . He had his own favorite works, favorite poets, and favorite songs—and for us, those works, poets and songs have since become the most precious testament that he bequeathed to us.[91]

Repertory mattered; performance style was of utmost importance. Both laid the groundwork for his legacy in music.

Of these hymns that flanked the services, the most recently composed, "My Fatherland," took on direct association with the Fatherland masses (see Figure 4.3). Popiełuszko asked for its performance by lining out the first

---

89 Quoted in Gołębiewski, Mysiakowska, and Piekarska, eds., *Aparat represji*, 166. See also the testimony reprinted on page 240 of the same volume.

90 Quoted in Gołębiewski, Mysiakowska, and Piekarska, eds., *Aparat represji*, Volume 1, 196.

91 Quoted in Szczepkowska, *Ks. Jerzy Popiełuszko*, 143.

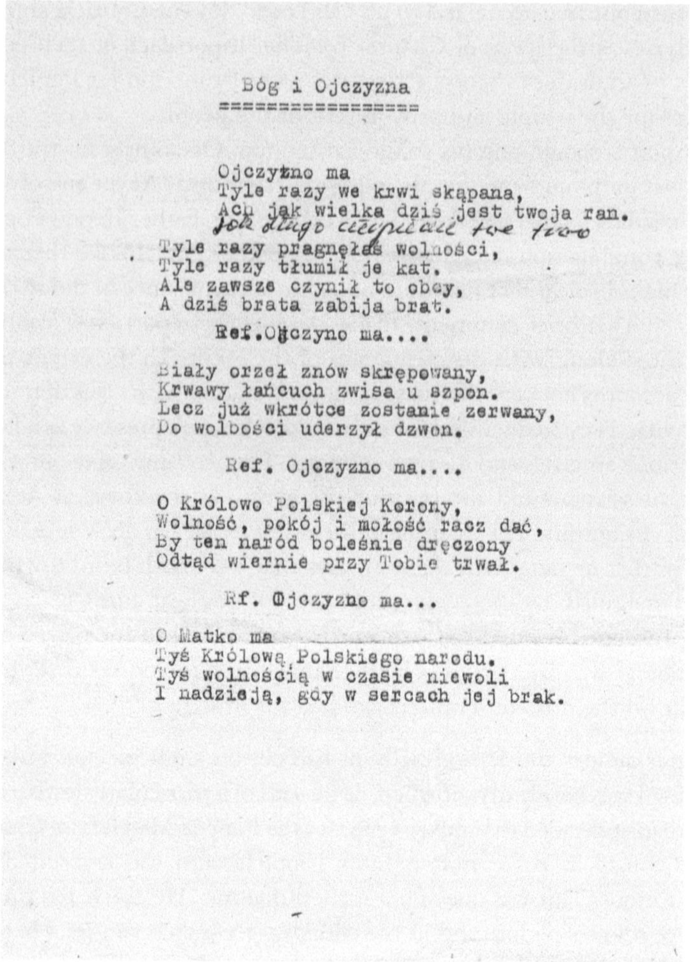

```
        Bóg i Ojczyzna
        ==================

        Ojczyzno ma
        Tyle razy we krwi skąpana,
        Ach jak wielka dziś jest twoja ran.
        Jak długo cierpiał będzie twe rany
        Tyle razy pragnęłaś wolności,
        Tyle razy tłumił je kat.
        Ale zawsze czynił to obcy,
        A dziś brata zabija brat.

           Ref. Ojczyzno ma....

        Biały orzeł znów skrępowany,
        Krwawy łańcuch zwisa u szpon.
        Lecz już wkrótce zostanie zerwany,
        Do wolności uderzył dzwon.

           Ref. Ojczyzno ma....

        O Królowo Polskiej Korony,
        Wolność, pokój i możość racz dać,
        By ten naród boleśnie dręczony
        Odtąd wiernie przy Tobie trwał.

           Rf. Ojczyzno ma...

        O Matko ma
        Tyś Królową Polskiego narodu.
        Tyś wolnością w czasie niewoli
        I nadzieją, gdy w sercach jej brak.
```

FIGURE 4.3. Drugi obieg pamphlet with hymn text.
Archiv der Forschungsstelle Osteuropa an der Universität Bremen, FSO 02-003-K30-33.

words at the end of services. After his death, it became his. In 2014 Roma Bratkowska remembered its meaningful performance at the 1984 funeral mass, "I will never forget, how the wife of the US Ambassador—or maybe Great Britain—sang the hymn, 'Ojczyzno ma tyle razy we krwi skąpana,' in Polish. Of course I should not have been surprised, because she had been at the Masses for the Fatherland."[92] When "My Fatherland" is reprinted in

---

92 Quoted in Jerzy Milewski, "Pogrzeb księdza; Cała Polska na Żoliborzu," *Gazeta Wyborcza,* October 13, 2014; http://wyborcza.pl/alehistoria/1,121681,16788913,Pogrzeb_ksiedza__Cala_Polska_na_Zoliborzu.html.

the pamphletry of the drugi obieg it is often labeled as Popiełuszko's hymn, or noted that it was "sung at all Masses for the Fatherland."[93] It is rarely dated or credited to the priest who composed it shortly after December 1981. Instead, the anthologies suggest the hymn's authentic emergence out of the opposition, out of a collective, patriotic love.

Instead, the tune's origin story goes like this, according to its author, the Michaelite priest Karol Dąbrowski, who spoke with a Catholic online news portal in 2013.[94] In the days after December 13, 1981, he fretted about his audiences, depleted of energy and resources. Inspiration came to him:

> I was reminded again of the words from the Wajdelote's Song: "the song remains."[95] I took my guitar, thought a bit, and started to tease out the first sounds of a melancholy melody. It evoked in me a symbolic image from [the Basilica of Our Lady of Licheń]: a shackled white eagle who still tries to rise in flight. I sensed that once again the nation was craving freedom and all those things that were expressed by the people of Solidarity.[96]

Shrouded in romantic ghosts, the lure of music is intuitive for Dąbrowski, and the song emerged out of his mission (see Example 4.1). He performed the song that evening in a friend's home, sitting at their piano, already confident in its significance and insisting on its capture: "I asked them to record it on tape. I said, I am performing it for the first time, and it is going to be a historic song." From this evening, the song began to be amplified in performance. It was taken up by an ensemble of Michaelite clergy, who had received the score from Dąbrowski. They eventually offered a performance to Popiełuszko when he called them to worship with him in December 1983. One month later, the chaplain asked the actor Leon Łochowski to sing the song as part of the Fatherland Masses: Łochowski learned the song from that first tape. He had taken on the responsibility of organizing performance within the liturgy of the masses, and the actor often sang himself. Eventually his performance practice, which included the omission of the song's first verse, would be crystalized in the public's imprint of the song as Popiełuszko requested it—called out for it—at every commemorative Mass. Dąbrowski, worried about arrest following Popiełuszko's death, even requested that his name be omitted from the anthologies and broadsides that disseminated the song's text until 1990.

---

93 Popiełuszko, *The Price of Love*, 6.

94 "W rocznicę stanu wojennego, historia pieśni, która dawała nadzieję," *Dziennik Parafialny*, December 13, 2013; http://dziennikparafialny.pl/2013/w-rocznice-stanu-wojennego-historia-piesni-ktora-dawala-nadzieje/.

95 A key song performed within Adam Mickiewicz's canonic Romantic epic poem *Konrad Wallenrod* (1828).

96 "W rocznicę stanu wojennego."

EXAMPLE 4.1. "My Fatherland" ("Ojczyzno ma," 1981), refrain.

Ojczyzno ma (My Fatherland), refrain

Ojczyzno ma,
Tyle razy we krwi skąpana!
Ach jak wielka dziś twoja rana,
Jakże długo cierpienie twe trwa.

Biały orzeł znów skrępowany,
Krwawy łańcuch zwisa u szpon,
Lecz już wkrótce zostanie zerwany,
Bo wolności uderzy dzwon.

My fatherland!
So many times bathed in blood.
Oh, how bad is your wound today,
How long your suffering has lasted.

Second Verse
The white eagle is fettered once again,
A blood-stained chain hangs from his claws.
But soon it will be torn away,
Because the bell of freedom will toll.

Let us read "My Fatherland" as a kind of portrait—even if it clearly was not designed, but rather heard, as such. The text is saturated with symbols of national pride, such as the white eagle from Poland's coat of arms and the Holy Mother of Poland (*Matka Polska*). The hymn, which musically satisfies the conventions of range, periodic structure, and simple tonality associated with the Roman Catholic tradition, aligns the recurring violent occupations of Poland from the late eighteenth century through martial law, integrating symbols more typical of the Book of Psalms than a devotional hymn (Example 4.1) ▶. It begins grounded in the Fatherland (*ojczyzna*) and concludes with an upward gaze to the Holy Mother (*Matka*), a transition from the earthly to the spiritual that encompasses both the Polish earth and the powerful, transcendent images of Polish Catholicism.[97] Reproductions of the Black Madonna of Częstochowa are cherished icons in Polish homes, and popular religious songs call often on her intercession—her reach toward Heaven.

As one research associate, Piotr, told me—we were sitting beneath a portrait of Pope John Paul II in his kitchen as this 85-year-old engineer sang Popiełuszko's hymn—the reference to the Polish Fatherland meant

---

97 See Maria Anna Harley's study of maternal themes and Marian Catholicism in Henryk Mikołaj Górecki's compositional output for another musical reference in Harley, "Górecki and the Paradigm of the 'Maternal'," 82, 86–96.

land and earth: *ziemia*. The concept had two immediate, heart-wrenching reference points for him. The mass and messy deaths that were the goal of the murder campaigns of the Second World War doused the Polish soil in the blood of innocent victims—a large portion of the "human geography of victims" that historian Timothy Snyder has called the "bloodlands."[98] Piotr also asked me if I had been to Piłsudski Square in Warsaw. There, on the ground, was another text about Polish lands from one of the "most important events during communism," he said. Upon his first pilgrimage to Poland as Pope, John Paul II held mass and concluded his sermon with a prophetic message of hope that he would repeat each time: "Let Thy Spirit renew the land, this land!" ▶.[99]

Piotr's voice cracked as he tried to relay the quote to me, which I encountered in many conversations and accounts of papal pilgrimages. In his break, however, I hear the gap between representations of voice and experiences of oration by many faithful during within the Church's opposition. The identificatory power of land was embedded in the sermon's delivery. The Pope placed himself on the square and among his congregation: "And I cry—I who am a Son of the land of Poland and who am also Pope John Paul II." As communications scholar Cesar Ornatowski describes this historical moment in his study of the Polish Pope's rhetoric: "When he uttered the key words . . . he said them like an incantation, slowly, enunciating every word and with a pause after the first 'land' and an emphasis on 'this.'"[100] In Piotr's uncomfortable and traumatized explanation of Fatherland, he combined the concrete fear that a nation can be occupied with the emotional relief of a spiritual presence prophesizing

---

98 Timothy Snyder, *Bloodlands: Europe between Hitler and Stalin* (New York: Basic Books, 2010), xviii.

99 Homily of His Holiness John Paul II, Victory Square, Warsaw, June 2, 1979. Available in English on the Vatican website, https://w2.vatican.va/content/john-paul-ii/en/homilies/1979/documents/hf_jp-ii_hom_19790602_polonia-varsavia.html.

100 Cesar Ornatowski, "Rhetoric of Pope John Paul II's Visits to Poland, 1979–1999," in *The Rhetoric of Pope John Paul II*, edited by Joseph R. Blaney and Joseph P. Zompetti (Lanham, MD: Lexington Books, 2009), 116. In the same analysis he provides a thick description of the Pope's voice based on extensive study of rhetoric, education, and theology in Communist Poland. "In 1979, the fifty-nine-year-old Pontiff spoke beautifully, in a powerful, melodious, charismatic baritone, enunciating every word clearly, unhurriedly, with beautiful modulation and cadence that enhanced the impact of his statements. . . . When, in the same Victory Square homily he said 'I, son of this land, and I, Pope, call . . . ,' slowly, rhythmically, in a booming voice, the words sounded like the tolling of a bell and, amplified through loudspeakers spread around the square, appeared to originate in space itself" (116).

its concrete permanence. His exegesis of Popiełuszko's song triangulates the personal and the performative, lending ethnographic perspective on its prominence from 1982 to 1989. In the movement from earth and nation to the heavens and freedom, from bodies suffering toward bells resounding in the air, the hymn is a kind of intermediary and, by extension, an intercessional medium for the collective.[101] Bells plead, too. As the engineer and Solidarity delegate Karol Szadurski called out during his funeral service, "Jerzy! My friend! Do you hear the bells of freedom that are ringing today?"[102]

Instruments and/of Death

Many faithful experienced Popiełuszko's assassination as the loss of a prophet—a closing of a portal to spirituality with the strangling of his voice. The murder articulated the fundamentally criminal nature of the communist state. Pope John Paul II eulogized the priest in his Christmas Eve address: "[Popiełuszko's] death is a testimony in which we Poles—and not only we—are reading the fundamental truths and values for which man and a society should live."[103] Across the many artistic responses to this catalytic event, composers commemorated their loss and confronted the priest's trauma with works that explicitly called out the murder's perpetrators. As had the broadsides that told the story of December 13, these set the historical record straight. Composers conjured Popiełuszko's voice and, by extension, his person. As on Muslimgauze's track, they did not isolate recordings of his voice, entombing it as a sound object within their musical compositions. Krzesimir Dębski's *Pie Jesu Domine* (1986), Augustyn Bloch's *Thou Shalt Not Kill!* (1990), Łukasz Urbaniak's *Missa in memoriam Beati Georgio Popiełuszko* (2012/13), and Michał Lorenc's *Light of Truth* (2014) represent just a selection of the consistently composed commemorative works that reference the melodic modes of the Catholic Church and the personal rhythmic cadence of Popiełuszko. Across them, the materiality of his voice is referenced through recitation as mediation.[104] I follow the priest's voice into two such

---

101 On Mary and intercession through song, see David Rothenberg, "Angels, Archangels, and a Woman in Distress: The Meaning of Isaac's *Angeli archangeli*," *Journal of Musicology* 21, no. 4 (2005), 523–24.

102 Szczepkowska, *Ks. Jerzy Popiełuszko*, 125.

103 Quoted in *The Price of Love*, 7. Accessible in Polish at the Vatican's webportal: https://w2.vatican.va/content/john-paul-ii/pl/speeches/1984/december/documents/hf_jp-ii_spe_19841224_pellegrini-polacchi.html.

104 On technologies, materiality, and recitation, see, for example, Natasha Heller, "Buddha in a Box: The Materiality of Recitation in Contemporary Chinese Buddhism," *Material Religion* 10, no. 3 (2014), 294–315; Tore Tvarnø Lind, *The Past*

compositions to conclude this chapter: Krzysztof Knittel's String Quartet (1985) and Andrzej Panufnik's Concerto for Bassoon (1986).

The music of these two compositions summons Popiełuszko as he had summoned audiences: through merciful chant and with frightened pleas. Chant is the hinge: Michel Poizat imagines the liturgical practice as "the articulation between vocal jouissance and worship, between vocal jouissance and the relation of the human to the divine, between the lyric and mystical ecstasy."[105] The voice is transformed in new compositions. Sparse stepwise motion allows musical audiences to imagine themselves in the presence of an orator, or even as part of the congregation at one of the Masses for the Fatherland.[106] Music becomes spiritual offering. These instrumental intonations of the medium through which the Word of God is transmitted combine devotional practice and aesthetic experience.

Krzysztof Knittel's String Quartet (1985) in memory of Popiełuszko was premiered in the Żoliborz parish on the anniversary of the priest's death.[107] The piece, which lasts approximately eighteen minutes and is scored for the ensemble's traditional instrumentation as well as pre-recorded tape, has been the touchstone for my conversations with and hearings of the now-influential composer. This is perhaps an unusual aperture. Knittel's work in Polish new music circles is usually of an experimentalist stripe that threads together experience improvising and collaborating with theater performers and electroacoustic forays (discussed in Chapter 2). He is also a generous teacher and leader for whom work with young people often means inviting them on stage with him to be creative. Knittel's activity has forward momentum and he doesn't attenuate earlier moments in his career. Born 1947, Knittel's biography is that of postwar

---

Is Always Present: The Revival of the Byzantine Musical Tradition at Mount Athos (Lanham, MD: Scarecrow Press, 2012), 199–202; and Albert B. Lord, *The Singer of Tales*, 2nd edition (Cambridge, MA: Harvard University Press, 2000), 124–26.

105 Michel Poizat, *The Angel's Cry: Beyond the Pleasure Principle in Opera* (Ithaca, NY: Cornell University Press, 1992), 47.

106 Adrian Thomas hears monody as a central element in Górecki's *Miserere* (begun in March 1981, premiered September 1987), too, noting its motto phrase, range of a perfect fifth, and aeolian mode. That work orbits through the opposition's context, since it is dedicated to the city of Bydgoszcz, which in March 1981 had hosted a tense altercation between Solidarity (organizing strikes) and the authorities (threatening violent intervention), resolved through peaceful negotiation. Thomas suggests that the work might have helped audiences mourn Popiełuszko when it was premiered in Włocławek. See Adrian Thomas, *Górecki* (Oxford: Clarendon Press, 1997), 101–3.

107 Musicologist Cindy Bylander describes her attendance at the one-year memorial event, which lasted nearly all day at the Stanisław Kostka parish. Cindy Bylander, "Responses to Adversity: The Polish Composers Union and Musical Life in the 1970s and 1980s," *The Musical Quarterly* 95 (2012), 490.

Europe. In living the reemergence of Poland after the Holocaust and the Second World War, he is—as the theater critic Jan Kott wrote of his generation—"as old as Europe."[108]

In our discussions of his activism over an extended meeting in April 2010, the composer painted a portrait of himself as driven by a kind of Aristotelian ethics to live a life of good: "As a human, I occupy myself with what is happening in the world, and in Poland, and I think that we should respond to reality."[109] He did not grow up attuned to oppositional discourses, whether on Radio Free Europe or around the dinner table. While enrolled at the Music Academy in Warsaw in the 1960s, he wrote music for the student cabaret "Abacus," a project that brought him into touch with the prominent satirist Andrzej Rosiewicz and rising crooner Magda Umer ▶. Knittel credits his early friendship with actors and visual artists with an awareness of his own political everyday. Following extended residencies abroad that shaped his professional development—the Darmstadt International Summer Courses (1974–75) and a year at State University of New York, Buffalo's Center for the Creative and Performing Arts (1978)—he devoted himself to organizing in Polish music circles.[110] He occasionally helped facilitate the illegal "import" of banned literature during the dire censorship of the 1970s. Following August 1980, he and music critic Tadeusz Kaczyński both became members of the Solidarity Union's Committee on Independent Culture. He also sought to establish a "House of Culture" for Solidarity in central Warsaw with other artists who supported the trade union, but martial law intervened in their organizational momentum. Knittel contributed to the Warsaw-based Circle of Independent Artists (Koło Twórców Niezależnych) until he contracted tuberculosis and was ordered to convalesce outside the city. None of this, he emphasized in 2010, was unusual.[111]

After Popiełuszko's murder, Knittel began to compose a work dedicated to the priest. The quartet, he underscored, is a personal—not commemorative—response to a horrific event. Throughout our conversation, he insisted that imagining catastrophe and thinking rationally about trauma are beyond human capacity, a poignant comment just two weeks

---

108 Introduction of Stanisław Barańczak and Biddle Memorial Lecture at Harvard Law School (1982), Woodberry Poetry Room Audio Collection, Lamont Library, Harvard University, Cambridge, MA.

109 Interview with author, April 26, 2010; quotation confirmed June 6, 2012.

110 This organizational investment continues to the present. He served as president of the Polish Composers' Union, curates the Ad Libitum festival at the Center for Contemporary Art at Warsaw's Ujazdowski Palace, and is a dynamic presence as a professor at the Music Academy in Łódź.

111 Interview with author, April 26, 2012.

after the plane crash in Smolensk had killed 96 Polish dignitaries. He held up Miron Białoszewski's *Memoir of the Warsaw Uprising* (published 1970) as a central model for his efforts to work through trauma in the quartet.[112] Like Białoszewski, he tried to lay out the facts, to portray the murder as an incident in cold blood. Monody and homophony—pared-down writing—resonate the string ensemble. Regular rhythmic pulses undergird the entire piece; out of these non-distinct or even quotidian patterns, warmth vibrates.[113]

Knittel builds a simple calendar into the quartet's structure that taps into the importance of time in figuring this murder's cultural potency. The three parts map the passing months: (1) October, (2) November, (3) December—January—February. Waiting and learning about Popiełuszko's fate was a practice of oral transmission and of the 24-hour news cycle. As one activist remembered in 1985, "Throngs around the boards and newspapers until quite late into the night. With flashlights or candles, people read the texts—often out loud. Some copied them down. Representatives of Western news agencies were also there from the early-morning hours. More and more people came from all over Poland."[114] The collective anticipation paved the way, even set the tone, for communal mourning.

Knittel's mensural labels are about communication. As John Durham Peters, attuned in particular to the relation between religion and technology, describes devices for periodic measure: "They are at once modes of representation and instruments of intervention: they constitute time in describing it. Calendars negotiate between the heavens and the state and orient us to time and eternity."[115] An audience in the know—an audience who had lived through that Polish winter—might be prompted to reexperience the confusion of the priest's abduction, the revelation of his murder, and the process of mourning his death. But the titles are merely hints at a narrative program that the composer, both in program notes and conversation, leaves the listener to expound upon individually. Or, these flags reorient listeners to the

---

112 In 2004 he composed incidental music for a dramatization of Białoszewski's account.

113 I hear Knittel through Joanna Niżyńska's study of Białoszewski. Joanna Niżyńska, *The Kingdom of Insignificance: Miron Białoszewski and the Quotidian, the Queer, and the Traumatic* (Chicago: Northwestern University Press, 2013), 51–98.

114 Collected by B. B. in Szczepkowska, *Ks. Jerzy Popiełuszko*, 74.

115 John Durham Peters, "Calendar, Clock, Tower," in *Deus in Machina: Religion, Technology, and the Things in Between*, edited by Jeremy Stolow (New York: Fordham University Press, 2013), 26.

continued march of time, marking distance from 1984 rather than collapsing history, as did the "trans-temporal" barrage of the 2009 reenactment.[116] They confront eschatology and phenomenology.

Musical inflections of meditation, chant, and unity set each part of the quartet into motion, establishing a reflective space. Slow tempi and homophonic textures evoke the practices of each of these touchstones (see Example 4.2a/b/c). Despite a recurring tension between unpitched percussive sound and pitched sustained tranquility, the composer dwells in a comforting aesthetic through the first two parts. Knittel, who has practiced meditation in many religious traditions, has written of the transformative space of reflection as a non-emotional state that effects change in an individual. He recollects in a personal note:

> From time to time it happens to me that I praise or deride something in exaggerated language, in [my] music I try to reject emotion, and especially negative emotion. This is very important and maybe it happens like this because I brought myself to a meditative state at some point. And because I have gone through different religious phases in my life, so the world seems a little bit different to me than it did before.[117]

Knittel frames music, happening, and subjectivity as process: static and transformative. Over the first ten minutes of the piece, Knittel's Popiełuszko story

EXAMPLE 4.2. Krzysztof Knittel, String Quartet No. 1 (1984), ostinato rhythms.
Reprinted with permission of Polskie Wydawnictwo Muzyczne S.A., Cracow, Poland.
EXAMPLE 4.2A. Part 1 (October), mm. 1–7.

116 Zubrzycki, "History and the National Sensorium," 22.
117 "Knittel sprawdzony," Krzysztof Knittel Private Collection.

EXAMPLE 4.2B. Part 2 (November), mm. 1–7.

EXAMPLE 4.2C. Part 3 (December–January–February), mm. 1–8, mm. 1–9, mm. 1–9.

OBJAŚNIENIA

- mały bębenek z dwoma kulkami
- płaski bęben i filcowa pałka
- mały dzwonek

Tuż przed rozpoczęciem tej części pierwszy skrzypek powinien uruchomić magnetofon kasetowy z nagranymi szumami trwającymi około 8–10 minut (co odpowiada przybliżonemu czasowi trwania całej trzeciej części kwartetu). Potencjometr głośności powinien być otwierany i zamykany tylko w określonych miejscach oznaczonych ; znak oznacza „trochę głośniej"; znak oznacza „trochę ciszej".

Szumy odtwarzane z magnetofonu kasetowego mogą być nagrane na urządzeniach elektronicznych lub na dowolnych instrumentach. Szumy, ich struktura, barwa i gęstość są dowolne — najprostszym dźwiękiem może być filtrowany biały szum z syntezatora lub zwykły szum z radia.
Uwaga: podczas wykonywania tej części muzycy, którzy grają akord G-dur mogą jednocześnie śpiewać grany przez siebie dźwięk.

EXPLANATION

- small drum with two balls
- flat drum with felt stick
- small bell

Before beginning this movement first violinist sets in motion the casette tape-recorder with the recording of noises lasting about 8–10 minutes (which equals the approximative duration of the whole third movement of the string quartet). The volume potentiometer should be opened and closed only in places indicated by ; the sign means "open a little"; the sign means "close a little".

The noises played back from the casette can be recorded either by means of electronic devices or with the help of any instruments. The noises, their structure, colour and density are free — the simplest sound may be the filtered white noise from synthesizer or the ordinary noise from the radio.
Note: when performing this movement, the musicians who play the G-major chord may simultaneously sing the played sound.

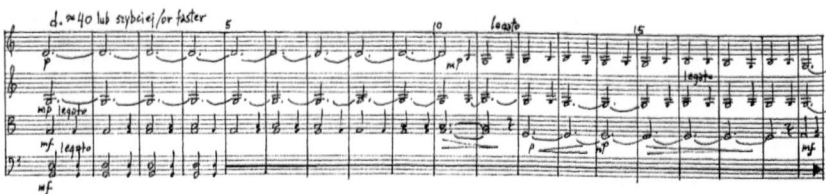

sounds nothing like Muslimgauze: repetition grounds a spiritual aesthetic that I would hitch, at least in retrospect, to the contemporaneous asceticism that Jeffers Engelhardt situates across Poland and the Baltic Soviet Socialist Republics.[118] Compounding the spiritual impulse of the work's dedication to the murdered priest is its musical resonance with Górecki's imploring *Miserere*, Opus 44 (1981) for unaccompanied choir, Arvo Pärt's tintinnabulist echoes in his *Stabat Mater* (1985), and one of the hits of the 1983 Warsaw Autumn Festival, Bronius Kutavičius's oratorio *Last Pagan Rites* (1978), which was performed in the sanctuary of an unlit church.

In the first movement, the instruments plead together before resolutely confirming a major tonality. The sonic confirmation gives way to duos and trios that hover around recitation tones. The reference to chant comes through stacked fifths in rhythmic unison. The final movement is constructed around a G major rhythmic ostinato with a gradual increase in tempo. Extended techniques sneak in and around the string parts: from the outset the musicians are invited (but not commanded) to sing the pitches they play when they are within the diatonic G space. So the voice hovers near as possibility in this instrumental work, this time as optional, additional tonal substance.

The months of the third part begin with pulses against the prepared tape track, the volume of which the performers are instructed to modify while they play. They come to a close as the string playing fades out. The pitch-centric string writing gives way to rustles, clanks, electronic zaps and hisses, and other electronically generated effects ▶. Left to their own devices, the instrumentalists are to prepare the noise track themselves, with either electronic or *concrète* sounds:

> Before beginning this movement first violinist sets in motion the cassette tape recorder with the recording of noises lasting about 8–10 minutes. . . . The volume potentiometer should be opened and closed only in places indicated. . . . The noises played back from the cassette can be recorded either by means of electronic devices or with the help of any instruments. The noises, their structure, colour and density are free—the simplest sound may be the filtered white noise from synthesizer or the ordinary noise from the radio.[119]

Live sounds become noisier at the same time. Knittel brings the piece toward his own musical aesthetic, one in which the quiet clicks and clacks

---

118 Jeffers Engelhardt, "Asceticism and the Nation: Henryk Górecki, Krzysztof Penderecki, and Late Twentieth-Century Poland," *European Meetings in Ethnomusicology* 9 (2002), 197–207.

119 Krzysztof Knittel, *Kwartet smyczkowy '84–'85, partytura* (Cracow: Polskie Wydawnictwo Muzyczne, 1992), 4.

of technology become integral textures in chamber music.[120] While fiddling with their potentiometers, the musicians rest their instruments to play others, adding timbres: a small bell and two drums, one played with a felt stick. This pattern of two-part months continues through the movement; to bring the piece full circle, Knittel revisits the two-voice counterpoint and stacked fifths of the work's opening measures, the effects wash over, and a diminuendo to nothingness closes the reflection.

Knowing the instruments that brought about Popiełuszko's death, it is hard not to hear the non-string sounds in this piece as representational rattles, shaking, clattering, and punches. One can only imagine the effect of the performance at the work's premiere, on the first anniversary of Popiełuszko's death at St. Stanisław Kostka. The work became prominently associated with the priest's story, especially when it was awarded the "Solidarity" Prize from the Committee on Independent Culture.[121]

The Limits of Popiełuszko's Voice

The émigré composer Andrzej Panufnik crafted his Bassoon Concerto (1986) in memory of Popiełuszko, building the musical material out of the three central components of his historical vocal profile: chant, sermon, and plea. Panufnik understood himself as a victim of state socialism, a persona non grata in Poland, and an outsider in the music circles of his adopted home, London. His autobiography recounts the struggles he endured under Stalinism and gives an engrossing account of the chase that ushered in his London-based exile beginning in 1954.[122] His widow, Lady Camilla Panufnik, remembers that as a result of socialist realism's vice on his compositional output and life story, he "looked on politics as a curse."[123] Nation, however, was another matter. His own body was of Polish land and culture, he suggested in a 1987 conversation with a Polish-language monthly in London: "In my compositions, I try to reflect

---

120 Knittel also employs this technique on *Lapis Sounds* (Alma Art 007, 1987).

121 *Kultura Niezależna* 16 (1986), 3. See Chapter 1 for further discussion of the "Solidarity" Prize.

122 Andrzej Panufnik, *Composing Myself* (London: Methuen, 1987). For a careful reconsideration of several key claims in the autobiography, see David Tompkins, "Composing for and with the Party: Andrzej Panufnik in Stalinist Poland," *The Polish Review* 54, no. 3 (2009), 271–85.

123 Camilla Panufnik, "Andrzej Panufnik's Ethos of Life and Work," in Jadwiga Paja-Stach, *Andrzej Panufnik's Music and Its Reception* (Cracow: Musica Iagellonica, 2003), 23.

the events that I personally experience. These are mostly the social, political, and religious problems of our country. This is because Poland is everything to me. My heart and my soul belong to it."[124]

Panufnik's voice could return if he could not. Writing in the mid-1980s, he mourned:

> My presence in Poland meanwhile can sadly still be only in voice, through my music. Although I would love to walk again through the city of my birth, to see my ageing relatives before they die and meet again with dear old friends, my physical presence in Poland is hardly essential. It matters to me infinitely more that my musical voice is occasionally allowed to be raised in my native land. In what I compose, I stand right by my countrymen with all my heart.[125]

Though composed in London for a US-based ensemble, Panufnik's Bassoon Concerto performed both "visits" to Poland he alludes to here. First, it explicitly thematizes Polish symbols and political concepts with its program, as did many of his compositions during the 1980s. The *Sinfonia Votiva* (1982, rev. 1984) responded to Solidarity's power and vulnerability with a setting of a medieval *carmen patrium* (the "Bogurodzica") that was dedicated to the Black Madonna of Częstochowa; he reworked his work that explicitly thematized Polish Marianism, the *Song to the Virgin Mary* (1964, 1987) for string sextet; and one of his final completed works, the Third String Quartet, "Wyciniaki" (1990), draws inspiration from paper-cutting traditions in Poland.[126] Second, like Knittel's String Quartet, it was animated within the Solidarity chaplain's parish in his memory. The concert brought Panufnik's and Popiełuszko's voices back to Warsaw, back into a political and religious space. As had Knittel before him (and without knowledge of this precedent), Panufnik uses plainchant as a programmatic reference in music to Popiełuszko (see Example 4.3).

Upon Panufnik's ultimate return to Poland in October 1990, after a terminal cancer diagnosis and the end of communism, he visited the priest's grave.[127] During the visit, he explained his relationship to Polish nationalism

---

124 Interview in *Dziennik Polski*. Quoted in Beata Bolesławska, *The Life and Works of Andrzej Panufnik (1914–1991)*, translated by Richard J. Reisner (Farnham, UK: Ashgate, 2015), 245.

125 Interview in *Dziennik Polski*.

126 For a discussion of Polish symbols in Panufnik's music, see Thomas, *Polish Music since Szymanowski*, 286–87.

127 Tadeusz Kaczyński, *Andrzej Panufnik i jego muzyka* (Warsaw: PWN, 1994), 75–78.

EXAMPLE 4.3. Andrzej Panufnik, Bassoon Concerto, transition between Prologue and Recitative 1.
© 1986 by Boosey & Hawkes Music Publishers Ltd. All rights reserved. Used with permission.

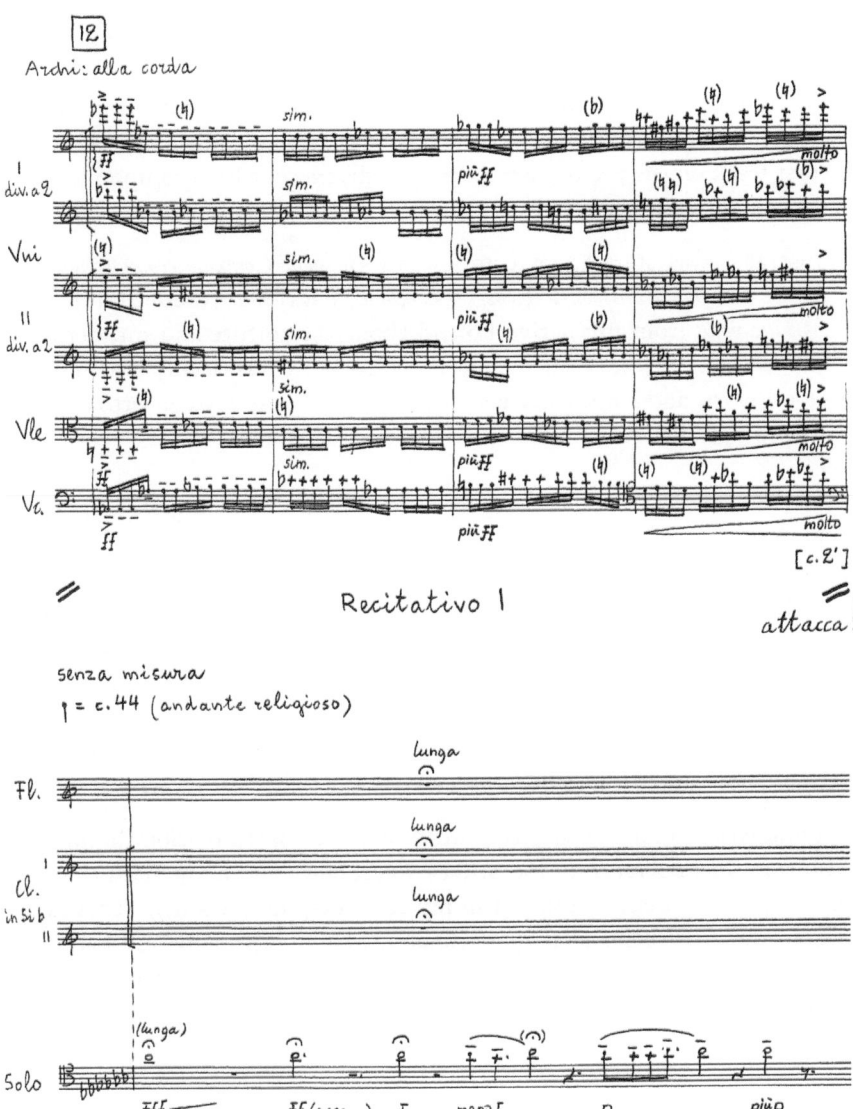

to an audience of journalists and musicians at a House of Culture. With his compositions he was "trying, in my own way, to do exactly what the democratic, anti-communist opposition in our country were doing—to awaken a sense of national identity, to prepare the ground for the rebirth of another, non-communist Poland."[128] At the same time, despite the limited—that is, essentially "Polish"—network in which Popiełuszko's sermons received close hearing, the path of Popiełuszko's voice into the Concerto reminds us that his death, as media event, had transnational meaning. Panufnik, like the Western readers bombarded with coverage of his suffering, learned of the murder through the news. This is the spur for the work he provides in his program note, reprinted in the score.

At the request of the commissioning performer, bassoonist Robert Thompson, Panufnik spoke—recorded—a variation on this program note as the first track on the premiere recording of the piece, which compounded the emotional nature of the piece and emphasized its urgent affective tenor:[129]

> Just as I was starting to compose *my Bassoon Concerto, commissioned by the American bassoonist Robert Thompson, I was told* [there came] *the horrific news* from my native Poland about the torture and murder of the Catholic priest, Father Jerzy Popiełuszko. I was deeply shaken *by this atrocity,* and I immediately decided to compose my concerto *to the* memory of this Polish martyr of faith and fatherland.
>
> . . .
>
> The concerto is an abstract work with no literary programme, but Fr. Popiełuszko was so much in my mind while I was composing that inevitably the Concerto conveys some feeling of Popiełuszko's ideals and the tragedy of his death. Perhaps in *Recitativo I*, (bassoon and three woodwind instruments) the listener might hear his humble prayer to the Virgin Mary. Possibly *Recitativo II*, where the bassoon is supported by the interjected chords of the string instruments, is related to the priest's fatal encounter with the secret police—the very last interrogation before his tortured body was thrown into the Vistula River.[130]

Panufnik enacts a form of spiritual worship and commemoration through the dedication. His reference to the priest's voice, faith, and body maps the symbols of the 2009 mass I observed in my ethnographic encounter. These symbols are the crux of his sonic performance. Many voices sing and haunt the Concerto: musical vocality, the bassoon as "evocative, rather modest voice,"[131] and Popiełuszko's "humble prayer." The titles of the five sections (Prologue,

---

128 Quoted in Kaczyński, *Andrzej Panufnik i jego muzyka*, 85.

129 Words in italics are modified from the score's written note for spoken delivery. Andrzej Panufnik, *Concerto for Bassoon and Small Orchestra*, 8105 (London: Boosey & Hawkes, 1986). The spoken text was released on *Panufnik: Symphony No. 9 and Bassoon Concerto*, Heritage Records, HTGCD266, 2014.

130 Andrzej Panufnik, Concerto for Bassoon and Small Orchestra, 8105 (London: Boosey & Hawkes, 1986).

131 Panufnik, *Composing Myself*, 345.

Recitatives I and II, Aria, Epilogue) invoke preaching, singing, and speaking. In the note, Panufnik explains that the recitatives are *"parlando"* and that in the aria, the bassoon sings. In an alternative version of the program note, a typescript held among Tadeusz Kaczyński's papers at the Library of the University of Warsaw, there is again greater sensory detail in the last paragraph: "Listeners, especially those with some knowledge of Father Jerzy Popiełuszko's religious life and horrific death, might recognize in my music *an echo—just an echo—of, say, the priest's patriotic sermon*, his humble prayer, or *even* his last fatal interrogation by the secret police before his tortured body was thrown into the reservoir by the Vistula river" (emphasis on text variants mine).

I heard the concerto's story from Thompson, who approached Panufnik in an effort to expand the solo repertory for his instrument.[132] The two were a good match, facilitated by a musicologist employed by Boosey and Hawkes, Bernard Jacobson. Panufnik's Polishness was also a boon, as a Milwaukee-based Polish-American society, "Polanki," underwrote the commission and supported its world premiere, in Wisconsin, and its Polish premiere, at St. Stanisław Kostka. As Thompson generously shared with me, the two artists met only a few times, and the conversation always hovered around the material peculiarities of the bassoon. He played for Panufnik. Later they rehearsed together. They found common ground in their affection for the bassoon's timbre—"colors and techniques."[133] Unlike the humorous solos of Chabrier, Dukas, Shostakovich, and Prokofiev, Thompson and Panufnik discussed the Interlude of Ernest Chausson's *Poème de l'amour et de la mer*, Opus 19 (1882–92). The composer wrote against "jocularity": "In my own ears I heard [the bassoon's] sounds as deep brown, velvet black. I imagined it singing dramatically, almost operatically."[134] In my conversations with Thompson, he almost repeated these words in a coincidental communication loop: "[The Bassoon] has a beautiful mellow voice. I like the mellow sound of it. It sounds like dark velvet, black or red velvet, the color of it."

The proximity—even equivalence—of the instrument with the human voice, along with the work's devotional dedication, shaped the nature of the virtuosity Thompson could showcase in his performance. Instead of something "like Paganini," he received a score with very different challenges. First, to interrupt the jagged sixteenth-note passage work of the Prologue, the soloist begins Recitative I with a D-sharp in its upper range (but not the top! see Example 4.3).

132 Skype conversation with author, December 25, 2016.

133 "But he wanted to know about lyrical possibilities. So I played him a solo from the middle movement of Chausson's *Poème de l'amour et de la mer*—and the notes of that passage are the essential tones of the 'Aria' of the Bassoon Concerto! It couldn't be more different though." In "Lines, Colours and Textures: Stephen Johnson Talks to Conductor Mark Stephenson and Bassoonist Robert Thompson," *Gramophone*, July 1990, 177.

134 Panufnik, *Composing Myself*, 345.

This pitch, which also concludes the Aria and the Epilogue, is reiterated in almost manic rhythms and different articulations until it relaxes into the "humble prayer" Panufnik describes. The entire section is a chain of elaborations around reciting tones, slowly dropping register. Through the stepwise motion of these breath-length chant echoes, the soloist is free to push and pull at the eighth-note ornaments' rhythm. The orchestration is sparse to accommodate the *parlando*: the hollow timbres of a flute and two clarinets is sustained *"alla organo"* beneath the solo line. Their breath is, per the instructions, to be unnoticeable in comparison with the structuring element of the soloist's exhale. Thompson gave himself homework to shape the unusual recitative:

> In order to do the second movement, I had to study Catholic liturgy a little bit. The bassoon has to play through the whole prayer without having a squalk or crack. It is quite a challenge, because you're all out there by yourself and that particular part is rather long. I took it that that was the priest praying and I was executing a prayer. Anyone who knows their Gregorian chant knows that prayers don't end abruptly. Phrases or sentences: "Forgive us, Mother." Or, "We pray to you, Mary!" There is a tender ending to each line. Because you're a supplicant. So that's what I tried to achieve theatrically.[135]

His comments position chant as the technology through which he can perform Popiełuszko. The details and close reading that Thompson performed, as I heard him explain it, made the commission intimate. This is how he extended respect to Panufnik's national sorrow, a project that he noted was occasionally a psychological burden. The programmatic suggestion of the piece, too, elicited the performance of ethical solidarity and emotional empathy among critics, as well, some of whom wrote of shedding tears when they heard the work performed live.[136]

The second pillar of virtuosity Thompson located in the score was that of physical limits. The pulse of the confessional core of the work, the Aria, is determined by the physical conditioning and fit embouchure of the soloist, since Panufnik marks it *adagio lamentoso*, "the slowest the soloist can possibly play" (Example 4.4). In his performances, Thompson was always mindful of the greatest challenge, the moments just before the Aria began when "the

---

135 Skype conversation with author, December 25, 2016.

136 For example, Martin Anderson, Review of Andrzej Panufnik, *Sinfonia Sacra, Arbor Cosmica* by New York Chamber Symphony; and Panufnik: Violin Concerto. Hommage à Chopin. Bassoon Concerto by Krysztof Smietana, Karen Jones, Robert Thompson, London Musici, Mark Stephenson and Panufnik, *Tempo* 175 (1990), 51. Thompson mentioned this review in our conversation, as well as another conversation in which the Aria was linked with the lament from Purcell's *Dido and Aeneas* as one of the most sorrowful moments in Western art music.

EXAMPLE 4.4. Andrzej Panufnik, Bassoon Concerto (1986), Aria, opening. © 1986 by Boosey & Hawkes Music Publishers Ltd. All rights reserved. Used with permission.

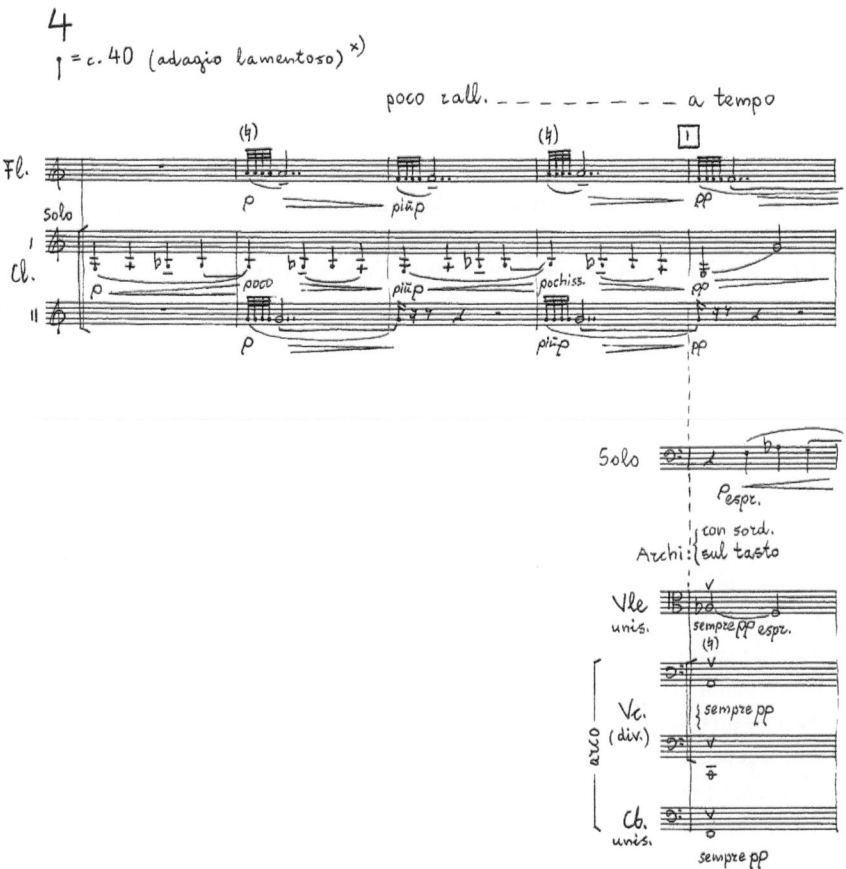

x) The slowest that the soloist can possibly play.

bassoon dies" at the hands of the SB. The elongated trill on a high D-sharp resolves to "the highest [note] at the end. He ended there. I knew I had to have the strength to do that note at the end of the movement." Panufnik explicitly pushes the performer and the music to limits, writing a crescendo under the pitch that is meant to grow as loud as possible.

Panufnik's Bassoon Concerto is patently a commemorative work. Through its fabric, the composer rebuilds and captures the dead priest. This is not merely a portrait Panufnik shapes, as when we hear Popiełuszko's demeanor and prayer throughout the Aria. It is inherent in the bassoon's presence and its technology. The bassoon is a kind of prosthetic for Popiełuszko, enabling him to continue to speak.[137] Thompson made Panufnik's voice when he shaped the reeds that were suited to the unusual demands of this work. As he recalled: "When you make your own reeds you're making your own voice.... You can change your voice, you can control your voice." Thus, the work's Polish premiere—noted in St. Stanisław Kostka's chronicle as a concert of mourning music (*koncert muzyki żałobnej*)—could shape for those assembled a kind of re-presencing.[138] On November 30, 1987, the Polish-American conductor Joseph Herter, who had lived in Warsaw since the mid-1970s, conducted Robert Thompson with an ad hoc orchestra of musicians from the Warsaw Philharmonic. The church was full, and those assembled held candles to honor Popiełuszko's memory. Tadeusz Kaczyński wrote up the concert for the classical music periodical *Ruch Muzyczny* (*Musical Movement*), moved by the attendance, Thompson's compassionate and expert performance that sounded "like a Pole, like a Catholic," and the continued significance of Popiełuszko's passing.[139] Police cars surrounded the church, though it was unclear at the time whether their perch at the border helped them keep an eye on the congregation, served to protect them, or articulated a warning.[140] The effect, according to Thompson, was to heighten the sense of community. He remembers that "afterward nearly the whole audience came up and shook my hand. They were crying."[141]

With the 1987 performance, Popiełuszko's voice crossed from its outerbounds—the bassoon—back into the space shaped as political through his sermons. With such sobbing, the work of Popiełuszko's voice becomes embodied, again, in those who heard him and mourn him. In this extended media archaeology of Popiełuszko's vocality, I have shown the vibrations and breaks in voice, along with its shouts and mediations of faith, to shape and route a network of hearing and singing, mourning and weeping. Though his work, as priest, was always in transcendent relation with the voice of God, it is also a story inextricable from the aesthetics and poetics of Polish Catholicism, the sound technologies of the 1980s, and the expediency of the mass as a political—oppositional—gathering and space. It is a particular story of voice. In her study of the Ilongot people, the anthropologist Michelle

---

137 Jonathan De Souza, *Music at Hand: Instruments, Bodies, and Cognition* (New York: Oxford University Press, 2017), 23–27.

138 I am grateful to Father Marcin Brzeziński for this archival information. Email with author, May 19, 2017.

139 Tadeusz Kaczyński (as "tk"), "Koncert fagotowy Andrzeja Panufnika," *Ruch Muzyczny* 31, no. 26 (20 December 1987), 16–17.

140 Joseph Herter, Skype interview with author, May 18, 2017.

141 Skype interview with author, December 25, 2016.

Rosaldo emphasized that "[a]ccounts of verbal action cannot reasonably proceed without attention to the relations between social order, folk ideas about the world, and styles of speaking."[142] This sociocultural—and, I would add, historical—situatedness of not just speaker and audience, but also of subject formation, linguistic practice, physical health, and sacred worship, have anchored this new portrait of Popiełuszko. Through him, the opposition's political action continues to work. Popiełuszko is steeped in voice and threaded through life after death in sound.

---

142 Michelle Z. Rosaldo, "The Things We Do with Words: Ilongot Speech Acts and Speech Act Theory in Philosophy," *Language in Society* 11, no. 2 (1982), 213.

5 | Megaphone

Society must be able to speak with its full voice, to express various social and political opinions; it must be able to organize in such a way as to guarantee a fair share in the material and spiritual achievements of the nation for all as well as to liberate all the nation's possibilities and creative forces.
—Solidarity's Program, October 1981

Music history shows that certain composers, within their own countries, in the hearts of their own people, assume an importance due almost as much to political reasons as to musical ones. . . . Viva Penderecki! Viva Polonia!
—Paul Moor in High Fidelity Magazine (1984)

Tadeusz Kaczyński took the mic at the International Radio University in Paris in January 1981 to deliver a brief address, "Penderecki's Secret."[1] Just a few months after the Solidarity Union had been legalized, all things Polish remained in the international spotlight. The music critic seized his opportunity to speak to a broad audience with a celebration of the composer's success among audiences worldwide. Kaczyński spoke of Krzysztof Penderecki's unprecedented position as a specifically Polish composer, citing both his positive critical acclaim and the respect accorded him by fellow composers. Just

---

1 "Tajemnica Pendereckiego," annotated typescript, Tadeusz Kaczyński Papers, Music Department, Special Collections, Library of the University of Warsaw, Poland. Epigraphs taken from: "Uchwała programowa I Krajowego Zjazdu Delegatów Niezależnego Samorządnego Związku Zawodowego 'Solidarność' "; http://www.wszechnica.solidarnosc.org.pl/?page_id=1370; Paul Moor, "Penderecki's Te Deum: Another Milestone from a Modern Master," *High Fidelity* 34, no. 5 (May 1984), 63.

what was Penderecki's ticket to pleasing such diverse audiences? Kaczyński spoke in search of an explanation for his "universal" approval:

> What is the source of such a strong compositional character as Penderecki's in Poland?—there is no answer to this question. Just like there is no answer to the question: what is the source of such a strong religious—and not only religious—character as Karol Wojtyła[?] Or—if we to stay in a strictly musical sphere—the origins of Frédéric Chopin's genius.

The critic spoke just four months after the remarkable strikes of August 1980 that had brought about Solidarity's legalization, shaping his comments with reference to the indescribable significance of Karol Wojtyła's selection as Pope in 1978. Both events ignited Kaczyński's nationalist hope.[2]

After August 1980, many with large platforms and prominent voices, like Kaczyński, dreamed big for the Polish nation. For example, the agenda for Solidarity's first national meeting, held in October 1981, would explicitly dream for—loud and fair—representation, as evident in the herald that serves as one epigraph to this section. This central manifest makes specific the need for "full voice" expression. Citizens are entitled to voices, the program suggests, as its authors invoke the pervasive Western metaphor of voice as agency.[3] For the organizers of Solidarity, to have a voice is to be a democratic subject. To call out the right to a voice is to demand representational politics. It is to explicitly critique the Communist Party as a hegemonic system of silencing. Kaczyński, too, puts questions about representation and individuality into play as he collects national heroes to suggest their inexplicable exceptionalism and their power as Poles on the international stage. In this chapter, I consider how these actors took to the mic and embraced their moment on the stage. Cultural work amplified Solidarity's nascent energy.

For the Polish opposition, singing, speaking, and metaphorical voices enabled the negotiation of multiplicity—nation as society—in tandem with symbolic work by individuals on behalf of the nation. Sociologist Andrzej Walicki captured this dynamism already in 1987 as he tried to take the pulse of the social movement: "National banners and singing the national anthem on the occasion of every strike . . . are, I think, clear evidence that

---

2 Jan Kubik, *The Power of Symbols against the Symbols of Power: The Rise of Solidarity and the Fall of State Socialism in Poland* (State College: Pennsylvania State University Press, 1994).

3 J. Martin Daughtry, "Afterword: From Voice to Violence and Back Again," in *Music, Politics, and Violence*, edited by Susan Fast and Kip Pegley (Middletown, CT: Wesleyan University Press, 2012), 250–51; Amanda Weidman, "Voice," in *Keywords in Sound*, edited by David Novak and Matt Sakakeeny (Durham, NC: Duke University Press, 2015), 232–33.

the Polish workers, united in 'Solidarity,' have become a 'national class' not only in the sense of representing all national interests, but also in the sense of inheriting the traditional virtues and faults of the Polish national character."[4] Walicki, among many observers of collective song across public gatherings across the nation during this time, weaves a national voice—singular—out of voices.[5] He has his eyes on what Rogers Brubaker, writing in the mid-1990s, would diagnose as spirit and politics "moving *back to* the nation state."[6] Affective politics and music's affects reconfirm a sameness across class, ethnic, and regional differences.[7] Lech Wałęsa, whom I have already mentioned, and Krzysztof Penderecki took the stage as international stars: they took up Solidarity's literal and metaphorical megaphones. To sound Polish, for Kaczyński's Penderecki, was not a question of citing national symbols or taking up national texts. (Krzysztof Meyer's *Polish Symphony*, discussed in Chapter 6, comments on martial law through these techniques.) Instead, Kaczyński anoints the composer as voice because of his musical gift—his secret.

Lech Wałęsa worked through sound, too: as the mouthpiece of the movement. He was Solidarity's star, from the moment he rallied for workers' rights in Gdańsk 1980 through Solidarity's ascent as a political party during the post-socialist transition. By 1989, US newspapers tracked his movements in celebrity watch columns.[8] The director Andrzej Wajda—a close friend, also, of Penderecki—cast him as the *Man of Hope* (*Człowiek z nadziei*) in his 2013 film about the Solidarity

---

4 Andrzej Walicki, "The Three Traditions in Polish Patriotism and Their Contemporary Relevance," address delivered March 26, 1987 at the Polish Studies Center, Indiana University (Bloomington, IN: Polish Studies Center, 1987), 19.

5 On the singular nation in musical plurality in a contemporary context, see Jonathyne Briggs, *Sounds French: Globalization, Cultural Communities, and Pop Music, 1958–1980* (New York: Oxford University Press, 2015). Walicki's comments between philosophy and on-the-ground being resonate in Slavoj Žižek's tripartite dissection of theoretical work: "*Universal* philosophy, *particular* Science, the *singularity* of the political," in Slavoj Žižek, *The Parallax View* (Cambridge, MA: MIT Press, 2006), 10.

6 Rogers Brubaker, *Nationalism Reframed: Nationhood and the National Question in the New Europe* (Cambridge: Cambridge University Press, 1996), 2.

7 Both Walicki and Kaczyński write along a strand of oppositional discourse that ignores the multiethnic history of Poland and its troubled relationship with Jewish history, as well as the impact of globalization upon the People's Republic—all issues barely beneath the surface, and politics that would demand a clearer confrontation with cultural pluralities. See Karen Auerbach, *The House at Ujazdowskie 16: Jewish Families in Warsaw after the Holocaust* (Bloomington: Indiana University Press, 2013); and Christopher B. Balme and Berenika Szymański-Düll, eds., *Theatre, Globalization, and the Cold War* (Cham, Switzerland: Palgrave Macmillan, 2017).

8 "Celebrity Watch: Arrive Early to Spot Poland's Lech Walesa," *Chicago Tribune*, November 17, 1989, p. NW21A.

movement. Consider again Timothy Garton Ash's evocative description of Wałęsa's charisma from the negotiation hall in Gdańsk over August 1980:

> I notice how skillfully Wałęsa manages this unruly assembly. Whenever the arguments become furious and voices from the floor are raised in anger he summons up the ghosts of General Dąbrowski's Polish legions, whose splendid marching-song is now the national anthem.
> "Poland is not yet lost so long as we live . . ." he intones, and all controversy is stilled as everyone rises to their feet, "March, march Dąbrowski, From Italian soil to Poland . . ." and the roof nearly lifts off, all dissension swept away in this never-failing catharsis, "Under thy command, We rejoin the nation . . ." and is it of Wałęsa or Dąbrowski that they sing? It is pure Polish magic. You know that magician has turned it on deliberately, almost cynically. Yet as he sings he is transformed: no longer is he the feisty little electrician in ill-fitting trousers. The sharp talker with many human weaknesses; no longer does his authority derive merely from his patter and repartee; now he stands up straight, head thrown back, arms to his sides, strangely rigid and pink in the face, like a wooden figure by one of the naive sculptors from the Land of Dobrzyn where he was born.⁹

I have already suggested the powerful command of Wałęsa as leader in song. When he speaks, his accent and plain language make clear that he is one of the workers. As Garton Ash has it, Wałęsa's rhetoric and repertory make him Polish. Performance casts Wałęsa at Solidarity's helm ▶.

I posit a composer—his works—and union man—as worker—as megaphones for the vocal trajectory of one from many across the Polish opposition. I also attend to the power of absent figures—in this case the murdered student, Zbigniew Godlewski—to assume a central role. These are canonic heroes of the Polish 1980s, and this chapter investigates how they crafted this power and how power was crafted through them. In politics, Lech Wałęsa, an electrician turned union activist, took on the role of rallying crowds in Gdańsk and negotiating on their behalf with authorities. Like Penderecki, whose charisma was a product of his public persona and his music's contribution to ideas about community, personhood, and nation, Wałęsa was fundamentally shaped by his communications' affect and content. Both were celebrated and scrutinized for "specifically exceptional powers" in the Weberian sense. Yet their charisma placed them outside the rational order of the state. Godlewski, too, whose funeral presented him as a tragic stifled voice, became a persona on Solidarity's stages. A song conjured his re-presence and organized affective release. As we have already seen in the case

---

9 Timothy Garton Ash, *The Polish Revolution: Solidarity*, 3rd ed. (New Haven, CT: Yale University Press, 2002), 64. See a discussion of this quote in the context of the national anthem in Chapter 3.

of Jerzy Popiełuszko, the opposition's "claims to legitimacy" depended on such individuals' presence or larger-than life absence.[10]

Penderecki and Wałęsa were magnetic leaders, credited with extraordinary character and metaphysical power on ethical terms across narrative accounts and in song. People had faith in these men to speak for them. To quote Max Weber, their performances manifest "devotion" to a collective cause: Polish independence.[11] Both delivered public addresses and invested in abstracting the voice to hear and discuss human, musical, and Polish character, to echo Kaczyński again. As such, this chapter builds on my analysis of Popiełuszko's voice to investigate their stardom and the "imaginary drive" they lent to the opposition.[12] However, I want to be careful not to further enshrine these two men as the motors behind the popular national imaginary. I ground their larger-than-life personae on the scene in Poland. I take seriously that extraordinary human needs, such as the peaks and valleys that define social movements, impute charisma upon others; charisma is relational.[13] I unpack these figures' "presence" on one of Solidarity's most important stages: the commemoration of the December 1970 massacre of Polish workers at the unveiling of its monument in 1980.

This moment—and my own emphatic return to Gdańsk after the study of August 1980 in Chapter 3—sets the tone for a broader analysis of the opposition's iconic figures, including Godlewski, as they are cast through music and across collective audiences. Anthropologist Laura Kunreuther traces vocal agency as fundamentally social: "The voice, conceived of as a material sound uniquely generated within the human body, has a social life associated with its role as the primary medium of human utterance. In this life, it is an embodied mode of transmission, imbued with an irreducible authenticity, yet itself ubiquitously mediated through a range of always more pervasive technologies."[14] Kunreuther's trajectory for the voice from fleshy utterance

---

10 Max Weber, *Economy and Society: An Outline of Interpretive Sociology*, edited by Guenther Roth and Klaus Wittich (Berkeley: University of California Pres, 1947), 241–42.

11 Max Weber, "Discipline and Charisma [1914]," in *Weber's Rationalism and Modern Society: New Translations on Politics, Bureaucracy, and Social Stratification*, edited and translated by Tony Walters and Dagmar Walters (New York: Palgrave Macmillan, 2015), 64.

12 Brandon LaBelle, *Lexicon of the Mouth: Poetics and Politics of Voice and the Oral Imaginary* (London: Bloomsbury, 2014), 13.

13 Charles Camic, "Charisma: Its Varieties, Preconditions, and Consequences," *Sociological Inquiry* 50, no. 1 (1980), 5–23. Camic analyzes Weber's writings in chronological order and underscores the heterogeneity of his data, offering Freudian psychoanalytical thought as a clarifying framework for understanding "extraordinary needs."

14 Laura Kunreuther, *Voicing Subjects: Public Intimacy and Mediation in Kathmandu* (Berkeley: University of California Press, 2014), 4.

across media motivates my comparison of three figures—as vocalists as well as as transcendent figurative voices. I situate sound and speech as a dynamic force for their elevation and configuration as representatives of a greater goal and greater polity.[15]

In Gdańsk with Penderecki

Penderecki is perhaps not the most obvious composer to have been cast as Solidarity's star. Witold Lutosławski reprimanded the Polish Composers' Union for their lack of professional attention to the Gdańsk strikes in September 1980, delivered a brief speech at the Congress of Culture in 1981, stood through the vigil at Jerzy Popiełuszko's graveside in October 1984, recused himself from Polish stages from 1982 to 1987 as part of the so-called boycott of state-sponsored culture, and eventually was selected as a member of Tadeusz Mazowiecki's Cultural Council as part of the transformation of the Communist Party. But he preferred to stay socially distant from politics.[16] Henryk Mikołaj Górecki was, for the most part, gravely ill and withdrew himself from public engagements.[17] Penderecki, however, was visible and audible: this is a peek behind his scenes.

Let us first turn to the portrait of the composer by one champion, Kaczyński. The 1981 radio address is littered with attention to the remarkable in Penderecki's career, compounding the description of a larger than life personality. The composer has the ability to create new sounds out of some of the most well-known instruments of the symphony orchestra in *Threnody for the Victims of Hiroshima* (1960), he explains. Penderecki's music is saturated with creativity and innovation, despite the fact that his formative years were during—as Kaczyński describes it—the Polish cultural void before 1956. He writes that the composer's religious music shows his humanistic ethics. The critic claims that, without pandering to his audience, Penderecki responds to people, to his audience's emotions. He switched *Threnody*'s title from its duration, 8'37", to its commemorative inscription, for example, a move that Kaczyński understands as engagement with the emotional responses

---

15 John Durham Peters, "The Voice and Modern Media," in *Kunst-Stimmen*, edited by Doris Kolesch and Jenny Schrödel (Berlin: Theater der Zeit, 2004), 85–100.

16 Andrea F. Bohlman, "Lutosławski's Political Refrains," in *Lutosławski's Worlds*, edited by Lisa Jakelski and Nicholas Reyland (Woodbridge, UK: Boydell and Brewer, 2018), 273–300.

17 He discusses and apologizes for his health in a discussion transcribed in *Aktualna sytuacja muzyki religijnej i liturgicznej w Polsce*, edited by Maria Bogusławska (Warsaw: Akademia Teologii Katolickiej, 1988), 54–55. See also Adrian Thomas, *Górecki* (Oxford: Clarendon Press, 1997), 101.

of his audiences, who would hear the nuclear in his sound world anyway.[18] Peppered with excitement, the address outlines a larger than life persona at the zenith of his impact, nationally and internationally. In 1981, this energy and prominence distinguishes Penderecki from his contemporary, Henryk Mikołaj Górecki, and the sage elder, Witold Lutosławski, whom Kaczyński is careful to assert are at least as talented.

As Ruth Seehaber has illustrated, music critics on both sides of the Iron Curtain reductively and strategically branded Lutosławski, Górecki, and Penderecki as the "Polish School," a label that located a place for this Warsaw Pact nation in the European avant-garde while also marking it as Other—a border that also had stylistic resonances.[19] They participated in the mid-twentieth-century (and, indeed, still ongoing) tendency to mark Eastern Europe with national labels, while the "European avant-garde" comfortably enveloped and universalized the contrasting compositional techniques and technologies funded by the Darmstadt International Summer Courses, IRCAM (the Paris-based Institute for Research and Coordination in Acoustics/Music), and the Studio di fonologia at the state radio in Italy.[20] One result of this act of grouping was that the career trajectories of these three composers, as different as their home cities of Warsaw, Katowice, and Cracow, were set in comparison with each other. Whatever reason for Kaczyński's selection of Penderecki, he does not mean to elevate him above the others. He makes

---

18 Penderecki in fact responded to a marketing suggestion by the director of the Polish Music Publishers (PWM), see Adrian Thomas, *Polish Music since Szymanowski* (Cambridge: Cambridge University Press, 2005), 205.

19 Ruth Seehaber, *Die "polnische Schule" in der neuen Musik: Befragung eines musikhistorischen Topos* (Cologne: Böhlau, 2009). To be sure, the generation gap between Lutosławski and his younger colleagues—along with his distance from the "sonoristic" timbral manipulations of the orchestra associated with the School—often excluded him from the explicit label. But, as the name of the webportal hosted in the 2010s by the National Audiovisual Institute of Poland— "Three Composers"—makes explicit, he is essential to the trinity. For an extended discussion of the many categories at stake in the early Cold War avant-garde in Poland, see Lisa Jakelski, *Making New Music in Cold War Poland: The Warsaw Autumn Festival, 1956–1968* (Oakland: University of California Press, 2017), in particular 11–35.

20 Richard Taruskin baldly describes the "covert" nationalism of the universalizing spirit behind unlabeled German music in the *New Grove Dictionary on Music and Musicians*: "Thus what began as a philosophy of diversity became, in the case of music, one of hegemony. The programme of German nationalism quickly metamorphosed, for music, into one of German universalism. In the history of no other modern art has nationalism been so pervasive—yet so covert—an issue." In Richard Taruskin, "Nationalism," *Grove Music Online, Oxford Music Online*. Oxford University Press; https://www-oxfordmusiconline-com.libproxy.lib.unc.edu/grovemusic/view/10.1093/gmo/9781561592630.001.0001/omo-9781561592630-e-0000050846.

clear that Penderecki is part of a larger-scale sensation, what he calls "Polish music of our times," an unmissable conflation of the vibrant and powerful energy of music with the ethos of political change underfoot.[21]

Through Solidarity's nascence and perseverance, Penderecki was visible on the podium and at public events; he was prolific as a composer. This presence and power emerges as mighty across political viewpoints. A report from the Polish Consulate in the Soviet Union waxed as euphorically as Kaczyński about the composer's visit to Leningrad in November 1986.[22] At the helm of that city's Philharmonic for two concerts, Penderecki conducted Dmitri Shostakovich's Fourteenth Symphony. He attracted capacity audiences and elicited from them extended "enthusiastic" applause. In the write-up the correspondent to the Communist Party's Culture Department is careful to underscore that the "enormous occasion" of these appearances stems from his work "as a conductor as well as as a composer."

"Penderecki's Secret" captures the spirit of an exceptional moment of international relevance and reach for the composer. Kaczyński is captivated by what he considers pronounced and sustained popularity. From 1976 to 1990, Penderecki received some of the most prominent commissions of his career. On the occasion of the US bicentennial, the Lyric Opera of Chicago commissioned *Paradise Lost*. For the Berlin Philharmonic's hundredth anniversary in 1982, he composed his Second Cello Concerto, to be performed by Mstislav Rostropovich, who conducted the US premiere of his major religious work of the decade, the *Polish Requiem* (1980–84). The Corpuzulia of Venezuela marked the two hundredth birthday of its military hero, Simón Bolívar, with Penderecki's *Concerto per Viola* in the hands of José Vazquez. An opera, *Die schwarze Maske* (*The Black Mask*, 1986), was instigated by and premiered at the Salzburger Festspiele. The French government asked the Polish composer to participate in their extensive campaign to mold the two hundredth anniversary of the outbreak of the French Revolution as a rearticulation of the Declaration of the Rights of Man and of the Citizen, and he responded with his Fourth Symphony, a one-movement work with the subtitle "Adagio." Through the decade he received recognition from a range of powerful institutions: Penderecki was decorated with a First Class Award from the Polish state (1983), a Grammy (1988), and the Jean Sibelius Award (1983).

"Penderecki's Secret" also bubbles with Kaczyński's thirst for Penderecki's prominence, for a composer whose power is "not only musical, but also for broader culture [*ogólno-kulturowo*]." It shines a light on the prestige and prominence Penderecki had in the moment of Solidarity's coherence. The critic

---

21 Kaczyński, "Penderecki's Secret," 2.
22 LVI-1738, WK KC PZPR, AAN.

positions Penderecki as the "artistic witness" of the political moment, one in which it is possible that "uncertain sovereignty of particular nations" and the "continued existence of humanity" is under threat. Dark allusions cloud the speech's conclusion. Though Kaczyński does not mention it—two brief mentions of Pope John Paul II (Karol Wojtyła) are as close as he comes to discussing Polish current events—Penderecki had taken bold moves to affiliate himself with Solidarity just weeks before. His most recent commission, *Lacrimosa* for soprano, choir, and orchestra, had become inextricably linked with Solidarity because of its prominence at the unveiling of the Monument to the Fallen Workers of 1970 at the entrance to the Lenin Shipyards in Gdańsk on December 16. Penderecki's dedication of the piece to Lech Wałęsa and Solidarity cemented the connection between Penderecki and Solidarity at the time of Kaczyński's address. By 1984 the movement was the cornerstone of his *Polish Requiem* (1984), a work that enacts the synergy between Polish Roman Catholicism and musical nationalism through liturgy.[23]

The 1980 commemoration event itself was a major triumph for the newly legal union, bringing to close a decade of demands that the government acknowledge the lives lost in its suppression of labor demonstrations across factories along the Baltic coast. Lech Wałęsa and an advisory committee pulled out the stops to create an occasion that would illustrate what Solidarity could do. They invited Party officials, who sat and observed instead of orchestrating the event. A photography exhibition brought to light the violated bodies, and late in the evening performances of Mozart's Requiem at the Cathedral of Saint Brigid in Gdańsk and at the Parish of the Sacred Heart in Gdynia by regional orchestras provided strains of solemnity.[24]

On December 16, 1980, in Gdańsk, the greatest symbolic weight was on the newly erected monument, a trio of crosses that catapult upward for forty-two meters. Its air of authenticity stemmed out of its design by an engineer employed at the shipyard, Bogdan Pietruszka. Each cross bears an anchor crucified across it, bringing the trades of the region—dockworker, sailor, and shipyard worker—in touch with the sacrifice of the four workers killed on precisely this ground in 1970.[25] Though Czesław Miłosz turned down the commission to write a poem to engrave upon its base, a verse of his translation of Psalm 29 serves as an epitaph, along with two other inscriptions,

---

23 Regina Chłopicka, "Krzysztof Penderecki's St. Luke Passion, Polish Requiem and Credo in the Context of Polish History," in *Krzysztof Penderecki: Musik im Kontext*, edited by Helmut Loos and Stefan Keym (Leipzig: Gudrun Schröder Verlag, 2006), 41–63.

24 Marcin Gugulski, "Od grudnia do grudnia," *Głos* 34, no. 1 (1982), 9–17.

25 The authoritative discussion of the monument remains Jan Kubik, *The Power of Symbols*, 196–206. The fourth worker died from injuries acquired in the initial assault in the days that followed, a nuance that explains the recourse to the heavily laden symbolism of the triad.

one a quote from a sermon by Pope John Paul II. The permission to build the monument, extended in response to the August demands after years of unofficial and illegal commemorations, made the exegesis of the looming artwork's materials and symbols a central talking point for discussions about art's capacity to support resistance. Preceding the unveiling, the official newspaper most closely associated with the opposition, Cracow's *Catholic Weekly* (*Tygodnik Powszechny*), published a front-page spread, "Monument and People," complete with large photographs of its mounting.[26] In his influential essays on the "ethics of solidarity," the philosopher, priest, and "Solidarity chaplain" Józef Tischner isolated this monument to claim that "one work of solidarity is the work of art—work among people, for people, and with people."[27] His theological analysis of the monument is grounded in the Bible, but also driven by a hope that individuals will stand at the monument and ask: "What does this artwork tell me?"[28]

We might imagine that we also stand at the monument—at its historical unveiling in Gdańsk when Penderecki's vocal writing (via soprano Jadwiga Gadulanka) unfolded across the grounds (Figure 5.1). *Lacrimosa* received its most significant performance through tape playback during that commemoration of the dead on a cold and inclement December dusk. Andrzej Wajda, the celebrated film director, presided over the evening's dramaturgy. His career to date, from *Ashes and Diamonds* (*Popiół i diament*, 1958) to *Man of Marble* (*Człowiek z marmuru*, 1976), had touched on issues of Polish identity and the struggle for sovereignty. He would be an outspoken advocate of Solidarity from 1980 through the dissolution of the People's Republic—even one of Lutosławski's select and few confidants on politics.[29] Under Wajda's supervision, the ceremony was laden with multimodal nationalist narratives.

Organized sound and ceremonial music telescoped the attention of those gathered over the course of the event, an extended litany of the dead. A carillon at a cathedral within audible range rang out "The Oath" ("Rota"), a 1910 hymn with text by Maria Konopnicka, as people gathered over the course of the afternoon.[30] As government officials arrived, the army band performed the "March of the Generals" (1924) by Henryk Melcer-Szczawiński.[31]

---

26 Jacek Susuł, "Pomnik i ludzie," *Tygodnik Powszechny*, December 12, 1980, 1, 8.

27 Józef Tischner, *The Spirit of Solidarity* (San Francisco: Harper & Row, 1984), 35.

28 Tischner, *The Spirit of Solidarity*, 36.

29 Grzegorz Michalski, *Lutosławski w pamięci: 20 rozmów o kompozytorze* (Gdańsk: słowo/obraz terytoria, 2007), 227–36.

30 An amateur film produced by Janusz Wisiński, which he posted to YouTube on May 7, 2010, captures this moment; https://www.youtube.com/watch?v=lSR7DT2am1Y. On the early arrival of the public, see Kubik, *The Power of Symbols against the Symbols of Power*, 200.

31 The Radio Free Europe broadcast of the event, as part 123 of its documentary series *How Solidarity Was Formed*, gives the impression that the march flanked the

FIGURE 5.1. Unveiling of the Monument to the Fallen Workers, Gdańsk, December 16, 1980.
Photographer unknown, Ośrodek Karta.

official beginning signaled by the simultaneous bells and alarms. ("Jak kszałtowało się Solidarność, cz. 123," broadcast December 18, 1981, accessible at the Radio Freedom archive http://www.polskieradio.pl/68/2461/Audio/297222). I have not come across a first-person account that mentions this musical performance, though none contains an inventory of all of the sounds or songs. It is notable, for example, that the ceremony seems not to have contained the national anthem, as had the illegal commemoration one year earlier, as described in Andrzej Friszke, *Opozycja polityczna w PRL 1945–1980* (Aneks: London, 1984), 574.

Moments later, factory whistles, church bells, and other sirens cleared the air—this is the choreographed beginning of the ceremony ⏵.[32] Those gathered were led by an amplified voice in a communal performance of "The Oath," this time with orchestral playback. The five-minute *Lacrimosa* was piped in over the loudspeakers before the actor Daniel Olbrychski recited first Psalm 11 ("For the Lord is righteous, / he loves justice; / the upright will see his face.") and then the names of the dead. The public's involvement continued through the litany: they responded, "Is among us!" after bearing witness to each name.

A collective moment of silence followed, broken by Lech Wałęsa as the first to address the crowd, followed by the Party's first secretary in Gdańsk. At the outset of his speech, Wałęsa lit a torch at the monument's base; after the government official spoke, delegations laid floral arrangements in the same place—their symmetrical attendance in counterpoint with the enumeration of those who perished. Catholic liturgy framed the final portion of the ceremony as the archbishop of Cracow, Cardinal Franciszek Macharski, held mass. Called to worship by the communal performance of "God Save Poland" (see Chapter 6), Macharski's firm tenor voice makes his twenty-minute service, which included a sermon based on an exegesis of Psalm 37 (on the destiny of the wicked and the righteous), stand out as the brightest and most sustained oration of the event.

The mass is the contribution that attracted the applause most audible across recordings. In movie theaters, people could watch a short documentary film of the ceremony as part of a long-standing series, the *Polish Film Chronicle*.[33] This composition begins with a hollow and repetitive drum pattern, a foreboding underlay to the black-and-white footage. It omits the musical overtures and keeps communal sounds (besides clapping) from the final cut. The source sounds beyond the addresses, however, are not unimportant, however: it foregrounds an (abbreviated) minute of silence. In contrast, the audiotape recording kept by the Solidarity Union "for internal union use" and broadcast on the anniversaries from 1982 onward through Radio Solidarity, adds music.[34] The introductory text specifies the date and time of the location over one of their musical signals, the first statement of the theme of Antonín Dvořak's Ninth Symphony ("From the New World"), fourth movement,

---

32 The tape recording of this event for Radio Solidarity is archived digitally online; http://www.wszechnica.solidarnosc.org.pl/?page_id=2036. The introductory text specifies the date and time of the location over one of their musical signals.

33 *Polish Film Chronicle* 80/52F (1981).

34 Archived online, http://www.wszechnica.solidarnosc.org.pl/?page_id=2036.

mm. 10–25. Janina Jankowska's documentary, *Polish August*, grabs sounds from this recording (see Chapter 3).

The event was saturated with secular and sacred rituals across the sensorium. The sonic diversity and pagaentry at this event kept in motion what Halina Filipowicz describes as the "intersecting spheres of cultural mythology and historical fact" of Solidarity's historical commemorations.[35] What did the between five and seven thousand gathered at the monument's base hear?[36] The distance of audio and video recordings obscure elements of the experience on the ground, however. Witness the ambivalence transcribed and interrogated by Marcin Gugulski in the oppositional periodical *Voice* (*Głos*), published in the *drugi obieg* (second circulation), in one of the first written reports:[37]

> The terrible calm of the crowd, frost, drizzle, no reaction to the sermon or to the address at all: this all exploded in an urgency, in silence, and in short, nervous bravos. What does it mean, that instead of genuinely and joyously applauding, as they usually do, they perform just strong and swift little bravos? They are cold, or they are afraid of how Big Brother might respond? They feel like they are at a funeral and want to guard the seriousness of the moment? Or are they suggesting it is dumb to applaud for colleagues from the branches of the trade unions? I have heard all four answers.[38]

Gugulski is attuned to the power of public theater, the public's ability to perform an event's mundanity. He is disappointed that after the "years of silence" following the attacks, the ceremony is poorly received. His uncertainty and even vulnerability about the affective resonance suggest that the commemoration was unsettled as it unfolded in real time. Retrospective accounts obscure this ambiguity. In 1994 sociologist Jan Kubik recalled the peace he found standing at the monument, in the fact that "society was celebrating itself without the state's participation."[39] In 1987, journalist Neal Ascherson framed his own experience with a particular focus on music: "In [1980],

---

35 Halina Filipowicz, "Re-Envisioning Solidarity: History, Agency, and the Politics of Performance," *Theatre Journal* 62, no. 3 (2010), 335.

36 This commonly quoted rough estimate is based on Marcin Gugulski's claim that there were between three and six people per square foot ("Od grudnia do grudniu," 15). Penderecki himself claimed there were two million in an interview, an exaggeration that has had traction in Polish-language musicology. See Chłopicka, "Krzysztof Penderecki's St. Luke Passion, Polish Requiem and Credo in the Context of Polish History," 53.

37 See chapter 1 for a discussion of the unofficial print culture of the opposition, known as the drugi obieg.

38 In Gugulski, "Od grudnia do grudniu," 15.

39 Kubik, *Power of Symbols against the Symbols of Power*, 200.

the *Lacrimosa* was about reconciliation as well as grief, about the hope—background to the whole ceremony—that Solidarity and the Communist State would be able to work together in a cleaner, freer Poland."[40]

Wałęsa (as dedicatee) and Wajda (as commissioner) guided Penderecki toward Gdańsk. Through that performance, Penderecki's vocal writing emanates out of that scene, and takes on its meaning for Solidarity's history ▶. The solo soprano lament that *Lacrimosa* supports is the linchpin for the composition's power as musical mourning. Buttressed by full orchestra, she stands out of the musical texture: the soloist carves out ascending minor sixths with step-wise resolution as she repeats, "Full of tears!"[41] A homophonic chorus responds to her pleading, as she crescendos from near silence to forte through each musical phrase. After every line, the collective soothes at greater length with rhythms that invoke a heartbeat. Their regular pulse in compound time complements, even resolves, the suspensions strained between the soloist and orchestra against measured quarter notes. At the assertion of guilt ("Judicandus homo reus"), Penderecki inverts the crucial interval in the solo line and the movement concludes with the chorus at rest and a Picardy third. The two-part structure of this brief movement has a rather straightforward dramaturgy: the sorrowful are first summoned together and then beg for mercy as a collective. Well-established in the return to romantic harmonic language and timbral preferences he had begun in the *St. Luke Passion* (1966), Penderecki converses most explicitly with the same discrete movement from Verdi's Requiem, which shares several aspects of orchestration. Strings and winds sustain (and occasionally echo), buoying the vocal work toward a place of rest. The four-part chorus meditates in prosodic declamation of the final pleading text: "Therefore spare him, O God, Merciful Lord Jesus, Grant them eternal rest."

Sparse chimes ring—rarely on the downbeat—through the second half of the movement. They almost clang, functioning as a seam between the composition's thorough notation and the less ordered open-air environment of the December commemoration. The larger ritual in which the playback occurred was, after all, itself structured through the tolls of time. The expansive four-octave register outlined by the lyric soprano and lower strings in the opening texture allowed the sobbing motives carried by Jadwiga Gadulanka to stand out in that first recording (Example 5.1). Outdoors, Penderecki's orchestration also allowed the orchestra's rumbling and pulsing sounds to

---

40 Neal Ascherson, "Requiem for an Old Piano Banger," *The Observer*, January 11, 1987, p. 7.

41 Perhaps because *Lacrimosa* is the germinal movement and the sixth is the seed within, the resolution of this minor-sixth sigh also provides formal unity for the larger composition, the *Polish Requiem*, appearing across its movements.

EXAMPLE 5.1. Krzysztof Penderecki, *Lacrimosa* (1980), mm. 1–10.
© 1982 Schott Music GmbH & Co. KG, Mainz, Germany. All rights reserved.
Used by permission of European American Music Distributors Company, sole US and Canadian agent for Schott Music GmbH & Co. KG, Mainz, Germany.

commingle with the ambient space of the capacious plaza through which they were amplified.

In the radio playback of the live event, the rumble of the lower strings as the movement begins are barely audible as music instead of as ambient sounds. The soprano line was easily distorted through the capture: when I have heard re-transmissions on the home recordings of Radio Solidarity, the signal is clipped so that Gadalunka bleats and there are halos of fuzz.[42] The television broadcast had access to the source recording, and its non-synchronous

---

42 For example, at the Archiv der Forschungsstelle Osteuropa an der Universität Bremen and the Solidarity Collection at the Museum of Independence, Warsaw. See Chapter 1 for further discussion of these taping practices.

EXAMPLE 5.1. (Continued)

edit on top of the religious service situated the occasional offering as the musical summary of its affective power. As discussed in Chapter 3, the playback recording played a crucial role in the definitive radio reportage of the strikes of August 1980 by Janina Jankowska. Jankowska and her team gave music, and particularly *Lacrimosa*, pride of place in the bricolage of sound documents that shape the narrative. The composition adds stereo sound *and* affective power to an otherwise mono and often monotonous collection of source recordings of negotiations and street sounds. With this swift kaleidoscopic hearing of *Lacrimosa*'s live sound and refracted amplification in mind, Ascherson's emphasis on the work—and his choice to frame it as "background"—takes on new significance. He captures the way in which Penderecki's contribution can sum up the symbolic power of the monument on its own. As the composer put it in a 2004 interview, "There was something seething at the time, and that work had to arise."[43] He has reinvested his pride in the work's politics—a move quite contrapuntal to, for example, Jacek Kaczmarski's mournful rejection of the adoption of "Walls" by the opposition as anthem (see Chapter 3).

The signifying work of *Lacrimosa* at the monument reveals a thirst for classical—even monumental—music at the foundation of Poland's Solidarity. For Mieczysław Tomaszewski, a musicologist who is also a close friend of the composer, Penderecki "dares" to write a work for the commemoration, and the movement itself is "brimming with an expression evoking an aura of Mozart's Requiem, becomes a part of history in the making."[44] Almost a quarter century removed, he reads a synergistic relationship between memory work and ethical leadership. "In both spheres of the composer's life—in terms of his compositional activity and on a level of purely human behavior—one of the principal characteristics of his personality is discernible: the courage of his convictions."

Lacrimosa is neither a commentary on Solidarity nor a commemorative work that responds specifically to 1970, though it has taken on cultural significance as both. The more complex origin story does not, to my mind, undermine the work that *Lacrimosa* did to shape a musical politics. It does, however, undermine the hand-in-hand image of Penderecki with his activist compatriots. In her 2013 documentary film, *Paths through the Labyrinth*, director Anna Schmidt captured a conversation between the composer and his 1980 patron, Wajda.[45] *Lacrimosa* was the first of their many collaborations, securing a professional relationship between Cracow-based artists that approached difficult topics in Polish history. It would continue through the 2007 film *Katyń*, which itself honors and narrates another massacre, that of Polish generals by the NKVD (predecessors to the KGB) in 1940. In the filmed conversation they casually recall the circumstances of *Lacrimosa*'s genesis with contradictory understandings of its inspiration and instigation. "The

---

43 In Paweł Strzelecki, *"Nowy romantyzm" w twórczości kompozytorów polskich po roku 1975* (Cracow: Musica Iagiellonica, 2006), 443.

44 Mieczysław Tomaszewski, *Penderecki* (Warsaw: Adam Mickiewicz Institute, 2003), 27.

45 Anna Schmidt, *Paths through the Labyrinth: The Composer Krzysztof Penderecki*, DVD, Berlin: C Major Entertainment, 2014.

committee behind the monument very much wanted Krzysztof Penderecki to write the music that would accompany its unveiling," Wajda recalls telling Penderecki over the telephone. "And you responded," he continues, "'Yes, I have such a work: *Lacrimosa*.'" As he continues, it is clear that Wajda wants to commend Penderecki's knack for the right music at the right time. The film director did not, at first, realize the poignancy of Penderecki's offering, he relates, because he was unaware of the liturgical function of the requiem mass portion.

As soon as Wajda sets one mythical origin story in place, Penderecki interrupts with his own version. "But!" the composer says with a smirk, "That's actually not what happened. Because at the time I hadn't even conceived of a piece like *Lacrimosa*." He explains that he didn't want to lose the commission, so he felt the need to stretch the truth: "I had the desire to write such a work." Penderecki had recently revisited the text from the Latin mass for the dead, so, "the text came to mind, and what better text could there be?" The assembly of the *Polish Requiem*, first with the addition of the *Agnus Dei* (in memoriam Cardinal Stefan Wyszyński, 1981) and the completion of the mass for its 1984 premiere, is rooted, he explains, in the impetus from Wałęsa and Wajda, flattering his guest and embracing their mutual historical importance.

During the People's Republic, however, Penderecki was happy to make explicit the connection between the opposition and *Lacrimosa*. In an influential (and somewhat controversial) interview published in 1987 by the West German magazine *Der Spiegel*, the conversation veered to the relative political and creative freedom that composers enjoyed over writers in Poland. The magazine provoked him: "Would [he] dare set the text of an underground poet?" Penderecki offered a confident response:

> Of course, why not? In the end, everyone knows that I wrote the *Lacrimosa* on commission from Lech Wałęsa, and that piece is performed everywhere. When it was performed for the first time, then, on December 16, 1980, for the vernissage of the Memorial for the Victims of the Gdańsk Uprising [*sic*], almost two million people were there, and all the streets were full. Some people cried. One experiences something like that rarely and never in a concert hall. Hereby I want to say: I, too, have been engaged (*engagiert*).[46]

He might have nodded to other moments when he stood in solidarity. For example, as rector of the State Academy of Music in Cracow, Penderecki had

---

[46] "'Ein Verlangen nach reinem Dur': Spiegel-Gespräch mit Krzysztof Penderecki," *Der Spiegel* 41, no. 2 (1987), 144–46. This interview is likely the origin of the previously discussed exaggerated figure of attendance.

lent his name, with ten other intellectuals, to a student initiative in that city to uncouple student trade unions from the state.[47] He attended and allowed his compositions to be performed at the oppositional and surveilled Weeks of Christian Culture, semi-annual symposia about the relationship between artists, society, and the church.[48]

Instead, it is Penderecki's presence in Gdańsk—via his music—that makes the strongest case for his political engagement (*działanie*). He has evoked that stage's cultural historical importance to make sweeping assertions and assumptions about personal politics and the professional risk he undertook during this decade. In a 1985 interview for *Tydzień Polski* (*Polish Weekly*), an émigré weekly printed in London, Penderecki framed his role heroically. "I was practically the only one who supported Solidarity. None of my musician colleagues would go to the trouble. Wałęsa asked Lutosławski and many others, but no one dared compose [something] for Gdańsk. In Gdynia, in Gdańsk, in Szczecin, in Poznań: everyone was afraid. And only I did it."[49] As part of the press that excited a Polish audience for the work's London performance under Penderecki's baton, the comment's self-serving nature is perhaps understandable, even expected. Explicitly framing his actions in relation to others' weaknesses, the composer played up the cultural power ascribed to him by people like Kaczyński. This 1985 narrative of *Lacrimosa*'s commission also circulated in a later, contrapuntal rendition—by Wajda. When asked to confirm Penderecki's anecdote for a 2005 publication, Wajda explained that only Penderecki could have received the commission: Wałęsa had only heard of "one contemporary composer's name."[50] Already in the spring of 1981, Wajda had expressed frustration at the light-speed organization of the Gdańsk event, with many organizational decisions made as quickly as possible.[51] While Penderecki would have his audience

---

47 Jan Józef Lipski, *KOR: A History of the Workers' Defense Committee in Poland, 1976–1981* (Berkeley: University of California Press, 1985), 403; Friszke, *Opozycja polityczna w PRL 1945–1980*, 535. The letter served to support the "flying university"—a network of unofficial educational settings. This particular moment of friction is discussed in Ryszard Terlecki, *Uniwersytet latający i towarzystwo kursów naukowych, 1977–1981* (Instytut Europejskich Studiów Społecznych w Rzeszowie: Cracow and Rzeszów, 2000), 175.

48 The Party tracked those who participated, though it was not illegal to do so. One such report mentions Penderecki among a list of other musicians that included Stefania Woytowicz, Witold Lutosławski, Stanisław Sojka, and Maciej Zembaty; LVI-1416, WK KC PZPR, AAN.

49 "Krzysztof Penderecki dyryguje 'Polskim Reqiuem,'" in interview with J. Motylewicz, *Tydzień Polski* 3 (January 19, 1985), 15.

50 Danuta Gwizdalanka and Krzysztof Meyer, *Lutosławski: Droga do mistrzostwa* (Cracow: Polskie Wydawnictwo Muzyczne, 2005), 315.

51 "Uzupełniam swój życiorys: Rozmowa z Andrzejem Wajdą," *Tygodnik Solidarność* 2 (April 10, 1981), no page number.

believe Solidarity was desperate for music, the director paints a picture of a musically naive and haphazard coincidence.

Through the 1980s, audiences increasingly heard a narrative of defiance in and experienced emotional catharsis through the *Lacrimosa*. Westerneas critical reception fueled the myth in particular, as Eastern Europe became the focus of "Western desire for lofty political meditations and courageous nonconformism."[52] A music critic for the *Washington Post* described an audience transfixed at the 1986 Boston premiere of the entire mass for the dead. "At about 4 this afternoon, the audience rose in Symphony Hall here and stood silently for several minutes. The vivid, brilliant *Lacrimosa* movement of Penderecki's 'Polish Requiem' was what brought the audience to its feet in a gesture echoed at the end of the concert by a ten-minute standing ovation."[53] Joseph McLellan insists this "deeply emotional" music greater than itself:

> But words and music were not the main reason for standing—a gesture audiences usually reserve for the "Star-Spangled Banner" and Handel's "Hallelujah" chorus. The *Lacrimosa*, the first part of the requiem composed by Penderecki, was commissioned by the Polish union Solidarity in memory of the dockworkers massacred in Gdansk in 1970. Now this music is treated as a sort of Solidarity anthem—music that cannot be heard sitting down. Although this was the first Boston performance of the Polish Requiem, the audience clearly knew the meaning of the music. Symphony Hall was packed and many in the audience were wearing Solidarity buttons.[54]

He conjures Penderecki's magic with the emphasis on the music's enchantment.[55] His exegesis of the audience's reverent rise links an act of violence and the resonance of this vocal music. He describes a congregational response and uprising at once.

Other critics focused on the work's express religiosity and commitment to tonality. In the program note for the New York Philharmonic's first performances of the movement on May 7–9, 1981, Benjamin Folkman explains Penderecki's turn from the avant-garde on universalist devotional terms: "The

---

52 Jonathan Bolton, *Worlds of Dissent: Charter 77, The Plastic People of the Universe, and Czech Culture under Communism* (Cambridge, MA: Harvard University Press, 2012), 2.

53 Joseph McLellan, "Resounding 'Polish Requiem,'" *The Washington Post,* January 27, 1986, p. B7.

54 Joseph McLellan, "Resounding 'Polish Requiem.'"

55 I gesture here toward what Jeffers Engelhardt calls "secular enchantment," or "the religious absolute given voice according to and against the limits and norms of the secular" (4). See Jeffers Engelhardt, *Singing the Right Way: Orthodox Christians and Enchantment in Estonia* (New York: Oxford University Press, 2014), 14–16.

music is notably restrained in expression and utilizes materials of extreme simplicity, almost as if Penderecki were deliberately cultivating a stylistic anonymity suitable to the selfless universality of worship."[56] Folkman positions the work as a community invitation. The 1987 *Spiegel* interviewer describes the movement as "cuddly and innocuous" (*kuschelig und harmlos*), but Penderecki pushes back, almost suggesting its simplistic profundity: "If you listen properly, you will realize that it sounds different."[57]

Penderecki under Watch

Media spotlights shone *Lacrimosa*'s scenes in Gdańsk and Boston. Behind the scenes, the Party (PZPR) handled Penderecki's persona. The bureaucratic machine focused on nitty-gritty details—absent was the grand vision of someone like Kaczyński. When Penderecki spoke in the name of Poland, he came under close scrutiny; otherwise he was largely left alone. The Department of Culture kept tabs on Penderecki's public appearances. He maintained their confidence in him even as they tracked him—probably enjoying some kind of reciprocal understanding not made explicit in the documentary record. Pushed to critique the Party by *Der Spiegel*, the composer does not comply, instead waxing on about his home: "I am not forced to live there, and I am frequently in the West. But I live there purposefully, not least because the present moment [*Gegenwart*] and my music are very important for Poland."[58] Penderecki's remarks ring out in accordance with what Miklós Haraszti influentially called a "mutual embrace." This cooperation between the artistic and political elite to craft a symbiotic relationship under state socialism, he suggested, had aesthetic consequences. For the Hungarian dissident, the comfort of the nation, of being at home, is the condition for this implicit contract: "The state is able to domesticate the artist because the artist has already made the state his home."[59] With the normalization policies of the 1980s in effect, the Party worked to nurture the cultural status quo and to keep artistic celebrities innocuous (see Chapter 1). As the Chair of the Subcommittee on Music (1984–87), luthier Włodzimierz Kamiński, put it: "Poland's musical society is too strong to allow a general collapse of musical arts."[60]

---

56 Benjamin Folkman, "Notes for May 7–9, 1981 (subscription season)," *Digital Archives of the New York Philharmonic*, 28D.

57 "Ein Verlangen nach reinem Dur," 145.

58 "Ein Verlangen nach reinem Dur," 146.

59 Miklós Haraszti, *The Velvet Prison: Artists under State Socialism*, translated by Katalin and Stephen Landesmann with Steve Wasserman (New York: Basic Books, 1987), 5.

60 Włodzimierz Kamiński, "Polska kultura muzyczna: Stan i potrzeby," LVI-210, WK KC PZPR, AAN. See Chapter 1 for a more extensive discussion of the Party and this Subcommittee.

In the PZPR, Penderecki's name had a certain cachet at the end of the Cold War, even though he was never a member. In the late 1970s the Central Committee, following Penderecki's (disorderly, from their perspective) genuflection in front of Cardinal Wyszyński, had "demanded that the incident be passed over in silence" because of the composer's renown.[61] One document that screened artists for a Cultural Committee described him as "loyal."[62] Soprano Stefania Woytowicz's citation for her 1985 Individual Award, First Class, makes special note of the prominence she achieved as a performer of Penderecki's works.[63] The mention, which recognized her activities as a vocalist and in the promotion of Polish music, underscores that she is the "single performer to have all of [Penderecki's] vocal-instrumental works in her repertory."[64] Woytowicz, who also made the premiere recording of the soprano solo in Henryk Mikołaj Górecki's now-celebrated Third Symphony, was linked exclusively with Penderecki in this release, further evidence of his supreme notoriety and respect.

Other discussions of Penderecki's activities balanced the composer's status as an international celebrity with the close watch on his publicly visible activities. In 1987, his most recent opera, *The Black Mask* (*Die schwarze Maske*, 1986), was given its Polish premiere in Poznań. Its success at the Salzburg Festival in August 1986 meant that the production was highly anticipated.[65] The October performance was designed to fête the composer's successful career. It coincided with a ceremony awarding him an honorary doctorate from the city's renowned academic institution, the Adam Mickiewicz University. Party officials and musical luminaries descended

---

61 Discussed in Andrzej Paczkowski, *The Spring Will Be Ours: Poland and the Poles from Occupation to Freedom,* translated by Jane Cave (University Park: Pennsylvania State University Press, 1995), 396.

62 See a discussion of these committees as formalities in the face of financial and political weakness during the late 1980s in Wolfgang Schlott with Ivo Bock and Hartmute Trepper, *Kultur im Umbruch: Polen—Tschechoslowakei—Rußland* (Bremen: Temmen, 1992), 24.

63 "Wniosek o przyznanie nagrody indywidualnej i stopnia za wybitne osiągnięcia w dziedzinie wokalistyki i propagandę muzyki polskiej," LVI-1735, WK KC PZPR, AAN.

64 LVI-1735, WK KC PZPR, AAN.

65 Penderecki had presented the opera to composers and musicologists at the annual Baranów seminar, and it was previewed in the biweekly music periodical *Ruch Muzyczny* with two articles ("Krzysztof Penderecki w Baranowie," 20–21, and Izabella Grzenkowicz, "O 'czarnej masce' bez maski," 3–4, *Ruch Muzyczny* 30, no. 26 [1986]). Two productions, one in German and one in Polish, would be performed by the Poznań and Warsaw companies, respectively, at the Warsaw Autumn Festival in 1988. It also received a rave review, from the composer as well as one of Poland's premiere critics, Ludwik Erhardt, after the Poznań premiere ("Die schwarze Maske' in Poznań," *Polish Music* 23, no. 1 [1988], 33–35).

upon the production's opening night, working to ensure that the composer would project a positive image of Polish musical culture in his acceptance speech.

The Black Mask was a vehicle to promote the composer's music in Poland for Grzegorz Wiśniewski, the opera enthusiast and literary scholar who liaised for contemporary music within the Party in the 1980s. In a report for the PZPR, he described the national premiere of Penderecki's operatic *danse macabre* with fervor and attention to the musical work's status: this is typical of the attention to musical material one finds in Polish Party discourse after the haranguing debates about new music's formal abstraction and Western association of the early years of Władysław Gomułka's government in the 1960s.⁶⁶ In a handwritten letter to the director of the Culture Department, he asserts, "We have here one of the *most influential phenomena and artistic events in all of Polish artistic culture of the 1980s* in the making. There has been nothing equal, not in literature, nor in theater, nor in film, not even in music itself."⁶⁷

Writing with such brazen praise, Wiśniewski defended the composer against backwater politics: the composer had actually also gotten himself into trouble in Poznań. In his official report, Wiśniewski noted provocations in the acceptance Penderecki had delivered upon receipt of the honorary doctorate.⁶⁸ The composer, Wiśniewski notes, had specifically isolated Nietzschean and Marxist philosophies as Promethean. He claimed these two "opponents" of Christianity were jointly responsible for the "most tragic repressive systems of the last century." From the perspective of the PZPR, Penderecki also provoked when he listed three public intellectuals from Poland—all of whom had been on the Party's blacklist at some point during the People's Republic—as his greatest living influences from Poland: Karol Wojtyła, the émigré Nobel laureate Czesław Miłosz, and the prominent philosopher émigré Leszek Kołakowski. The only commendation Wiśniewski's account supplies is that Penderecki was grateful to be associated with the heroic duo from the interwar period, Józef Piłsudski and Ignacy Paderewski, who had also received the honorary doctorate bestowed upon him.

Wiśniewski's report shows that the PZPR could easily craft Penderecki's Poznań speech as an attack on the government. But they hardly meddled. The

---

66 Lisa Jakelski's study of the Warsaw Autumn Festival of Contemporary Music in transnational perspective reveals the bureaucratic, aesthetic, and political strife, concessions, and agendas of post-stalinist musical policy. See Lisa Jakelski, *Making New Music in Cold War Poland.*

67 Letter to Sawic from Wiśniewski, October 26, 1987, LVI-1734, WK KC PZPR, AAN; emphasis in original.

68 "Notatka o pobycie Krzysztofa Pendereckiego w Poznaniu," October 27, 1987, LVI-1734, WK KC PZPR, AAN.

speech was published at the front of *Tygodnik Powszechny* with a single sentence removed. The exclusion was even indicated through a suggestive ellipsis.[69] The missing sentence is the one in which Penderecki pointed his finger at communism: "In the complex processes of history, these two ideas [the philosophies of Nietzsche and Marx], profoundly anti-Christian as they are, gave rise to the two most evil tyrannies [i.e., Nazism and stalinism], such as the world had not seen for ages."[70] Though Wiśniewski had drawn attention to the excised statement in his report, it was not the meat of Penderecki's argument, which centered on the Christian faith as universal inspiration.[71] In this minor elision, however, Penderecki gained traction as a dissenting citizen. The complete Poznań text was published by at least two drugi obieg periodicals that indicated his censure.[72]

Matters were not always so easily handled on Penderecki's behalf. The *Spiegel* article from that same year sent up a number of red flags: the duplicate circulated within the Culture Division contains heavy-handed underscoring to mark politically sensitive statements.[73] The text had been processed by the department itself: it was translated into Polish and annotated by a bureaucrat before circulation to the Vice Director of the Ministry for Foreign Affairs.[74] What had caught their attention? As in the Poznań speech, naming the wrong names set off alarms, as did statements that emphasized Christian belief despite communism's presence in his homeland. They underlined Penderecki's assertion that "this music is an expression of my faith and my political conviction and evidence that faith and church can have tremendous meaning in a communist state." The bureaucrat also tracked close affiliations between musical style and belief, as when the interviewer summarized,

69 "Kulturotwórcza moc chrześciaństwa," *Tygodnik Powszechny* January 3, 1988, p. 3. This censorship is far less than the intrusion suggested in Mieczysław Tomaszewski, "Listening to Penderecki," in *Krzysztof Penderecki: The Black Mask: Contemporary Dance of Death from Idea to Performance* (Cracow: The International Cultural Centre, 1998), 39, n3.

70 The *Tygodnik Powszechny* print also omits the *Polish Requiem* in a list of works Penderecki claims are sacred.

71 Mieczysław Tomaszewski, writing against actually existing socialism, likewise reads the speech as the first instance of a critique that would shape Penderecki's career through the late twentieth century: artistic decay in the absence of the sacred; in Mieczysław Tomaszewski, *Krzysztof Penderecki i jego muzyka: Cztery eseje* (Cracow: Akademia Muzyczna, 1994), 108.

72 *Kultura Niezależna* 6 (1987), 15–21; *Puls* (London) 35 (1987), 73–77.

73 LVI-1734, WK KC PZPR, AAN.

74 The interview, prepared by Adela Suchodolska of the Culture Department for Jerzy Piątkowski, director of the Department for Foreign Affairs, had been published in February 1987 after the premiere of *The Black Mask* in Salzburg, but before its Poznań production; see "'Ein Verlangen nach reinem Dur.'" It followed an essay on the tonal turn, which Penderecki believed himself to pioneer, in European new music; see Klaus

"Traditional harmony for sacred music is good, but with the blessing of the church [becomes] better."[75] Other comments deemed potentially volatile touched on the state of artistic freedom.[76] Ultimately, however, the documentation was, like so many other wrinkles in the Party's cultural management, filed away without recourse.

Back to 1970 in 1980

Penderecki's was not the only absent presence that hovered over the events in Gdańsk on December 16, 1980. The elaborate choreography of the monument unveiling recuperated a past trauma—murdered protesters—with a performance of compensation. It derived this power over and between historical narrative (telling and organizing) and collective memory (living and present) through repetition. Consider the important elements: the return *en masse* to the shipyards where both massacre and strike had happened; the voicing of the names of the dead while laying wreaths bearing witness to a legalized trade union; and, finally, the trinity of anchored crosses. In more abstract terms, the ceremony pushed for the "embodiment of a memorial consciousness" specific to this place—a relationship to memory, history, and place that Pierre Nora has influentially theorized as *lieux de mémoire*.[77] The participants were called upon to identify with those murdered, as well as with those who had occupied the Lenin Shipyards. Many had, of course, witnessed and even participated in the triumphant strikes. The two pasts, August 1980 and December 1970, coexisted in the place and in the repertories of song, silence, prayer, and slogan summoned for the commemoration. The event created a dynamic, embodied archive.[78]

Pierre Nora observed the obsession to collect data in the late twentieth century, arguing that the modern condition hushed and dismissed other modes of knowing about the past. The Polish opposition in some senses exemplifies this frenetic impulse. Fact-oriented eyewitness accounts like

---

Umbrich, "Mit Gloria und Glykol in den Rückwärtsgang," *Der Spiegel* 41, no. 2 (1987), 142–44.

75 "Tradycyjna harmonia jest dobra, ale z błogosławieństwem kościoła jeszcze lepsza." LVI-1734, WK KC PZPR, AAN.

76 "In literature there are obviously certain difficulties. Some writers do not publish officially. But they communicate themselves in illegal publications that reach an even broader readership"; LVI-1734, WK KC PZPR, AAN.

77 Pierre Nora, "Between Memory and History: Les *Lieux des Mémoire*," *Representations* (1989), 7.

78 Diana Taylor, *The Archive and the Repertoire: Performing Cultural Memory in the Americas* (Durham, NC: Duke University Press, 2003).

Gugulski's, which I discussed previously, flow through the reams of mimeographed newsletters that made up the drugi obieg and that counter official accounts. By the mid-1980s, the opposition had founded its own archive, still housed outside of the state at the Karta Organization. The Solidarity Union's materials—including tape recordings of Radio Solidarity and uncataloged boxes of songbooks—were housed in the basement of the Union's twenty-first-century offices when I began this project; as of 2019 they are curated and advocated for by the European Solidarity Centre. Memories and memory objects have been central to the ethos of the Polish opposition.

Music throws the multimodal nature of these processes and objects into relief. Nora, too, is sensitive to the way in which recording (even the fungible format of tape) is culturally understood as inscription: "Modern memory is, above all, archival. It relies entirely on the materiality of the trace, the immediacy of the recording, the visibility of the image. What began as writing ends as high fidelity and tape recording."[79] His comments resound with the story of the 1980 commemoration I have told, from its murky beginnings and distorted transmission.

Lacrimosa gains power and its sound becomes ever clearer over time, as it is replayed on documentary audio and video tape or written about on the pages of newspapers. The *Polish Requiem* archives the *Lacrimosa*: the larger work presents a transcendent text for symphonic performing forces, an ensemble that Penderecki later figured as a preserve on biblical terms—as a "musical ark."[80] The *Requiem* also organizes. Penderecki catalogs other significant deaths for Poland: the Agnus Dei in memory of Cardinal Stefan Wyszyński upon his death in 1981; the Recordare (1982) for a Franciscan friar who sacrificed himself for another prisoner at Auschwitz; the Dies irae in memory of those who fell in the 1944 Warsaw Uprising; the Libera me in honor of those massacred at Katyń; and, ultimately, a supplemental Ciaconna that postdates the People's Republic, written upon the death of Pope John Paul II in 2005. With each addition, Gdańsk is absorbed into the ever more comprehensive project of cataloging the losses of the Polish nation as a historical series to be kept in circulation and mourned anew with each performance.

Contra Penderecki's chronological narrative, let us return again to Gdańsk, beginning again with Wajda, in order to hear a different mode of performing 1970 in 1980. In his Palme d'Or-winning 1981 film, *Man of Iron*, the director offers a fictionalized account of a cast involved in both protests. At the end of the film—set after the agreement of August 1980 had been reached—the director overlays the cover of a song, "The Ballad of Janek Wiśniewski"

---

79 Nora, "Between Memory and History," 13.

80 Krzysztof Penderecki, *The Labyrinth of Time* (Chapel Hill, NC: Hinshaw Music, 1998), 59.

("Janek Wiśniewski padł"). The audience follows the main characters departing the scene of protest. The song turns the narrative back to December 1970 as a woman sings:

Chłopcy z Grabówka, chłopcy z Chylonii,	Boys from Grabówek, boys from Chylonia,
Dzisiaj milicja użyła broni.	The militia used force today.
Dzielnieśmy stali i celnie rzucali:	We bravely stood and hit our targets:
Janek Wiśniewski padł.	Janek Wiśniewski fell.

As the closing credits roll, a guitar duo hammers out simple minor chords in a manner that recalls a military march ▶. The vocalist is accompanied by Jacek Kaczmarski and Przemysław Gintrowski, musicians whose meaning for the opposition was also amplified by their participation here (see Chapter 3). The squareness of the meter sets the tone for the curt and almost declamatory recitation of a simple narrative verse by the actress Krystyna Janda, whose sustained eminence in Polish theater stems in part from her gritty performances of tragically heroic women on stage and screen, as well as from the distinctive cabaret-trained voice grounded in her chest.

Each four-line stanza unfolds over an antecedent and consequent phrase with internal melodic repetition. In this particular performance, Janda disrupts the accent pattern of the original song, raising tension for Polish audiences by displacing the metrical downbeat to the middle of each sentence (Example 5.2b). The move has the peculiar effect of emphasizing a weakness in the song's text setting: the music's strong beats mark unaccented syllables in the Polish language. The last line of each verse is always the same, announcing the death of Janek Wiśniewski. It interrupts the previous

EXAMPLE 5.2. Comparison of syntactic emphasis in performances of "Janek Wiśniewski Fell."

EXAMPLE 5.2A. Mieczysław Cholewa's original declamation of the melody (1980).

218 | MUSICAL SOLIDARITIES

EXAMPLE 5.2B. Krystyna Janda's 1981 cover from *Man of Iron* with Jacek Kaczmarski's instrumentals.

EXAMPLE 5.2C. Kazik's cover in *Black Thursday* (2011).

lines' parallel decasyllabic structure with a stabbing and percussive shout that he has fallen—*padł*. The final syllable wallops, snapping the march into step. The relative simplicity and predictability through the ballad alert my hearing to her voice. With each stanza, Janda raises the volume and allows the strain on her voice to be audible; she pleads through the final stanza, abandoning the melodic contour. This deliberate escalation culminates in a wail in her climax. "Breath, spit, gristle and desire in equal parts . . . sonic scar-tissue," to borrow a hearing from Steven Connor.[81]

The resolute rhythmic manipulation is Janda's performative intervention. She does not modify the text of Krzysztof Dowgiałło's ballad, which summarizes the details of the police attacks on protesters on December 17, 1970. The text—melody-less for ten years—teaches a lesson: witnessing history may empower the oppressed to unite, but it also makes those bodies vulnerable to violent intervention. In a 2014 interview Dowgiałło, an architect, recalled composing the lyrics immediately after observing a funeral procession on the streets of Gdynia. He describes what he had seen forty-four years previous: a young man, having been fatally shot by the militia, carried by protesters through the streets on a door.[82] Not knowing the youth's

---

81 Steven Connor, *Beyond Words: Sobs, Hums, Stutters and Other Vocalizations* (London: Reaktion, 2014), 71.

82 He was interviewed for the YouTube channel of the city of Gdynia and recounts his experience as witness ("Z historii Gdyni: Krzysztof Dowgiałło o powstaniu ballady 'Janek Wiśniewski padł'"; https://www.youtube.com/watch?v=m750G_Qqnxg). Jerzy Eisler,

name—Zbigniew Godlewski—he supplied the dead protester a pseudonym made of common Polish names, cultivating a sense of familiarity, just as he did with the references across the narration to local streets (St. John's), local workers (at the shipyards in Gdynia and Gdańsk), and towns in northern Poland. His funeral procession was also a demonstration. A journalist in the region observed the proliferation of nationalist symbols in her first-person account of the march: waving flags, they sang the national anthem and "The Oath."[83]

The snapshot that Dowgiałło frames to give his ballad a historical beginning was also captured in an actually existing photograph by Edmund Pepliński. The chilling image of the dead student activist being marched to his grave traversed the print culture of the opposition (Figure 5.2a, b).[84] Barthes, evoking the photograph's intimacy with dying, writes that cameras are "clocks for seeing."[85] These two cultural artifacts, the frozen frame of the photograph and that image as projected in the poem, maintained the memory of the unjust death. A visible analog to the song's refrain, the image amplified memory. It gave 1970 affective impact; the song gave it affective resonance.

Dowigiałło's text maps the coast as the home of Polish dissent, a theme in memory work that links 1970 to 1980. Many drugi obieg periodicals place the opposition on the Baltic coast. From the *Coastal Gazette* (Gazeta Wybrzeża, edited by Anna Walentynowicz) to the *Coastal Songbook* (Śpiewnik Wybrzeża), the popular association of the tri-city region of Gdańsk, Opole, and Gdynia with summer resort activity and song festivals was replaced with protest stages on which workers united. "Janek Wiśniewski" was often a

---

using witness accounts and materials from the scene, makes the connection to Godlewski in Jerzy Eisler, *Grudzień 1970: Geneza, przebieg, konsekwencje* (Warsaw: Wydawnictwo Sensacje XX wieku, 2000), 219–21.

83 Wiesława Kwiatkowska, *Grudniowa apokalipsa* (Gdynia, 1993), 56, quoted in Eisler, *Grudzień 1970*, 220.

84 See, for example, the discussion in a program on Polish Radio from December 2011 (the available with a reproduction of the original photo at http://www.polskieradio.pl/39/1240/Artykul/282993,Prawdziwa-historia-Janka-Wisniewskiego). The "Road to Freedom" exhibit at the Solidarity Museum in Gdańsk sells reproductions of a child's sketch of the photograph in its gift shop. In 1980, the photograph was reproduced with the song's text on a pamphlet of verses circulated in Gdańsk; see "Przestańcie stale nas przepraszać . . . : Wiersze sierpień 1980" (Gdańsk: Wydawnictwo im. konstytucji 3. maja, 1980). I have come across the photo reproduced with the song in broadsheet collections at the University of Bremen, the Karta archive, the Solidarity Union's own archive, the University of Warsaw, and the Solidarity Collection at Harvard University.

85 Roland Barthes, *Camera Lucida: Reflections on Photography*, translated by Richard Howard (London: Cape, 1982), 15.

keystone in print. For example, it opens a collection of songs and poems written for and about the two surges in popular dissent, *December–August: Songs and Poems of the Coast*.[86] Whether at the end of Wajda's film or on the first page of a collection, the prominent song served as a kind of binding agent, an interface between writing and hearing, learning and remembering, and place and memory.

In his recollection, Dowgiałło situates the text of "Janek Wiśniewski" as an organic, immediate creative response to the scene it describes, a move toward authentication that parallels the cultural work upon Jacek Kaczmarski's "Walls" that I discussed in Chapter 3. The music, however, is a treatment of 1970 *in* 1980. Mieczysław Cholewa gave the text a tune in 1980 and performed the song, guitar in hand, throughout Poland (see Example 5.2a), including at the Review of Authentic Song in August 1981 ▶. Cholewa claims to have written the song in September 1980, after the peaceful negotiations at the Lenin Shipyards.[87] Many layers—lenses of interpretation—separate the murdered student from the song about him. He died when police fired ruthlessly and recklessly at a crowd of protesters on the street. He was an unnamed and unrecognized victim; his ad hoc unofficial funeral took on symbolic significance for its poignant theatrics first witnessed, then written about. For Dowigiałło, the victim was captured on camera. The pseudonym he was given obscures his identity further. Memorial practices—spoken, then sung; heard, then recorded—stiffen the story.

Cholewa's recollection that the song and the strikes did not emerge at the same time holds up. None of the archival recordings of the August strikes contains the song. Nevertheless, the authenticity that such a double genesis in situ would provide has been alluring, with historians claiming that the *song*, rather than the *text*, was present in Gdańsk at the strikes in 1980.[88] Such slips and hopes configure anthems as instrumental, the musical performance as more visible and more powerful than the written text or the bound songbook. This is the real imagined promise of musical solidarity. Locational specificity, perhaps, implicates the music's history with the defining moment

---

86 *Grudzień–Sierpień: Piosenki i wiersze wybrzeża* (Warsaw, 1980, Zespół BL i H).

87 Cholewa later owned up to his work as an officer for the Security Service (Służba Bezpieczeństwa, SB) in the 1990s in a published interview with a member of the Senate who had also been a signatory of the Gdańsk Accord, Bogdan Borusewicz, in the Polish newspaper of record, *Gazeta Wyborcza* (Roman Daszczyński, "Agent SB przeprasza Bogdana Borusewicza," Feburary 11, 2005, http://wiadomosci.gazeta.pl/wiadomosci/1,114883,2546256.html).

88 In her monograph on music and politics, Iwona Massaka makes the claim for Jacek Kaczmarski's "Walls" ("Mury") and Vladimir Vysotsky's "Wolf Hunt" ("Okhota na bolkov") alongside that for Cholewa's tune; see Iwona Massaka, *Muzyka jako instrument wpływu politycznego* (Łódź: Wydawnictwo Naukowe Ibidem, 2009), 401.

(a)

(b)

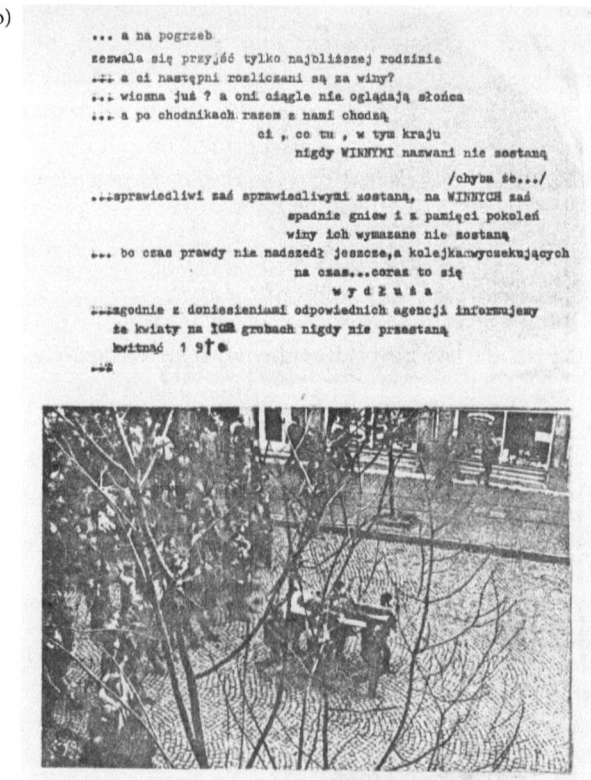

FIGURE 5.2. Zbigniew Godlewski in (a) Edmund Pepliński's photograph, Ośrodek Karta, and (b) narrated as "Janek Wiśniewski" on a broadside in the drugi obieg.
Archiv der Forschungsstelle Osteuropa an der Universität Bremen, FSO 02-003-K30-29.

that was Solidarity. The song's mediation across diverse media and historical time nurtures it as a perennially renewable germ for the cultural memory and history of 1970/1980, often through performative repetition. Nonetheless, as with Penderecki's *Lacrimosa*, the myth of political inspiration clouds the scene(s) in Gdańsk.

Take, for example, the documentary account of Solidarity's sounds presented in 1981 to North American audiences by Folkways Records, *Solidarity! Postulat 22*.[89] "A Song about Janek from Gdynia" is the second track on the A side of the Folkways imprint of an album recorded and edited by Swedish producer Lars Holmberg in Gdynia with a team of local assistants who are left uncredited to maintain their anonymity. To the studio take of Cholewa— or someone who sounds like Cholewa—they add two pieces of front matter: a recording "in possession of the trade union" from December 17, 1970, and a voice-over text, also recorded and mixed in Poland ▶.[90] A bass voice gives a brief history of the militia attack during which Godlewski (as Wiśniewski)— "on his way to work"—was murdered. Low-fidelity source recordings crackle quietly beneath, with suggestive textures that the liner notes explicate. "The trainwhistle heard is the warning from the driver of the local train to the workers that they would be met by militia, and you can also hear the militia firing and people screaming." This is not a collage of acousmatic sounds, or a production with invisible hands at mixing boards. With the Polish voice unnamed and activists seated at the recording technology, the project takes on a present tense. Before the declaration of martial law, "Janek Wiśniewski padł" is an urgent cry still and again: he has fallen, but he is not yet buried. His historical moment is not yet past.

Music and sound stretch the storytelling capacity of this ballad. Building on Janda's performance—circulating it and recomposing it at once—Elżbieta

---

89 *Solidarity! Postulat 22*, Folkways Records (FSS 37251), 1981. Italian trade unions circulated a very similar cassette along with a booklet of lyrics in Italian translation (AO IV/206.2, Opposition Archive, Karta Organization, Warsaw, Poland). The Archiv der Forschungsstelle Osteuropa an der Universität Bremen holds West German and Swedish imprints.

90 Liner notes, *Solidarity! Postulat 22*. Among the many audio compilations composed between 1970 and 1980, the "Sound Chronicle of the Strikes in the Lenin Shipyards, Part 1" (CD 352) is most comprehensive with respect to the events on the street in December 1970 (Archive of the Solidarity State Commission). This is probably the source for the archival recording on Holmberg's production. Notably, the 1970 source material also frames Andrzej Wajda's film and Janina Jankowska's radio montage of the incident, *Sierpień 1980*. I compare the performance here, which has a slightly less frenetic guitar accompaniment but shares the vocal timbre, with Cholewa's performance at the Review of Authentic Song, released as *Piosenki Solidarności* on the Echo Original Country Recording Label in 1981 (E 901-2).

Sikora utilizes the actress's striking declamation of "padł" as a sonic impetus for her electronic composition, *Janek Wiśniewski-Décembre-Pologne* (1982–84). Realized at the Groupe de Recherches Musicales (GRM) while she was studying with Betsy Jolas, the work has none of the explicit communication of the ballad or the clear routes through the social movement's media.[91] Sikora cuts out and reframes key moments from the Janda performance. At the same time, the composer positions the sixteen-minute tape piece as a direct affective response to the declaration of martial law with her title and as part of her public performance of citizenship. "I was shocked," Sikora explained in 2013.[92]

For Polish listeners, her concrète techniques trade on the game of recognition and affective resonance. "Padł" frames her piece. Sikora grabs the exclamation and the guitar chords for her piece, stripping the syllable of its vocal inflection. For the first gesture of the work, she generates an avalanche of pitches to clear the air that point to the one-two punch of the syllable, pronounced [*padw*]—with a light rebound off the open a to the soft ł. This is also the last sound we hear, though with noisier filters (see Figure 5.3). Throughout the work, she weaves distorted sounds identifiable as sirens, helicopters, and the unstable overtone series of church bells through the sinewaves she generates. She sets the story within a whirl of alarm sounds that are not so different from those on the Folkways album—or from Wajda's choreography in December 1980. The guitar chords, distorted in the first and last moments, are maniacal. Sikora has explained the composition through her hearing of the Janda performance: "Four introductory guitar chords of the song 'Janek Wiśniewski Fell' became the most recognizable element in the piece. After numerous transformations, they still break the silence at the beginning and resound with bells in the end."[93] The guitar refrain orients again as the piece comes to a close ⏵. I hear strumming, the treble snaps of the metallic strings tapping out the acoustic instruments' resonance. Or perhaps I have heard the Janda so many times that I am predisposed to a moment of recognition. Whatever the case, Sikora sets up aural comparison. I notice that song and voice are missing. The final minutes of the piece take me back to the credit music of *Man of Iron*. The splice of the guitar chords feels open-ended, as though she leaves her tape unspooled, pushing a listener who recognizes the chords to hear Janda sing in their mind.

---

91 Though Sikora was working and studying at multiple institutions in Paris through this time, the Groupe des Recherches Musicales provided the support for this project. See Évelyn Gayou, *Le GRM, Groupe de Recherches Musicales: Cinquante ans d'histoire* (Paris: Fayard, 2007), 216.

92 Liner notes, *Blanc et rouge*, Warsaw: Bôłt Records, 2012; BR ES07.

93 Liner notes, *Blanc et rouge*.

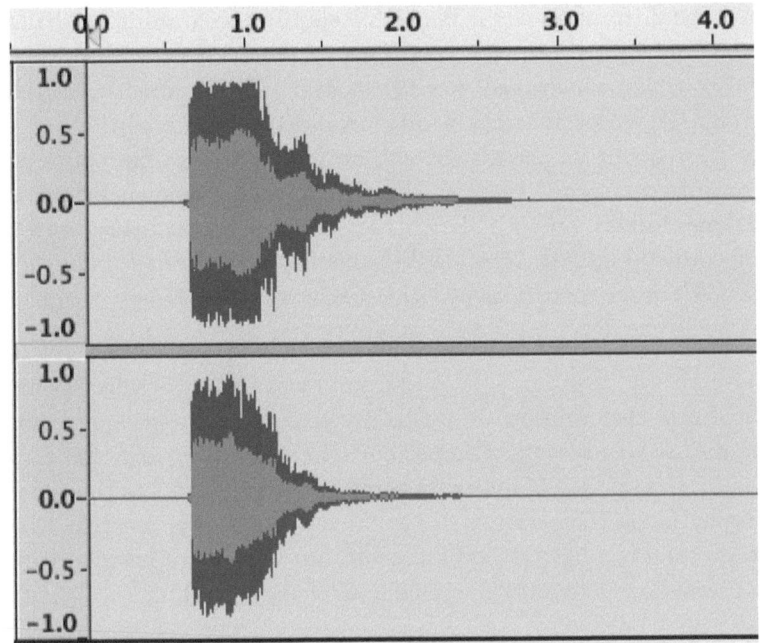

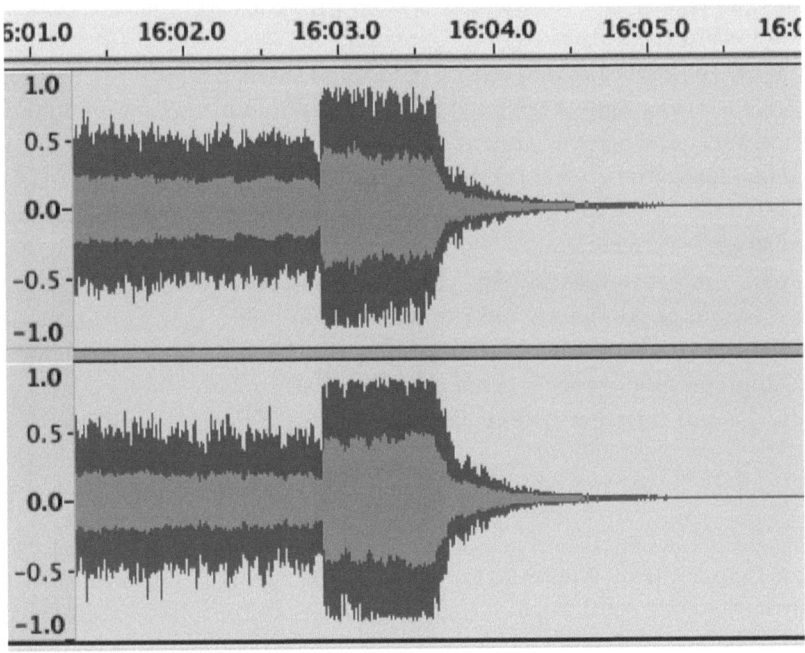

FIGURE 5.3. Elżbieta Sikora's samples of "*padł*" in *Janek Wiśniewski-Décembre-Pologne* (1982–84), 0'00"–4'00", 16'01"–16'07".

After the dissolution of the People's Republic, performing the ballad has continued to become a crucial component of the memory work surrounding December 1970, which itself has faded from its symptomatic relationship with 1980. These continued performances provoke reflections through which we can learn about its percolation and currency through the 1980s outside of recordings and print. In 2011, Kazik Staszewski (known simply by his stage name, Kazik), one of Poland's most enduringly successful rock musicians, recorded the Janek Wiśniewski ballad for a docudrama about the 1970 protests, *Black Thursday* (*Czarny Czwartek*, 2011, see Example 5.2c) ▶. His reflections in the film's press material are tinged with nostalgia:

> I have known this song for a long time. I was singing it when I didn't even know that singing would be my profession. Long, long before. For me, it was a song of hope, hope for something big, for a victory... I didn't like [Cholewa's] better known version, but the version sung by Janda. This song is one of the best songs ever written. I have always sung it, I have always known it, but I could not have imagined that somebody would ever ask me to sing and record it.[94]

The song's longevity, even timelessness, emerges as a leading factor in Kazik's musical affinity. The rocker's interpretation is driven by the big ideas—hope, victory, downfall—which, while associated with battles of the past, direct his vision toward the future.

"Janek Wiśniewski" tells a story of loss and absence through an insistence on presence. As a song, a bounded unit, it reclaims a history for an unknown victim and casts a place of work as a place of change. Its cultural work extends beyond depth of repetition (1) through the song, (2) by its reprints, reflected and refracted in visual culture, and (3) via amplification and fragmentation in rock and electronic music. Both song and story bind. They merge 1970 to 1980, protest to Gdańsk, and death (*padł*) to outcry. That is, they intertwine sound, performance, and the social to do political work—something akin to the elusive notion of musical gestus. The real Janek Wiśniewski is not Zbigniew Godlewski, but the powerful abstract icon of the ballad across its media and unstable history, sounded out in its audible syllabic grip.[95]

---

94 Quoted in Olga Bieniek, *Czarny Czwartek: Janek Wiśniewski padł; Album o filmie* [Black Thursday: Janek Wiśniewski Fell; Making of the Movie], ed. by Ewa K. Jaskulska (Gdynia: Nordfilm, 2011), 201.

95 While gestus is usually employed to think through an Austro-German lineage of protest songs from the Brecht/Weill *Lehrstücke* through workers' songs by Hanns Eisler and Marc Blitzstein, I find the importance of "emancipation" for the concept useful in thinking through the beneath-the-surface simmering of "Janek Wiśniewski." For a lucid introduction to gestus in the postwar context, see Anicia Chung Timberlake, "Brecht for

Where Penderecki's *Lacrimosa* synthesizes and mourns, creating a "backdrop" or shroud of sorrow on the memorial stage, "Janek Wiśniewski" relates and summons. In my triangulation of its covers, I have pushed Sikora's sample far and have reduced it to a single sound or slogan. Now I take a different cue from her: I return to Gdańsk again, this time to revisit Lech Wałęsa as the mouthpiece of a movement.

In Gdańsk with Lech Wałęsa

Again, the August 1980 strikes: the heart of the activity is a set of meetings—negotiations even—between the Inter-Factory Strike Committee (Międzyzakładowy Komitet Strajkowy) and delegates from the PZPR. Inside the Work Health and Safety Hall of the Lenin Shipyards, these men engage in heated conversation, speaking into microphones. Other workers with leadership positions within the movement sit with journalists at tables; some must stand. The hall is full. The proceedings are transmitted and transcribed. It is broadcast on the radio, amplified across the grounds on speakers. Announcements come through the factory's loudspeakers or are transmitted on walkie-talkies. At the end of each day, there are official and unofficial radio and television broadcast excerpts. Stenographers transcribe every word spoken—this is work that has accompanied the hundreds of thousands of meetings of government committees and state-sponsored unions through state socialism's many phases. Journalists clutch mini-cassette recorders, capturing the sound while they scribble notes and speak with witnesses (see Chapter 3).

As the "secular pilgrimage" to Gdańsk continued, more and more crowds gathered.[96] Outside the halls, people gathered. They waited. They wrote. They chatted; they chanted. They sang. Some brought their guitars to accompany legion songs, cabaret tunes, and simple laments. This was guitar poetry, scouting music, spontaneous covers, rock, patriotic anthems, and then some. A weary—but short—little song, "Our Lord," wove its way through the groups and was covered in different genres: "Oh, Lord, Lord of ours, Lord of ours / how this strike, how this strike / lasts so long."

Children: Shaping the Ideal GDR Citizen through Opera Education," *Representations* 132 (2015), 36–40.

96 Colin Barker, "Fear, Laughter, and Collective Power: The Making of Solidarity at the Lenin Shipyards in Gdansk, Poland, August 1980," in *Passionate Politics: Emotions and Social Movements,* edited by Jeff Goodwin, James M. Jasper, and Francesca Polletta (Chicago: University of Chicago Press, 2001), 187.

The theatricality of the negotiations cast everyone present as a participant and as an onlooker at some point: the birthday song "One Hundred Years" ("Sto lat") stood out as raucous (Example 5.3) ▶. The song's text conveys well-wishes for a long life, and its melody is easily sung when hoarse, intoxicated, or elated, something like the English-language "For (S)He's a Jolly Good Fellow." For decades, this song's lack of specificity served to communicate rousing support *or* critique in public spaces. When, in 1978, the Polish Jewish composer Alexandre Tansman returned to Poland for the first time since his displacement in 1941, he clung to that song in the account of the concert in his honor. In a letter to Tadeusz Kaczyński, he provided a political interpretation of this joy: "I had never expected such a triumphant reception: encores, standing ovations, flowers, the whole hall at the end was singing 'Sto lat,' etc. I talked a lot about Israel and I had the impression that . . . Poland is the most pro-Israeli country in Europe!"[97]

EXAMPLE 5.3. "One Hundred Years."

Sto lat, sto lat,	One hundred years, one hundred years,
Niech żyje, żyje nam.	May he live, live with us.
Sto lat, sto lat,	One hundred years, one hundred years,
Niech żyje, żyje nam.	May he live, live with us.
Jeszcze raz, jeszcze raz, Niech żyje,	Once more, once more,
żyje nam,	May he live, live with us,
Niech żyje nam!	May he live with us!

The practice of using "Sto lat" in protests extends at least as far back as October 1956, the crest of the civil resistance that would instigate the relaxation of Stalinism known as the Thaw. On October 24 a crowd of 300,000 outside the Communist Party's Seventh Plenum in the center of the capitol rallied for political change and transparency; they sang "Sto lat" in support of

---

97 Translated by Maja Trochimczyk in "Aleksander Tansman to Tadeusz Kaczyński: Selected Letters (1971–1985)," *Polish Music Journal* 6, no. 1 (2003); https://polishmusic.usc.edu/research/publications/polish-music-journal/vol6no1/tansman-kaczynski-letters/.

Władysław Gomułka, the communist at the helm of the demands for reform who spoke at their rally.[98]

In November of that year, the writer Maria Dąbrowska recounted another performance of the song for Gomułka in her diary: "Everywhere the crowd sang 'Sto lat.' Gomułka had to say: 'I didn't know that "Sto lat" is a revolutionary song.' And so from then on 'Sto lat' was established as a song of that 'Polish revolution.'"[99] Just over a decade later, still on the streets of downtown Warsaw, the song protected activists. One economist, who had been enrolled at the University of Warsaw during the 1968 protests, remembered standing and singing the song *at* police: "They knew what we meant, but we knew they couldn't do anything."[100] When George H. W. Bush hosted the leaders of the new democratic government at the White House in 1990, he recounted how well he had been received in Poland. He commented to Tadeusz Mazowiecki, the new prime minister, "Let me return the kind wish that your countrymen made me in the Hall of the Sejm [a house of parliament], in the streets of Warsaw, and the square of Gdańsk: *Sto lat*, may you live 100 years."[101]

In Gdańsk, the song was directed at Lech Wałęsa. "May he live with us!" the workers shouted toward him to underscore the communal rapture they felt at crucial moments in the negotiations.[102] The song welcomed their focus on progress and the future, rather than the past and history: the call, "one more time," rebounds with a simplicity that is anything but fatalist. Stenographers note when the negotiation hall erupted in this song, but with the text in mind, the song was also actually a meaningful escalation of purpose (not just an open signifier). Recordings of these moments—whether excerpted for documentary purposes, or archived as reference material—do not capture mayhem. They sound like unison.[103]

---

98 A detailed account of the street atmosphere, including songs, as it punctuated Gomułka's leadership is in Andrzej Friszke, *Opozycja polityczna w PRL 1945–1980* (Aneks: London, 1984), 78–83.

99 Maria Dąbrowska, *Dzienniki 1951–1957*, Volume 4, edited by Tadeusz Drewnowski (Warsaw: Czytelnik, 1988), 313.

100 Recounted by an audience member at a book launch in central Warsaw for Piotr Wierzbicki's *Muzykalny kosmos* in May 2010.

101 "Toasts at the State Dinner for Prime Minister Tadeusz Mazowiecki of Poland, March 21, 1990," *Public Papers of the Presidents of the United States: George Bush, January 1 to June 30, 1990*, Washington, DC, 399.

102 *Polski Sierpień 1980: Reedycja Almanachu gdańskich Środowisk Twórczych "Punkt" nr 12/80* (New York: Biblioteka Pomostu, 1981), 107, 93.

103 The first ten minutes of Solidarity's first documentary (*Robotnicy '80*) and Janina Jankowska's radio documentary *Polski Sierpień* feature representative performances.

Wałęsa rose to prominence on the stage of Solidarity through action. On August 14, 1980, it had been four years since he had been employed at the Lenin Shipyards as an electrician. That morning he climbed back into the grounds by scaling a wall, tasked by other organizers to rally a strike. This wall, the Berlin Wall (and, as I suggested in Chapter 3, the walls of Jericho): these are the real barriers that stand in for the metaphor of the Iron Curtain in the symbolic history of the 1980s. Writing before the end of the Cold War, poet, translator, and essayist Stanisław Barańczak wrapped the character and charisma of Wałęsa in praise in his essay, "Wałęsa: The Uncommon Common Man." He describes Wałęsa as gymnast and come-from-behind insurgent:

> It was only seven years ago last August that an obscure unemployed electrician climbed the wall surrounding the Lenin Shipyard in Gdańsk, Poland. In jumping down from that wall, he jumped into the limelight of History. Seldom does the course of human events depend so much on an individual's decision as it did that August morning in 1980. Had Lech Wałęsa not joined the shipyard strike to lead it to its triumphant conclusion two weeks later, and had he not served as his nation's unofficial leader throughout its subsequent seven-year ordeal, our world would look different today.[104]

Across accounts of the strikes, Wałęsa is built up as an intuitive political leader and representative of the populace. Foreign journalists, for example from *Le Figaro,* draw attention to this indescribable character as "larger than life."[105] Wałęsa took physical risks. On August 18 he stood on the gates at the Shipyards with a bullhorn, inviting people to join in their strikes.[106] He also receives acknowledgment for the aura at the negotiations as much as he does for their measured progress. In *Man of Iron*, Wałęsa is also a champion in song. Wajda's canonic filmic treatment includes extended audio and audio-video footage from the 1980 negotiations. Moments before the credits roll in "Janek Wiśniewski," audiences rewatch Solidarity's euphoric conclusion. Wałęsa signs the agreement and is carried out of the gates of the Shipyards on the shoulders of the exuberant crowd. They chant, "Thank you!" (*Dźiękujemy!*). They sing "Sto lat" ▶.

Lech Wałęsa embraced his celebrity. His approval meant the approval of Solidarity, even when he was imprisoned or otherwise stepping out of public

---

[104] Stanisław Barańczak, *Breathing under Water and Other East European Essays* (Cambridge, MA: Harvard University Press, 1990), 39.

[105] Quoted by Radio Free Europe in *August 1980: The Strikes in Poland* (Munich: Radio Free Europe Research, 1980), 339.

[106] Colin Barker, "Fear, Laughter, and Collective Power," 182.

appearances. The drugi obieg record of songs from Gdańsk, *Postulat 22*, with the nod to Janek Wiśniewski, had his approval. On the record's sleeve, a validating blurb, a photo of him with his trademark mustache, and, in the case of the German and Swedish pressings, a facsimile of his signature gave the recording a stamp of authenticity and placed Wałęsa within the strikes' sounding ethos (Figure 5.4). Wałęsa's quick text is strident: "The songs and poems, which were created during the strikes, kept our solidarity spirit high and carried us to victory. We would like freedom-lovers throughout the world to share this experience by listening to this record." The instruments of freedom are to be held and circulated, he would have us believe—solidarity on wings of song.

The declaration of martial law only enabled further amplification (through reproduction) of Wałęsa's voice and persona to project him as figurehead through the 1980s. Transcripts of Radio Solidarity show that fragments from

FIGURE 5.4. *Solidarity! Postulat 22: Songs from the Polish Labour Movement*, FW37251.
Courtesy of Smithsonian Folkways Recordings. © 1981. Used by permission.

his addresses, in particular his rallying speech at the first national assembly of the trade union in August 1981, flanked evening news reports at least through 1985.[107] He demands, "We must work together [*solidarnie*]" and Jacek Kaczmarski sings, "And the walls fall, fall, fall. . . ." On the news in the United States, his voice and charisma caught the ear of US singer Joan Baez, who, hearing historical echoes with the police's persecution of Martin Luther King Jr., was compelled to speak out against his 1981 imprisonment and write a song in solidarity. "Do you hear us, Lech Wałęsa? . . . We hear you, Lech Wałęsa!" She lauds him and comforts him with the lilting refrain of a song whose fundamental register is a jeer at Leonid Brezhnev. "Happy Birthday, Leonid Brezhnev" (1982) sarcastically lists the "accomplishments" of the Soviet Party Secretary: the harms he has done and the power he has claimed. This song, which Baez performed alongside other global protest ballads like Mercedes Sosa's "Gracias a la Vida," rubbed US music critics the wrong way. Despite her "truly oracular folk-pop instrument," as Stephen Holden wrote in the *New York Times*, it is Baez's covers of Bob Dylan that capture his attention and foreground her vocal talent.[108]

In *Tygodnik Mazowsze*, the editorial board embraced the buzz that someone of Baez's status accelerated in the media—or at least they understood the song on media theoretical terms as part magic, part news. A critic celebrated her solidarity song and Wałęsa at once in a 1984 article:

> They are singing songs about Lech Wałęsa: in Polish, in Spanish, in various languages. Joan Baez sings in English: "But the courage of you and your man of the year / Is a symphony the world has seldom seen or heard . . . They didn't know that there would always be within you / And we hear you, Lech Walesa." And they talk about him in different languages. They repeat to each other what he has done—what he has said—simple people and politicians, and correspondents for major newspapers, calling out the latest news into the world's attentive ears. Man of song. Man of sensational dispatch. Man of contemporary legend. What luck that we are able to see him up close, almost to touch him—and to satisfy ourselves that he is real.[109]

With the triplicate reference to Wałęsa as "man of" immaterial substance, the author weaves Wałęsa and Wajda together again, casting him now as a

---

107 "FSO-2-003 Flugschriften, Flugblätter, Dokumente aus dem poln. zweiten Umlauf," Archiv der Forschungsstelle Osteuropa an der Universität Bremen, Bremen, Germany.

108 Stephen Holden, "Joan Baez's Voice," *New York Times*, July 4, 1982, http://www.nytimes.com/1982/07/04/arts/pop-joan-baez-s-voice.html. He also explicitly critiques that she takes a political stance.

109 "em," "Nasz kandydat—Lech Wałęsa," *Tygodnik Mazowsze* 91 (July 7, 1984), 1.

mythic hero in the director's film dynasty of Polish history (*Man of Marble, Man of Iron*).

Baez traveled to Gdańsk, a story she retells with enthusiasm and conviction in her 1987 memoir, *A Voice to Sing With*.[110] She delights in the highs and high risk of the November 1985 trip: smuggling cassettes of Dire Straits, U2, Paul Young, and Hall and Oates (along with her own) around in her guitar case, being kissed upon walking into Wałęsa's home, dancing with a priest, and navigating the careful watch of the Security Service (Służba Bezpieceństwa, SB) in the wake of the Western media coverage that she notes her visit attracted (NBC, BBC). She is compelled by Wałęsa, and he—it would seem—by her. During her weekend in Gdańsk, she is absorbed into family dinners, learns the first verse of Maciej Pietrzyk's "Song for My Daughter" in Polish (Chapter 3), and attends mass and sings during its communion. She also gives a concert of songs that tell stories of women resisting and that she understands as nonviolent tools to work for peace, always turning to the audience to sing with her.[111] Held in Wałęsa's home parish, Saint Brigid, the "Concert for Solidarity" offers Baez the opportunity to bring one more community into her orbit. I learn as much from the drugi obieg recording of the event as from her excited written-down retelling. The tape recording has little acoustic resonance of the space. Baez banters only briefly; a sequential translator faithfully transmits her political exegesis of songs to "create a global hope network." This is no bootleg: the vocal track and guitar accompaniment are mixed across the take. With Pietrzyk's waiting song and the skewer of Brezhnev, she tailors the evening to the Polish audience. She jokes a bit about her own composition, drawing attention to her privilege as traveler: "This is a very sarcastic song. Still, I get to leave Poland."[112] The move she makes before singing in Polish, from leader to collective, inverts the trajectory I have highlighted through this chapter. Instead of the leader whose voice amplifies the people, we hear the celebrity engender the crowd to join in: to work toward unison. Baez galvanizes the audience with whom she will sing "Our God" ("Boże nasz") in chorus: "I always try to learn a song for the country I'm in, but they've kept me so busy that all I've only learned one refrain. And so I'm asking my friends whom I met last night to please come and sing the song, which you also know, and we'll all sing the refrain" ▶.

---

110 Joan Baez, *A Voice to Sing With* (New York: Summit Books, 1987), 340–52.

111 *Joan Baez: Koncert dla Solidarności*, Wydawnictwo Wtrwałość, Kaseta 013, Archiv der Forschungsstelle Osteuropa an der Universität Bremen, Bremen, Germany. She sang in Lublin over the following week, at the Catholic University. Tapes of that concert, which had the same program, also circulated with almost identical script.

112 The translator softens the assertiveness of her statement: "This is a very sarcastic song, still I think I will get to leave Poland."

6 | Chorus

W. Ziembiński sentenced to 3 months in prison: *Undeterred by divergent witness statements, on the 15th of October the District Court in Warsaw upheld the magistrates' court's decree of punishment for a rally that had taken place on August 15, the anniversary of the Battle of Warsaw. . . . Witnesses from the traffic police consistently declared that the rally had been peaceful and that police intervention had been unnecessary. Officers from the SB {Security Service}, however, spoke of "anti-governmental excesses," i.e. hands raised in the "V" sign and the singing of an altered version of "God Save Poland" {"Boże, coś Polskę"}. They also claimed that Ziembiński insulted the authorities of the People's Republic by demanding that plaques commemorating the war of 1918–1920, removed from the Tomb of the Unknown Soldier under Stalin, be reinstalled.*
—Tygodnik Mazowsze *(October 18, 1984)*

In October 1984 the weekly newsletter of Solidarity's Warsaw branch, *Tygodnik Mazowsze* (*Mazovian Weekly*), reported on the minor incursions experienced by leaders of the opposition in a crime blotter to unpick the Security Service's (Służba Bezpieczeństwa, SB) strategy for assembling evidence.[1] In this particular case, Wojciech Ziembiński had been persecuted for his work organizing a public manifestation. He had attempted to replace a memorial tablet to those Polish soldiers who had fallen in the Polish-Soviet War (1918–20) at the Grave of the Unknown Soldier.[2] The previous inscription had been removed from the landmark in Warsaw's largest public square by

---

1 *Tygodnik Mazowsze* 102 (October 18, 1984), 2. Emphasis original.

2 Ziembiński, a signatory in the Workers' Defense Committee's early activities, was primarily active in the right-wing Movement for Defense of Human and Civil Rights (Ruch Obrony Praw Człowieka i Obywatela) in 1984.

the stalinist authorities in the 1950s; Ziembiński was rectifying this erasure of Polish national heroes.

But this was not the activity that caught the attention of the SB, at least as Solidarity understood the watchdog organization's logic. The activity had "anti-excesses," according to the official court ruling. The journalists behind *Tygodnik Mazowsze* are doubtful that this assertion was based on real events, citing witness descriptions of the public assembly as peaceful. They emphasized that the police had not needed to intervene. The report confirms some details, however, and quotes the ruling directly. The demonstrators raised their fingers in the shape of a V. And they sang. They sang the "changed" version of a church hymn so well-known that its incipit only need be quoted: "God Save Poland" ("Boże, coś Polskę"; see Example 6.1).[3]

This story, captured in one brief paragraph, offers a glimpse into a routine mode of protest in Poland in the 1980s: small gatherings around patriotic monuments to commemorate anniversaries. Recall the power of anniversaries to propel the work of Tadeusz Kaczyński and the Traugutt Philharmonic and the monumental occasion that connected Krzysztof Penderecki, Lech Wałęsa, and Andrzej Wajda as representatives of Solidarity. The SB kept detailed tabs on the full range of smaller-scale public demonstrations, aware that even if individual events had low numbers, the anniversaries could coordinate dispersed efforts.[4] Intimate oppositional groups—perhaps individuals with family ties to a particular historical skirmish, scout groups with respect for predecessors of their own banded youth resistance, or church congregations devoted to the memory of clerics who took a political stand—rallied in the streets of cities. These performed an alternative, and presumably more authentic, commemorative force to the grand May Day parades and Labor Day celebrations that flooded the stalinist-built boulevards (like Marszałkowska Street in Warsaw) and manufactured factory cities (iconically Nowa Huta along the eastern reach of Cracow).[5] By the end of the 1980s, the opposition's

---

3 I use the most common English translation of the hymn's title through this chapter, which glosses the meaning of the refrain. Among its alternate translations are "God Protect Poland" and "God Bless Poland."

4 This was the case even before martial law. One report within the Ministry of Internal Affairs suggests that they were concerned with foreign correspondents at a "patriotic" manifestation with 500–700 people in attendance in Warsaw, but also with the fact that those gathered sang the national anthem. "Informacja dot. przebiegu wiecu zorganizowanego w dniu 8 marca br. na pl. Na Rozdrożu," March 10, 1981, IPN BU 0365/67, Institute of National Memory, Warsaw, Poland.

5 Malte Rolf's authoritative study of Soviet parades and celebrations considers the way the "Red Calendar" offered the Community Party the opportunity to squash local rituals and values with mass-scale and forced participation in Malte Rolf, *Soviet Mass Festivals, 1917–1991*, translated by Cynthia Klohr (Pittsburgh: University of Pittsburgh Press, 2013).

EXAMPLE 6.1. "God Save Poland," as printed in the standard-issue hymnal in twenty-first century Poland.
Jan Siedlecki, *Śpiewnik kościelny*, 40th edition (2009), p. 541.

subcultures, especially the Orange Alternative in Wrocław, poked fun at these triumphalist performances with explicitly carnivalesque parodies of the state-organized gatherings ▶. As Padraic Kenney has shown, these ludic protests were reframed as happenings by their organizers. Costumes and puppets openly mocked the government, the crowds reappropriated top-down slogans, and any musical repertory was fair game.[6]

---

6 Padraic Kenney, *A Carnival of Revolution: Central Europe 1989* (Princeton, NJ: Princeton University Press, 2002), 1.

At Orange Alternative events, figureheads and defiant youths often were detained as a kind of slap on the wrist to keep things in check. Such petty interventions—though on significant occasions the arrests did escalate, even reaching brutality—were rather common. They were even expected in the atmosphere of dissent by the 1980s and are unremarkable in hindsight—or such is the story I was told by former members of the punk group Praffdata, who once stormed an anti-nuclear youth festival screaming and carrying a giant poster of Lenin ▶.[7] Wojciech Ziembiński's arrest, just one moment in an activist career that was increasingly devoted to the commemoration of Poles murdered by the Soviet Army in the east, is not registered in any of the official sources on his life.[8]

Consider again the news summary, this time as a window onto how music sounds at scenes of protest: we are not just told what music was sung, or that music was sung. The description suggests that *how* this hymn was sung was important for those keeping protest in check and those organizing dissent alike. The protesters are accused of "changing" a lyric of "God Save Poland." If we take the charge of "excess" at face value, I imagine the Catholic hymn sung firmly, and that many sang along. But this evidence is far removed from the scene, and the interpretation plays out my own fantasy of political song through a sound bite that is actually the oppositional scribe's interpretation of a court's interpretation of a SB report on witness accounts transcribed by stenographers after being coerced out of informants.[9] Instead of tracing this trail into historical archives to verify—here I evoke that term with its impossible suggestion of truth—I stop at this aperture onto communal protest through sound to find

---

7 This is a notable contrast to stakes and strategies of arrest for musician protesters in the context that many of the youth protests referenced: 1968. See Beate Kutschke, "Anti-Authoritarian Revolt by Musical Means on Both Sides of the Berlin Wall," in *Music and Protest in 1968*, edited by Beate Kutschke and Barley Norton (Cambridge: Cambridge University Press, 2013), 195–96. For a theoretical discussion of the high stakes of arrest for making sound in a very different time and place, see Noriko Manabe, *The Revolution Will Not Be Televised: Protest Music after Fukushima* (New York: Oxford University Press, 2016), 56–59, 164–66.

8 Grzegorz Waligóra, "Wojciech Ziembiński (1925–2001)," *Biuletyn Instytutu Pamięci Narodowej* 88–89 (2008), 166–71; Alina Czerniakowska, *Był taki ktoś* (2006 Polish Television film). His entry on the Institute of National Memory's encyclopedia of the opposition references earlier arrests; see Krzysztof Biernacki, *Encyklopedia Solidarności*, "Wojciech Ziembiński;" http://www.encysol.pl/wiki/Wojciech_Ziembi%C5%84ski.

9 This is what Todd May, in his reading of Foucault's *Discipline and Punish*, calls "continuance in the face of [the prison's] failure." The opposition's report reveals some breakdown of the chain of information control set into motion by the penal system. In May's words: "Prisons, parole officers, police, informants: all these become relays in a larger system of surveillance where criminality can be overseen, at times even utilized, when it cannot be eliminated." See Todd May, *The Philosophy of Foucault* (Chesham: Acumem, 2006), 78.

others like it, to understand oppositional singing practices as they cohered in this specific Catholic hymn. This "change" to the text worth noting became intuitive; it was always subversive, as we shall see. I dwell in the hymn's chorus by tracing the performance practice of "God Save Poland" from the Congress of Vienna well through Solidarity's moment: into the summer of 2017. For all of this book's contention with the equation of musical unison with political consensus, this Catholic hymn was—and is—a powerful vehicle of communal coherence through music. The chorus's tremendous affective power in Poland resonates with the powerful work of singing in the Baltic states, where the revolution was predicated on "living truth" in song.[10] With the granular focus of the history presented here, however, I also position "God Save Poland" as a limited anthem that, contra the amplification and circulation of sound in Chapter 5, has been trapped in the particularities of its national context.[11] The Polish opposition built its evanescent foundation on diverging identities, cultures, histories, and political ideologies to undo state socialism. The aesthetic and cultural inaccessibility—even irrelevance—of this hymn outside Poland is a crucial component of this book's insistence that there is no universal playbook for the sounds of revolution.

Chorus, Politics, Polity

"Chorus" here refers both to the hymn's formal refrain and to the musical ensembles that gave "God Save Poland" voice. Scholars have traditionally

---

10 Guntis Šmidchens centers song in his story of the "Singing Revolution" and the enormous festival culture that supported the Baltic independence movement. His history provides close literary and historical analysis of the non-Soviet repertory deemed politically meaningful by the movement's participants. Guntis Šmidchens, *The Power of Song: Nonviolent National Culture in the Baltic Revolution* (Seattle and London: University of Washington Press, 2014).

11 Shana Redmond's work on Black anthems, which she insists are founded in politico-diasporic mobility, shapes this sense of limitation in the "God Save Poland" context. Nevertheless, her writing on ritual performance illuminates: "Through anthems, the delineation between art and politics as well as listener and actor is blurred. Anthems demand something of their listeners. In performance they often occasion hands placed over hearts or standing at attention. Yet more than a physical gesture, anthems require subscription to a system of beliefs that stir and organize the receivers of the music. At its best this system inspires its listeners to believe that the circumstances or world around them can change for the better—that the vision of freedom represented in the song's lyrics and/or history are worth fighting for in the contemporary moment." See Shana L. Redmond, *Anthem: Social Movements and the Sound of Solidarity in the African Diaspora* (New York: New York University Press, 2014), 2.

interpreted the power of the chorus as a musical manifestation of collectivity, one that crucially forms political communities.[12] From the civic identity enacted by the ensemble in ancient tragedies to the intimate sense of belonging provided by church choirs, to the crowd organizing shouts of sports fans, to the anthems sung at commemorative performances of the modern nation state: the chorus both multiplies and unifies.[13] It turns up the volume on affect, on discourse, on sound. Analyses that are anxious about unisonality's power over the crowd complement those that underscore the resistance facilitated through the grouping that is the choir.[14] This tension between coercion and inspiration distinguishes mass song from workers' song. It also explains the modulation from Aaron Copland's optimistic exhortation in 1934 that "Workers Sing!" to Witold Lutosławski's weary recollection in 1981 that clear and direct vocal music was the state mandate in postwar Poland until 1956.[15]

The instrumentalization of collective singing as social control by the two totalitarian regimes that bartered Poland in the Molotov-Ribbentrop Pact has threaded much scholarly attention to the chorus through the Russian and German national contexts. For example, in Ryan Minor's analysis of nineteenth-century German choral music, the participatory nature of the chorus models citizenship.[16] Alexander Rehding connects the legacy of these choral celebrations of *das Volk* into the monumental mass-media spectacles of National Socialist Germany. The repertory born in Minor's historical context

---

12 Steven Connor calls this the "strange and powerful plural-singular." See Steven Connor, "Choralities," *Twentieth-Century Music* 13, no. 1 (2016), 3.

13 Renaud Gagné and Mariann Govers Hopman, eds. *Choral Meditations in Greek Tragedy* (Cambridge: Cambridge University Press, 2013); Byron Dueck, *Musical Intimacies and Indigenous Imaginaries: Aboriginal Music and Dance in Public Performance* (New York: Oxford University Press, 2013), 100–26; Robert Woltering. "Unusual Suspects: 'Ultras' as Political Actors in the Egyptian Revolution," *Arab Studies Quarterly*, 35, no. 3 (2013), 290–304; Celia Applegate, "The Building of Community through Choral Singing," in *Nineteenth-Century Choral Music*, edited by Donna M. Di Grazia (New York: Routledge, 2013), 3–20; Karen Ahlquist, ed., *Chorus and Community* (Urbana and Chicago: University of Illinois Press, 2006).

14 See Stefan Michael Newerkla, Fedor B. Poljakov, and Oliver Jens Schmitt, eds., *Das politische Lied in Ost- und Südosteuropa* (Vienna: LIT Verlag, 2011), which shines light on communist regimes' ideological dreams for mass songs, as well as protest movements grounded in singing as dissent.

15 Copland wrote with confidence: "A good mass song . . . creates solidarity and inspires action." See Aaron Copland, "Workers Sing!" *New Masses* 11, no. 9 (1934), 28. Witold Lutosławski, "Wokół zagadnienia prawdy w dziele sztuki," in *50 Lat Związku Kompozytorów Polskich*, edited by Ludwik Erhardt (Warsaw: Związek Kompozytorów Polskich, 1995), 140.

16 Ryan Minor, *Choral Fantasies: Music, Festivity, and Nationhood in Nineteenth-Century Germany* (Cambridge: Cambridge University Press, 2008), 1–7.

confirmed the collective adoration of Adolf Hitler half a century later.[17] Pamela Potter zooms in on one such event in her study of Richard Wagner and the Third Reich. After the performance of *Die Meistersinger* at Bayreuth in 1933, she writes, Hitler halted the audience's customary collective performance of the national anthem and "Horst Wessel Song." Instead, Joseph Goebbels gave a radio address on the opera and its relation to the German nation. He exhorted the work's final chorus. Its message—"Awake!" (*Wach auf!*)—was a charge to those listening in.[18]

In their discussion of the politics of inclusion and exclusion of the US anthem, Judith Butler and Gayatri Spivak turn their eyes and ears to singing in public spaces as they celebrate a contested public performance of the "Star Spangled Banner" in Spanish. For their conversation, both the audibility and visibility of the chorus confer performative agency:

> The point is not simply to situate the song on the street, but to expose the street as the site for free assembly. At this point, the song can be understood not only as the expression of freedom or the longing for enfranchisement—though it is, clearly, both those things—but also as restaging the street, enacting freedom of assembly precisely when and where it is explicitly prohibited by law.[19]

Both power and danger of groups in league shape the ubiquitous choralities of Solidarity in Poland: the chanted slogans, the hymns, and the euphoric rock anthems to which people sang along. These are songs that exert the counter-hegemonic power of the symbol ▶.[20] The 1980 choruses—sing-a-longs—performed the popular assembly as unorchestrated: as critical through their transience, in contrast to the top-down mass spectacles of, for example, song festivals and official parades.[21] Though lyrics described

---

17 Alexander Rehding, *Music and Monumentality: Commemoration and Wonderment in Nineteenth-Century Germany* (New York: Oxford University Press, 2009), 188.

18 Pamela Potter, "Wagner and the Third Reich: Myths and Realities," *The Cambridge Companion to Wagner* (Cambridge: Cambridge University Press, 2008), 241.

19 Judith Butler and Gayatri Chakravorty Spivak, *Who Sings the Nation-State?: Language, Politics, and Belonging* (London: Seagull Books, 2007), 62. This coauthored book differentiates the authors' voices; these words are attributed to Butler.

20 In the Polish context, the most prominent analysis remains Jan Kubik, *The Power of Symbols over the Symbols of Power: The Rise of Solidarity and the Fall of State Socialism in Poland* (University Park: Pennsylvania State University Press, 1994). Observing the 1989 protests in Tianamen Square, Valerie Samson offered the pithy observation: "Almost any kind of music could have value as political protest depending on the circumstances of performance." See Valerie Samson, "Music as Protest Strategy: The Example of Tianamen Square, 1989," *Pacific Review of Ethnomusicology* 6 (1991), 36.

21 Judith Butler, *Notes toward a Performative Theory of Assembly* (Cambridge, MA: Harvard University Press, 2015), 7.

and often responded to contemporary woes by prescribing action, as sung anthems they enact collectivity and project authenticity. In these terms, the Polish case is another node in the global anthem fabric in which, through communal performance, people ordain publics with the capacity to reassert sovereignty.[22] Theologian Helmut Juros plainly remarked as he opened a 1985 congress on religious music in Poland: "Communal singing [is] valued not for its aesthetic value, but its functionality."[23] Through the 1980s, the power of the individual in the collective was at stake, as was the power of the collective beyond itself.

But the chorus is not merely an ideal. Bernard Lortat-Jacob suggestively writes that the social and sonic formulation that is the chorus "give[s] an acoustic form to shared experiences."[24] His description focuses on the physical connection between choristers who sing side by side, who feel and transmit embodied vibration. The story of "God Save Poland" offers insight into the value of co-presence and the stakes of bodily vulnerability in the dissenting contexts of the 1980s. The hymn's choral performance, I suggest following the apt formulation of Lortat-Jacob, gives acoustic form to shared history.

"God Save Poland" is among the handful of anthems along which one might string Solidarity's story. There are euphoric rock choruses, drunken renditions of "One Hundred Years," international resistance anthems like "Walls," patriotic legion songs that conjure the military hero Józef Piłsudski, and other strophic hymns out of Polish Catholic history (see, for example, Chapter 3).[25] In this chapter, however, I focus on one particular chorus again and again, reading its history in conversation with some of the first scholarly studies of its history, written in the 1980s.[26] I underscore some of the discrete

22 Thomas R. Hilder, *Sámi Musical Performance and the Politics of Indigeneity in Northern Europe* (Lanham, MD: Rowman and Littlefield, 2015), 19–21. On emboldened communities as publics, see Redmond, *Anthem*, 9–10.

23 "Powitanie," in *Aktualna sytuacja muzyki religijnej i liturgicznej w Polsce*, edited by Maria Bogusławska (Warsaw: Akademia Teologii Katolickiej, 1988), 6.

24 Bernard Lortat-Jacob with Marc Benamou, "Concord and Discord: Singing Together in a Sardinian Brotherhood," in *Chorus and Community*, edited by Ahlquist, 93.

25 There is a long history of putting anthems in competition with one another as the most representative, as discussed in Maja Trochimczyk, "Sacred/Secular Constructs of National Identity: A Convoluted History of Polish Anthems," in *After Chopin: Studies in Polish Music*, edited by Maja Trochimczyk, Polish Music History 6 (Los Angeles: Polish Music Center at the University of Southern California, 2000), 263–94.

26 The establishment of the Museum of the National Anthem in 1978 near Gdańsk, as well as the increased presence of singing patriotic anthems across political contexts, spurred renewed scholarly and popular interest in the history of songs. See Hanna Domańska, *Muzeum Hymnu Narodowego w Będominie* (Gdańsk: Krajowa Agencja Wydawnicza, 1981). There was also special interest in "God Save Poland." The 1980s histories of the song end with the Second World War but do print the contested lyric; see,

moments in which "God Save Poland" was sung or otherwise mobilized for the collective in order to write one history of the chorus. By plumbing the richness of its political-theological work in the nineteenth century, another constellation of spaces and functions emerges. In a final analysis, I explore the hymn off the streets and unsung, as one of three citations that anchors Krzysztof Meyer's *Polish Symphony* (1982). The first of these inroads—presented here without the concatenating work of scholarly prose—is perhaps the most kaleidoscopic and perfunctory, but its detail drives the flexibility and ubiquity of "God Save Poland" home.

"Boże, coś Polskę": 1977–89

- July 6, 1978: Composer and cultural critic Zygmunt Mycielski writes to émigré poet Czesław Miłosz and describes a mass on the 35th anniversary of General Władysław Sikorski's death. On July 4, 1943, the prime minister of the Polish Government in Exile perished in a plane crash off Gibraltar. "He was *my* general," Mycielski mulls, "[The Church of the Holy Cross] is full. A wreath, an eagle, 'God Save Poland,' a good sermon, a Bach Toccata is played beautifully at the end. But everyone had already left, with the wreath, for the Grave of the Unknown Soldier."[27]
- August 18, 1980: At 5 p.m. the striking workers at the Lenin Shipyards pray together and share an "emotional moment.... The workers compose new texts for 'The Oath' and 'God Save Poland' and their collective singing keeps sounding better."[28] Over the course of the month, the hymn is sung often in the meeting hall,[29] as part of the masses held across the open grounds of the shipyards,[30] and in the churches of the

---

for example, Bogdan Zakrzewski, *"Boże, coś Polskę" Alojzego Felińskiego* (Wrocław: Zakład Narodowy im. Ossolińskich, 1983); and Alina Nowak-Romanowicz, "Przyczynek do dziejów pieśni 'Boże, coś Polskę,'" *Ruch Muzyczny* 7 (April 3, 1983), 24–25. Tadeusz Matulewicz, "Boże, coś Polskę," *Kultura* 42 (October 18, 1981), 14. Wawrzykowska-Wierciochowa's monumental edition was also begun during this time: Dioniza Wawrzykowska-Wierciochowa, *"Boże, coś Polskę": Monografia historyczno-literacka i muzyczna* (Warsaw: Instytut Wydawniczy Pax, 1999).

27 Czesław Miłosz Correspondence, Box 45, Folder 653, Bienecke Rare Book and Manuscript Library, Yale University, New Haven, CT.

28 "Kalendarium," *Bratniak* 24 (July–August 1980), 8.

29 See the discussion of Adam Orchowski's reconstruction in Chapter 3, based on *Polski Sierpień 1980* (New York: Biblioteka Pomostu, 1981).

30 At approximately 1'20" in *Robotnicy '80* (dir. Andrzej Chodakowski and Andrzej Zajaczkowski, 1981).

tri-city region.[31] Many of these recordings are re-broadcast over Radio Solidarity in the months to come ▶.[32]

- November 10, 1980: At a four-hour concert celebrating Solidarity ("Solidarity's first gala event") at Warsaw's Grand Theater, the audience sings along to many of the cherished songs of the nascent union and listens in rapt attention as actors recite poetry. Two years later, when the concert is rebroadcast on Radio Free Europe, the commentators remember people singing "God Save Poland" after the concert had formally ended.[33] A cassette recording of the concert captures Lech Wałęsa leading the crowd in the hymn.[34]

- Undated (ca. 1980–85): The hymn appears on broadsides typewritten, mimeographed, copied by hand, and photocopied by the opposition. Within the corpus held at the University of Bremen, for example, one copy contains the melody (only), another in an A5 notebook is itself a carbon copy that includes only two verses, and one is included in what appears to be a collection of patriotic-religious prayers (see Figure 6.1).[35]

- May 17, 1981: A homemade cassette tape that tells the story of the assassination attempt on Pope John Paul II five days earlier includes an amateur recording of the hymn sung by a congregation.[36] Many of the cassettes of the opposition with religious themes include "God Save Poland."

- September 20, 1981: The regional bulletin for Solidarity's Lublin-based union, *Wprost*, includes a photograph of Lech Wałęsa flanked by

---

31 Interview by author with Anna Tarnowska-Waszak, July 31, 2009.

32 It is the second song, after the national anthem on a tape (with the handwritten label "Gdańsk spotkanie delegatów MKZ 25 IX 1980") at the People's Republic of Poland Archive, Museum of Independence, Warsaw, which indicates that this documentation of a meeting of delegates was recorded off the radio.

33 The event is described in Timothy Garton Ash, *The Polish Revolution: Solidarity*, third edition (New Haven, CT: Yale University Press, 2002), 89–91. Fragments broadcast on Radio Free Europe December 31, 1982; http://www.polskieradio.pl//68/2461/Audio/307136.

34 CD 515, Nagrania ze zbiory MSW, National Commission of the Independent and Self-Governing Trade Union "Solidarity," Gdańsk, Poland.

35 "FSO-2-003 Flugschriften, Flugblätter, Dokumente aus dem poln. zweiten Umlauf," Archiv der Forschungsstelle Osteuropa an der Universität Bremen, Bremen, Germany.

36 "Po zamachu na Jana Pawła II," CD 477, Nagrania ze zbiory MSW, National Commission of the Independent and Self-Governing Trade Union "Solidarity," Gdańsk, Poland.

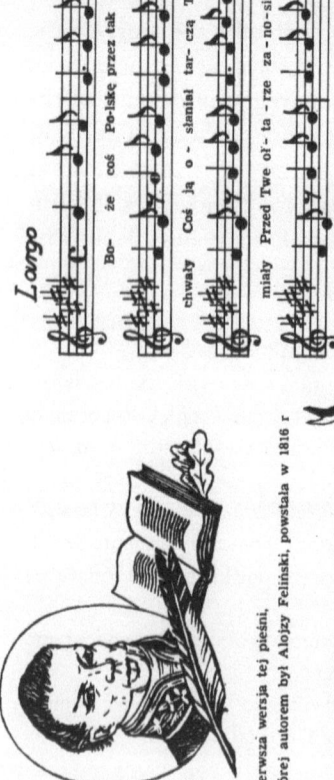
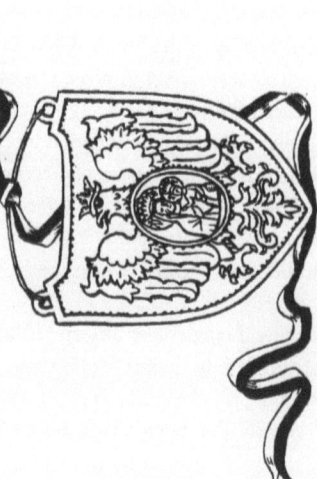

FIGURE 6.1. Examples of "God Save Poland" within the paphletry of the Polish opposition. Collected at Archiv der Forschungsstelle Osteuropa an der Universität Bremen. FSO 02-003-K30-1, FSO 02-003-K30-54, FSO 02-003-K30-54.

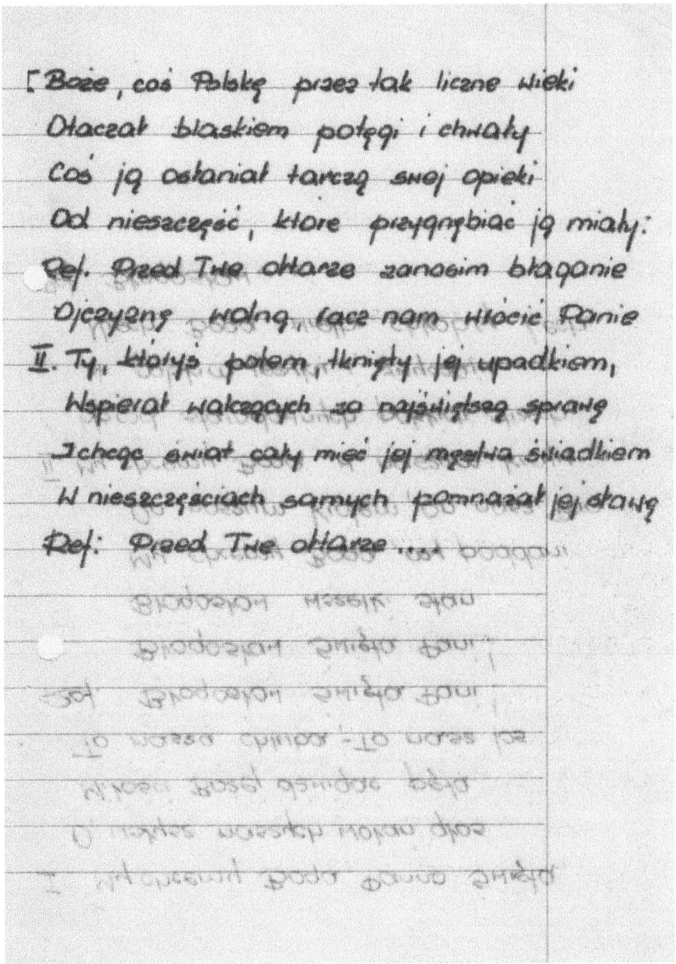

FIGURE 6.1. (Continued)

Zbigniew Bujak and other leading activists singing together, with the hymn's first line—in large font—emblazoned beneath the transcript of Wałęsa's address (Figure 6.2).[37]

- 1982: The State Folk Song and Dance Ensemble, "Mazowsze," releases a new album on vinyl and cassette. The eponymous song of the album concludes the first side of *Boże, coś Polskę: Prayer for the Country*.[38] The studio recording of the arrangement by Romuald

---

37 *Wprost* 47 (September 20, 1981), 1.

38 Mazowsze, *Boże, coś Polskę: Prayer for the Country*, LP, cassette, Veriton SXV-848, VK-010.

Modlitwa Pańska

Ojcze nasz, któryś jest w niebie,
Święć się Imię Twoje, przyjdź królestwo Twoje,
bądź wola Twoja, jako w niebie, tak i na ziemi.
Chleba naszego powszedniego daj nam dzisiaj
i odpuść nam nasze winy, jako i my odpuszczamy
naszym winowajcom, i nie wódź nas na pokuszenie,
ale nas zbaw ode złego. Amen.

Modlitwa za Ojczyznę

Ks. Zachowaj, Panie, Ojczyznę naszą.
W. Która w Tobie, Boże mój, nadzieję pokłada.
Ks. Ześlij jej, Panie, pomoc z przybytku swego.
W. Z nieba wysokiego ją wesprzyj.
Ks. Niech nie bierze nad nią góry nieprzyjaciel.
W. A duch nieprawości niechaj jej nie szkodzi.
Ks. Niech Bóg sprowadzi pokój do domów jej.
W. I bezpieczeństwo do jej posiadłości.
Ks. Panie, wysłuchaj modlitwy mojej.
W. A wołanie moje niech do Ciebie przyjdzie.
Ks. Módlmy się: Prosimy Cię, Panie, za przyczyną Najświętszej Maryi
  Panny, Królowej Polski, i za wstawiennictwem Świętych
  Patronów naszych, ochraniaj Ojczyznę naszą od wszelkich
  przeciwności, gdy całym sercem którzy się przed Tobą,
  zasłoń ją łaskawie od zasadzek nieprzyjacielskich. Amen

1. Boże, coś Polskę przez tak liczne wieki
   otaczał blaskiem potęgi i chwały,
   Coś ją osłaniał tarczą swej opieki
   od nieszczęść, które przygnębić ją miały:
   Ref.: Przed Twe ołtarze zanosim błaganie
   Ojczyznę wolną, racz nam wrócić Panie.
2. Ty, któryś potem tknięty jej upadkiem,
   wspierał walczących za najświętszą sprawą,
   I chcąc świat cały mieć jej męstwa świadkiem,
   w nieszczęściach samych pomnażał jej sławę.
   Ref.: Przed Twe ołtarze...

1. MY CHCEMY BOGA, Panno Święta!
   O usłysz naszych wołań głos,
   Miłości Bożej dźwigać pęta
   to nasza chluba, to nasz los,
   Ref.: Błogosław, Święta Pani, błogosław wszelki stan!
   My chcemy Boga, my poddani! On naszym Królem, On nasz Pan!
2. My chcemy Boga w naszym kraju,
   Wśród starodawnych polskich strzech.
   W polskim języku i zwyczaju,
   Niech Boga wielbi Chrobry, Lech.
   Ref.: Błogosław...

FIGURE 6.1. (Continued)

Twardowski for SATB choir and organ is clean and light, especially compared with the slow and chorally sloppy August 1980 recording from a Gdańsk church released in 1981 by, among many labels, Folkways Records.[39]

39 See Chapter 3.

FIGURE 6.2. Solidarity dignitaries singing "God Save Poland."

- June 25, 1982: An inmate at the internment camp sends a letter describing the celebration of Corpus Christi on June 10 behind walls: "for three hours the prison was a church." The visiting chaplain leaves after concluding mass with a collective performance of "God Save Poland." As he departs, they continue singing to him.[40] There is voluminous evidence of the hymn sung at religious services and as part of the activities to pass time in the internment camps and prisons of martial law—not least in the songbooks they craft see (Chapter 2).

- January 30, 1983: The Traugutt Philharmonia performs its first concert under the title "God Save Poland" in Warsaw's Church of St. Hyacinth (Św. Jacka). It is dedicated to songs from the January Uprising on its 120th anniversary. "The concert concluded with the hymn 'God Save Poland,' sung by the entire ensemble—and the refrain once with the entire public. Ten verses of the post-uprising original version."[41]

- May 5, 1983: Ewa Ostrowska's 30-minute audio documentary, "Democrats," is broadcast on Radio Free Europe to celebrate May Day and Poland's Constitution Day (May 3). The broadcast's opening three minutes are punctuated by a recording of a performance of "God Save Poland" in a large sanctuary with organ accompaniment.[42]

- June 21, 1983: A woman in attendance at Pope John Paul II's pilgrimage to Wrocław's racecourse is interviewed by Janina Jankowska. She weeps about the feeling his Holiness inspires: "That we are in solidarity, that we arranged a cross and sang 'God Save Poland,' and lit candles. And we prayed for all those who had perished through the events of August 31, for those dead, and for Wałęsa and for the freedom . . . of Poland."[43]

- June 26, 1983: Leszek Polony reviews Krzysztof Meyer's *Polish Symphony* (1982). He listens to the quotation of the song carefully: "The melody of the hymn 'God Save Poland' emerges from [a held bass note], led by the cellos and contrabasses. From the third verse of the song the violins' sighing motive, a leading tone that takes over the pleading, serves as counterpoint."[44]

- May 1984: The review by Paul Moor of Krysztof Penderecki's *Te Deum* leads with an excerpt of the composer's musical arrangement of the hymn within the choral work. He explains this typographic decision: "Everyone else will hear this melody merely as an unexpected

---

40 AO IV/56.8, Archive of the Opposition, Karta Organization, Warsaw, Poland.

41 Rafał Bracki, "Filharmonia imienia Traugutta," *Kultura Niezależna* 3 (1983), 56.

42 Ewa Ostrowska, "Demokraci," http://www.polskieradio.pl/68/2461/Audio/299562,Demokraci.

43 Jan Gall, *Pielgrzym trudnych chwil: Cz. 2, "Odzyskać nadzieję,"* NowaKaseta 010 (1983). Solidarity Collection, Houghton Library, Harvard University. Jan Gall is the pseudonym of Janina Jankowska and Marek Mądrzejewski.

44 Leszek Polony, "Nie znacie? A szkoda: Krzysztof Meyer, Symfonia Polska," *Ruch Muzyczny* 13 (June 26, 1983), 5.

choral-like interlude, but for Poles it assumes the profoundest significance and has the power to move a comprehending audience to tears."[45]
- October 24, 1984: Jerzy Popiełuszko's death is announced at the parish of St. Stanisław Kostka in Żoliborz. The hymn is sung, with, as one witness remembers, its new text.[46]
- November 4, 1984: The *Los Angeles Times* reports on Popiełuszko's funeral, including the tour his coffin makes through the steelworks where the priest held mass for workers. "The crowd surged forward and thurst up their hands in V-for-victory signs. They sang 'Boze Cos Polske' [*sic*] (God Who Watches Over Poland), a religious hymn that has become a symbol of defiance of the Communist authorities."[47]
- June 4, 1975: During a roundtable discussion at a musicological conference on religious music, Tadeusz Kaczyński challenges Jan Węcowski for abbreviating and modifying "God Save Poland" on his 1966 recording of Polish religious songs.[48] Kaczyński accuses him of not honoring patriotic fights for Polish independence in the past; Węcowski counters that he picked the music with the most beautiful texts.
- ca. 1985: As he reads news items of interest to lead off the 16th edition of his *Sound Gazette* (see Chapter 1), Stefan Bratkowski remarks:

> In truth: Wałęsa, the Provisional Council [Tymczasowa Rada] and the [Temporary Coordinating Council] have a couple of hundred thousand—yes, *a couple of hundred thousand*—in their industrial unit structures. The rest, for now, are just forests of bunnies singing "God Save Poland" by the church on high holidays. But I wouldn't advise anyone to belittle those bunnies. A favorable situation, one signal, and there's going to be a million behind Wałęsa. Another signal—three million. A third—ten million. The authorities know that, the authorities remember, the authorities . . . the authorities . . . anyway, this is suggested by sociological studies, I'd reckon.[49]

---

45 Paul Moor, "Penderecki's *Te Deum*: Another Milestone from a Modern Master," *High Fidelity* 34, no. 5 (May 1984), 63–64.

46 Roma Szczepkowska, ed., *Ks. Jerzy Popiełuszko: Życie i śmierć, Dokumenty i wspomnienia* (Paris: Polemika, 1986), 74.

47 "3 More Involved in Priest Death: Thousands Gather on Eve of Cleric's Funeral," *Los Angeles Times*, November 4, 1984, 12.

48 *966–1966: Polskie pieśni religijne*, Veriton, VX-706 (1966). Discussion transcribed in *Aktualna sytuacja muzyki religijnej i liturgicznej w Polsce*, edited by Maria Bogusławska (Warsaw: Akademia Teologii Katolickiej, 1988), 98–100.

49 Stefan Bratkowski, *Gazeta Dźwiękowa* 16 (undated), Muzeum Niepodległości, People's Republic of Poland Collection, Warsaw, Poland.

FIGURE 6.3. Drugi obieg stamps commemorating the performance of "God Save Poland."
Fundacja CDCN, Zn 434 III; Ple 878 III.

- 1988: For the 50th anniversary of the steel mill town Stalowa Wola, built from nothing, an artist affiliated with Solidarity designs four underground postage stamps to celebrate the city, a hotspot for strikes that summer (Figure 6.3). The fourth stamp has a hand raised in a "V," a crucifix, and the text, "God Save Poland."

As is no doubt clear, the list goes on; this sedimented history's particles are infinite. Another methodological approach, the one that is the heart of this chapter, is to figure these performances as the residue, or even accumulation, of a longer historical practice of singing "God Save Poland" that is the crucible of Solidarity's musical solidarity. How did it come to be that Timothy Garton Ash observed, "There is no doubt that anyone who spoke, wrote, or (best of all) sung about national independence could be sure of a great and growing response"?[50] As we shall see, the "change" to the final line of "God Save Poland" mentioned in *Tygodnik Powszechny* is the hymn's political power and thorn.

50 Garton Ash, *The Polish Revolution*, 263.

1816

Boże, coś Polskę przez tak liczne wieki	God, for centuries thou hast enveloped Poland
Otaczał blaskiem potęgi i chwały	With the radiance of thy power and thy glory
I tarczą swojej zasłaniał opieki	And with the shield of thy care hast protected it
Od nieszczęść, które przywalić ją miały:	From disasters drawing nigh:
Przed Twe ołtarze zanosim błaganie,	At thy altars we lay down our prayers,
Naszego Króla zachowaj nam, Panie!	God, save our King!

The hymn's story begins along the complex terrain of nineteenth-century Polish nationalism. Alojzy Feliński (1771–1820) originally published the hymn's text in 1816 to celebrate the Russian Tsar's role in the formation of the Kingdom of Poland at the Congress of Vienna.[51] A poet, playwright, and translator, Feliński frequently incorporated historical and nationalist themes into his works. The piece remained in the repertory of theater troupes through the nineteenth century: the great madame of Polish theater, Helena Modejska, cut her teeth playing the title role of his *Barbara Radziwiłł* (1817) in 1865.[52] Feliński was also personally connected with a national hero from the Polish pantheon: he served as the correspondence secretary for Tadeusz Kościuszko, the leader of the 1794 uprising against Imperial Russia—who had also been decorated for his contributions to the Continental Army in the American Revolutionary War.

The hymn's original text bears no relation to the nostalgic (and even love-lorn) turn of the 1817 play, which glorifies the Polish-Lithuanian Commonwealth in classical verse. Instead, Feliński praises the Tsar, grateful for his protection and hopeful that God will in turn keep Poland's guardian safe. In the immediate aftermath of partition, state sovereignty was not the driving ambition of Polish nationalism, and the text's praise of the Russian head of state did not hinder the song's power to cohere a public.[53] The final line echoed the popular and frequently parodied "God Save the King," which had also circulated in Polish translation and adaptation in praise of the Polish monarch.[54] In fact, the first publication of "God Save Poland," on the front

---

51 *Gazeta Warszawska* 58 (July 20, 1816), 1.

52 This anecdote is a point of pride in 1980s biographies of Feliński; see Tadeusz Matulewicz, "Boże, coś Polskę."

53 On the complex strains and symbols of Polish nationalism through nineteenth-century commemorations, see Patrice M. Dabrowski, *Commemorations and the Shaping of Modern Poland* (Bloomington: Indiana University Press, 2004).

54 Dioniza Wawrzykowska-Wierciochowa, *"Boże, coś Polskę,"* 13–15.

FIGURE 6.4. The first publication of "God Save Poland."

page of the *Warsaw Gazette* (*Gazeta Warszawska*), positions the English hymn as the prompt for the new anthem (see Figure 6.4). The anonymous description observes that Feliński's text is in "that spirit."

There are westward and eastward gazes toward empire in the impetus for the hymn. None of the musical settings of "God Save Poland"—more about which later—bears resemblance to the eighteenth-century English anthem that Malcolm Boyd has suggested is a "model" for many European national anthems that are topically hymns.⁵⁵ And while "God Save Poland" was decidedly Catholic, "God Save the King" signaled support for King George II against his Catholic detractors.⁵⁶ But both exhortations firmly give God a hand in the fate of modern nation states and thus complemented the emphasis on penitence within Polish Catholicism.⁵⁷ The familiarity and popularity of the English hymn certainly also augmented the power of the final line of "God Save Poland." Even from this textually stable beginning, the intertextual work of this anthem upholds J. Martin Daughtry's suggestion that (national) anthems are best understood as "polysemous text[s] through which national identity is constantly being negotiated."⁵⁸

The first publication of "God Save Poland" falls under the newspaper header "News from the Country" (*Krajowe wiadomości*), an unwitting transmission resonant with the arrest account that organized this chapter's beginning. The paper issues the following report from Warsaw, followed by the hymn's text, as seen in Figure 6.4:

> The English people's best-loved song, *"God Save the King,"* often mentioned in this paper, has inspired Mr. Aloizy *Feliński*, a noted man of letters in this country, to write a national song in the same spirit, but in Polish. It is reproduced below. Owing to this fact, His Imperial Majesty Konstantin has deigned to make his satisfaction known to the author. Captain *Kaszewski* from the Fourth Infantry Regiment has created appropriate music to this hymn, following which voices of soldiers of various ranks perform this hymn every Sunday during the church army parade in the Holy Carmelite Church, while the remainder of the army sings the *chorus* that concludes each stanza. May these prayers, which come from the depths of hearts overflowing with gratitude and raised to God in the Kingdom's capital, and which are then repeated by the loyal people across the entire country, prolong unto

---

55 Malcolm Boyd, "National Anthems," *Grove Music Online, Oxford Music Online*. Oxford University Press; https://www-oxfordmusiconline-com.libproxy.lib.unc.edu/grovemusic/view/10.1093/gmo/9781561592630.001.0001/omo-9781561592630-e-0000019602.

56 Glenda Goodman, "Transatlantic Contrafacta, Musical Formats, and the Creation of Political Culture in Revolutionary America," *Journal of the Society for American Music* 11, no. 4 (2017), 392–419.

57 Brian Porter-Szűcs, *Faith and Fatherland: Catholicism, Modernity, and Poland* (Oxford and New York: Oxford University Press, 2011), 226–27.

58 J. Martin Daughtry, "Russia's New Anthem and the Negotiation of National Identity," *Ethnomusicology* 47, no. 1 (2003), 42.

TABLE 6.1 Adaptations of the Final Line of "God Save Poland" for Political Purposes

1816:	"Save our King, Lord!" (Naszego Króla zachoway nam Panie!)
1830:	"Return our Homeland to us, Lord!" (Naszą Ojczyznę racz nam wrócić Panie!)
1956:	"Return our free Homeland to us, Lord!" (Ojczyznę wolną racz nam wrócić Panie!)
1989:	"Bless our Homeland and freedom, Lord!" (Ojczyznę, wolność, pobłogosław Panie!)
1996:	"Bless our free Homeland, Lord!" (Ojczyznę wolną pobłogosław Panie!)

advanced age the most precious life of *ALEXANDER I*, the most beloved Monarch our Father, to whom we owe so much benefaction.[59]

The explanatory text is part program note, part performance instruction, laying out the hymn's dramaturgical power during military parades. The music is to be performed by a trained army choir of mixed voices. The chorus that concludes each verse expands the singing ensemble. The news item explains that the two repeated lines drive at the heartfelt emotions of those assembled. The blurb, too, instrumentalizes the debut performance within state pomp and circumstance.

The public theatrics chronicled here shaped the first performance tradition for "God Save Poland." In her monumental study of the song's written sources and material history, Dioniza Wawrzykowska-Wierciochowa argues that it was first and foremost a military song until 1820. Through the late 1820s, it was still sung at every public celebration and at Sunday masses.[60] Ultimately, however, faith in the Tsar to protect civil liberties in the Russian partition—which included the nation's then-and-now capital Warsaw—weakened as the promise of autonomy for the Kingdom of Poland specified at the Congress went unfulfilled. Public and printed declarations of adoration of the Tsar ceased to have patriotic resonance; the hymn fell out of favor across political camps. Only much later, when Poland regained independence after the First World War, would the state recoup the hymn and its ceremonial affect. In the increasingly polarized political climate of the 1820s, "God Save Poland" rallied the fight for independence. The original music for the hymn by Jan Neopomucen Kaszewski, however, became passé. His tune, with its ornamental melodic turns, disappeared from the paper trail and performance record of the hymn at this point in its history (see Example 6.2a and 6.2b).

---

59 *Gazeta Warszawska* 58 (July 20, 1816), 1. Emphasis in original.
60 Dioniza Wawrzykowska-Wierciochowa, *"Boże, coś Polskę,"* 19, 26.

EXAMPLE 6.2. Melodic settings of "God Save Poland" compared: the standard melody, the 1815 melody, and an 1828 version set to a popular Marian Song.

EXAMPLE 6.2A. Opening phrase.

EXAMPLE 6.2B. Final plea.

Adaptation as/to Resistance

"God Save Poland" re-entered performance practice in public spaces when it was adapted to new and resistant political contexts during the failed November Uprising against Russia (1930–31). In his monumental history of nineteenth-century literature, Stanisław Tarnowski described communal performance and oral transmission in this moment: "Never have [little patriotic songs] blossomed so, never have they come into being in so many ways and so often, never were they loved so much, never were they taken up so willingly, sung and heard with such delight, as in the years between 1831 and 1846."[61]

---

61 Quoted in Maria Janion, "Słowo i symbol w miesiącach przełomu," in *Kongres Kultury Polskiej, 11–13 grudnia 1981*, edited by Władysław Masiulanis (Warsaw: Oficyna Wydawnictwa Volumen Instytut Kultury, 2000), 41.

In public memory, the song fortified those on crusade: they sang while fighting, it was "on soldiers' lips" as they went into battle.[62] Two major changes were permanent: "God Save Poland" received a new choral refrain and a new melody. The ultimate plea for intercession was reoriented: protect Poland, not the Tsar. The adaptation of text to address the contemporary plight of the Polish nation became a custom—indeed, it is the "change" that ruffled the feathers of the SB and became a badge of honor, of sorts, for the Solidarity periodical that launched this chapter. Table 6.1 compares the five political choruses of the hymn, each pleading for Poland as its status as a sovereign nation has shifted over time.

The "blossoming" of song in print and oral transmission confirmed this new text as standard. Thanks to the painstaking work of the historian Wawrzykowska-Wierciochowa, undertaken as a response to the song's significance for the 1980s, we can observe just how malleable the text was across the many formats that capture the frenzy for the song—pamphlets, song collections, hymnals, newspapers, sheet music, piano paraphrases, to name just the most accessible in urban print culture. The hymn's flexibility has grounded its popularity, its choral refrain ever-adaptable to past, present, and future concerns for freedom and national independence from 1828 onward. Musical adaptation and arrangement have also bolstered its circulation—Chopin himself arranged a nonstandard version.[63] In Wawrzykowska-Wierciochowa's critical edition of "God Save Poland," she notes dialogisms with other patriotic hymns; some versions contain additional verses that address current events. After the song was revived without mention of the Tsar, the chorus remained the same across the variants: "Return our fatherland to us, Lord!"[64]

Print sources contained various attributions for the new melody. It was designated a folk melody, attributed to the nationalist composer Karol Kurpiński (1785–1857), claimed as a borrowing from an aria by Jean Pierre Solié, and attributed to a religious song.[65] Maja Trochimczyk has emphasized the false link many have made with the religious folk song "Dearest Mother" ("Serdeczno Matko").[66] The Czech-Jewish musicologist Paul Nettl, writing

---

62 Tadeusz Matulewicz, "Boże, coś Polskę."

63 Published in *Chopin: Suplement; Hexameron, mazurki, wariacje fletowe i inne*, edited by Jan Ekier (Warsaw: Polskie Wydawnictwo Muzyczne, 2010).

64 See, in particular, the appendices to her study, which annotate the original sources according to 18 foundational variants; see Wawrzykowska-Wierciochowa, "*Boże, coś Polskę,*" 464–562.

65 The aria in contention is "Qu'on soit jalouse" from *Le secret* (1796).

66 See Trochimczyk, "Sacred/Secular Constructs of National Identity," 276, for a full discussion of the song's relationship to folk music. In the twenty-first century this spurious association still appears in texts that emphasize the music's "religious character." See Balázs Trenscényi and Michal Kopecek, eds., *Discourses of Collective Identity in Central and*

the first history of "God Save Poland" in English, values the song's mobility.[67] "This anthem too is a migrating melody," he colorfully narrates its ubiquity, characteristically attuned to tunes' variance and interested in the politics of musical geography.[68] Writing in the United States after fleeing Nazi-compromised Prague, Nettl hears the hymn not as Polish, despite a strong conceit that "the song fully deserves the title of honor often bestowed upon it, that is, the Polish Anthem of the Opposition."[69] He hears references to it in Solié's comic opera, as well as in an Italian folk song that Carl Maria von Weber treated to a set of variations.[70] More revealing, perhaps, is that Nettl maps the hymn's regional resonance across the Austro-Hungarian Empire and the Third Reich—that is, along the military mights that shaped his own biography. These are, he writes, "blood relations."[71] A songbook from Upper Silesia contains lyrics in Czech translation. He notes its performance by German soldiers under Hitler. Nettl's interest in dissemination (rather than origins) also makes clear that a tune's flexibility carries with it not only the potential for Herderian collective plurality, but also the performance of exclusion and difference.[72] Nettl draws attention to a performance instruction from a German school book: "lively and spirited [*flott und lustig*] and not after the sentimental fashion of the Poles."[73] It matters, again, not just that it is sung, but how.

Across all these references—localizations of text, musical adaptations to function—hovers the importance of national belonging and tradition. The song pleads for the protection of a nation not (yet, or again) granted a state. Though the "change" to its text defines the political expediency of "God Save Poland" to this day, the hymn has retained Feliński's original narrative arch. After asserting a broad claim of adoration (of the Tsar, of God), the text delves into specifics: those giving voice ask for action on behalf of Poland. The poet Jacek Bierezin, among many who observed the powerful presence of this song in the mid-1980s, made casual reference to the fact that the hymn

---

Southeast Europe (1770–1945): Texts and Commentaries, Volume 1: Late Enlightenment-Emergence of the Modern "National Idea" (Budapest and New York: Central European University Press, 2004), 294–95.

67 Paul Nettl, *National Anthems*, 2nd edition (New York: Frederick Ungar, 1967), 122–24.

68 Paul Nettl, *National Anthems*, 124. Annegret Fauser, *Sounds of War: Music in the United States during World War II* (Oxford: Oxford University Press, 2013), 71–72.

69 Nettl, *National Anthems*, 122.

70 He is referencing Weber's *7 Variations sur l'air "Vien quà, Dorina bella,"* Op. 7 (1807).

71 Nettl, *National Anthems*, 125.

72 Johann Gottfried Herder and Philip V. Bohlman, *Song Loves the Masses: Herder on Music and Nationalism* (Oakland: University of California Press, 2017), 44–49.

73 *Gesangbuch für Bürgerschulen* (1924). Quoted in Nettl, *National Anthems*, 123–24.

had "achieved the status of a second national anthem" precisely because of its observable and palpable popularity. For him, the song had itself worked its way through the competition, surviving (with the national anthem) as one of the fittest.[74] Other critics in the opposition located its power in its evergreen message to Poles looking ahead. Writing in 1980 in the literary weekly *Kultura*, Tadeusz Matulewicz commented, "The Biblical belief in the nation's exceptionality, the remembrance of former glory in years of slavery, the trust in the help of higher powers—all this, along with music, was consistent with the social feeling (*uczucie społeczne*), lingered in the atmosphere, determined the success of the song."[75] In music (and singing), the song enmeshes trust in the nation and belief in the Holy Scripture—divine transcendence with the power of community.

Singing "God Save Poland"

The hymn's material history illustrates a broad range of social functions when sung and places it at the intersection of many sociabilities.[76] There are pianovocal scores in songbooks that indicate domestic use, piano paraphrases for salons (in Poland and in Paris), sheet music editions for amateur and military choral performance, and hymnals. The latter reveal the hymn's increased functionality as a liturgical regular, not just as the occasional offering as it had served in the 1810s.

The work is paraliturgical. It shares four-part harmonization with the hymns that ground Catholic liturgy, making its inclusion in services feasible. The melody's similarity to hymns of praise, for example, supplied the justification for its legitimate incorporation into the mass in the Austro-Hungarian partition. When the Cracow-based Bishops of Galicia officially shifted their allegiance from support of a Polish-Austrian allegiance to the celebration of national independence in 1918, they asked that the hymn be intoned for congregational singing following the Te Deum.[77] In the Russian partition—in contrast—it was occasionally sung within church walls but without organ accompaniment to keep it less audible.[78] Historian Ted Weeks describes an incident that anticipates Ziembiński's 1984 arrest. In 1861, one imperial agent substantiated a claim that

---

74 Jacek Bierezin, "Fenomen: Jacek Kaczmarski," in Jacek Kaczmarski, *Wierszy i piosenki* (Paris: Instytut Literacki, 1983), i.

75 Matulewicz, "Boże, coś Polskę."

76 Kate van Orden, *Materialities: Books, Readers, and the Chanson in Sixteenth-Century Europe* (New York: Oxford University Press, 2015), 4–7.

77 Neal Pease, *Rome's Most Faithful Daughter: The Catholic Church and Independent Poland, 1914–39* (Athens: Ohio University Press, 2009), 19.

78 Report on Warsaw in *Süddeutsche Zeitung* 184 (April 11, 1861), 2.

political resistance was born in the church with evidence that priests led congregations in song, naming "God Save Poland" as one.[79] The texts also aroused controversy in the Prussian partition. In 1866, under the pretext of liturgical reform, the Archbishop of Poznań developed a policy of political disengagement for the Church. He forbade "God Save Poland" in sanctuary spaces, claiming that its performance brought politics into weekly devotion.[80]

Example 6.2 compares the two nineteenth-century melodies with the simplified and stately version that was learned by ear in the 1980s.[81] (In common devotional practice within Polish Catholic Church, the hymnal is rarely consulted.) The increased simplicity of the melody's rise and fall and elimination of rhythmic complexity over time likely have contributed to "God Save Poland's" flexibility as a freedom anthem. Most variants—as seen in these three archetypes—conform to a shared melodic shape. Seeking resonance of Feliński's text in the musical material, I hear the simple downward gestures in the vocal line and sparing use of harmonic tension as a kind of musical salve that suggests the stability of God's protection.

Those individuals who were interested in speaking at length with me about "God Save Poland" focused on the experience of hearing and singing the hymn—its affect instead of its history. "That's a tune like a lullaby," one retired French teacher told me as we shared a February afternoon in Warsaw discussing her humanitarian work making and doling out soup to activists at churches during martial law. "It was inviting. My friends and I felt strong when we began singing, 'God!,'" an academic responded when I pushed him to explain why performing this anthem at protests in the late 1980s had been comfortable for him, then a Protestant student in Warsaw. Music makes the work safe and secure, whether because of its might or calm.

I likewise hear the chorus of "God Save Poland" with attention to its particular features and personal histories. A melody in rising stepwise motion frames the presentation of the prayer at God's altar, so that the twice repeated supplication is at the height of the vocal line. Singing the word *błaganie* (prayer) offers the amateur singer the greatest difficulty, so that the desperation on behalf of Poland is mimicked in a singer's vocal strain. This

---

79 Ted Weeks, "Religion, Nationality, or Politics: Catholicism in the Russian Empire, 1863–1905," *Journal of Eurasian Studies* 2, no. 1 (2011), 53.

80 William Fiddian Reddaway, *The Cambridge History of Poland, Volume 2* (Cambridge: Cambridge University Press, 1941), 416. The historian connects citizenship and faith: "In all this he showed himself the true churchman—*civis Romanus, subditus Borussiae*; whose resolve it was to keep his office above national controversies, and to wage no wars unless in defense of the faith."

81 Based on *Śpiewy burszów polskich z muzyką na trzy głosy ułożoną* (Lviv) and *Śpiewnik strzelecki szkoły junaka dla organizacyj przysposobienia wojskowego* (Warsaw), originally reproduced in Dioniza Wawrzykowska-Wierciochowa, *"Boże, coś Polskę,"* 478–79.

physiological break stood out to me during the spontaneous performances of this hymn that I witnessed through my fieldwork. I listened to my neighbors while I sang along in churches, at commemorations, and at festivals, trying to fit in. Or, in feedback interviews, I worked to hear care, devotion, and personal history when the older patrons of the Traugutt Philharmonic sang the melody for me, either by supplying eye contact or moving my body to face them more directly. Across these live choruses, that first melodic peak, approached from below, rarely had the fortitude of its reiteration with an open vowel at the start of the final phrase: *Ojczyznę* (Fatherland).

A Hymn in Between

The hymn has maintained its significant status as liminal: at the boundaries of devotional practice and as a bridge between intimate communities of faith and assembled publics. Its prominence at the end of Father Jerzy Popiełuszko's Masses for the Fatherland, discussed in Chapter 4, has its roots in nineteenth-century practice when it was sung at the end of the service. It was also first published in the final pages of hymnals, for example in sections specifically designated as soldiers' songs.[82] These peripherals in the vernacular would eventually receive permission—at least in some parishes—to be sung within services and thus also reflect the increased Polonization of Catholic worship in the Austro-Hungarian partition through the nineteenth century.[83]

The 1828 musical setting entwined "God Save Poland" with the Polish Catholic Church and its public interfaces, usurping the original melody entirely.[84] The new tune was more singable, and, as Wawrzykowska-Wieciochowa establishes, it was already in the public domain as the unattributed religious fanfare, "Hail to You, Blessed Mary" ("Bądź pozdrowiona, Panienko Maryja"). This source's musical genre expands the ceremonial and religious elements of the hymn. As a *hejnał*, a genre of morning trumpet call specific to Poland, the fanfare was among the repertory of brief pieces performed from atop St. Mary's Church in Cracow onto the Market Square. These signals functioned as the city's "sonic armature," as theorized by Niall Atkinson.[85] They called (and call) attention to the time of day and,

---

82 Wawrzykowska-Wieciochowa, *"Boże, coś Polskę,"* 408.

83 Theo Hamacher, "Das Kirchenlied der Romantik," in *Geschichte der katholischen Kirchenmusik*, Volume 2, edited by Karl Gustav Fellerer (Kassel: Bärenreiter, 1976), 262–70.

84 Wawrzykowska-Wieciochowa,*"Boże, coś Polskę,"* 411.

85 Niall Atkinson, "Sonic Armatures: Constructing an Acoustic Regime in Renaissance Florence," *Senses and Society* 7, no. 1 (2012), 39–52.

on occasion, the time of year. They also directed (and direct) visual attention to the church as the trumpeter positions the instrument through the bell tower's windows to amplify the call through the medieval town center. As the loudest music blasted into Cracow's primary plaza, it reached a lot of ears. In 1861 this particular song still flagged that genre and geography: Stanisław Moniuszko arranged it with six other *hejnał*s for publication in a weekly magazine.[86] The popular familiarity of some of these is captured in the vague titles some are given in the printing: "A *hejnał* sung by everyone."

I have positioned "God Save Poland" at three interfaces that position it as an inclusive link between the Church and other publics: at the fringes of buildings, ritual ceremonies, and civic institutions. The hymn is thus an exemplary conduit through which to observe—and understand the significance of—historian Brian Porter-Szűcs's claim that "the church was never the *only* space within which Poles could express and cultivate the myths, customs, or practices of their ethnicity."[87] It reveals, too, that the division between the texts (e.g., hymnals), rites (e.g., mass), and spaces (e.g., sanctuaries) of the Catholic Church and corollaries in other public domains (e.g., newspapers, memorial ceremonies, squares) was porous.

"God Save Poland" functions simultaneously as a patriotic hymn and a church hymn through its music and appellation. During the interwar period, it was published under the heading of national anthem (*hymn narodowy*), even after the Dąbrowski March was officially granted this status in 1926.[88] It circulates as explicitly Catholic and/or as secular—generating what George Mosse influentially called the "worked-out liturgy" of nationalism as "civic religion."[89] When Józef Piłsudski commanded the first celebration of Independence Day on November 11, 1926, it was "God Save Poland" that was sung at the end of the service in Warsaw's Orthodox churches—and described in the newspaper reports of the coordinated celebration of national sovereignty.[90]

Recall the hymn's paraliturgical work. Ethnomusicologist Antoni Zoła has illustrated how the porous separation of sacred and profane continues to define Catholic singing in Poland.[91] He argues that many

---

86 Included as the illustrations for "O hajnałach krakowskich," *Tygodnik Ilustrowany* 3, no. 84 (1861), 169.

87 Brian Porter-Szűcs, *Faith and Fatherland*, 8.

88 Jan Siedlecki, *Śpiewnik kościelny z melodjami na dwa głosy* (Lwów, 1928), 535.

89 George L. Mosse, *Nationalization of the Masses: Political Symbolism and Mass Movements in Germany from the Napoleonic Wars through the Third Reich* (New York: Fertig, 1975), 2.

90 M. B. B. Biskupski, *Independence Day: Myth, Symbol, and the Creation of Modern Poland* (Oxford: Oxford University Press, 2012), 52–53.

91 Antoni Zola, CD booklet for *Polskie pieśni religijne*, Polish Radio Folk Collection 25, edited by Maria Baliszewska, Małgorzata Jędruch-Włodarczyk, and Antoni Zoła, PRCD 174.

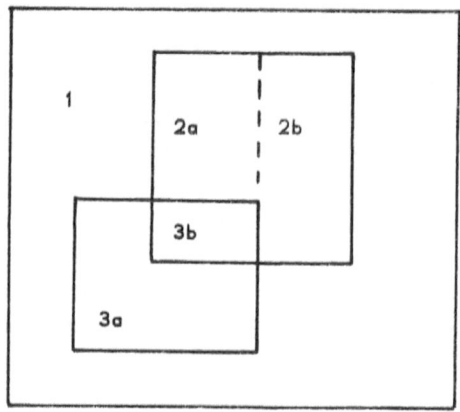

FIGURE 6.5. Bolesław Bartkowski's model for religious music.
1: Religious songs; 2a: Non-liturgical hymns; 2b: Liturgical hymns/songs;
3a: Songs outside the church; 3b: Songs with an ambivalent function.

tunes with origins outside of the Church sound like hymns. Zola focuses on songs as the locus of interaction between system and adaptation. When paraliturgical songs are adapted to the church space, they absorb the influence of organ accompaniment. Sung outside of liturgical contexts, they bear sonic reference to their "other" use. In a 1987 monograph on the living tradition of Polish religious song, Bolesław Bartkowski argued more explicitly that "paraliturgical" music builds a relationship between the Church as container and expanding spaces of collective action. He presented a typology of religious music with a diagram that maps the dynamism or "religious music" in interlocking and overlapping boxes (see Figure 6.5).[92] This Venn-diagram variant organizes repertories that have traversed the church's threshold in both directions. It also abstracts the sanctuary space and public religious life, so that Bartkowski projects the meaningful movement of paraliturgical singing between or among both groups of people, activities, and physical enclosures.

Polishness under Pressure

It is tempting to seek out pivotal moments in which performances of "God Save Poland" propagated the essential germ of its appellation: Polish Catholic identity

---

[92] Bolesław Bartkowski, *Polskie śpiewy religijne w żywej tradycji: Style i formy* (Cracow: Polskie Wydawnictwo Muzyczne, 1987), 25.

as normative. Without question, the hymn's affiliation with the Church explains some of its loudest performances. I have listened back, for example, to its performance by and with Pope John Paul II on June 7, 1979, in Lower Silesia during the pontiff's first pilgrimage to his homeland.[93] When the Polish community in London celebrated the Millennium of Polish Christianity in May 1966, announcers for Radio Free Europe reported that 70,000 were in attendance to sing the hymn, with its demand for a free Poland.[94] When Tadeusz Mazowiecki, the first democratically elected prime minister, visited Chicago, he spoke to the Polish-American community at a Catholic Church, where a mass was held in his honor. The *Chicago Tribune* reported: "The brief address was the last of the prime minister's visit, which ended with a spirited singing of 'Boze, Cos Polske,' the Polish hymn."[95] These performances of "God Save Poland" complement church history.

The hymn connects generations, weaving communities of dissent with communities of descent.[96] For example, in the Polish silent film *Hurricane* (*Huragan*, 1928), it is performed by the main characters, a heroic couple, during the January Uprising of 1863. Succinct intertitles convey lessons about the restrictions on the freedom of expression. From the first text, singing is politically loaded: "The year 1863. [Adam] Mickiewicz's songs have been silenced, but have rendered a flame of self-sacrifice in all hearts. Everywhere the nation finds an eagerness to seek out unity and independence."[97] In a later scene, the couple prays for an end to the violence of the uprising in a local church. We are told that they sing "God Save Poland" with the congregation. Closeups and crowd shots in alternation suggest that this is a devotional and unisonal rendition of "God Save Poland," even if the live music that would have accompanied its original screening has not survived.[98] During another violent revolt, the Warsaw Uprising in August 1944, the hymn was certainly sung within the walls of the cinemas following mass.[99] References to the

---

93 "Audycje specjalne rada Solidarność Dolny Śląsk - Jan Paweł II i prymas Stefan Wyszyński," CD 419, Nagrania ze zbiory MSW, National Commission of the Independent and Self-Governing Trade Union "Solidarity," Gdańsk, Poland.

94 "Materiały dźwiękowe z uroczystości zorganizowanej z okazji Sacrum Millenium Poloniae w Londynie;" http://www.polskieradio.pl/68/2461/Audio/294314.

95 Christi Parsons, "2,000 Pack Church to Catch Glimpse of Polish Leader," *Chicago Tribune*, March 26, 1990, S3.

96 Kay Kaufman Shelemay, "Musical Communities: Rethinking the Collective in Music," *Journal of the American Musicological Society* 64, no. 2 (2011), 349–90.

97 Quoted in Ewa Mazierska and Elżbieta Ostrowska, *Women in Polish Cinema* (New York: Berghahn Books, 2006), 39.

98 A similar scene (though with playback of the hymn with organ accompaniment) occurs in Bogdan Poręba's 1973 *Hubal*, this time set in Nazi-occupied Warsaw.

99 Joanna K. M. Hanson, *The Civilian Population and the Warsaw Uprising of 1944* (Cambridge: Cambridge University Press, 2004), 249.

hymn are littered through personal accounts of this traumatic event. One memoirist claimed that singing the hymn stalled a street skirmish, buying time for the arrival of more insurgent machine guns.[100]

In the heat of resistance in 1944, singing along to "God Save Poland"—allowing one to be absorbed into its emotional power—allowed people to pass as Polish Catholics. In his first-person account of the Warsaw Uprising and his eventual flight from Poland, Benjamin Mandelkern explains that being a part of the chorus for the hymn's renditions was a means of disguising (or distracting from) his Jewishness:[101]

> The Poles observe all ceremonies where religion is concerned. . . . To give the greatest number of people the opportunity to pray collectively and receive the priest's blessing, a different courtyard was chosen every time for the service. . . . It was "natural" that all the residents of the block attended the mass. Unless on a military mission, I went to the service too. I followed all the movements the others made, kneeling and crossing myself at the right moments. When the mighty sound of the national religious hymn ["God Save Poland"] filled the air, I would sing loudly, I knew the words and the tune well. Everything then was so emotional I always made sure that my neighbours heard me singing and saying *amen* when the occasion called for it.[102]

He approaches the hymn as one more way to physically perform his belonging.[103] His passing is dependent on understanding the song's meaning for others and knowing the performance rituals that are intuitive to this group. Mandelkern engages his body, to "fill the air" with his breath, in accordance with the Catholic rite.

"God Save Poland" appears in poetry written by Zbigniew Jasiński while fighting in the 1944 rebellion against the occupying forces. His four-stanza verse registers a complaint about how performances of the

---

100 Discussed in Antoni Przygoński, *Powstanie warszawskie w sierpniu 1944 r.*, Volume 1 (Warsaw: Polskie Wydawnictwo Naukowe, 1980), 426.

101 His relationship to the song is in counterpoint with its performance within nineteenth-century campaigns for Jewish assimilation by the Polish Jewish brotherhood, for example. See Magdalena Opalski and Israel Bartal, *Poles and Jews: A Failed Brotherhood* (Hanover, NH, and London: Brandeis University Press, 1992), 42, 53.

102 Benjamin Mandelkern, with Mark Czarnecki, *Escape from the Nazis* (Toronto: James Lorimer, 1988), 156–57.

103 It was also, according to Stanisław Lachowicz, sung in the Cracow Ghetto already in 1941. See Stanisław Lachowicz, *Muzyka w okupowanym Krakowie 1939–1945* (Cracow: Wydawnictwo Literackie, 1988).

hymn can sound. According to historian Norman Davies, the BBC Polish Service had selected the tune as its theme.[104] Jasiński found it too resigned against the "elated" (*radośne*) energy of the Warsaw Uprising on the ground—apparently the recording was one of the more lugubrious. His poetry borrows the language of the Polish underground radio ("This is Warsaw speaking!"), which would eventually broadcast the author's reading of the poem, read aloud, to propose a counter-effect. Throughout, exclamatory punctuation transmits some of the enthusiasm he misses in the BBC broadcast.

Żądamy amunicji (We Demand Ammunition, final three verses)

A wy tam wciąż śpiewacie, że z kurzem krwi bratniej,	And you're still singing about Warsaw's destruction
Że w dymie pożarów niszczeje Warszawa,	In the smoke of conflagrations, in the dust of our brothers' blood.
A my tu nagą piersią na strzały armatnie,	While we, naked breasts facing cannon fire,
Na podziw wasz, na śpiewy i na wasze brawa.	Earn your admiration, songs and applause.
Czemu żałobny chorał śpiewacie wciąż w Londynie,	Why are you still singing that somber chorus in London
Gdy tu nadeszło wreszcie oczekiwane święto!	When here the long-awaited celebration has begun!
U boku swoich chłopców walczą tu dziewczęta	At the side of our boys we have girls fighting
I małe dzieci walczą, i krew radośnie płynie.	And little children fighting, and the blood flows joyously.
Halo! Tu serce Polski! Tu mówi Warszawa!	Hello! This is the heart of Poland! This is Warsaw speaking!
Niech pogrzebowe śpiewy wyrzucą z audycji!	Tell them to scratch those funereal songs from the radio program!
Nam ducha starczy dla nas i starczy go dla Was!	Our spirit is enough for us and there's enough of it for you!
Oklasków nie trzeba! Żądamy amunicji!	There's no need for applause! We demand ammunition!

A Choral Symphony

The prominence of "God Save Poland" was also marked in new art music from Poland. In the 1970s and 1980s, new symphonic music tracked the

---

104 Norman Davies, *Rising '44: The Battle for Warsaw* (New York: Viking, 2004), 731.

contemporary importance of religious music.[105] Cindy Bylander and Paweł Strzelecki have understood this stream after Penderecki's *St. Luke Passion* (1966) as Polish "neo-romanticism," a path away from the fascination with and of the international avant-garde that had dominated the new music scene.[106] Long before Henryk Mikołaj Górecki's Third Symphony (1976) topped *Billboard* charts in the early 1990s, it stood out among many works that were built out of folk, religious, and patriotic textures and tunes.[107] Composers orchestrated for conventional ensembles and constructed formal scaffolding out of tonal spaces. In his symphony, Górecki builds harmonic patterns and formal sections (canons) out of the songs he cites. Górecki's *Miserere*, Opus 44 (1981), is a notable example in the orbit of oppositional culture. Adrian Thomas hears in the choral work dedicated to the March 19, 1981, conflict between Solidarity and the militia in Bydgoszcz "elements of massed choralism typical of a choral congregation."[108] Through timbre, the work negotiates along the paralitugical axis of "God Save Poland." Górecki himself said in conversation in 1985, "I don't want to differentiate liturgical songs from others."[109] In Krzysztof Meyer's sixth symphony, the *Polish Symphony* (1982), the composer cites three choral anthems for and from Solidarity. My sustained analysis of this work is a final take on the hymn as itself a cultural history of music in Poland. Meyer, as I shall show, leaves his citations hanging, appended, and somehow between the work he writes and the world in which his audience (usually) sings these tunes. His work enacts spiritual resistance in a symphony and choral singing out of an orchestra.

At the conclusion of the first movement, Meyer intones the melody of "God Save Poland" (Example 6.3). It grows out of a sustained cluster in the double basses. The tune remains unadorned in the orchestra's lowest strings, the cadences at the end of each four-bar phrase elaborated upon by ever-lengthier sinuous counterpoint in the upper strings. Meyer subtly distorts the square meter to effect a lingering *morendo* before briefly returning to the

---

105 Adrian Thomas, *Polish Music since Szymanowski* (Cambridge: Cambridge University Press, 2005), 253–55. He highlights oratorios and text settings, as well as compositions for sacred spaces.

106 For an overview of the stylistic unities and influences within neo-romanticism and an argument for the school's existence, see Paweł Strzelecki, *"Nowy romantyzm" w twórczości kompozytorów polskich po roku 1975* (Cracow: Musica Iagiellonica, 2006). See also Cindy Bylander, "Charles Ives and Poland's Stalowa Wola Festival: Inspirations and Legacies," *The Polish Review* 59, no. 2 (2014), 43–60.

107 Adrian Thomas, *Górecki* (Oxford: Clarendon Press, 1997), 81–93; Luke B. Howard, "Motherhood, *Billboard,* and the Holocaust: Perceptions and Receptions of Górecki's Symphony No. 3." *Musical Quarterly* 82, no. 1 (1998), 131–59.

108 Thomas, *Górecki*, 102.

109 *Aktualna sytuacja muzyki religijnej i liturgicznej w Polsce*, edited by Maria Bogusławska (Warsaw: Akademia Teologii Katolickiej, 1988), 55.

EXAMPLE 6.3. Krzysztof Meyer, *Polish Symphony*, melodic paraphrases of religious songs.

EXAMPLE 6.3A. Krzysztof Meyer, *Polish Symphony*, "God Save Poland," mvt. 1.

EXAMPLE 6.3B. Krzysztof Meyer, *Polish Symphony*, "Mother of God," mvt. 3.

EXAMPLE 6.3C. Krzysztof Meyer, *Polish Symphony*, "The Oath," mvt. 4.

movement's hesitant first theme. Just as the hymn (usually) was sung at the end of masses and meetings, protests and memorial rituals, it is positioned at the end of the movement. It leads us as listeners out of the first bounded unit of the symphony and invites us to reflect on our own relationships to the song.

The hymn is one of three religious and patriotic songs that the composer quotes in structurally significant moments of this symphony, a musical response to martial law. A former student of Lutosławski and Penderecki, along with Nadia Boulanger, in 1982 Meyer was a music theory docent at the Cracow Music Academy. Along with the "Bogurodzica" ("Mother of God") and "The Oath" ("Rota"), the paraliturgical hymn resonates collectivity and participation, making audible Meyer's political allegiance. Indeed, "God Save Poland," because of its power to flag the struggle for Polish independence, had been already been quoted in art music as (following David Metzer's formulation) cultural agent—even before 1944.[110] In Franz Liszt's interlude from his unfinished Stanislaus Oratoria, *Salve Polonia* (ca. 1863) for piano, it opens the second section. Alexandre Tansman arranged it as the final piece in *Vingt pièces faciles sur des mélodies populaires Polonaises* (1925), written after the Łódź-born Polish Jewish composer had moved to Paris. The arrangement is slow and *solenne*. Its concluding two measures are the only ones marked forte in the entire piece: Tansman catches his listeners' attention at the pivotal final chorus.

Meyer joined at least two of his colleagues by citing this work in the late twentieth century.[111] One of Zygmunt Krauze's collage pieces with tape and live performance, *Soundscape* (1975), teases apart "God Save Poland"; he returned to the anthem in *Tableau vivant* (1982) for chamber orchestra. In the 1980s composition, the citation comes at a moment of tremendous reduction of instrumentation, tempo, and texture. The pulse of the work (already quarter note = 60) becomes *molto tranquillo*. Individual instrument sections line out the hymn's first lines, repeating each pitch multiple times so that only listeners primed to seek a long line will recognize that there is a melody in this wisp of a musical presence. The performers quiet from *ppp* to *pppp*.

Krzysztof Penderecki represents the populace as a chorus on stage. He explicitly instructed them to sing the adapted chorus of the hymn when it appears as a crystalline injection in his *Te Deum*, completed in 1980. At figure 30—about two-thirds through the forty-minute work—the orchestra drops out and a four-part vocal ensemble sings the hymn's first two lines within. The lush and tonal harmonization by Penderecki is all the more comfortable because a sinewy and atonal solo soprano line bridges the first and second halves of "God Save Poland." Toward the capstone concluding lines, Penderecki winds down the musical flow: with a fermata before the plea

---

110 David Metzer, *Quotation and Cultural Meaning in Twentieth-Century Music* (Cambridge: Cambridge University Press, 2003).

111 Both are discussed within Bogumiła Mika's typology of citation in Bogumiła Mika, "Pieśń Boże, coś Polskę w funkcji cytatu w polskiej muzyce artystycznej XX wieku," in *Muzyka religijna: między epokami i kulturami*, Volume 2, edited by Krystyna Turek (Katowice: Wydawnictwo Uniwersytetu Śląskiego, 2009), 114–34.

for protection begins, instructions that they sing *poco meno mosso*, and—as in Krauze's work—ever more quietly. Musicologist Mieczysław Tomaszewski, a close friend of Penderecki's, explained the political meaning of this surfacing, in which he felt—like my interlocutors—strength:

> In the cantata's penultimate verse a religious hymn ["God Save Poland"] . . . which had become an anthem of the liberation movement, resounds defiantly—this time also *quasi da lontano*. Its symbolic interpretation acts cathartically—in any event on Polish audiences. The more so, as ignoring obligatory censorship, Penderecki instructs the chorus to sing a version of the hymn to words sung only during the years of captivity.[112]

Tomaszewski's hint at the specific symbolic work that "God Save Poland" does *in Poland* underscores a crucial point here: what to outsiders might come across as the redundant, excessive, or predictable is, for those at home in the hymn, an invitation to emotional intimacy.

Ruch Muzyczny *under Review*

Let us meet Meyer's *Polish Symphony* as many of his Polish audience members did, through a review published in June 1983 in *Ruch Muzyczny* (*Musical Movement*).[113] The title of the regular column devoted to new works, "You don't know it? Too bad," has particular resonance for Meyer's symphony: premiered in Hamburg, it had not yet been performed in Poland. The review's sprawling length—nearly two A3 pages—was typical of the column inches that important new works, like Meyer's, received. Critic Leszek Polony saturates the review with technical details, drawing attention to every orchestration decision and carefully delineating form. The article's text captures the fine line that journalists walked as they continued to write about contemporary musical culture after the essential periodical of the classical music community had been suspended by the government during martial law.

Polony begins by describing his first encounter with the work, deploying a roster of references to the political situation.

> I heard Krzysztof Meyer's new work for the first time last year on December thirteenth, among friends the composer had invited to

---

112 Mieczysław Tomaszewski, *Penderecki* (Warsaw: Adam Mickiewicz Institute, 2003), 26. While Tomaszewski streamlines the hymn's history, it is worth noting that Penderecki's score, published by the West German press Schott, does include the "changed" text. *Te Deum* (Mainz: Schott, 1980), ED 7107 Schott.

113 Leszek Polony, "Nie znacie? A szkoda," 5–6.

his home. Not even a full three weeks earlier, on the twenty-fifth of November, the premiere of the *Polish Symphony* by the North German Radio Symphony Orchestra had occurred. . . . An amateur, but completely technically successful recording, made during the concert in Hamburg with the help of a miniature tape recorder from Japan, was replayed here, in Cracow, on a superb stereo system, allowing for full evaluation of the quality of both the music and the performance.[114]

The review's opening paragraph follows convention, covering the details surrounding the premiere and subsequent "performance." At the same time, Polony cultivates a sense of intimacy, ushering the reader into the composer's home and bringing the *Polish Symphony* to Cracow. In 1983, Polish readers, however, would have dwelled on the opening, because the critic suggests a political stance without taking one. Right off the bat, Polony situates the work within the opposition to communist rule by being specific with his details. December 13, 1982, the date on which Meyer, Polony, and friends heard the work, marked one year since the declaration of martial law. "The thirteenth of December in the year remember," the song at work in Chapter 2, leaves proof of its powerful legacy here.

In less numerical code, the critic alludes to two musical practices associated with life under martial law: gatherings in the home and the trafficking of bootleg cassette tapes.[115] By foregrounding his domestic listening and the Japanese cassette player, Polony signals the opposition's activities but does not implicate himself in dissident activism. Microcassette recorders were not illegal, but they were most often imported hand to hand across the border or via stores that only accepted Western currency, like any technology from outside the Warsaw Pact zone.[116] The use of the recorder at the *Polish Symphony*'s West German premiere to bootleg shared little with that of the Polish opposition, who used hand recorders to capture meetings that would be re-broadcast over Solidarity's underground radio stations (see Chapter 3). The review is positive. Polony praises the communicative power of the *Polish Symphony* specifically, as do the German reviews of the premiere. The latter draw attention to the

---

114 Polony, "Nie znacie? A szkoda," 5.

115 See Chapter 2. See Joanna Krakowska-Narożniak, Wojciech Miszczuk, and Marta Fik, *Teatr drugiego obiegu: Materiały do kroniki teatru stanu wojennego 13 XII 1981–15 XI 1989* (Warsaw: Oficyna Wydawnicza Errata, 2000).

116 In interview with the author, several former Solidarity members spoke lightly of their activity covertly bringing such technology across the border between 1980–85, acknowledging the actions had low stakes, though they could have attracted SB attention (Małgorzata Pietkiewicz, July 2, 2010; Stanisław Krupowicz, January 10, 2011; Judyta Szylar, June 3, 2010).

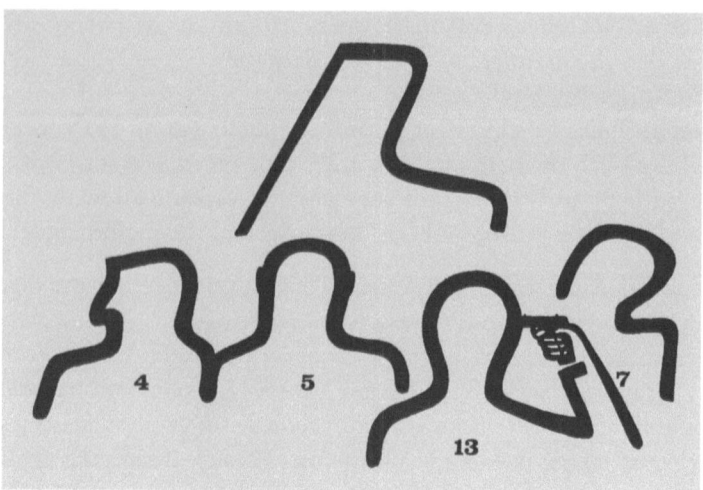

FIGURE 6.6. Cover of *Ruch Muzyczny*, July 1982. Designed by Marian Jankowski.

exalting applause in the concert hall as evidence of the work's accessibility, as does an anonymous Polish review of a later Cracow performance.[117]

In the official music press, there was some explicit writing about politics during the 1980s. Criticizing martial law on pages one could purchase at any good bookstore—as was the case with the art music periodical *Ruch Muzyczny*— drew the attention of the Censorship Bureau. The periodical's presses had been halted in December 1981, and, shortly after the magazine resumed publication in June 1982, the Party's Central Committee issued a warning, prompted by the not-so-subtle symbolism of the front-page image on July 25 to the periodical's editor-in-chief (see Figure 6.6). "Musicologists and musicians constituting the editorial board of this periodical repeatedly assumed unfavorable or even hostile attitudes toward the processes underway in Poland."[118] The bureaucrat who filed the August 20, 1982, report explicated the sketch's political critique:

> There's the emphasis of a black, fat line that outlines an open grand piano and a row of listeners' silhouettes with the symbolic numbers four, five, seven, and thirteen. The figure marked with the number thirteen holds a pistol to his own head. This is a clear allusion to the thirteenth of December, the date of martial law's declaration, and puts

---

117 See Georg Borchardt, "Sein jüngstes Werk ist eine polnische Sinfonie," *Die Welt* (April 29, 1982); Walter Labhardt, "Polnische Gegenwartsmusik," *Neue Zürcher Zeitung* (April 10–11, 1982); and Lutz Lesle, "Neue Werke von Krzysztof Meyer in Hamburg," *Das Orchester* 7 (1981). "Symfonia polska Meyera," *Przekrój* 2017 (January 1984), 12.

118 536 897/88, WK PZPR, AAN.

forth the legible suggestion: martial law—this is suicide for Polish culture.[119]

The cover art most clearly indicates the periodical's "aggression" to the censor's eyes, but the author of the report goes on to substantiate the warning with examples from throughout the issue.

The Party bureaucrat claims that something suspicious is afoot: *Ruch Muzyczny* does not assess the Polish musical present in a positive light. According to the missive, a number of concert reviews threaten Polish musical life by disparaging the lack of financial support and through outspoken advocacy for Polish musicians abroad. In fact, columns devoted to festivals and recordings beyond national borders were staples of the journal, and this issue additionally portrayed the richness of musical culture in Poland by including an interview with the Minister of Culture and the Arts (Izabella Bojkowska), fragments from the composer Grażyna Bacewicz's personal papers, and a rave review of the LaSalle Quartet's recent performance in Warsaw. The censors quantify the periodical's Westward gaze, noting that 60 percent of the writings in this publication are devoted to non-Polish musicians. The witty, frequently elitist, and conflict-driven debates of the music criticism that characterized *Ruch Muzyczny* irk the bureaucrat because of their frequent pessimism. As of 2017, the files of the Censorship Bureau, PZPR, and SB contained no other concern for *Ruch Muzyczny* in the 1980s.[120] Having paged through the 1980s run of the periodical, I do not consider this issue remarkable for its content. Perhaps the lengthy report is a product of a bureaucratic routine in the segmented structure of the party.[121] Perhaps, by the time the review of Meyer's symphony was published, it had been filed away, its fact-finding rendered useless.[122]

The Party would not have first heard of the *Polish Symphony* through Polony (or even Polony's cassette) anyway. To some extent, it took ownership of the work's "Polishness." A 1986 document that tracks the distribution of state funds to "serious music" (*muzyka poważna*) from 1980 to 1986 lists

---

119 536 897/88, WK PZPR, AAN.

120 The SB coverage contains unannotated, identical copies of the reports at AAN on this same issue, as well as correspondence that the journal was being issued again after the post-martial law break. IPN BU 1585/21370, Institute of National Memory, Warsaw, Poland.

121 For an application of Max Weber's theories of bondage and bureaucracy to communist Poland, see Maria Hirszkowicz, *The Bureaucratic Leviathan: A Study in the Sociology of Communism* (Oxford: Robertson, 1980).

122 On the lure of objectivity for archive makers, see Antoinette Burton, ed., *Archive Stories: Facts, Fictions, and the Writing of History* (Durham, NC: Duke University Press, 2005).

Meyer's symphonic work.[123] The list, an attachment to a report on patronage, presents empirical evidence that cultural life had been renewed after the official conclusion of martial law. Meyer benefited—when, how, and how much is not clear, since there is no evidence the work was written on commission. That a composition quoting "God Save Poland" could receive party funding while someone singing it in protest was at risk reveals just how disinvested the Culture Department was in censoring musical content in the 1980s (see Chapter 1).[124]

Polony did not assume music's political impact or import. Instead, martial law prompted him to question music's power to ameliorate everyday life. In the Meyer review he commented:

> It has been difficult for the last while to focus our attention upon music. Thoughts have hovered outside the world of sounds, penetrated the walls of the concert hall, returned to the abandoned external conflicts, disputes, and problems. Our constant, external discourse upon the present lasted without our having a chance to articulate it. What trace do the events of the past years leave in Polish music? And do they leave [one]? Is the reaction to the world's mundane affairs generally the stuff of music?[125]

Polony's skepticism and oblique reference to martial law again rely on the power of suggestion. But his turn against music's political expediency—consider the many who did turn to musical routines in Chapter 2—is a challenge. Does Meyer contend that music is relevant and instrumental with this symphony? I suggest that the composition bears vestiges of oppositional practices within its form, not apparent without hearing it in conversation with the extended historical looping I have undertaken in my choral fantasy on "God Save Poland."

A Symphony for the Polish 1980s

Meyer's music had its Polish premiere at the 1984 Warsaw Autumn Festival, along with Penderecki's *Polish Requiem* (discussed in Chapter 3). In his program note for that first performance, Meyer hoped his work would have meaning for Polish listeners. Like Polony, he assiduously avoided explicit reference to politics: "The composition is about contemporaneity, the present,

---

123 LVI-210, WK PZPR, AAN.

124 As one report summarized: "The support and stimulation of musical creation, including inspiration, commission, purchase, and stipends—particularly state patronage—is one of the most important activities with respect to cultural and artistic activities." LVI-210, WK PZPR, AAN.

125 Leszek Polony, "Nie znacie? A szkoda," 6.

the problems preying on our minds. The Symphony is the composer's view on everything we have witnessed and experienced."[126] Placing himself as a member of his Polish audience, he casts himself as a fellow citizen and the work as a composition that speaks both out of and to everyday life in Poland. He gives the audience permission to hear this work through their reality, drenched in "problems."

Meyer's musical decisions also convey an interest in communication as he leans hard on traditions within the Western canon. Composed for a full orchestra with the fortification of a percussion battery, the symphony is built of four movements that conform to the narrative arc of the nineteenth-century symphony: a moderate lament, a brusque scherzo, a contemplative elegy, and a martial finale. In an interview with Maciej Jabłoński, the composer has clarified his symphonic language as strategically accessible. He explains that nineteenth-century performing forces and formal outlines are instrumental for fashioning a language that reaches audiences primarily educated through eighteenth- and nineteenth-century repertory.[127]

Among late twentieth-century symphonies, the work most directly references Dmitri Shostakovich, Meyer's mentor and friend, whose music he has promoted through multiple creative channels. He completed Shostakovich's opera *The Gamblers* over the course of 1980–81 and compiled the first Polish biography of the Russian composer in the late 1970s.[128] Using textures that recall the military onslaught in Shostakovich's Seventh Symphony and allusions to the melancholic solos of the Fifth Symphony's storied third movement, Meyer evokes him in the 1982 work.[129] The *Polish Symphony* sounds in step with a composer noted for his struggles with communist authorities.

Meyer understands the Soviet composer's musical politics as dissident. In his 1973 Shostakovich biography, he frames his mentor's commitment to the symphony as an investment in accessibility. Meyer extolls, for

---

126 Krzysztof Meyer, program book for the 1984 Warsaw Autumn Festival (Archive of the Warsaw Autumn Festival, Polish Music Information Center, Warsaw), 181.

127 Maciej Jabłoński, "Gespräche," in *Krzysztof Meyer: Ein Komponistenporträt* (Poznań/Cologne: Ars nowa/Bela Verlag, 1998), 49.

128 Krzysztof Meyer, *Szostakowicz* (Cracow: Polskie Wydawnictwo Muzyczne, 1973). It is worth noting that this book was published before the controversial memoirs, which were published in Polish translation out of the 1979 English-language version in the drugi obieg, the unofficial print culture of the opposition, in 1987, with a 1989 second edition. See Solomon Volkov, ed., *Testimony: The Memoirs of Dmitri Shostakovich*, translated by Antonina W. Bouis (New York: Harper and Row, 1980); and Solomon Wołków, ed., *Świadectwo: wspomnienia Dymitra Szostakowicza*, translated by Barbara Maluch (Warsaw: Niezależna Wydawnicza Oficyjna, 1987).

129 Compare Shostakovich, Symphony No. 7, mvt. 1 (fig. 45) to Meyer, *Polish Symphony*, mvt. 2 (fig. 66); and Shostakovich, Symphony No. 5, mvt. 3 (fig. 86) to Meyer, *Polish Symphony*, mvt. 3 (fig. 73).

example, Shostakovich's return to a musical language that is "simplified, [and] beholden to tradition" in the fifth symphony.[130] He also concedes that timely music has its value—but not always an aesthetic one. For him, the "Leningrad" Symphony's power lies in its message to Soviet audiences under military siege, rather than in its musical merits. Meyer praises its timeliness and is deferential to the "extraordinary circumstances" (*ungewöhnliche Umstände*) in which it was composed.[131] The 1984 program note projects—almost verbatim—this same political action onto Meyer's work.

In the *Polish Symphony*, Meyer encodes a range of musical references, much as Polony did in the text of his review. The composer explains that the symphony "contain[s] various quotations, analogies, and references, thanks to which—I hope—the composition is readable even to a less sophisticated audience."[132] Thus prompted, a listener might hear the recurring chimes and strong double bass fundamental that open the third movement as recalling Modest Mussorgsky's catacombs in *Pictures at an Exhibition*, Hector Berlioz's *dies irae* in *Symphonie Fantastique*, or the meeting of the star-crossed lovers with Friar Lawrence in Sergei Prokofiev's *Romeo and Juliet*. Of course, a Polish listener would hear the familiar tunes I have already flagged for attention more than these dialogisms with other program music.

Like "God Save Poland," each patriotic song stands out when it is introduced. The first notated chant in the Polish language, "Mother of God" ("Bogurodzica"), serves as the opening melody of the reserved third movement.[133] A supplication to the Virgin Mary, it is the first preserved document of Polish-language poetry, notated in approximately 1407 and assumed to have its origins in the thirteenth century.[134] Already in the fifteenth century, Polish chronicler Jan Długosz made the case that the hymn served as a *carmen patrium* because of the sustenance it had provided the Polish army at

---

130 "Shostakovich made admirable use of his material . . . , which was supported by traditional, classical formal models. Like almost no other work of his, the 5th symphony makes an impression through its colossal power"; Krzysztof Meyer, *Dmitri Schostakowitsch*, translated by Ilona Reinhold (Leipzig: Verlag Philipp Reclam, 1980), 99.

131 Meyer, *Dmitri Schostakowitsch*, 126.

132 Meyer, program book for the 1984 Warsaw Autumn Festival, 181.

133 Meyer's citation in the *Polish Symphony* is not the only example of a reference to the "Mother of God" in Polish new music during the Cold War. Wojciech Kilar camouflaged the tune with spectral clamor in his *Bogurodzica* (1975), while Henryk Mikołaj Górecki heard it as the inspiration for *Songs of Joy and Rhythm* (1960); see Thomas, *Górecki*, 8–10. Only Andrzej Panufnik's *Sinfonia Sacra* (1963) presents the melody in the sparsely scored and unaltered manner that Meyer does.

134 Hieronim Feicht, "Bogurodzica" in *Studia nad muzyką polskiego średnowiecza* (Cracow: PWM, 1975), 131–85.

symbolic battles, before which legions would sing the song together.[135] In Henryk Siekiewicz's tale of the Teutonic Knights' fall, the Polish cavalry sing it before entering battle. In this historical novel, the chorus radiates vibrational power: "There was a measureless victorious force in those voices and in that hymn, as if thunder had really begun to roll in the sky."[136] From fifteenth-century sources, scholars have established that the "Mother of God" was not only associated with coronations and the battlefield; it was also sung in church, first as a devotional hymn during certain processionals and later incorporated into the mass, preceding the sermon.[137] Many of Polish musicology's first publications studied the "Mother of God" to understand the beginnings of Polish music and positioned it as a monument of Polish heritage.[138] Pope John Paul II, addressing a youth gathering in Poland in 1979, celebrated its relevance:

> It is simultaneously a confession of faith, it is a Polish symbol, a Polish credo, it is a catechism, it is even a document of Christian education. The primary truths of belief and tenets of morality entered [our world] in it. It is not only a monument. It is a document of life. . . . We sing it always with profound concern, with exultation, remembering, that it was sung in celebratory and defining moments. And we read it with great emotion. . . . It gave Polish culture its fundamental, basic outline.[139]

"Mother of God" appears either as melody or ostinato throughout the movement. Meyer evokes the pastness of the anonymous medieval chant. After three measures of hesitant pizzicato in the lower strings and a subdued sonorous carpet in the lower brass, an irregular and prolonged chime sets time into motion, inciting an ostinato pizzicato in the second violins. White-note writing, as in Górecki's settings of Wacław z Szamotuł's hymns in *Three Pieces in Old Style* (1963) two decades earlier, provides an early music-inspired texture.

---

135 Trochimczyk, "Sacred/Secular Constructs of National Identity," 270.

136 Henryk Sienkiewicz, *The Teutonic Knights*, translated by Alicia Tyszkiewicz, revised by Mirosław Lipiński (New York: Hippocrene Books, 1993), 769. Quoted in Maja Trochimczyk, "Sacred/Secular Constructs of National Identity," 274.

137 Religious indulgences were granted for singing the anthem in church from 1450; Katarzyna Morawska, *The History of Music in Poland: The Middle Ages Pt. 2; 1320–1500*, translated by John Comber (Warsaw: Sutkowski Edition, 2001), 114.

138 Roman Pilat, *Pieśń "Bogurodzica": Restytucyja tekstu pieśni* (Cracow: Drukarnia Uniwersytetu Jagiellonskiego, 1879). *Bogurodzica*, musicological edition by Hieronim Feicht, philological introduction by Ewa Ostrowska, edited by Jerzy Woronczak (Wrocław: Zakład Narodowy im. Ossolińskich, 1962).

139 Quoted in Antoni Posiad, *Bogarodzico-Dziewico: Polski Almanach Maryjny* (Warsaw: Instytut Wydawniczy PAX, 1983), vii.

Meyer briefly—but audibly—cites "The Oath," a homophonic setting of Maria Konopnicka's 1910 patriotic poem, near the work's conclusion, in the coda to the fourth movement. A muted trumpet plays the melody's phrases in ever more distorted rhythm over a driving eighth-note passage in the strings: this quotation sounds in the symphony as *hejnał*. The rhythmic stability of this bar-form hymn is undone, though the composer is faithful to the pitch contour. The point in "The Oath" at which God is asked for assistance—a refrain that hints at the chorus of "God Save Poland"—follows a hesitation in the trumpet's herald above increasingly agitated clusters in the strings.

Singing Vulnerability

> Their hands swollen from clapping,
> Bored by singing, people called for action.
>
> —*Cyprian Kamil Norwid,* Vade-mecum *(1865–66)*

With its link to resistance under partition, prominence in the 1980s, and oversimplification as Polish Catholic anthem, "God Save Poland" has become central to the isolationist and anti-European Union platforms of the Law and Justice Party (Prawo i Sprawiedliwość) in the early twenty-first century, a part of the symbolic saturation to confirm "intrinsic Catholicity."[140] It is still sung at official masses: on July 31, 2017, I stood with a large crowd in front of the monument that commemorates the Warsaw Uprising and witnessed its performance at the end of the mass in celebration of that historical event ▶. Contemporary performances still lean on the final line ("Bless our free Homeland, Lord!"). When crowds sing for the protection of freedom at a louder volume than any other congregational participation, the now-*unchanged* text takes on a conservative tone, as though the country were on the brink of attack.

In April 2017, the hymn concluded official commemorations of the seventh anniversary of the 2010 plane crash in Smolensk that killed 96 dignitaries. Among those who perished on board a Polish governmental jetliner was the brother of Law and Justice chairman Jarosław Kaczyński (2003–present). Standing on a stage in front of the President's Palace in central Warsaw, the head of the Office for War Veterans and the Victims of Oppression, Jan

---

140 Geneviève Zubrzycki, "History and the National Sensorium: Making Sense of Polish Mythology," *Qualitative Sociology* 34 (2011), 26. Epigraph: "Klaskaniem mając obrzękłe prawice, / Znudzony pieśnią, lud wołał o czyny." Cyprian Kamil Norwid, *Poems*, translated by Danuta Borchardt (Brooklyn, NY: Archipelago Books, 2011), 23, 26.

Józef Kasprzyk, led those assembled—a crowd that filled the streets—in the hymn, singing that post-1990 chorus that confirms an already free Poland. At the moment in which the chorus repeated, the event's producers faded his microphone out, instead tapping the audience to illustrate the ad hoc participation of all in this confirmational moment ▶. Kasprzyk explained, "For years we concluded this song with a request that God would give us back our freedom. And, Poland is [free]. Poland was resurrected. As was Christ."[141] With this equivalence: of Poland's sacrifices with those of Jesus Christ, his audience—"we Poles"—can only be Catholic. With bodies assembled and singing, he gestured to the collective: "We are free" (*Jesteśmy wolni*).

One month later, there were protests. The Smolensk anniversary is not only marked every year upon its return on April 10, but every month on the tenth. There is a mass, followed by a procession—a "March of Memory"—through downtown Warsaw. This 500-meter walk keeps the wound of the crash fresh and concern about its cause vital for those, predominantly supporters of the Law and Justice Party, who contend it was a conspiracy with Russia. Out of frustration with the obsessive practice and the endorsement of the ritual by the party, a tradition of counter-demonstrations has taken shape. This protest project has consequently been regulated by a December 2016 law that privileges "periodic meetings" over other public gatherings, which must be held at 100-meter distance. As I write in the summer of 2017, the right to assemble remains hotly debated, often on the street. The counter-protesters risk arrest; those marching out of belief that the crash was a foreign attack are protected by the police and militia. "God Save Poland" is sung again. But instead of the provocation by subversive anti-demonstrations, the anthem belongs to those with the power to control the historical narrative. Adam Borowski gave an account from inside the singing crowd:

> It turned out that some so-called Citizens of Poland [a social movement] had mixed with the Commemorative March. . . . When we had reached the Presidential Palace, they pulled out roses and started waving them about, whistling, yelling and causing disruption. During the speeches, when the commemorative roll was read out and we sang "God Save Poland," they joked about and mocked us. Their behavior showed no respect.[142]

---

141 The televised performance was at 1:10:45 in "Obchody 7. rocznicy katastrofy smoleńskiej - Apel Pamięci przed Pałacem Prezydenckim w Warszawie," the official ceremonies as released on Radio Maryja's YouTube channel; https://www.youtube.com/watch?v=leGiUdFboOw (currently inaccessible).

142 Interview with niezalezna.pl; http://niezalezna.pl/98554-adam-borowski-dla-niezaleznapl-w-pewnym-momencie-poczulem-uderzenie-w-twarz.

Outside of the music—which he projects as sacred—there is hurtful noise. What Borowski conjures as harsh sounds and threats of physical violence (he later complains that someone tugged at his suit jacket) provide a sense of cacophonic claustrophobia; they vilify the counter-protesters. In Borowski's rendering, their noise reveals that the song is not theirs. They show a lack of unity through a lack of chorality. The hymn itself is no longer under scrutiny. Now, it seems, it has lost the malleability that has always defined its performance. It is that world outside the safety in numbers provided by the chorus that receives attention and, ultimately, is felt as having political agency. Noisy dissent—its instability, scrim, and inherent conflict—may no longer be obviously musical. But it is set into motion by the sung, collective, and choreographed.

SELECTED REFERENCES

Archives

Academy of Sciences, Phonogram Archive, Warsaw, Poland.
Akademie der Künste, Zofia Lissa Collection, Berlin, Germany.
Archiv der Forschungsstelle Osteuropa an der Universität Bremen, Bremen, Germany.
Archiwum Akt Nowych, Warsaw, Poland.
Bienecke Rare Book and Manuscript Library, Czesław Miłosz Papers, Yale University, New Haven, CT, United States.
Deutscher Akademischer Austauschdienst, Artist-in-Berlin Program, Berlin, Germany.
Hoover Archives, Polish Independent Periodicals Collection, Stanford University, Stanford, CA, United States.
Houghton Library, Solidarity Bibliographic Center, Harvard University, Cambridge, MA, United States.
Institute of National Memory, Warsaw, Poland.
Karta Organization, Opposition Archive, Warsaw, Poland.
Muzeum Niepodległości, People's Republic of Poland Collection, Warsaw, Poland.
National Commission of the Independent and Self-Governing Trade Union "Solidarity," Gdańsk, Poland.
National Digital Archives, Warsaw, Poland.
New York Philharmonic, Digital Archives.
Oddziałowe Archiwum Instytutu Pamięci Narodowej, Gdańsk, Poland.
Polish Composers' Union (ZKP), Archives, Warsaw, Poland.
Polish Radio, Archives, Warsaw, Poland.
Polish Radio, Archiwum Radia Wolności, Warsaw, Poland.
Special Collections, National Library, Poland.
St. Stanslaus Kostka Church, Archives, Warsaw, Poland.
University Libraries, University of North Carolina at Chapel Hill, United States.
University of Warsaw, Special Collections, Ephemera and Department, Warsaw, Poland.
University of Warsaw, Special Collections, Music Department, Warsaw, Poland.
Woodberry Poetry Room Audio Collection, Lamont Library, Harvard University, Cambridge, MA, United States.

Periodicals

Gazeta Dźwiękowa (1983–88).
Index on Censorship (1977–90).
Kultura Niezależna (1983–91).
Polish Music/Polnische Musik (1966–92).
Ruch Muzyczny (1975–92).
Tygodnik Mazowsze (1977–92).
Tygodnik Powszechny (1976–90).
Warsaw Autumn Festival of Contemporary Music: Programs (1975–92).
Wprost (1977–92).

Printed Media

Abe, Marié. *Resonances of* Chindon-ya: *Sounding Space and Sociality in Contemporary Japan.* Middletown, CT: Wesleyan University Press, 2018.
Agnew, Vanessa. "What Is Reenactment?" *Criticism* 46, no. 3 (2004), 327–39.
Ahlquist, Karen, ed. *Chorus and Community.* Urbana and Chicago: University of Illinois Press, 2006.
"Akt oskarżenia przeciwko Jerzemu Aleksandrowi Popiełuszce." *Zeszyty Historyczne* 71 (1984), 64–78.
Aleksandrowicz, Dariusz, Stefani Sonntag, and Jan Wielgohs, eds. *The Polish Solidarity Movement in Retrospect: A Story of Failure or Success?* Berlin: Gesellschaft für sozialwissenschaftliche Forschung und Publizistik, 2009.
Anderson, Ben. *Encountering Affect: Capacities, Apparatuses, Conditions.* London: Routledge, 2014.
Anderson, Martin. Review of Andrzej Panufnik, *Sinfonia Sacra, Arbor Cosmica* by New York Chamber Symphony; and Panufnik: Violin Concerto, *Hommage à Chopin*, Bassoon Concerto. *Tempo* 175 (1990), 50–51.
Ansari, Emily Abrams. "Aaron Copland and the Politics of Cultural Diplomacy." *Journal of the Society for American Music* 5, no. 3 (2011), 335–64.
Antologia poezji ulotnej. Gdańsk: REDAKCJA Terytorialno-Związkowego Komitetu Samoobrony Społeczno SOLIDARNOŚĆ, 1982.
Applegate, Celia. "The Building of Community through Choral Singing." In *Nineteenth-Century Choral Music*, edited by Donna M. Di Grazia, 3–20. New York: Routledge, 2013.
Arendt, Hannah. *On Revolution.* London: Penguin Books, 1990.
Ascherson, Neal. "Requiem for an Old Piano Banger." *The Observer*, January 11, 1987.
Ash, Timothy Garton. *The Polish Revolution: Solidarity.* 3rd edition. New Haven, CT: Yale University Press, 2002.
Assman, Jan. "Communicative and Cultural Memory." In *Cultural Memory Studies: An International and Interdisciplinary Handbook*, edited by Astrid Erll and Ansgar Nünning, 109–18. Berlin: de Gruyter, 2008.
Atkinson, Niall. "Sonic Armatures: Constructing an Acoustic Regime in Renaissance Florence." *Senses and Society* 7, no. 1 (2012), 39–52.
Attali, Jacques. *Noise: The Political Economy of Music.* Translated by Brian Massumi. Minneapolis: University of Minnesota Press, 1986.

Auerbach, Karen. *The House at Ujazdowskie 16: Jewish Families in Warsaw after the Holocaust.* Bloomington: Indiana University Press, 2013.

August 1980: The Strikes in Poland. Munich: Radio Free Europe Research, 1980.

Baez, Joan. *A Voice to Sing With.* New York: Summit Books, 1987.

Balme, Christopher B., and Berenika Szymański-Düll, eds. *Theatre, Globalization, and the Cold War.* Cham, Switzerland: Palgrave Macmillan, 2017.

Barańczak, Stanisław. *Breathing under Water and Other East European Essays.* Cambridge, MA: Harvard University Press, 1990.

Barbieri, Anthony, Jr. "Polish Government Discloses Walkout at Site of Bloody 1970 Workers' Riots." *The Sun,* August 15, 1980.

Barker, Colin. "Fear, Laughter, and Collective Power: The Making of Solidarity at the Lenin Shipyards in Gdansk, Poland, August 1980." In *Passionate Politics: Emotions and Social Movements,* edited by Jeff Goodwin, James M. Jasper, and Francesca Polletta, 174–94. Chicago: University of Chicago Press, 2001.

Barthes, Roland. *Camera Lucida: Reflections on Photography.* Translated by Richard Howard. London: Cape, 1982.

Bartkowski, Bolesław. "Polnische Kirchenlieder in der katholischen Liturgie." In *Kirchenmusikalisches Erbe und Liturgie,* edited by Karlheinz Schlager and Hubert Unverricht, 171–82. Tutzing: Hans Schneider, 1995.

Bartoszewski, Gabriel, ed. *Bogosławiony Jerzy Popuiełuszko: Zapiski, listy i wywiady ks. Jerzego Popiełuszki, 1967–1984.* Warsaw: Oficyna Wydawniczo-Poligraficzna "adam," 2010.

Bartoszewski, Władysław. *Dziennik z internowania: Jaworze 15.12.1981–19.04.1982.* Warsaw: Świat Książki, 2006.

Bates, Eliot. "Mixing for *Parlak* and Bowing for a *Büyük Ses*: The Aesthetics of Arranged Traditional Music in Turkey." *Ethnomusicology* 54 (2010), 81–105.

Bates, John M. "From State Monopoly to a Free Market of Ideas? Censorship in Poland, 1976–1989." In *Censorship and Cultural Regulation in the Modern Age,* edited by Beate Müller, 141–67. Critical Studies 22. Amsterdam: Rodopi, 2004.

Bauman, Zygmunt. *Modernity and Ambivalence.* Ithaca, NY: Cornell University Press, 1991.

Bayat, Asef. "Islamism and Social Movement Theory." *Third World Quarterly* 26, no. 6 (2005), 891–908.

Beckles Willson, Rachel. *Ligeti, Kurtág, and Hungarian Music during the Cold War.* Cambridge: Cambridge University Press, 2007.

Beckles Willson, Rachel. "Whose Utopia? Perspectives on the West-Eastern Divan Orchestra." *Music and Politics* 3, no. 2 (2009). http://quod.lib.umich.edu/m/mp/9460447.0003.201?view=text;rgn=main.

Bell, Catherine. *Ritual: Perspectives and Dimensions.* Revised edition. Oxford: Oxford University Press, 2009.

Benhabib, Seyla. "The Strange Silence of Political Theory: Response." *Political Theory* 23, no. 4 (1995), 674–81.

Bergeron, Katherine. *Decadent Enchantments: The Revival of Gregorian Chant at Solesmes.* Berkeley: University of California Press, 1998.

Bernhard, Michael, and Jan Kubik, eds. *Twenty Years after Communism: The Politics of Memory and Commemoration.* New York and Oxford: Oxford University Press, 2014.

Beyrau, Dietrich, and Wolfgang Eichwede, eds. *Auf der Suche nach Autonomie: Kultur und Gesellschaft in Osteuropa*. Bremen: Donat & Temmen, 1987.

Bhabha, Homi K. *The Location of Culture*. London and New York: Routledge, 1994.

Bieniek, Olga. *Czarny czwartek: Janek Wiśniewski padł; Album o filmie*. Gdynia: Nordfilm, 2011.

Bierezin, Jacek. "Fenomen: Jacek Kaczmarski." Preface to *Wierszy i piosenki*, by Jacek Kaczmarski. Paris: Instytut Literacki, 1983.

Biernacki, Krzysztof. "Wojciech Ziembiński." In *Encyklopedia Solidarności*, edited by Mirosława Łątkowska et al. Instytut Pamięci Narodu, 2010; online edition. http://www.encysol.pl/wiki/Wojciech_Ziembi%C5%84ski.

Bilica, Krzysztof. "Wspomnienie o Tadeuszu Kaczyńskim." *Ruch Muzyczny* 53, no. 18 (September 6, 2009), 36–37.

Biskupski, M. B. B. *Independence Day: Myth, Symbol, and the Creation of Modern Poland*. Oxford: Oxford University Press, 2012.

Biuletyn, Jan. "Czy kultura może wybić się na niezależność?" *Kultura Niezależna* 3 (1984), 8–9.

The Black Book of Polish Censorship. New York: Vintage Books, 1984.

Bloom, Jack M. *Seeing through the Eyes of the Polish Revolution: Solidarity and the Struggle against Communism in Poland*. Leiden: Brill, 2013.

Bogusławska, Maria, ed. *Aktualna sytuacja muzyki religijnej i liturgicznej w Polsce*. Warsaw: Akademia Teologii Katolickiej, 1988.

Bohlman, Andrea F. "Lutosławski's Political Refrains." In *Lutosławski's Worlds*, edited by Lisa Jakelski and Nicholas Reyland, 273–300. Woodbridge, UK: Boydell and Brewer, 2018.

Bohlman, Andrea F. "Making Tapes in Poland: The Compact Cassette at Home." *Twentieth-Century Music* 14, no. 1 (2017), 119–34.

Bohlman, Andrea F. "Orienting the Martial: Polish Legion Songs on the Map." In *Hearing Crimea*, edited by Gavin Williams, 105–28. New York: Oxford University Press, 2018.

Bohlman, Andrea F. "'Where I Cannot Roam, My Song Will Take Wing': Polish Cultural Promotion in Belarus, 1988." In *Music and International History*, edited by Jessica C. E. Gienow-Hecht, 226–55. New York and Oxford: Berghahn Books, 2015.

Bohlman, Andrea F., and Peter McMurray. "Tape: Or, Rewinding the Phonographic Regime." *Twentieth-Century Music* 14, no. 1 (2017), 3–24.

Bohlman, Philip V. *The Music of European Nationalism*. Santa Barbara, CA: ABC-CLIO, 2004.

Bohlman, Philip V., and Jeffers Engelhardt. "Resounding Transcendence: An Introduction." In *Resounding Transcendence: Transitions in Music, Religion, and Ritual*, edited by Philip V. Bohlman and Jeffers Engelhardt, 1–25. New York: Oxford University Press, 2016.

Bolecki, Włodzimierz. "*Kultura* (1946–2000)." In *The Exile and Return of Writers from East-Central Europe: A Compendium*, edited by John Neubauer and Borbála Zsuzsanna Török, 144–88. Berlin: Walter de Gruyter, 2009.

Bolesławska, Beata. *The Life and Works of Andrzej Panufnik (1914–1991)*. Translated by Richard J. Reisner. Farnham, UK: Ashgate, 2015.

Bolton, Jonathan. *Worlds of Dissent: Charter 77, The Plastic People of the Universe, and Czech Culture under Communism*. Cambridge, MA: Harvard University Press, 2012.

Borchardt, Georg. "Sein jüngstes Werk ist eine polnische Sinfonie." *Die Welt*, April 29 1982.

Born, Georgina. "Introduction." In *Music, Sound and Space: Transformations of Public and Private Experience*, edited by Georgina Born, 1–69. Cambridge: Cambridge University Press, 2013.

Boyd, Malcolm. "National Anthems." In *Grove Music Online. Oxford Music Online*. Oxford University Press, 2001. https://www-oxfordmusiconline-com.lib-proxy.lib.unc.edu/grovemusic/view/10.1093/gmo/9781561592630.001.0001/omo-9781561592630-e-0000019602.

Briggs, Jonathyne. *Sounds French: Globalization, Cultural Communities, and Pop Music, 1958–1980*. New York: Oxford University Press, 2015.

Brooks, Jeanice. "Nadia Boulanger and the Salon of the Princesse de Polignac." *Journal of the American Musicological Society* 46, no. 3 (1993), 415–68.

Brubaker, Rogers. *Nationalism Reframed: Nationhood and the National Question in the New Europe*. Cambridge: Cambridge University Press, 1996.

Burton, Antoinette, ed. *Archive Stories: Facts, Fictions, and the Writing of History*. Durham, NC: Duke University Press, 2005.

Butler, Judith. *Excitable Speech: A Politics of the Performative*. New York: Routledge, 1997.

Butler, Judith. *Notes toward a Performative Theory of Assembly*. Cambridge, MA: Harvard University Press, 2015.

Butler, Judith, and Gayatri Chakravorty Spivak. *Who Sings the Nation-State? Language, Politics, and Belonging*. London: Seagull Books, 2007.

Bylander, Cindy. "Charles Ives and Poland's Stalowa Wola Festival: Inspirations and Legacies." *The Polish Review* 59, no. 2 (2014), 43–60.

Bylander, Cindy. "Responses to Martial Law: Glimpses of Poland's Musical Life in the 1980s." *Musicology Today* (2010), 176–77.

Calico, Joy H. *Arnold Schoenberg's* A Survivor from Warsaw *in Postwar Europe*. Berkeley: University of California Press, 2014.

Calico, Joy H. "The Trial, the Condemnation, the Cover-up: Behind the Scenes of Brecht/Dessau's *Lucullus* Opera(s)." *Cambridge Opera Journal* 14, no. 3 (2002), 313–42.

Camic, Charles. "Charisma: Its Varieties, Preconditions, and Consequences." *Sociological Inquiry* 50, no. 1 (1980), 5–23.

"Celebrity Watch: Arrive Early to Spot Poland's Lech Walesa." *Chicago Tribune*, November 17, 1989.

Cenckiewicz, Sławomir, and Piotr Gontarczyk. *SB a Lech Wałęsa: Przyczynek do biografii*. Warsaw: Instytut Pamięci Narodu, 2008.

Chanan, Michael. *The Politics of Documentary*. London: British Film Institute, 2007.

Chłopicka, Regina. "Krzysztof Penderecki's *St. Luke Passion, Polish Requiem* and *Credo* in the Context of Polish History." In *Krzysztof Penderecki: Musik im Kontext*, edited by Helmut Loos and Stefan Keym, 41–63. Leipzig: Gudrun Schröder Verlag, 2006.

Chomsky, Noam, and Edward S. Herman. *Manufacturing Consent: The Political Economy of the Mass Media*. New York: Pantheon Books, 1988.

Cioffi, Kathleen. *Alternative Theatre in Poland, 1954–1989*. London: Routledge, 1996.
Ciołek, Erazm. *Sierpień Solidarności*. Warsaw: Centrum Sztuki Współczesnej, 2010.
Clayton, Jace. "Muslin Gaze: The Enigmatic Afterlives of Bryn Jones," *Bidoun* 11, Special Issue: Failure (2007). http://bidoun.org/articles/muslin-gaze.
Clover, Joshua. *1989: Bob Dylan Didn't Have This to Sing About*. Berkeley: University of California Press, 2009.
Connor, Steven. *Beyond Words: Sobs, Hums, Stutters and Other Vocalizations*. London: Reaktion, 2014.
Connor, Steven. "Choralities." *Twentieth-Century Music* 13, no. 1 (2016), 3–23.
Copland, Aaron. "Workers Sing!" *New Masses* 11, no. 9 (1934), 28.
Corbin, Alain. *Village Bells: Sound and Meaning in the Nineteenth-Century French Countryside*. Translated by Martin Thom. New York: Columbia University Press, 1998.
Crowley, David. "People's Warsaw/Popular Warsaw." *Journal of Design History* 10, no. 2 (1997), 203–23.
Culbert, David. "Memories of 1945 and 1963: American Television Coverage of the End of the Berlin Wall, November 9, 1989." In *Television Histories: Shaping Collective Memory in the Media Age*, edited by Gary R. Edgerton and Peter C. Rollins, 230–43. Lexington: University of Kentucky Press, 2001.
Czaczkowska, Ewa, and Tomasz Wiścicki. *Ksiądz Jerzy Popiełuszko*. Warsaw: Świat Książki, 2004.
Czapińska, Wiesława. "Budujcie arkę przed potopem—czyli Jacek Kaczmarski." *Ekran* 26 (1981), 10–11.
Czapliński, Przemysław. "O realizmie antysocjalistycznym." *Teksty Drugie* 1 (1995), 31–48.
Dabrowski, Patrice M. *Commemorations and the Shaping of Modern Poland*. Bloomington: Indiana University Press, 2004.
Daszczyński, Roman. "Agent SB przeprasza Bogdana Borusewicza." *Gazeta Wyborcza*, February 11, 2005. http://wiadomosci.gazeta.pl/wiadomosci/1,114883,2546256.html.
Daughtry, J. Martin. "Afterword: From Voice to Violence and Back Again." In *Music, Politics, and Violence*, edited by Susan Fast and Kip Pegley, 243–64. Middletown, CT: Wesleyan University Press, 2012.
Daughtry, J. Martin. *Listening to War: Sound, Music, Trauma, and Survival in Wartime Iraq*. New York: Oxford University Press, 2015.
Daughtry, J. Martin. "Russia's New Anthem and the Negotiation of National Identity." *Ethnomusicology* 47, no. 1 (2003), 42–67.
Daughtry, J. Martin. "'Sonic Samizdat': Situating Unofficial Recording in the Post-Stalinist Soviet Union," *Poetics Today* 30 (2009), 27–65.
Dave, Nomi. "The Politics of Silence: Music, Violence and Protest in Guinea," *Ethnomusicology* 58, no. 1 (2014), 1–29.
Dąbek, Krzysztof. *PZPR—Retrospektywny portret własny*. Warsaw: Wydawnictwo TRIO, 2006.
Dąbrowska, Maria. *Dzienniki 1951–1957*. Volume 4. Edited by Tadeusz Drewnowski. Warsaw: Czytelnik, 1988.
Davies, Norman. *God's Playground: 1795 to the Present*. Volume 2. New York: Columbia University Press, 2005.

Davies, Norman. *Rising '44: The Battle for Warsaw.* New York: Viking, 2004.

De Souza, Jonathan. *Music at Hand: Instruments, Bodies, and Cognition.* New York: Oxford University Press, 2017.

Dębska, Agnieszka, ed., *Stan wojenny: Ostatni atak systemu.* Warsaw: Karta, 2006.

Djagalov, Rossen. "Guitar Poetry, Democratic Socialism, and the Limits of 1960s Internationalism." In *The Socialist Sixties: Crossing Borders in the Second World*, edited by Anne E. Gorsuch and Diane P. Koenker, 148–66. Bloomington and Indianapolis: Indiana University Press, 2013.

Dolar, Mladen. *A Voice and Nothing More.* Cambridge, MA: MIT Press, 2006.

Domańska, Hanna. *Muzeum Hymnu Narodowego w Będominie.* Gdańsk: Krajowa Agencja Wydawnicza, 1981.

Drott, Eric. *Music and the Elusive Revolution: Cultural Politics and Politics of Culture in France, 1968–81.* Berkeley: University of California Press, 2011.

Drott, Eric. "Resistance and Social Movements." In *The Routledge Reader on the Sociology of Music*, edited by Kyle Devine and John Shepherd, 171–79. New York: Routledge, 2015.

Drużyńska, Jolanta, and Stanisław M. Jankowski. *Kolacja z konfidentem: Piwnica pod Baranami w dokumentach Służby Bezpieczeństwa.* Cracow: Przedsięwzięcie Galicja, 2006.

Drzycimski, Andrzej, and Tadeusz Skutnik, eds. *Zapis wydarzeń: Gdańsk-Sierpień 1980; dokumenty.* Warsaw: Niezależna Oficyjna Wydawnicza NOWA, 1999.

Dueck, Byron. *Musical Intimacies and Indigenous Imaginaries: Aboriginal Music and Dance in Public Performance.* New York: Oxford University Press, 2013.

Dydycz, Antoni Pacyfik. *Homilie 1994–2000.* Drohiczyn: Drohiczyńskie Towarzystwo Naukowe and Kuria Diecezjalna w Drohicznie, 2011.

"'Ein Verlangen nach reinem Dur': Spiegel-Gespräch mit Krzysztof Penderecki." *Der Spiegel* 41, no. 2 (1987), 144–46.

Eisler, Jerzy. *Grudzień 1970: Geneza, przebieg, konsekwencje.* Warsaw: Wydawnictwo Sensacje XX wieku, 2000.

Ejmont, Sylwia D. "The Troubadour Takes the Tram: Experience in Polish Poetry and Music." Ph.D. diss., University of Michigan, 2008.

Engelhardt, Jeffers. "Asceticism and the Nation: Henryk Górecki, Krzysztof Penderecki, and Late Twentieth-Century Poland." *European Meetings in Ethnomusicology* 9 (2002), 197–207.

Engelhardt, Jeffers. *Singing the Right Way: Orthodox Christians and Enchantment in Estonia.* New York: Oxford University Press, 2014.

Erhardt, Ludwik, ed. *50 lat Związku Kompozytorów Polskich.* Warsaw: Polish Composers' Union, 1995.

Erhardt, Ludwik. "Die schwarze Maske' in Poznań." *Polish Music* 23, no. 1 (1988), 33–35.

Eugster, David, and Sibylle Marti. "Das Imaginäre des Kalten Krieges." In *Das Imaginäre des Kalten Krieges: Beiträge zu einer Kulturgeschichte des Ost-West-Konfliktes in Europa*, 3–17. Essen: Klartext, 2015.

Evans, Kristi S. "The Argument of Images: Historical Representation in Solidarity Underground Postage, 1981–87." *American Ethnologist* 19, no. 4 (1992), 749–67.

Eyerman, Ron, and Andrew Jamison. *Music and Social Movements: Mobilizing Traditions in the Twentieth-Century.* Cambridge: Cambridge University Press, 1998.

Falk, Barbara J. *Dilemmas of Dissidence in East-Central Europe.* Budapest: Central European Press, 2003.

Fauser, Annegret. *Sounds of War: Music in the United States during World War II.* Oxford: Oxford University Press, 2013.

Feicht, Hieronim. *Studia nad muzyką polskiego średnowiecza.* Cracow: PWM, 1975.

Feld, Steven, Aaron A. Fox, Thomas Porcello, and David Samuels. "Vocal Anthropology: From the Music of Language to the Language of Song." In *A Companion to Linguistic Anthropology*, edited by Alessandro Duranti, 321–45. Oxford: Blackwell, 2004.

Filipowicz, Halina. "Re-Envisioning Solidarity: History, Agency, and the Politics of Performance." *Theatre Journal* 62, no. 3 (2010), 335.

Fitzpatrick, Sheila. "Intelligentsia and Power: Client-Patron Relations in Stalin's Russia." In *Stalinismus vor dem Zweiten Weltkrieg: Neue Wege der Forschung*, edited by Manfred Hildermeier, 35–53. Munich: R. Oldenbourg Verlag, 1998.

Frolova-Walker, Marina. *Stalin's Music Prize: Soviet Culture and Politics.* New Haven, CT, and London: Yale University Press, 2016.

Fulcher, Jane. *French Cultural Politics and Music: From the Dreyfus Affair to the First World War.* Oxford and New York: Oxford University Press, 1999.

Furlong, Alison. "Politics, Faith, and the East German Blues." *Colloquia Germanica* 46, no. 4 (2013): 435–62.

Fox, John. "Murder of a Polish Priest." *Reader's Digest*, December 1985, 65–72, 217–48.

Friszke, Andrzej. *Opozycja polityczna w PRL 1945–1980.* Aneks: London, 1984.

Gagné, Renaud, and Mariann Govers Hopman, eds. *Choral Meditations in Greek Tragedy.* Cambridge: Cambridge University Press, 2013.

Gajda, Krzysztof. *Poza państwowem monopolem—Jan Krzysztof Kelus.* Poznań: Wydawnictwo WiS, 1998.

Gajda, Krzysztof. *To moja droga.* Wrocław: Wydawnictwo Dolnośląskie, 2009.

Gawlikowski, Lechosław, with Yvette Neisser Moreno, "The Audience to Western Broadcasts to Poland during the Cold War." In *Cold War Broadcasting: Impact on the Soviet Union and Eastern Europe, A Collection of Studies and Documents*, edited by A. Ross Johnson and R. Eugene Parta, 121–41. Budapest and New York: Central European University Press, 2010.

Gayou, Évelyn. *Le GRM, Groupe de Recherches Musicales: Cinquante ans d'histoire.* Paris: Fayard, 2007.

Gitelman, Lisa. *Paper Knowledge: Toward a Media History of Documents.* Durham, NC: Duke University Press, 2014.

Goldberg, Halina. *Music in Chopin's Warsaw.* New York: Oxford University Press, 2008.

Goldberg, Halina. "'Remembering That Tale of Grief': The Prophetic Voice in Chopin's Music." In *The Age of Chopin: Interdisciplinary Inquiries*, edited by Halina Goldberg, 54–92. Bloomington: Indiana University Press, 2004.

Gołębiewski, Jakub, Jolanta Mysiakowska, and Anna K. Piekarska, eds. *Aparat represji wobec księdza Jerzego Popiełuszki, 1982–1984.* Volume 1. Warsaw: Institute of National Memory, 2009.

Goodman, Glenda. "Transatlantic Contrafacta, Musical Formats, and the Creation of Political Culture in Revolutionary America." *Journal of the Society for American Music* 11, no. 4 (2017), 392–419.

Górski, Roman. *Dziennik z internowania 1981–1982: Krasnystaw—Włodawa—Kwidzyń*. Boston: Roman Górski, 1991.

Graham, Bradley. "Glemp Curbs Radical Priest: Polish Primate Targets Political Activism." *The Washington Post*, December 2, 1984.

Green, Archie, David Roediger, Franklin Rosemont, and Salvatore Solerno, eds. *The Big Red Songbook*. Chicago: Charles H. Kerr, 2007.

Grudzień—Sierpień: Piosenki i wiersze wybrzeża. Warsaw: Zespół BL i H, 1980.

Gwizdalanka, Danuta, and Krzysztof Meyer. *Lutosławski: Droga do mistrzostwa*. Cracow: Polskie Wydawnictwo Muzyczne, 2005.

Hagen, Trever, with Tia Denora. "From Listening to Distribution in Hungary and Czechoslovakia from the 1960s to the 1980s." In *The Oxford Handbook to Sound Studies*, edited by Trevor Pinch and Karin Bijsterveld, 440–58. Oxford: Oxford University Press, 2012.

Haltof, Mark. *Polish National Cinema*. New York and Oxford: Berghahn Books, 2002.

Hamacher, Theo. "Das Kirchenlied der Romantik." In *Geschichte der katholischen Kirchenmusik*, Volume II, edited by Karl Gustav Fellerer, 262–70. Kassel: Bärenreiter, 1976.

Hanson, Joanna K. M. *The Civilian Population and the Warsaw Uprising of 1944*. Cambridge: Cambridge University Press, 2004.

Haraszti, Miklós. *The Velvet Prison: Artists under State Socialism*. Translated by Katalin and Stephen Landesmann with Steve Wasserman. New York: Basic Books, 1987.

Hardt, Michael, and Antonio Negri. *Assembly*. New York and Oxford: Oxford University Press, 2017.

Hardt, Michael, and Antoni Negri. *Multitude: War and Democracy in the Age of Empire*. New York: Penguin Books, 2004.

Harley, Anna Maria. "Górecki and the Paradigm of the 'Maternal.'" *Musical Quarterly* 82, no. 1 (1998), 86–96.

Heller, Natasha. "Buddha in a Box: The Materiality of Recitation in Contemporary Chinese Buddhism." *Material Religion* 10, no. 3 (2014), 294–315.

Herbst, Lothar. *Polska więzienna: Dziennik liryczny pisany od 16 lutego do 6 czerwca 1982 r. w Strzelcach Opolskich, Nysie, we Wrocławiu*. Warsaw: AD SUM, 1983.

Herder, Johann Gottfried, and Philip V. Bohlman. *Song Loves the Masses: Herder on Music and Nationalism*. Oakland: University of California Press, 2017.

Hilder, Thomas R. *Sámi Musical Performance and the Politics of Indigeneity in Northern Europe*. Lanham, MD: Rowman and Littlefield, 2015.

Hirschkind, Charles. *The Ethical Soundscape: Cassette Sermons and Islamic Counterpublics*. New York: Columbia University Press, 2006.

Hirschkind, Charles. "Religion." In *Keywords in Sound*, edited by David Novak and Matt Sakakeeny, 165–74. Durham, NC: Duke University Press, 2015.

Hirszkowicz, Maria. *The Bureaucratic Leviathan: A Study in the Sociology of Communism*. Oxford: Robertson, 1980.

Howard, Luke B. "Motherhood, *Billboard*, and the Holocaust: Perceptions and Receptions of Górecki's Symphony No. 3." *Musical Quarterly* 82, no. 1 (1998), 131–59.

Iwanicka, Katarzyna, and Małgorzata Romańska. *25 lat Duszpasterstwa Środowisk Twórczych: Księga jubileuszowa*. Izabelin: Rosikon Press, 2004.

Jabłoński, Maciej, and Martina Homma. *Krzysztof Meyer: Ein Komponistenporträt*. Poznań/Cologne: Ars nowa/Bela Verlag, 1998.

Jackowski, Jacek. "Folk Religious Songs Sung during the Peregrination of Virgin Mary's Icon: An Example of Traditional Polish Peasant Piety in Communist Times." *Musicology Today* 7 (2010), 182–211.

Jakelski, Lisa. *Making New Music in Cold War Poland: The Warsaw Autumn Festival, 1956–1968*. Oakland: University of California Press, 2017.

Jakelski, Lisa. "Pushing Boundaries: Mobility at the Warsaw Autumn International Festival of Contemporary Music." *East European Politics and Societies and Cultures* 29, no. 1 (2015), 189–21.

Jakelski, Lisa. "Witold Lutosławski and the Ethics of Abstraction." *Twentieth-Century Music* 10, no. 2 (2013), 169–202.

Jakubowska, Longina. *Patrons of History: Nobility, Capital and Political Transitions in Poland*. New York and London: Routledge, 2012.

Janion, Maria. "Mesjanizm to przekleństwo: List Marii Janion do Kongresu Kultury." *Gazeta Wyborcza*, October 10, 2016. http://wyborcza.pl/7,75410,20813344,mesjanizm-to-przeklenstwo-list-marii-janion-do-kongresu-kultury.html.

Janion, Maria. "Słowo i symbol w miesiącach przełomu." In *Kongres Kultury Polskiej, 11–13 grudnia 1981*, edited by Władysław Masiulanim, 37–44. Warsaw: Oficyna Wydawnictwa Volumen Instytut Kultury, 2000.

Jankowska, Janina. *Portrety niedokończone: Rozmowy z twórcami "Solidarności" 1980–81*. Warsaw: Biblioteka "Więzi," 2003.

Jastrzębski, Marek, and Ewa Krysiak. "Avoiding Censorship: The 'Second Circulation' of Books in Poland." *Journal of Reading* 36, no. 6 (1993), 470–73.

Johnson, Gaye Theresa. *Spaces of Conflict, Sounds of Solidarity: Music, Race, and Spatial Enlightenment in Los Angeles*. Berkeley: University of California Press, 2013.

Jóźwiakowski, Andrzej. *Internowanie we Włodawie i w Lublinie: 13 grudnia 1981–30 kwietnia 1982 roku*. Lublin: "EL-Press," 2004.

Judt, Tony. *Postwar: A History of Europe since 1945*. New York: Penguin Press, 2005.

Judt, Tony. "The Rediscovery of Central Europe." *Daedalus* 119, no. 1 (1990), 23–54.

Junes, Tom. "Facing the Music: How the Foundations of Socialism Were Rocked in Communist Poland." In *Youth and Rock in the Soviet Bloc: Youth Cultures, Music and the State in Russia and Eastern Europe*, edited by William Jay Risch, 229–54. Lanham, MD: Lexington Books, 2015.

Kaczmarski, Jacek. *Antologia poezji*. Warsaw: Demart, 2011.

Kaczyński, Tadeusz. *Andrzej Panufnik i jego muzyka*. Warsaw: PWN, 1994.

Kaczyński, Tadeusz. *Ze ściśniętym gardłem . . . : 10 lat Filharmonii im. Traugutta*. Warsaw, 1993.

Kafka, Ben. *The Demon of Writing*. New York: Zone Books, 2012.

Kallberg, Jeffrey. *Chopin at the Boundaries: Sex, History, and Musical Genre*. Cambridge, MA: Harvard University Press, 1998.

Kamiński, Marek M. *Games Prisoners Play: The Tragicomic Worlds of Polish Prison*. Princeton, NJ: Princeton University Press, 2004.

Karnes, Kevin C. "Recollecting Jewish Musics from the Baltic Bloodlands." *Acta Musicologica* 84, no. 2 (2011), 253–88.

Kater, Michael H. *The Twisted Muse: Musicians and Their Music in the Third Reich.* New York: Oxford University Press, 1997.

Katz, Mark. *Capturing Sound: How Technology Has Changed Music.* Berkeley: University of California Press, 2004.

Keff, Bożena. *Utwór o matce i ojczyźnie.* Cracow: ha!art Corporation, 2008.

Kelly, Elaine. *Composing the Canon in the German Democratic Republic: Narratives of Nineteenth-Century Music.* Oxford: Oxford University Press, 2014.

Kelus, Jan Krzysztof. *Był raz dobry świat.* Interview with Wojciech Staszewski. Warsaw: Prószyński i S-ka, 1999.

Kemp-Welch, A. *Poland under Communism: A Cold War History.* Cambridge: Cambridge University Press, 2008.

Kemp-Welch, Klara. *Antipolitics in Central European Art: Reticence as Dissidence under Post-Totalitarian Rule, 1956–1989.* London: I. B. Tauris, 2014.

Kennan, George. "Witness." *New York Review of Books*, March 1, 1990, 3–6.

Kennedy, Michael D. *Professionals, Power, and Solidarity in Poland: A Critical Sociology of Soviet-Type Society.* Cambridge: Cambridge University Press, 1990.

Kenney, Padraic. *A Carnival of Revolution: Central Europe 1989.* Princeton, NJ: Princeton University Press, 2002.

Kenney, Padraic. "The Gender of Resistance in Communist Poland." *American Historical Review* 104 (1999), 399–425.

Kenney, Padraic. "Opposition Networks and Transnational Diffusion." In *Transnational Moments of Change: Europe 1945, 1968, 1989*, edited by Gerd-Rainer Horn and Padraic Kenney, 207–23. Lanham, MD: Rowman & Littlefield, 2004.

Kernodle, Tammy L. "'I Wish I Knew How It Would Feel to Be Free': Nina Simone and the Redefining of the Freedom Song of the 1960s." *Journal of the Society for American Music* 2, no. 3 (2008), 295–317.

"Kidnapped Priest Pleaded for Life, Polish Court Told," *Globe and Mail*, December 29, 1984.

Kind-Kovács, Friederike, and Jesse Labov, eds. *Samizdat, Tamizdat, and Beyond: Transnational Media during and after Socialism.* Oxford and New York: Berghahn Books, 2013.

Kleyff, Jacek, with Kazimierz Malinowskia. *Rozmowa.* Warsaw: Wydawnictwo Czarne, 2012.

Konferencja Episkopatu Polski: Listy pasterskie Episkopatu Polski, 1945–1974. Paris: Éditions du Dialogue, 1975.

Kowalski, Miłosz. *Mikołaj w szkole PRL.* Illustrated by Masław. Warsaw: Rytm, 1986.

Krakowska-Narożniak, Joanna, Wojciech Miszczuk, and Marta Fik. *Teatr drugiego obiegu: Materiały do kroniki teatru stanu wojennego 13 XII 1981–15 XI 1989.* Warsaw: Oficyna Wydawnicza Errata, 2000.

"Krzysztof Penderecki dyryguje 'Polskim Reqiuem.'" Interview by J. Motylewicz. *Tydzień Polski* no. 3 (1985), 15.

Kubik, Jan. *The Power of Symbols against the Symbols of Power: The Rise of Solidarity and the Fall of State Socialism in Poland.* University Park: Pennsylvania State University Press, 1994.

Kulas, Jan. *Stan wojenny: Wspomnienia i oceny.* Gdańsk: Pepliń "Bernardinium," 1999.

"Kulturotwórcza moc chrześcijaństwa." *Tygodnik Powszechny*, January 3, 1988.

Kunreuther, Laura. *Voicing Subjects: Public Intimacy and Mediation in Kathmandu.* Berkeley: University of California Press, 2014.

Kur, Krzysztof. *Będziemy dalej uprawiać ten ogród: 25 lat Filharmonii im. Romualda Traugutta 1983–2008.* Warsaw: Traugutt Philharmonic, 2008.

Kuroń, Jacek. "Polityczna opozycja w Polsce." *Kultura* 326 (1974), 11.

Kuroń, Jacek. *Kuroń Opozycja: Pisma Polityczne 1969–1989.* Edited by Michał Sutowski, Maciej Kropiwinicki, and Sebastian Liszka. Warsaw: Wydawnictwo Krytyki Politycznej, 2010.

Kutschke, Beate. "Anti-authoritarian Revolt by Musical Means on Both Sides of the Berlin Wall." In *Music and Protest in 1968,* edited by Beate Kutschke and Barley Norton, 188–204. Cambridge: Cambridge University Press, 2013.

Kutschke, Beate. "In Lieu of an Introduction." In *Music and Protest in 1968,* edited by Beate Kutschke and Barley Norton, 1–11. Cambridge: Cambridge University Press, 2013.

Kwiatkowska, Wiesława. *Grudniowa apokalipsa.* Gdynia, 1993.

Kwiatkowski, Maciej Józef. *Wrzesień 1939 w Warszawskiej rozgłośni Polskiego Radia.* Warsaw: Państwowy Instytut Wydawniczy, 1984.

Laba, Roman. *The Roots of Solidarity: A Political Sociology of Poland's Working-Class Democratization.* Princeton, NJ: Princeton University Press, 1991.

LaBelle, Brandon. *Lexicon of the Mouth: Poetics and Politics of Voice and the Oral Imaginary.* London: Bloomsbury, 2014.

Labhardt, Walter. "Polnische Gegenwartsmusik." *Neue Zürcher Zeitung,* April 10–11, 1982.

Lachowicz, Stanisław. *Muzyka w okupowanym Krakowie, 1939–1945.* Cracow: Wydawnictwo Literackie, 1988.

Lammich, Siegfried. *Der "Popieluszko-Prozess": Sicherheitspolizei und katholische Kirche in Polen: Bericht und Dokumentation im Auftrag der Internationalen Gesellschaft für Menschenrechte.* Cologne: Wissenschaft und Politik, 1985.

Lange, Irena, ed. *Żelazowa Wola.* Warsaw: Wydawnictwo "Sport i Turystyka," 1970.

Łaś, Józef. "Rytmika polskich śpiewów liturgicznych." *Ruch Biblijny i Liturgiczny* 21 (1968), 266–83.

Lesiakowski, Krzysztof, Paweł Perzyna, and Tomasz Toborek. *Jarocin w obiektywie bezpieki.* Warsaw: Instytut Pamięci Narodu, 2001.

Lewek, Antoni. *Funkcja kerygmatyczna Kościoła w świetle Vaticanum II: Istota i zadania.* Volume 1. Warsaw: Akademia Teologii Katolickiej, 1984.

Lewis, Paul G. *Political Authority and Party Secretaries in Poland, 1975–1986.* Cambridge: Cambridge University Press, 1989.

Libera, Antoni. "Marek Nowakowski: Everyday Life under Communism." *Modern Drama* 27, no. 1 (1984), 59–63.

Lichau, Karsten. "'The moving, awe-inspiring silence': Zum 'emotionalen Potential' der Schweigeminute." In *Performing Emotions: Interdisziplinäre Perspektiven auf das Verhältnis von Politik und Emotion in der Frühen Neuzeit und in der Moderne,* edited by Claudia Jarzebowski and Anne Kwaschik, 69–92. Göttingen: V&R unipress, 2013.

Lind, Tore Tvarnø. *The Past Is Always Present: The Revival of the Byzantine Musical Tradition at Mount Athos.* Lanham, MD: Scarecrow Press, 2012.

"Lines, Colours and Textures: Stephen Johnson Talks to Conductor Mark Stephenson and Bassoonist Robert Thompson." *Gramophone*, July 1990, 177.

"Lipcowy apel Lecha Wałęsy," *Kultura Niezależna* 2 (1984), 95.

Lipski, Jan Józef. *KOR: A History of the Workers' Defense Committee in Poland, 1976–1981*. Berkeley: University of California Press, 1985.

Lord, Albert B. *The Singer of Tales*, 2nd edition. Cambridge, MA: Harvard University Press, 2000.

Lortat-Jacob, Bernard, with Marc Benamou. "Concord and Discord: Singing Together in a Sardinian Brotherhood." In *Chorus and Community*, edited by Karen Ahlquist, 87–110. Urbana and Chicago: University of Illinois Press, 2006.

Lukasiewicz, Mark. "Passion Fades, Life in Poland Back to Normal." *Globe and Mail*, December 24, 1982.

Lukasiewicz, Mark. "Repressed Arts Seethe with Life behind Curtains." *Globe and Mail*, April 4, 1983.

Lysloff, René T. A. "Mozart in Mirrorshades: Ethnomusicology, Technology, and the Politics of Representation." *Ethnomusicology* 41 (1997), 206–19.

MacFadyen, David. *Estrada?! Grand Narratives and the Philosophy of the Russian Popular Song since Perestroika*. Montreal: McGill-Queen's University Press, 2005.

MacFadyen, David. *Red Stars: Personality and the Soviet Popular Song, 1955–1991*. Montreal: McGill-Queen's University Press, 2001.

Machcewicz, Paweł. *Rebellious Satellite: Poland, 1956*. Translated by Maya Latynski. Stanford: Stanford University Press, 2009.

Madsen, Virginia. "'Your Ears Are a Portal to Another World': The New Radio Documentary Imagination and the Digital Domain." In *Radio's New Wave: Global Sound in the Digital Era*, edited by Jason Loviglio and Michele Hilmes, 126–44. New York: Routledge, 2013.

Manabe, Noriko. *The Revolution Will Not Be Televised: Protest Music after Fukushima*. New York: Oxford University Press, 2016.

Mandelkern, Benjamin, with Mark Czarnecki. *Escape from the Nazis*. Toronto: James Lorimer, 1988.

Manuel, Peter. *Cassette Culture: Popular Music and Technology in North India*. Chicago: University of Chicago Press, 1993.

Marotti, William. "Japan 1968: The Performance of Violence and the Theater of Protest." *The American Historical Review* 114 (2009), 97–135.

Masiulanis, Władysław, ed. *Kongres Kultury Polskiej: 11–13 grudnia 1981*. Warsaw: VOLUMEN, 2000.

Massaka, Iwona. *Muzyka jako instrument wpływu politycznego*. Łódź: Wydawnictwo Naukowe Ibidem, 2009.

Matulewicz, Tadeusz. "Boże, coś Polskę." *Kultura* 42, October 18, 1981.

Matynia, Elżbieta. *Performative Democracy*. Boulder, CO: Paradigm, 2009.

May, Todd. *The Philosophy of Foucault*. Chesham: Acumem, 2006.

Mazierska, Ewa, and Elżbieta Ostrowska. *Women in Polish Cinema*. New York: Berghahn Books, 2006.

Mazurek, Malgorzata, and Matthew Hilton. "Consumerism, Solidarity and Communism: Consumer Protection and the Consumer Movement." *Journal of Contemporary History* 42, no. 2 (2007), 315–43.

McLellan, Joseph. "Resounding 'Polish Requiem.'" *Washington Post,* January 27, 1986.
Melucci, Alberto. *Challenging Codes: Collective Action in the Information Age.* Cambridge: Cambridge University, 1996.
Metzer, David. *Quotation and Cultural Meaning in Twentieth-Century Music.* Cambridge: Cambridge University Press, 2003.
Meyer, Krzysztof. *Dmitri Schostakowitsch.* Translated by Ilona Reinhold. Leipzig: Verlag Philipp Reclam, 1980.
Meyer, Krzysztof. *Szostakowicz.* Cracow: Polskie Wydawnictwo Muzyczne, 1973.
Miazga, Tadeusz. *Z problematyki muzyki sakralnej w Polsce.* Graz: Akademische Druck- und Verlagsanstalt, 1986.
Michalski, Grzegorz. *Lutosławski w pamięci: 20 rozmów o kompozystorze.* Gdańsk: słowo/obraz terytoria, 2007.
Michnik, Adam. *The Church and the Left.* Translated by David Ost. Chicago: University of Chicago Press, 1993.
Michnik, Adam. *Letters from Prison and Other Essays.* Translated by Maya Latynski. Berkeley: University of California Press, 1985.
Michnik, Adam, ed. *Przeciw antysemityzmowi 1936–2009.* Volume 3. Cracow: Towarzystwo Autorów i Wydawców Prac Naukowych Universitas, 2010.
Mickiewicz, Adam. *Pan Tadeusz.* Translated by Kenneth R. Mackenzie. New York: Hippocrene Books, 1986.
Mika, Bogumiła. "Pieśń *Boże, coś Polskę* w funkcji cytatu w polskiej muzyce artystycznej XX wieku." In *Muzyka religijna: między epokami i kulturami.* Volume 2, edited by Krystyna Turek, 114–34. Katowice: Wydawnictwo Uniwersytetu Śląskiego, 2009.
Milewski, Barbara. "Chopin and the Myth of the Folk." *19th-Century Music* 23 (1999), 113–35.
Miller, Byron A. *Geography and Social Movements: Comparing Antinuclear Activism in the Boston Area.* Minneapolis: University of Minnesota Press, 2000.
Minor, Ryan. *Choral Fantasies: Music, Festivity, and Nationhood in Nineteenth-Century Germany.* Cambridge: Cambridge University Press, 2008.
Misniec, Stefan, ed. *Dialog kosciola i kultura: Materiały z IV i V Tygonia Kultury Chrześcijańskiej w Krakowie 1983, 1984.* Volume 1. Cracow: Kuria Metropolitalna, 1986.
Misztal, Bronisław, ed. *Poland after Solidarity: Social Movements versus the State,* edited by Bronisław Misztal. New Brunswick, NJ: Transaction Books, 1985.
Morawska, Katarzyna. *The History of Music in Poland: The Middle Ages Pt. 2; 1320–1500.* Translated by John Comber. Warsaw: Sutkowski Edition, 2001.
Morrison, Simon. *The People's Artist: Prokofiev's Soviet Years.* Oxford and New York: Oxford University Press, 2009.
Mosse, George L. *Nationalization of the Masses: Political Symbolism and Mass Movements in Germany from the Napoleonic Wars through the Third Reich.* New York: Fertig, 1975.
Mówię o was i za was: Trzecia pielgrzymka Jana Pawła II do Ojczyzny. Warsaw: Wydawnictwo Pelikan, 1988.
Mur, Jan. *A Prisoner of Martial Law: Poland 1981–82.* Translated by Lillian Vallee. San Diego, CA: Hancourt Brace Javanovich, 1984.
Naliwajek-Mazurek, Katarzyna. "The Racialization and Ghettoization of Music in the General Government." In *Twentieth-Century Music and Politics,* edited by Pauline Fairclough, 191–210. Aldershot: Ashgate, 2012.

Nancy, Jean-Luc. *The Inoperative Community*. Translated by Peter Connor, Lisa Garbus, Michael Holland, and Simona Sawhney. Mineapolis and Oxford: University of Minnesota Press, 1990.

Nancy, Jean-Luc. *Listening*. Translated by Charlotte Mandell. New York: Fordham University Press, 2007.

Nettl, Paul. *National Anthems*. 2nd edition. New York: Frederick Ungar, 1967.

Newerkla, Stefan Michael, Fedor B. Poljakov, and Oliver Jens Schmitt, eds. *Das politische Lied in Ost- und Südosteuropa*. Vienna: LIT Verlag, 2011.

Niewęgłowski, Ks. Wiesław Al. *Kościół i kultura w dialogu*. Warsaw: Oficyna Wydawniczo-poligraficzna "Adam": 2008.

Niżyńska, Joanna. "The Impossibility of Shrugging One's Shoulders: O'Harists, O'Hara, and Post-1989 Polish Poetry." *Slavic Review* 66 (2007), 463–83.

Niżyńska, Joanna. *The Kingdom of Insignificance: Miron Białoszewski and the Quotidian, the Queer, and the Traumatic*. Chicago: Northwestern University Press, 2013.

Nora, Pierre. "Between Memory and History: Les *Lieux des Mémoire*." *Representations* (1989), 7–24.

Norwid, Cyprian Kamil. *Poems*. Translated by Danuta Borchardt. Brooklyn, NY: Archipelago Books, 2011.

Nowak-Romanowicz, Alina. "Przyczynek do dziejów pieśni 'Boże, coś Polskę." *Ruch Muzyczny* 7 (April 3, 1983), 24–25.

Nowakowski, Marek. *The Canary and Other Tales of Martial Law*. Translated by Krystyna Bronkowska. London: Harvill Press, 1983.

Ochoa Gautier, Ana María. *Aurality: Listening and Knowledge in Nineteenth-Century Colombia*. Durham, NC: Duke University Press, 2014.

Ochoa Gautier, Ana María. "Silence." In *Keywords in Sound*, edited by David Novak and Matt Sakakeeny, 183–92. Durham, NC: Duke University Press, 2015.

Ong, Walter J. *The Presence of the Word: Some Prolegomena for Cultural and Religious History*. New Haven, CT: Yale University Press, 1967.

Opalski, Magdalena, and Israel Bartal. *Poles and Jews: A Failed Brotherhood*. Hanover, NH, and London: Brandeis University Press, 1992.

Orla-Bukowska, Annamaria. "New Threads on an Old Loom: National Memory and Social Identity in Postwar and Postcommunist Poland." In *The Politics of Memory in Postwar Europe*, edited by Richard Ned Lebow, Wulf Jansteiner, and Claudio Fogu, 177–209. Durham, NC: Duke University Press, 2006.

Ornatowski, Cesar. "Rhetoric of Pope John Paul II's Visits to Poland, 1979–1999." In *The Rhetoric of Pope John Paul II*, edited by Joseph R. Blaney and Joseph P. Zompetti, 103–50. Lanham, MD: Lexington Books, 2009.

Osa, Maryjane. *Solidarity and Contention: Networks of Polish Opposition*. Minneapolis: University of Minnesota Press, 2003.

Ost, David. *The Defeat of Solidarity: Anger and Politics in Postcommunist Europe*. Ithaca, NY: Cornell University Press, 2005.

Ost, David. *Solidarity and the Politics of Anti-Politics: Opposition and Reform in Poland since 1968*. Philadelphia: Temple University Press, 1991.

Oushakine, Serguei Alex. "The Terrifying Mimicry of Samizdat." *Public Culture* 12, no. 2 (2001), 191–214.

Paczkowski, Andrzej. *Revolution and Counterrevolution in Poland, 1980–1989*. Translated by Christine Manetti. Rochester, NY: University of Rochester Press, 2015.
Paczkowski, Andrzej. *The Spring Will Be Ours: Poland and the Poles from Occupation to Freedom.* Translated by Jane Cave. University Park: Pennsylvania State University Press, 1995.
Paczkowski, Andrzej, and Malcolm Byrne, eds. *From Solidarity to Martial Law: The Polish Crisis of 1980–1981; A Documentary History*. Budapest: Central European University Press, 2007.
Palmer, Roy. *The Sound of History: Songs and Social Comment*. Oxford: Oxford University Press, 1988.
Panufnik, Andrzej. *Composing Myself*. London: Methuen, 1987.
Panufnik, Camilla. "Andrzej Panufnik's Ethos of Life and Work." In Jadwiga Paja-Stach, *Andrzej Panufnik's Music and Its Reception*, 17–23. Cracow: Musica Iagellonica, 2003.
Papierowa Rewolucja: Z dziejów drugiego obiegu wydawniczego w Polsce 1976–1989/1990. Warsaw: Instytut Pamięci Narodu, 2010.
Parsons, Christi. "2,000 Pack Church to Catch Glimpse of Polish Leader." *Chicago Tribune*, March 26, 1990.
Patton, Raymond. "The Communist Culture Industry: The Music Business in 1980s Poland." *Journal of Contemporary History* 47, no. 2 (2012), 427–49.
Payerhin, Marek. "Singing Out of Pain: Protest Songs and Social Mobilization." *Polish Review* 37 (2012), 5–31.
Peace, Susan C. "Who Owns a Movement's Memory: The Case of Poland's Solidarity." In *Cultural Memories of Nonviolent Struggle: Powerful Times*, edited by Anna Reading and Tamar Katriel, 166–86. New York: Palgrave Macmillan, 2015.
Pease, Neal. *Rome's Most Faithful Daughter: The Catholic Church and Independent Poland, 1914–39*. Athens: Ohio University Press, 2009.
Penderecki, Krzysztof. *The Labyrinth of Time*. Chapel Hill, NC: Hinshaw Music, 1998.
Penn, Shana. *Solidarity's Secret: The Women Who Defeated Communism in Poland*. Ann Arbor: University of Michigan Press, 2005.
Peteri, György. "Nylon Curtain—Transnational and Transsystemic Tendencies in the Cultural Life of State-Socialist Russia and East-Central Europe." *Slavonica* 10, no. 2 (2004), 113–23.
Peters, John Durham. "Calendar, Clock, Tower." In *Deus in Machina: Religion, Technology, and the Things in Between*, edited by Jeremy Stolow, 25–42. New York: Fordham University Press, 2013.
Peters, John Durham. "The Voice and Modern Media." In *Kunst-Stimmen*, edited by Doris Kolesch and Jenny Schrödel, 85–100. Berlin: Theater der Zeit, 2004.
Picker, John M. *Victorian Soundscapes*. Oxford: Oxford University Press, 2003.
Pietrzak, Jan. *Jak obaliłem komunę*. Łomianki: Wydawnictwo LTW, 2010.
Pilat, Roman. *Pieśń "Bogurodzica": Restytucyja tekstu pieśni*. Cracow: Drukarnia Uniwersytetu Jagiellonskiego, 1879.
Platonov, Rachel S. *Singing the Self: Guitar Poetry, Community, and Identity in the Post-Soviet Period*. Evanston, IL: Northwestern University Press, 2012.
Poizat, Michel. *The Angel's Cry: Beyond the Pleasure Principle in Opera*. Ithaca, NY: Cornell University Press, 1992.
Polska 13 grudnia 1981: Wojna z narodem. Lund, Sweden: Stödkommitten för Solidaritet; Warsaw: Nowa, Krąg, and CDN, 1982.

Polski Sierpień 1980: Reedycja Almanachu Gdańskich Środowisk Twórczych "Punkt" nr 12/ 80. New York: Biblioteka Pomostu, 1981.
Popiełuszko, Jerzy. *The Price of Love: The Sermons of Fr. Jerzy Popiełuszko.* Translated by Zygmunt Lawrynowicz. London: "Veritas," 1985.
Porter-Szűcs, Brian. *Faith and Fatherland: Catholicism, Modernity, and Poland.* Oxford and New York: Oxford University Press, 2011.
Posiad, Antoni. *Bogarodzico-Dziewico: Polski Almanach Maryjny.* Warsaw: Instytut Wydawniczy PAX, 1983.
Potter, Pamela. "Wagner and the Third Reich: Myths and Realities." In *The Cambridge Companion to Wagner,* edited by Thomas S. Grey, 235–45. Cambridge: Cambridge University Press, 2008.
"Proces morderców ks. Jerzego Popiełuszki." *Zeszyty Historyczne* 73 (1984), 80–108.
"Przestańcie stale nas przepraszać . . . : Wiersze sierpień 1980." Gdańsk: Wydawnictwo im. konstytucji 3. maja, 1980.
Przyborska, Katarzyna, and Marta Markowska. *Salon Niezależni w "świetlicy" Anny Erdman i Tadeusza Walendowskiego 1976–79.* Warsaw: Karta, 2016.
Przygoński, Antoni. *Powstanie warszawskie w sierpniu 1944 r.* Volume 1. Warsaw: Polskie Wydawnictwo Naukowe, 1980.
Radziwon-Stefaniuk, Ewa, and Krzysztof Droba, eds. *Warszawska Jesień w zwierciadle polskiej krytyki muzycznej: Antologia tekstów z lat 1956–2006.* Warsaw: Polish Music Information Center, 2007.
Ramet, Sylvia P. *Nihil Obstat: Religion, Politics, and Social Change in East-Central Europe and Russia.* Durham, NC: Duke University Press, 1998.
Ratzinger, Joseph. *Introduction to Christianity.* Translated by J. R. Foster. San Francisco: Ignatius Press, 2004.
Reddaway, William Fiddian. *The Cambridge History of Poland.* Volume 2. Cambridge: Cambridge University Press, 1941.
Redmond, Shana L. *Anthem: Social Movements and the Sound of Solidarity in the African Diaspora.* New York: New York University Press, 2014.
Reed, T. V. *The Art of Protest: Culture and Activism from the Civil Rights Movement to the Streets of Seattle.* Minneapolis: University of Minnesota Press, 2005.
Rehding, Alexander. *Music and Monumentality: Commemoration and Wonderment in Nineteenth-Century Germany.* New York: Oxford University Press, 2009.
Reiss, Matthias, ed. *The Street as Stage: Protest Marches and Public Rallies since the Nineteenth Century.* Oxford: Oxford University Press, 2007.
Reyland, Nicholas. *Zbigniew Preisner's* Three Colors Trilogy: Blue, White, Red*: A Film Score Guide.* Lanham, MD: Scarecrow Press, 2012.
Ritter, Rüdiger. "Polnisch, litauisch oder weißrussisch? Stanisław Moniuszko und das Problem der nationalen Musik." In *Nationale Musik im 20. Jahrhundert: Kompositorische und soziokulturelle Aspekte der Musikgeschichte zwischen Ost- und Westeuropa,* edited by Helmut Loos and Stefan Keym, 182–204. Leipzig: Schröder Verlag, 2004.
Rolf, Malte. *Soviet Mass Festivals, 1917–1991.* Translated by Cynthia Klohr. Pittsburgh: University of Pittsburgh Press, 2013.
Rosaldo, Michelle Z. "The Things We Do with Words: Ilongot Speech Acts and Speech Act Theory in Philosophy." *Language in Society* 11, no. 2 (1982), 203–37.

Rosenberg, Neil V. "From the Sound Recordings Review Editor: Documentary Sound Recordings." *The Journal of American Folklore* 105 (1992), 344–58.

Rothenberg, David. "Angels, Archangels, and a Woman in Distress: The Meaning of Isaac's *Angeli archangeli*." *Journal of Musicology* 21, no. 4 (2005), 523–24.

Rothstein, Robert A. *Two Words to the Wise: Reflections on Polish Language, Literature, and Folklore*. Bloomington, IN: Slavica, 2008.

Rudka, Szczepan. *Radio "Solidarność" Wrocław 1981: Rozgłośnie wrocławskiej opozycji* Wrocław: Muzeum Miejskie Wrocławia, 2005.

Ruzikowski, Tadeusz. "Kultura niezależna." In *NSZZ Solidarność 1980–89; Tom 2: Ruch społeczny*, edited by Łukasz Kamiński and Grzegorz Waligóra, 315–85. Warsaw: Instytut Pamięci Narodu, 2010.

Ruzikowski, Tadeusz. *Stan wojenny w Warszawie i województwie stołecznym 1981–83*. Warsaw: Instytut Pamięci Narodu, 2009.

Samson, Jim. *Chopin*. New York: Schirmer, 1996.

Samson, Jim. *The Music of Chopin*. Oxford: Clarendon, 1985.

Samson, Valerie. "Music as Protest Strategy: The Example of Tianamen Square, 1989." *Pacific Review of Ethnomusicology* 6 (1991), 35–64.

Samuels, David W., Louise Meintjes, Ana María Ochoa, and Thomas Porcello. "Soundscapes: Toward a Sounded Anthropology." *Annual Review of Anthropology* 39 (2010), 329–45.

Sawicka, Jadwiga, and Ewa Paczoska, eds. *Bardowie*. Łódź: Ibidem, 2001.

Schafer, R. Murray. *The Soundscape: Our Sonic Environment and the Tuning of the World*. Rochester, VT: Destiny Books, 1977.

Schmelz, Peter J. "Music in the Cold War." *Journal of Musicology* 26, no. 1 (2009), 3–16.

Schmelz, Peter J. *Such Freedom, If Only Musical: Unofficial Soviet Music during the Thaw*. New York and Oxford: Oxford University Press, 2009.

Schlott, Wolfgang, with Ivo Bock and Hartmute Trepper. *Kultur im Umbruch: Polen—Tschechoslowakei—Rußland*. Bremen: Temmen, 1992.

Schneider, Wolfgang, ed. *Leipziger Demontagebuch: Demo, Montag, Tagebuch, Demontage*. Leipzig and Weimar: Gustav Kiepenheuer Verlag, 1990.

Scruggs, T. M. "(Re)Indigenization? Post-Vatican II Catholic Ritual and 'Folk Masses' in Nicaragua." *The World of Music* 47, no. 1 (2005), 91–123.

Seeger, Charles. *Studies in Musicology, 1935–1975*. Berkeley: University of California Press, 1977.

Seehaber, Ruth. *Die "polnische Schule" in der neuen Musik: Befragung eines musikhistorischen Topos*. Cologne: Böhlau, 2009.

Shelemay, Kay Kaufman. "Musical Communities: Rethinking the Collective in Music." *Journal of the American Musicological Society* 64, no. 2 (2011), 349–90.

Siedlecki, Jan. *Śpiewnik kościelny z melodjami na dwa głosy*. Lwów: n.p., 1928.

Sienkiewicz, Henryk. *The Teutonic Knights*. Translated by Alicia Tyszkiewicz, revised by Mirosław Lipiński. New York: Hippocrene Books, 1993.

Šmidchens, Guntis. *The Power of Song: Nonviolent National Culture in the Baltic Revolution*. Seattle and London: University of Washington Press, 2014.

Smith, Gerald S. *Songs to Seven Strings: Russian Guitar Poetry and Soviet "Mass Song."* Bloomington: Indiana University Press, 1984.

Snyder, Alvin A. *Warriors of Disinformation: How Lies, Videotape, and the USIA Won the Cold War*. New York: Arcade, 1995.

Snyder, Timothy. *Bloodlands: Europe between Hitler and Stalin*. New York: Basic Books, 2010.

Snyder, Timothy. *The Reconstruction of Nations: Poland, Ukraine, Lithuania, Belarus, 1569–1999*. New Haven, CT: Yale University Press, 2003.

Solak, Zbigniew, Jarosław Szarek, with Henryk Głębocki, Jolanta Nowak, and Adam Roliński. *Stan wojenny w Małopolsce: Relacje i dokumenty*. Cracow: Księgarnia Akademicka, 2005.

Solińska, Ewa. *W salonie muzycznym: Wywiady*. Bydgoszcz: Pomorze, 1986.

Śpiewnik ekstremisty, czyli Zakazane piosenki. Cracow: Quarter II, 1986.

Stefanowski, Roman, ed. *Poland under Martial Law: A Chronology of Events 13 December 1981–30 December 1982*. New York: Radio Free Europe Research, 1983.

Steiner, Peter. "On Samizdat, Tamizdat, Magnitizdat, and Other Strange Words That Are Difficult to Pronounce." *Poetics Today* 29, no. 4 (2008), 613–28.

Sterne, Jonathan. "The Theology of Sound: A Critique of Orality." *Canadian Journal of Communication* 36 (2011), 207–25.

Stępiński, Zygmunt. *A mury runą, runą, runą . . . : Pamiętki internowanych*. Warsaw: Wydawnictwo CDN, 1983.

Stjernø, Steinar. *Solidarity in Europe: The History of an Idea*. Cambridge: Cambridge University Press, 2004.

Stöcker, Lars Fredrik. "The Baltic Connection: Transnational Samizdat Networks between Émigrés in Sweden and the Democratic Opposition in Poland." In *Samizdat, Tamizdat, and Beyond: Transnational Media during and after Socialism*, edited by Friederike Kind-Kovács and Jesse Labov, 51–69. Oxford and New York: Berghahn Books, 2013.

Strzelecki, Paweł. *"Nowy romantyzm" w twórczości kompozytorów polskich po roku 1975*. Cracow: Musica Iagiellonica, 2006.

Susuł, Jacek. "Pomnik i Ludzie." *Tygodnik Powszechny*, December 12, 1980.

Świerczyńska, Dobrosława, Cecylia Gajkowska, Joanna Król, and Irena Stemplowska, eds. *Kto był kim w drugim obiegu: słownik pseudonimów pisarzy i dziennikarzy 1976–89*. Warsaw: Instytut Badań Literackich, 1995.

Szczepkowska, Roma, ed. *Ks. Jerzy Popiełuszko: Życie i śmierć. Dokumenty i wspomnienia*. Paris: Polemika, 1986.

Szewera, Tadeusz, ed. *Niech wiatr ją poniesie: Antologia pieśni z lat 1939–45*. 2nd edition. Łódź: Wydawnictwo Łódzkie, 1972.

Szulc, Paweł, ed. *Fikcja czy rzeczywistość?: Wybór audycji Polskiego Radia Szczecin z lat 1946–1989*. Szczecin: IPN, 2016.

Taruskin, Richard. "Nationalism." *Grove Music Online*. Oxford Music Online. Oxford University Press, 2001. https://www-oxfordmusiconline-com.libproxy.lib.unc.edu/grovemusic/view/10.1093/gmo/9781561592630.001.0001/omo-9781561592630-e-0000050846.

Taylor, Diana. *The Archive and the Repertoire: Performing Cultural Memory in the Americas*. Durham, NC: Duke University Press, 2003.

Taylor, Timothy. *Strange Sounds: Music, Technology, and Culture*. New York: Routledge, 2001.

Terlecki, Ryszard. *Uniwersytet latający i towarzystwo kursów naukowych, 1977–1981*. Cracow and Rzeszów: Instytut Europejskich Studiów Społecznych w Rzeszowie, 2000.

Thomas, Adrian. *Górecki*. Oxford: Clarendon Press, 1997.

Thomas, Adrian. *Polish Music since Szymanowski*. Cambridge: Cambridge University Press, 2007.

Timberlake, Anicia Chung. "Brecht for Children: Shaping the Ideal GDR Citizen through Opera Education." *Representations* 132 (2015), 30–60.

Tischner, Józef. *The Spirit of Solidarity*. Translated by Marek B. Zaleski and Benjamin Fiore. San Francisco: Harper and Row, 1984.

Titon, Jeff Todd. *Powerhouse for God: Speech, Chant, and Song in an Appalachian Baptist Church*. Austin: University of Texas, 1988.

Tochka, Nicholas. *Audible States: Socialist Politics and Popular Music in Albania*. Oxford and New York: Oxford University Press, 2016.

Tochka, Nicholas. "Pussy Riot, Freedom of Expression, and Popular Music Studies after the Cold War." *Popular Music* 32, no. 2 (2013), 303–11.

Tomaszewski, Mieczysław. *Frederic Chopin und seine Zeit*. Translated by Małgorzata Kozlowska. Laaber: Laaber Verlag, 1999.

Tomaszewski, Mieczysław. *Krzysztof Penderecki i jego muzyka: Cztery eseje*. Cracow: Akademia Muzyczna, 1994.

Tomaszewski, Mieczysław. "Listening to Penderecki." In *Krzysztof Penderecki:* The Black Mask: *Contemporary Dance of Death from Idea to Performance*, 25–39. Translated by Józef Rybicki. Cracow: The International Cultural Centre, 1998.

Tomaszewski, Mieczysław. *Penderecki*. Warsaw: Adam Mickiewicz Institute, 2003.

Tomoff, Kiril. *Creative Union: The Professional Organization of Soviet Composers, 1939–53*. Ithaca, NY: Cornell University Press, 2006.

Tompkins, David G. "Composing for and with the Party: Andrzej Panufnik in Stalinist Poland." *The Polish Review* 54, no. 3 (2009), 271–85.

Tompkins, David G. *Composing the Party Line: Music and Politics in Early Cold War Poland and West Germany*. West Lafayette, IN: Purdue University Press, 2013.

Trenscényi, Balázs, and Michal Kopecek, eds. *Discourses of Collective Identity in Central and Southeast Europe (1770–1945): Texts and Commentaries*. Volume 1, *Late Enlightenment-Emergence of the Modern "National Idea."* Budapest and New York: Central European University Press, 2004.

Trochimczyk, Maja. "Aleksander Tansman to Tadeusz Kaczyński: Selected Letters (1971–1985)." *Polish Music Journal* 6, no. 1 (2003). https://polishmusic.usc.edu/research/publications/polish-music-journal/vol6no1/tansman-kaczynski-letters/.

Trochimczyk, Maja. "Sacred/Secular Constructs of National Identity: A Convoluted History of Polish Anthems." In *After Chopin: Studies in Polish Music*, edited by Maja Trochimczyk, 263–94. Los Angeles: Polish Music Center at the University of Southern California, 2000.

Turner, Victor. "The Center Out There: Pilgrim's Goal." *History of Religions* 12, no. 3 (1973), 191–230.

Verdery, Katherine. "Theorizing Socialism: A Prologue to the 'Transition.'" *American Ethnologist* 18, no. 34 (1991), 28–33.

Vest, Lisa Cooper. "Educating Audiences, Educating Composers: The Polish Composers' Union and *Upowszechnienie*." *Musicology Today* 7 (2010), 226–42.

Villa, Dana R. *Politics, Philosophy, Terror: Essays on the Thought of Hannah Arendt.* Princeton, NJ: Princeton University Press, 2009.

Vissmann, Cornelia. *Files: Law and Media Technology.* Translated by Geoffrey Winthrop Young. Stanford, CA: Stanford University Press, 2008.

Volkov, Solomon, ed. *Testimony: The Memoirs of Dmitri Shostakovich.* Translated by Antonina W. Bouis. New York: Harper and Row, 1980.

Wajda, Andrzej, and Jarosław Iwaszkiewicz. *Korespondencja.* Edited by Jan Strzałka. Warsaw: Zeszyty Literackie, 2013.

Walicki, Andrzej. "The Three Traditions in Polish Patriotism and Their Contemporary Relevance," Address delivered March 26, 1987, at the Polish Studies Center, Indiana University. Bloomington, IN: Polish Studies Center, 1987.

Waligóra, Grzegorz. "Wojciech Ziembiński (1925–2001)." *Biuletyn Instytutu Pamięci Narodowej* 88–89 (2008), 166–71.

Wałęsa, Lech, Andrzej Drzyciński, and Adam Kinaszewski. *A Path of Hope.* London: Collins Harvill, 1987.

Wawrzykowska-Wierciochowa, Dioniza. *"Boże, coś Polskę": Monografia historyczno-literacka i muzyczna.* Warsaw: Instytut Wydawniczy Pax, 1999.

Weber, Max. *Economy and Society: An Outline of Interpretive Sociology.* Edited by Guenther Roth and Klaus Wittich. Berkeley: University of California Pres, 1947.

Weber, Max. *Weber's Rationalism and Modern Society: New Translations on Politics, Bureaucracy, and Social Stratification.* Translated and edited by Tony Walters and Dagmar Walters. New York: Palgrave Macmillan, 2015.

Weeks, Ted. "Religion, Nationality, or Politics: Catholicism in the Russian Empire, 1863–1905." *Journal of Eurasian Studies* 2, no. 1 (2011), 52–59.

Weidman, Amanda. "Voice." In *Keywords in Sound*, edited by David Novak and Matt Sakakeeny, 232–45. Durham, NC: Duke University Press, 2015.

White, Anne. *De-Stalinization and the House of Culture: Declining State Control over Leisure in the USSR, Poland, and Hungary, 1953–89.* London and New York: Routledge, 1990.

Wierzbicka-Rusiecka, Joanna, ed. *Głosy zza muru: Wiersze i piosenki z obozów dla internowanych (grudzień '81–listopada '82).* Warsaw: "W," 1984.

Więzienne tango, Śpiewnik internowanego: Opole, Kamienna Góra, Nysa, Zaborze, Głogów, Grodków. Uherce: Wolna Drukarnia im. Józefa Piłsudskiego, 1982.

Wiroński, Piotr. *Wbrew, pomimo i dlatego: Analiza twórczości Jacka Kaczmarskiego.* Cracow: Księgarnia Akademicka, 2011.

Wlodarski, Amy Lynn. *Musical Witness and Holocaust Representation.* Cambridge: Cambridge University Press, 2015.

Wojciechowski, Aleksander. *Czas smutku, czas nadziei.* Warsaw: Wydawnictwo Artystyczne i Filmowe, 1992.

Wojczuk, Grażyna. "Sacrosong jako nowe zjawisko w polskiej kulturze religijnej ostatnich dziesięcioleci." In *Dramat i teatr sakralny*, edited by Irena Sławińska, 209–16. Lublin: Redakcja Wydawnictw Katolickiego Uniwersytetu Lubelskiego, 1988.

Wolff, Larry. *Inventing Eastern Europe: The Map of Civilization on the Mind of the Enlightenment.* Stanford, CA: Stanford University Press, 1994.

Woltering. Robert. "Unusual Suspects: 'Ultras' as Political Actors in the Egyptian Revolution." *Arab Studies Quarterly* 35, no. 3 (2013), 290–304.

Worończak, Jerzy, ed. *Bogurodzica*. Musicological edition by Hieronim Feicht, philological introduction by Ewa Ostrowska. Wrocław: Zakład Narodowy im. Ossolińskich, 1962.
Woroszylski, Wiktor. *Lustro: Dziennik internowania*. Cracow: Oficyna Literacka, 1983.
Yurchak, Alexei. *Everthing Was Forever Until It Was No More: The Last Soviet Generation* Princeton, NJ: Princeton University Press, 2005.
Zak, Albin. *The Poetics of Rock: Cutting Tracks, Making Records*. Berkeley: University of California Press, 2001.
Zakrzewski, Bogdan. *"Boże, coś Polskę" Alojzego Felińskiego*. Wrocław: Zakład Narodowy im. Ossolińskich, 1983.
Ziemiański, Stanisław. "Ks. Józef Łaś SJ (1907–1990)—pizarz i kompozytor." In *Muzyka religijna między epokami i kulturami*. Volume 1, edited by Krystyna Turek and Bogumiła Mika, 117–25. Katowice: Wydawnictwo Uniwersytetu Śląskiego, 2008.
Žižek, Slavoj. *The Parallax View*. Cambridge, MA: MIT Press, 2006.
Zubrzycki, Geneviève. "History and the National Sensorium: Making Sense of Polish Mythology." *Qualitative Sociology* 34 (2011), 21–57.

Audiovisual Materials

966–1966: Polskie pieśni religijne. Veriton VX-706, 1966, long-playing record.
Baez, Joan. *Joan Baez: Koncert dla Solidarności*. Wydawnictwo Wtrwałość 013, n.d., audiocassette.
Blanc et rouge. Bôlt Records BR ES07, 2012, CD.
Chodakowski, Andrzej, and Andrzej Zajaczkowski. *Robotnicy '80*, 1981.
Czerniakowska, Alina. *Był taki ktoś*, 2006.
Gall, Jan. *Wałęsa*. NOWa Kaseta 013, 1983, audiocassette.
Jankowska, Janina. *Polski Sierpień*. NOWa Kaseta 006, 1981, audiocassette.
Kaczmarski, Jacek. *Godzina z Jackim Kaczmarskim*. CDN Oficyna Fonograficzna 23, 1987, audiocassette.
Kaczmarski, Jacek. *Litania*. Saturn Recording Company, Iron Curtain Records 3, 1987, long-playing record.
Kaczmarski, Jacek. *Mury*. Wifon audiocassette, 1981. Remastered Pomaton EMI CD 7243 522839 2 7, 1999, CD.
Kelus, Jan Krzysztof. *Piosenki ze starej kasety*. Oficyna Fonograficzna CDN 01, 1984, audiocassette. Re-released as *Kawał w bok od szosy głównej*, Altmaster 5385614, 1998.
Kelus, Jan Krzysztof. *Z nie skończoną wciąż piosenką: Lata 1980–83*. CDN, 1984, audiocassette.
Krzysztoń, Antonina, and Andrzej Michalski. *Piosenki Karela Kryla*. NOWa Kaseta 033, 1986, audiocassette.
Ksiądz Jerzy Popiełuszko: Zło dobrem zwyciężaj; Modlitwy, kazania, rozważania; Nagrania archiwalne z lat 1982–84. 4BNB, 2010, CD.
Księga Hioba. Galeria 2b/Stowarzyszenie STEP, TR 020, 2007, CD.
Lapis Sounds. Alma Art 007, 1987, long-playing record.
Mazowsze. *Boże, coś Polskę: Prayer for the Country*. Veriton SXV-848, VK-010, LP, cassette.

Nowa Huta '82–'84. Nowohucka Oficyjna Fonograficzna 002, 1986, audiocassette.
Panufnik, Andrzej. *Symphony No. 9 and Bassoon Concerto.* Heritage Records, HTGCD266, 2014, CD.
Pietrzak, Jan, et al. *Kabaret pod Egidą: Sezon słynny '80.* Telewizja Polska S.A., 2009, DVD.
Piosenki Solidarności—Songs of Solidarity. Echo Original Country E LP 901-2, 1981, long-playing record.
Piwnica pod Baranami: Piosenki piwniczych kompozytorów, Volume 2. Pomaton, POM CD 039, 1993, CD.
Polskie pieśni religijne. Polish Radio Folk Collection 25, PRCD 174, 2012, CD.
Przeboje z Niemieckiej Republiki Demokratycznej. Polskie Nagrania, SXL 1167, 1974, long-playing record.
Scena to dziwna . . . 1981–2001. Metal Mind Productions MMP5DVDBOX001, 2008, DVD.
Schlöndorff, Völker. *Strajk.* 2007.
Schmidt, Anna. *Paths through the Labyrinth: The Composer Krzysztof Penderecki.* C Major Entertainment, 2014, DVD.
Sierpień 80. Wifon LP 163, 1989, long-playing record.
Sikora, Tadeusz. *Okrakiem na barykadzie.* CDN Oficyna Fonograficzna 20, 1986, audiocassette.
Śląsk. Muza SX 182, long-playing record.
Słowo o ks. Jerzym. Arka 023, 1985, audiocassette.
Solidarity! Postulat 22. Smithsonian Folkways FSS 37251, 1981, long-playing record.
Ujica, Andrei, and Harun Farocki. *Videograms of a Revolution.* 1992.
Wajda, Andrzej. *Człowiek z żelaza.* 1981.
Zakazane piosenki. CDN, 1983, audiocassette.
Zielona wrona czyli obozowe piosenki z Łupkowa i Gołdapi. NOWa 001, 1982, audiocassette.

INDEX

For the benefit of digital users, indexed terms that span two pages (e.g., 52–53) may, on occasion, appear on only one of those pages.

Tables and figures are indicated by *t* and *f* following the page number

accessibility, 275
action
   and affect, 193–94, 195–96, 204–5, 206–8, 223–24
   defined against activism, 5–6
   gestus as, 226–27
   music as call to, 27–28, 78, 108, 111, 116–17
   music as response to, 274–75, 276
   nonviolent, 119–20, 233
   in social movements, 5–6, 116–17, 235
   sound in relation to, 25, 69–70, 111–12, 116–17, 157, 168, 261–62
   space for, 261–62
advertisements, 36*f*
Agnew, Vanessa, 155
Altenberger, Alicja, 23
ambivalence, 26–27, 84–85, 90, 204
amplification, 16, 28–29, 113, 122–23, 146, 203, 205–6, 260–61, 278–79
anarchy, 9
annotation, 215–16
anonymity, 105–6, 173
anthems
   as chorus, 238, 252–54, 276–77
   cabaret, 12–13
   national, 9–10, 71, 77–78, 101, 106, 116–17, 122–23, 123*t*, 124, 219–20, 238–40, 251–53, 256–57, 261
   protest, 4, 15, 58, 65–66, 67–71, 98–99, 100, 107, 117–18, 119, 137–38, 141, 159
anthology, 171–73, 206–8
anti-Semitism, 2, 9, 143–44, 194n.7, 256–57, 264
applause, 18, 49–50, 122–23, 125, 166, 199, 203–4
architecture, 75–77, 95
   and assembly, 94, 114, 119, 155–56, 169–71, 189–90, 205–6, 227
   walls, 80–81, 86, 95, 109–10, 114, 143–44, 230, 247, 274
archives
   bodies as, 216, 259
   documents, 51, 54, 62, 90–92, 112–13, 121–22, 273
   ephemera, 95–97, 113
   personal, 40–41, 69–70, 81–82, 96*f*, 100–1
   tape, 23–25, 26, 39, 40–41, 95–97, 99–100, 117–18, 122, 128–29, 149*t*, 157, 203–4, 216–17
Arendt, Hannah, 3–4, 116–17
arrangement, 184, 248, 256, 266–69, 277–78

arrest, 39, 66, 94, 164, 173, 234, 237
artistic freedom, 48, 209, 215–16
Ascherson, Neal, 204–5, 206–8
assembly, 50, 68, 75–78, 114, 169–71,
    201–5, 227–28, 235, 240, 278–79
  through music, 205
Atkinson, Niall, 260–61
atmosphere, 16, 119, 154
Attali, Jacques, 42–43
attendance, 204, 209, 235n.4, 249
attention, 106, 120, 201–3, 232,
    260–61, 274
audibility, 33, 201–4, 221–23, 240,
    269, 276
  inaudibility, 119–20, 258–59
audience participation, 82, 90–92, 108–9,
    119–20, 154, 156, 168, 211, 227,
    229, 233, 240–41, 278–79
  as ethical, 87–89
audiobooks, 31–32, 40
audio literature, 23–26
aurality, 32–33, 162, 163
Auschwitz concentration camp, 98, 217
authenticity, 111–12, 121, 200–1, 221
autobiography, 14–15, 127, 183–84,
    233, 264
autonomy, 42–43, 95, 142, 254
avant-garde, *see* contemporary music

Bacewicz, Grażyna, 273
Bach, Johann Sebastian, 83*t*, 89, 242
background music, 134, 151–52,
    204–5, 206–8
Baez, Joan, 134, 231–33
"Ballad of Janek Wiśniewski" ("Janek
    Wiśniewski padł"), 217–27
Barańczak, Stanisław, 81–82, 230
bards, *see* poezja śpiewana
Barthes, Roland, 220
Bartkowski, Bronisław, 261–62
Bartoszewski, Władysław, 82–84, 95, 98
bassoon, 187–89
Bauman, Zygmunt, 85
bells
  chimes, 205–6, 276
  church, 145, 149–50, 154, 174, 175–76,
    201–3, 224
  towers, 260–61
Benhabib, Seyla, 22
Berlin Wall, 109–10, 230

Białołęka internment camp, 84
Białoszewski, Miron, 178–79
Bible
  exegesis of, 161–63, 200–1, 203
  biblical allegory, 31–32, 69, 99, 155–56,
    200–1, 217
  biblical settings in music, 87, 89
bibuły, 95, 96*f*
Bierezin, Jacek, 257–58
Bieżan, Andrzej, 86–89
biography, 140–41, 155–56,
    256–57, 275
Blumsztajn, Seweryn, 77–78
bodies, 149–50, 175–76, 188–89, 238n.11
  athleticism, 230
  genuflection, 213, 264
  prosthesis, 189–90
"Bogurodzica," *see* "Mother of God"
bootleg recording, 14–15, 23–26, 28–29,
    31–32, 39, 65–66, 148, 149*t*, 233,
    243, 270–71
Borowski, Adam, 279–80
Boston, 23, 211
Boulanger, Nadia, 269
boycott, 165–66, 197
"Boże, coś Polskę," *see* "God Save Poland"
Bratkowski, Stefan, 33–34
  Sound Gazette (*Gazeta Dźwiękowa*),
    23–26, 249
  vocal performance, 26–27, 30
breathing, 100–1, 187–88
Brezhnev, Leonid, 231–32, 233
broadcasting, 9–11, 12–13, 58–59, 65–66,
    71, 115, 119, 203–4, 242, 248
broadsides, 34–35, 40, 67, 101, 121–22,
    173, 219–20
Brubaker, Rogers, 193–94
bullhorn, 230
bureaucracy, 34–35, 41, 59, 60, 76*f*,
    122n.57, 212, 272–74
  correspondence within, 54, 61, 63–64
Bush, George H.W., 229
Butler, Judith, 17, 240
Bylander, Cindy, 265–66

cabaret
  music, 12–13, 17, 26–27, 53–54, 64,
    115, 137–38, 218
  stage, 14–15, 47, 49–50, 61, 81–82,
    86, 113–14

Cabaret Cellar Under the Rams, 26–28
Cabaret Under the Aegis (*Kabaret pod Egidą*), 14–15
calendar, 179–80, 260–61, 279
call and response, 86–89, 116–17, 119, 177, 201–3, 230
cameos, 10, 49–50, 136–37
   from Poland, 192–94, 212
   Krzysztof Penderecki as, 212
   Lech Wałęsa as, 227
candles, 180–82, 189–90
canon
   historiographic, 2–3, 5, 70, 110–11, 116–17, 141–42, 278
   literary, 83–84
   musical, 2–3, 136, 275
capitalism
   sounds of, 62
Cash, Johnny, 58–59
cassette
   culture, 24–25, 29–30, 32, 38–41, 129–30, 135, 243
   labels, 29–30, 34–35, 40, 65, 84
   microcassette recorder, 95–97, 117–18, 130–31, 270, 272
   mixtapes, 135, 149*t*
   player or recorder, 14–15, 25, 122, 130–31, 182
   tapes, 23–26, 38–41, 45, 64–65, 134, 136, 149*t*, 166, 233, 243
   videos, 38–39
cataloging, 98, 105–6, 217, 242
Catholic Church
   and Polish identity, 261, 262–63, 264, 278
   and the Polish opposition, 89, 149–50, 159, 160, 167–68, 214–16
   as Western European, 159
   globalization, 161–62, 164
   music in (*see* plainchant; religious music)
   rituals of, 98–99, 166, 261, 264
   spirituality, 158–59, 164, 176–77, 214–16, 252–53
   value of the arts, 164
   voice within, 157, 161–63
CDN
   cassette label, 65, 84
   press, 81–82
celebrity
   and the Polish opposition, 21, 43–44, 195–96, 231–33

Cabaret Cellar Under the Rams, 26–28
censorship
   in the nineteenth century, 80, 256, 263–64
   of individuals, 14–15, 214
   of music, 64–65, 214n.66, 249, 273–74
   of sound, 129–30n.78
   of text, 33–34, 42, 64–65, 86, 100, 136–37, 148, 178, 214–15, 270, 272–74
   self-censorship, 25, 272–73
Censorship Bureau, 68, 272–73
charisma, 127–28, 148, 194–96, 230
Chicago, 14, 28, 199, 262–63
Chimiak, Marek, 40–41
Chłopecki, Andrzej, 68
Chodakowski, Andrzej, see *Workers '80*
Cholewa, Mieczysław, 221–23, 226
Chomsky, Noam, 146
Chopin, Frédéric, 10, 12–13, 57–58, 72–74, 91*t*, 115, 131–33n.81, 193, 256
choral performance, 87, 156, 238, 254, 265–66
   by church congregations, 169
   performance practice, 256–57, 258, 276–77
Christmas, 79, 92, 97–100, 176–77
   carols, 97–98, 99
churches
   acoustics of, 87, 154, 233, 248, 261–62
   concerts in, 86–89, 90–92, 180, 183, 189–90, 199–200, 248
   organizing in, 89, 165–66
church hymns, 21–22, 90–92, 95–97, 154, 164–65, 169, 234
   See also specific titles
circulation
   by music, 217
   of music, 136
civil society, 41–44, 46, 48–49, 86–87, 94, 192
class, 168
classical music (*muzyka poważna*), 53–54, 115, 208, 273
   early music, 89
clocks, 220, 260–61
   See also calendar
cold, 78–80, 179–80, 201, 204

Cold War
    and music, 5–6, 11–12, 140, 211
    emotional tenor of, 146–47, 204–5
    history, 7–10, 58, 74–75, 109–11, 146–47, 214, 274–75
    media, 9, 28–29, 34–35, 39, 58–59, 128–29, 146
collaboration
    artistic, 87, 131–33, 150–51, 208–9
    political, 117–18, 160, 231–32
collecting, 30, 65, 99–100, 101, 121–22, 123*t*, 135–36, 148, 216–17
commemoration, 20–21, 48–49, 90, 91*t*, 141–42, 145, 261
    and sound recording, 166, 201
    ceremony, 152, 197, 278
    concert in celebration in honor of Warsaw's liberation, 62–63
    in musical composition, 176
    of December 1970, 116–17, 131–33, 131*t*, 199–201, 216
commission, *see* patronage
Committee for Workers' Defense (Komitet Obrony Robotników, KOR), 6–7, 34
Committee on Independent Culture (Komitet Kultury Niezależnej), 43–44, 45*t*, 49, 178
Communist Party, *see* Polish United Workers' Party
community, 258, 262–63
    creative, 165
concerts
    domestic, 80–86, 108
    programming, 82, 136, 199–200
confession, 147, 168, 252–53, 277
Congress of Culture, 17–18
Congress of Polish Culture, 17, 75–77, 78, 95
Congress of Vienna, 251
consciousness
    national, 165
consonants, 31–32, 58–59, 107, 161–62, 166–67
contemporary music, 5, 11–12, 53–54, 86–87, 214, 265
    experimentalism, 87–89
    in global context, 198–99, 273
    neo-romanticism, 265–66
contrafacts, 97, 99, 101, 121, 125, 136, 152–54

Copland, Aaron, 239
copyright, 39
Corbin, Alain, 154
correspondence, 109, 160, 228, 242, 247
cover art, 31, 43*f*, 138*f*
cover songs, 102–3, 105–6, 121, 217–20, 224–26, 231–32
Cracow, 156, 158, 160–61, 235–36, 258–59, 260–61, 270–71
critical edition, 81–82, 100–1, 122–23, 241–42n.26, 254, 256
cultural diplomacy, 5–6, 56–57, 155–56, 178, 199
cultural management, 41, 46–47, 51–59, 69–70, 121, 212
    and work stoppage, 77, 80–81, 270
cultural thaw after 1956, *see* Thaw
culture
    debates about autonomy, 44–48
    expediency of, 165, 200–1, 274

Dąbrowska, Maria, 229
Dąbrowski, Andrzej, 63–64
Dąbrowski, Karol, 173
Daughtry, J. Martin, 140, 252–53
dedication, musical, 127n.72, 178–79, 186–87, 199–200, 205, 265–66
democracy, representative, 150, 193, 240
demonstrations
    1968, 84, 237n.7
    counter-demonstrations, 279–80
    December 1970, 116, 219–20
    during state socialism, 116, 228–29
    twenty-first century, 68, 278
detention, 66, 94, 101
    cultural programming during, 82–84
    of activists, 74, 192
diaries, 69–70, 74n.18, 82–84, 94, 95–100, 160, 229
diplomacy, 229, 262–63
displacement, 159, 228, 264
dissent
    as behavior, 69, 275–76
    ethics of, 28, 41, 136–37, 158–59, 164, 168, 178, 196, 200–1, 214–15
    songs as symbols of, 99–100, 140, 141, 223n.86, 228–29, 240–41, 264–65, 269
    Western value of, 3–4, 6–7, 33–34, 109–10, 145–46, 151–52, 209

308 | INDEX

Długosz, Leszek, 276–77
documentary, 141–42
  audio recordings, 40, 117–18, 122, 128, 201n.30, 206–8, 230, 248
  films, 62, 113–14, 152–54, 203–4, 208–9, 217–18, 226, 230
documents
  paper, 51–54, 61, 101, 220n.81
  sound, 112–13, 128, 135, 149*t*, 150–51, 206–8, 277
domestic
  listening, 65–66, 86, 174–75, 178, 271
  recording, 128–29, 157, 173, 206–8, 243
Dowigiałło, Krzysztof, 219–21
Drott, Eric, 5–6, 113
drowning, 158, 168
drugi obieg (second circulation), 24–25, 28–29, 31, 33, 74n.17, 81–82, 137–38, 146, 158–59, 171–73, 204, 214–15, 220–27, 230–31, 233, 234, 243, 275n.128
Durkheim, Emile, 5–6
Dvořák, Antonín, 132n.81, 203–4

East Central Europe, 7–9, 141–42
  as part of Central Europe, 145–46, 198–99, 256–57
  culture as transnational, 40, 48, 56–57, 58–59, 126, 134, 256–57
echo, 148, 186–87
economy
  alternative, 33, 157–58
  failure thereof, 51, 273
  free-market, 5, 271–72
  import and export, 29–30, 176–77, 178, 271–72
  music in, 5, 60
education, 56–57, 60
elections (June 4, 1989), 1–2, 137–38, 141n.110
electronic music, 45*t*, 86–89, 150–52, 182, 223–24
émigré, *see* Polish émigrés
empire, 13, 14
  Austro-Hungarian, 256–57
  Polish-Lithuanian Commonwealth, 251–52
  Russian, 251, 254
employment
  of musicians, 49, 61, 80

entertainment industry
  in Poland, 39, 54–55, 59, 245
  in the United States, 10, 60
estrada (music for the stage), 47, 59
eternity, 179–80
ethnography, 17–18, 84, 152, 259–60, 278
European Union, 152–54, 278
everyday, 7–9, 19–20, 31, 68–69, 80, 99, 123*t*, 143, 178–79, 274
exile, 29–30, 34–35, 90–92, 214, 242

family, 39, 95–97, 98, 133, 156, 184, 233, 278–79
fanfare, see *hejnał*
fear, 74–75, 77, 94, 100, 142, 147, 175–76, 210–11
Fedorowicz, Jacek, 16
Feliński, Alojzy, 251, 253–54, 257–58
feminism, 18
festivals, 5–6, 47, 56–57, 64, 136–40, 160–61, 213–14, 220–21, 240–41, 273
  See also individual titles
fidelity (recording), 64, 216–17, 223, 270
Filipowicz, Halina, 203–4
film, 48, 79, 105, 148, 166, 226, 263–64
first-person narratives
  in music, 115
  See also witness
flags, 14, 101, 106, 219–20
folk art, 127–28, 184
Folkman, Benjamin, 211
folk music, 53–54, 256–57
folk poetry, *see* poetry; vernacular
folksong, 12–13, 65, 121
Folkways Records, 223, 224, 230–31, 245
Fołtyn, Maria, 56–57
food, 10, 16, 68, 74, 77, 98
Forbidden Songs (*Zakazane piosenki*), 81–82, 105
Forman, Miloš, 48
freedom, 42–43, 95, 111, 127, 150, 173, 175–76, 278–79
  of speech, 116–17, 192, 263–64
  sounds of, 145, 174
friendship, 85, 86, 87, 92, 98, 138–40, 178, 184, 194–95, 208, 269–70, 275
funeral
  as political event, 148, 219–20
  music, 90–92, 115
  of Jerzy Popiełuszko, 160, 164–65, 171–73, 249

Gadulanka, Jadwiga, 201, 205–6
Gaertner, Katarzyna, 160–61
Garton Ash, Timothy, 1, 15, 119–21, 127–28, 194–95, 250
Gdańsk, 1, 13, 242
   Lenin Shipyards, 77, 114, 199–200, 216, 227
   See also demonstrations: December 1970
Gdańsk Agreement, 15, 114, 221
   commemoration of, 49–50, 110–11, 243
genocide, 174–75
genre, 32–33, 53–54, 59–60, 64, 72–74, 160–61, 260–61
geography
   European, 7–9, 174–75
   musical, 256–57
   of protest, 116, 219–21, 229
   urban, 70
Giedroyc, Jerzy, 34–35
Gintrowski, Przemysław, 31–32, 91*t*, 107, 218
Glemp, Józef, 157–58, 164
Głogów prison, 95–97
Godlewski, Zbigniew, 195–96, 219–20, 221
"God Save Poland" ("Boże, coś Polskę),” 89, 91*t*, 98, 101, 123*t*, 155–56, 157, 169–71, 234
"God Save the King," 252–53
Gołdap internment camp, 95, 100
Gombrowicz, Witold, 34–35, 160
Gomułka, Władysław, 228–29
Gorbachev, Mikhail, 26, 31
Górecki, Henryk Mikołaj, 45*t*, 197, 213, 265–66, 276n.133, 277
   Miserere, Op. 44, 180–82, 265–66
graffiti, 17
Greek chorus, 2–3, 238–39
Gugulski, Marcin, 204–5
guitar, 26–29, 31–32, 65–66, 72–74, 86, 115, 134, 160–61, 173, 218, 224, 233
   poetry (*see* poezja śpiewana)

Handel, George Frideric, 30, 211
happenings, 85, 235–36
Hardt, Michael, 120
Harvard University, 23, 26
hearing
   as witness, 72–74, 111–12, 162, 166–67
   in theological context, 163

overhearing, 78, 123*t*, 171, 264
silent, 224
heat, 16
hejnał (fanfare), 260–61, 278
Herbert, Zbigniew, 49–50
Herman, Edward S., 146–47
Herter, Joseph, 189–90
Heston, Charlton, 10–11
historiography
   Cold War, 3–4, 5, 7–9, 11–12, 74, 230
   compensatory, 93, 226–27
   grassroots, 95–97, 101, 109–11, 119, 121–22, 216–17
heroic figures, 21, 110–11, 229–33
   Lech Wałęsa as, 124, 127–28, 194–95, 227
   music, 5–6, 11–12, 69
   myths, 3–4, 18, 85, 109–11, 141–42, 204, 276–77
   of the Polish opposition, 5–6, 109–10, 111, 114, 116, 155
   political artists as, 110–11, 138, 165–66
history
   as communal, 136
   as embodied, 155, 156
Hitler, Adolf, and music, 239–40
Holland, Agnieszka, 148, 151–52
Holmberg, Lars, 223
Home Army (Armia Krajowa), 105
homophony, 178–79, 180, 205, 258–59, 269–70, 277
humanitarian aid, 6–7, 39, 74, 89, 95–97, 99, 146, 159–60, 259
humming, 134–35
hymnals, 256, 258, 259, 260
hymns, *see* church hymns

icons, religious, 133, 159–60, 173, 174, 184
identity
   multiethnic, 56–57
   Polish, 56–57, 75–77, 124, 159
imprisonment, 66, 94, 98, 146–47
   See also detention
improvisation, 86–89, 161–62
Independent Culture (*Kultura Niezależna*), 41, 90, 158
Independent Electroacoustic Music Studio, 49–50, 86–89, 161–62
Index on Censorship, 33
industry, 52–53, 63–64, 77–78, 116–17, 156–57, 158, 235–36, 249, 250

informant, 81–82, 161–62, 169–71, 221n.84
instruments, 176, 186
intelligentsia
  as audience, 72–74, 83–84, 108, 274–75
  as taste makers, 5, 34–35, 171
  disinterest in popular culture, 40–41, 59, 273
  in opposition, 160, 165, 214
  in detention, 95
intercession, 251–52, 256, 278–79
"Internationale," 119
internment camps, 94, 247
  See also detention; individual camp locations
interrogation, 157–58, 186, 189–90
interruption, 133, 163
interview, 15–16, 40, 65–66, 100–1, 131*t*, 188, 206–8, 209, 210–11, 215–16, 273, 275
  protest as, 114, 133
  sound as, 72–74, 124, 154, 201–3, 205–6, 224, 279
Intervision Song Festival, 56–57, 58–59, 220–21
Iron Curtain, 11–12
Israel, 228

Jabłoński, Maciej, 275
Janda, Krystyna, 218–20, 224, 226
"Janek Wiśniewski padł," *see* "Ballad of Janek Wiśniewski"
Janion, Maria, 17–18, 78, 135
Jankowska, Janina, 128, 149*t*, 206–8, 223n.87, 248
Jarocin Festival, 5, 80–81n.42
Jarre, Jean Michel, 110
Jaruzelski, Wojciech, 9–10, 64, 65, 71–74, 106, 150–51
Jaworze internment camp, 82–84, 95, 98
jazz, 5, 63–64, 160–61
Jazz Jamboree, 5
Jones, Bryn, *see* Muslimgauze
journalism
  in Poland, 16, 25–26, 33–34, 68, 99–100, 128, 136
  transnational coverage, 79–80, 85–86, 113–14, 119–21, 146, 150, 179, 209
journalists
  as politically vulnerable, 71

Judt, Tony, 7–9
justice, 168

Kaczmarski, Jacek, 28–30, 31–32, 69–70, 91*t*, 107–11, 138, 218
  "Walls," 107–11, 137–40, 142, 226–33
Kaczyński, Jarosław, 278–79
Kaczyński, Lech, 155–56, 278–79
Kaczyński, Tadeusz, 45*t*, 86–87, 90, 159–60, 161–62, 178, 186–87, 189–90, 192–93, 197–98, 199–200, 228, 249
Kalinowska, Tamara, 27–28
Kamiński, Włodzimierz, 54–55, 212
Karta Organization, 216–17
Kasprzyk, Jan Józef, 278–79
Kaszewski, Jan Neopomucen, 253–54
Katz, Mark, 30
Kazik, 226–27
Keff, Bożena, 2–6, 10, 13, 18
Kelus, Jan Krzysztof, 17, 39, 65, 72–74, 81–82, 84–85
Kenney, Padraic, 6–7, 235–36
Kieślowski, Krzysztof, 27–28
Kilar, Wojciech, 91*t*, 152n.19, 276n.133
Knittel, Krzysztof, 45*t*, 80, 86–89
  Black Water, White Water, Old Stream, 87–89
  String Quartet (1985), 176
Kołakowski, Leszek, 74–75, 214
Komorowska, Maja, 17
Komorowski, Bronisław, 111
Konopnicka, Maria, 82–83, 91*t*
  "The Oath" ("Rota"), 152–54, 168, 201–3, 219–20, 269, 278
Korcz, Włodzimierz, 13
Kościuszko, Tadeusz, 251
Krauze, Zygmunt, 269
Krupowicz, Stanisław, 86–89
Kryl, Karel, 40–41
Kubik, Jan, 204–5
Kunreuther, Laura, 196–97
Kuroń, Jacek, 6–7, 41
Kurpiński, Karol, 256–57
Kutavičius, Bronius, 180–82

labor history, 116, 121–22, 156–57, 199–201
language
  critique of quality, 17, 65, 249
  symbolic, 3, 34–35, 74–75, 136–37, 174

Łapiński, Zbigniew, 31–32, 91*t*, 107
laughter, 122–23
Law and Justice Party (Prawo i Sprawiedliwość), 278
leadership
  of musical performance, 127–28, 168, 199, 210–11
  of protests, 237
  of religious community, 148, 169–71
  See also Lech Wałęsa
legion songs, 82, 102–3, 115, 124–25, 127, 241–42, 253–54, 256, 277
Lewek, Antoni, 163
liminality, 169–71, 183, 220–21, 224, 260
  paraliturgical hymns and, 261–62
liner notes, 39, 230–31
Lipski, Jan Józef, 6–7
listening
  and subjectivity, 61, 79, 87–89, 148, 177, 240, 270
  as methodology, 11–12, 32–33, 69, 159, 206–8, 237–38
  as political work, 25–26, 40–41, 65–66, 135, 211, 224, 230–31, 272–73
  as silent, 111–12, 143
  as witness, 147, 230–31, 232
  theological perspectives on, 161–63, 177
Liszt, Franz, 269
literacy, 33
literary journals, 34–35, 40, 41, 214–15, 257–58, 260–61, 270
literature
  children's, 31–32, 99
  nineteenth-century, 140, 141, 165, 251, 255
  short story, 78–79
liturgy, 20–21, 89, 155–56, 160–61, 165–66, 188, 203
  music in, 160, 169, 199–200, 208–9, 258, 261, 265–66
  paraliturgical music, 261–62
Litwiński, Mieczysław, 86–89
live
  broadcast, 10–11
  performance, 13, 58–59, 61, 87–89, 122–23, 141, 182–83, 189–90, 221, 270
  recording, 28–29, 31–32, 270–71
liveness, 168, 206–8
Llach, Luís, 68
local history, 130–31, 150, 219–21

logo, 13
  See also Polish opposition; visual culture
Lortat-Jacob, Bernard, 241
loudness, 18, 62, 77, 79, 111, 143, 168, 169–71, 182, 187–89, 230, 278
  of singing, 99–100, 117–20, 124, 218–19, 258–59, 264
loudspeakers, 122–23, 130–31, 146, 156, 227
Lukasiewicz, Mark, 85–86
lullabies, 40–41, 93, 259
Lutosławski, Witold, 41, 43–44, 45*t*, 49–50, 75–77, 197, 209n.46, 210–11, 269

magnetic recording, 38–39, 113, 117–18, 122, 149–50, 157–58
Manuel, Peter, 39
march, 87, 143, 218–19, 279
martial law, 1–2, 9, 67, 269
  declaration of as event, 71, 270–72
  in fiction, 78–79
  See also Popiełuszko, Jerzy
martyrdom, 145, 164, 168, 186, 263–64
Marxist political thought, 3–4, 5–6, 214
mass
  during protests, 122, 123*t*, 156–57, 264, 279
  dramaturgy of, 165–66, 174–75, 242, 253–54
  in cinemas, 263–64
  in commemorative context, 49–50, 152, 203–4, 242
  in detention, 95–97, 247
  language of, 160–61, 260
  musical settings, 160–61
mass culture, 60
"Masses for the Fatherland," 146, 155–58, 163, 164, 169, 177, 249, 260
Mazowiecki, Tadeusz, 95, 99, 197, 229, 262–63
mazurka, 68, 126
  Dąbrowski mazurka (*see* anthems: national)
media
  affordances, 24–25, 33, 129–30
  archaeology, 20–21, 163, 190–91
  communication, 120, 122, 128, 178–79
  convergence, 30, 128–29, 135, 163, 182, 205–8, 223

312 | INDEX

distribution, 35–39, 61, 123*t*, 178–79
elements and, 168
format, 23–27, 38–39, 113, 256
ecology, 128, 227, 237–38
spectacle, 10–11, 60, 110–11,
  113, 239–40
state-sponsored, 26, 33–34, 39, 45,
  61, 129–30
transnational circulation, 11, 28, 29–30,
  33–34, 57–58, 121, 123*t*, 134,
  184–86, 223
unofficial, 33
meditation, 180–82
memoir, *see* autobiography
memory
  culture, 101, 141–42, 217, 220
  making music by, 95–97, 154, 226
  personal, 17, 148, 155, 163, 273
  public, 110–11, 116, 137–38, 152,
    197, 216
  work, 176, 190–91, 216–17,
    221–23, 224
meter, 218
methodology, 19, 69–70
Metzer, David, 269
Meyer, Krzysztof, 248, 265, 270, 274
  Polish Symphony, 265, 270, 274
Miazga, Tadeusz, 161–62
Michalski, Grzegorz, 75–77
Michnik, Adam, 49–50, 71, 160
Mickiewicz, Adam, 91*t*, 125, 165,
  173, 263–64
microfilm, 34–35, 38–39
microphones, 114, 123*t*, 168, 227, 278–79
Middle East, 150–51
migration, 47, 69–70, 124–25, 159, 183–
  86, 212, 233, 256–57
Mikołajska, Halina, 98
military band, 125, 201–3
military control, 17, 19–20, 67, 70–71, 80,
  157, 219–20
  Citizens' Militia (Zmotoryzowane
    Odwody Milicji Obywatelskiej,
    ZOMO), 77
military music, *see* legion songs
Millenium of Polish Christianity, 75–77,
  159–60, 262–63
Miłosz, Czesław, 34–35, 89, 145–46, 161–
  62, 200–1, 214, 241–42
mimeographs, 34–35, 216–17

Ministry of Arts and Sciences, 55–56
Minor, Ryan, 239–40
minute of silence, 101, 116–17, 131*t*,
  141–42, 203–4
Mitan, Andrzej, 86–89
mobility, 24–25, 124–25, 156–57, 184
Modejska, Helena, 251
Mokotów prison, 98
moment of silence, *see* minute of silence
Moniuszko, Stanisław, 56–57, 81–82, 91*t*,
  115, 260–61
monument, 28, 143, 234–35, 239–40, 278
Monument for the Fallen Shipyard Workers,
  28, 116
  unveiling of, 197
Mosse, George, 261
"Mother of God" ("Bogurodzica"), 91*t*, 184,
  269, 276–77
mourning of, 1–2, 131–33, 143–44, 155–56,
  188, 199–200, 205, 217, 248, 275
  Wolfgang Amadeus Mozart, Requiem, as
    ideal, 199–200, 208–9
Mur, Jan (Andrzej Drzycimski), 94, 97–98,
  99–100, 101
museums, 31–32, 45, 152–54, 156n.31,
  163, 220n.81, 241–42n.26
Museum of Independence, 23
music
  and ethics, 87–89, 136–37, 158–59, 178,
    188, 197–98, 208
  and political agency, 69, 93, 101, 106,
    128, 240–41, 274
  and socialism, 5, 11–12, 41, 57, 59,
    183–84, 238–39
  as articulation of humanity, 100, 136,
    149–50, 164–65, 274
  as asemantic, 55, 75–77, 90, 214
  as work, 32
  as universal language, 58, 192–93, 211
  definitions of, 40, 47–48, 93
  exceptionalism and, 32–33, 54–55, 214
  failure, 47, 62–63, 64–65, 115, 143–44,
    171, 264–65
  instrumentality, 22, 40–41, 124, 143–44,
    165, 189–90, 221–23
  mediation of, 31, 53–54, 101, 135, 177,
    186, 220–21
  political efficacy, 5–6, 19, 51, 64, 90,
    120, 206–8, 229, 230–31, 240–41,
    257–58, 274

INDEX | 313

music (cont.)
  political ideology, 11–12, 46, 52–53, 57–58, 127, 150–51, 230–31, 250
music criticism, 42, 87–89, 93, 100–1, 131–33, 188, 189–90, 192–93, 211, 231–33, 248, 270. *See also* journalism
music institutions, 56*t*, 58
musical autonomy, 47–48, 140, 143–44
musical form, 205, 265–69, 270
Musical Movement, see *Ruch Muzyczny*
musical notation, 97, 135, 248, 260–61, 276–77
musicians
  amateur, 90, 115, 133, 258, 259–60
  See also Polish opposition: musicians in
musicology, 95, 100–1, 158–59, 161–62, 249
Muslimgauze, 150–52
Mycielski, Zygmunt, 45*t*, 242
"My Fatherland" ("Ojczyzno ma"), 155–56, 169, 171–76

naming, 101–2, 131*t*, 133, 141, 156, 214, 221
  of dead, 201–3, 216, 279
nation
  as history, 217
  as homogenous, 3–4, 9
  as people, 13, 15, 173, 238–39
  as terrain, 7–9, 14, 124, 173–75
  as victim, 85, 169
  ideas of Johann Gottfried Herder about, 256–57
national heritage, 56–57, 83–84, 99
nationalism
  critique of, 17–18, 143–44, 273
  in Poland, 9, 21–22, 109–10, 159, 183–84, 193–94, 251
  in the nineteenth century, 21–22, 58, 90–92, 124, 165, 251
  singing and, 239–40, 252–53, 276–77
Nazi Germany, 7–9, 58, 238–39, 256–57
  occupation of Poland, 65–66, 80, 81–82, 104
negotiations, *see* organizing meetings
Negri, Antoni, 120
Nettl, Paul, 256–57
news, 28, 31–32, 104, 121–22, 143–44, 179, 186, 249
newspaper, 25–26, 34–35, 131*t*, 147–48, 194–95, 200–1, 253

New York Philharmonic, 211
Niewęglowski, Wiesław, 89–90
Niżyńska, Joanna, 141
noise, 77, 101, 147, 150–51, 168, 182–83, 206–8, 279–80
Nora, Pierre, 216–17
normalization, 51, 54–55, 59, 212, 273–74
Norwid, Cyprian Kamil, 91*t*, 278
NOWa (Niezależna Oficyna Wydawnicza, Independent Publishing House), 38n.33, 40, 41, 100–1
Nowakowski, Marek, 78–79
"The Oath" ("Rota"), *see* Maria Konopnicka

objectivity, 122
obscenity, 31
"One Hundred Years," 117–18, 122–23, 123*t*, 228–29
Ong, Walter J., 162
Ono, Yoko, 27–28
open letter, 17–18, 49, 209–10
opera, 56–57, 213–14, 275
oral history, 41, 67n.1, 69–70, 77, 78, 149–50
orality, 162
oral transmission, 101, 154, 173, 179, 255, 259
Orange Alternative, 45*t*, 235–36
oratory, 145
orchestration, 205–8, 265, 275
organ, 164–65, 171, 248
  as chorus, 92, 245, 261–62
  as technology, 154, 160–61, 187–88
organizing
  archival work, 23, 128–29, 136–37, 203–4, 216–17
  by clergy, 95–97, 99, 160, 258–59
  and the common, 120, 240–41
  domestic, 34–35, 74–75, 80–81, 86, 233
  grassroots, 3–4, 27–28, 120
  labor, 19, 26, 32, 40, 65–66, 78, 149–50
  meetings, 16, 68, 89, 95, 114, 124, 165–66, 193, 227
  space for, 201–3
  tactics, 46, 116–17, 120, 234–35
orientalism, 86–87, 91*t*, 150–51
Osiecka, Agnieszka, 62–63
Ostrowska, Ewa, 248
ovation, standing, 158–59, 228

pace, 168, 175–76, 180, 188–89, 269–70
Paderewski, Ignacy Jan, 48, 214
pamphlets, 35–39, 43–44, 81–82, 84, 104, 114, 152–54, 163, 172*f*
   See *also* zine
Panufnik, Andrzej, 184–90, 276–77n.133
paper, 95, 101–2, 121–22, 152–54, 243
   See also *bibuły*
paper shortage, 38–39, 94, 95
parades, 235–36, 240–41, 253–54
Paris, 34–35, 77–78, 223–24
   in Polish culture, 82
parody, 14–15, 26, 30, 61, 113–14, 121, 136–37, 231–32, 235–36
Pärt, Arvo, 180–82
partition of Poland, 7–9, 57–58, 80, 82, 90–92, 124, 125, 152–54, 251–52
   music in the partitions compared, 258–59
Patkowski, Józef, 49
patronage
   by friends, 68, 208–9, 210–11
   by the state, 46–47, 121, 273–74
   from abroad, 186, 187, 199
Penderecki, Krzysztof, 48–49, 192, 248, 265–66, 269
   and commemoration, 197
   and the communist state, 212
   and Solidarity, 197
   Lacrimosa, 38, 48–49, 197
   Polish Requiem, 199, 209, 215n.70, 217, 274–75
   Te Deum, 269–70
   The Black Mask (*Die schwarze Maske*), 213–14
Pepliński, Edmund, 220
perestroika, 31, 51
performance practice, 21–22, 92, 188–89, 254
photographs, 114n.28, 199–200, 219–20, 243
Pietkiewicz, Małgorzata, 81–82, 95, 96*f*, 100–1, 117–18n.39
Pietruszka, Bogdan, 200–1
Pietrzak, Jan, 13–16, 47
Pietrzyk, Maciej, 121, 133–34, 233
pilgrimage, 27–28, 152, 153*f*, 156, 163, 174–75, 227, 248, 262–63
Piłsudski, Józef, and music, 241–42, 261
pitch, 161–62, 176–77, 187–89
   range, 166–67

plainchant, 95–97, 148, 154, 160–62, 168, 171, 178–79, 182, 188, 276–77
   and theology of the voice, 177
playback, 33, 50, 71, 131*t*, 158–59, 201, 203, 270–71
plurality, 111–13, 143, 193–94, 256–57, 280
poetry, 2–3, 32, 40, 264–65, 276–77
   and messianism, 165
   and the opposition, 81–82, 121–22, 135, 145–46, 209
   sung (*see* poezja śpiewana)
   readings, 80, 152n.19, 243, 264–65
   vernacular, 17, 101–2, 121–22, 135–36, 156
poezja śpiewana (sung poetry), 26–30, 31–32, 40, 53–54, 90–92, 93, 121, 134, 138–41
   as national music, 109, 115
   in response to martial law, 72–74
   relationship to Russian traditions, 138–40
Poizat, Michel, 177
Polish Composers' Union (Związek Kompozytorów Polskich, ZKP), 49, 56*t*, 76*f*, 77, 125, 197
Polish constitution and music, 125
Polish émigrés
   as audiences, 10, 28, 211, 262–63
   as musicians, 28–30, 69–70, 124–25, 183–84, 189–90
   as organizers, 23–25, 77–78
   institutions, 29–30, 187, 242
   publications, 34–35, 36*f*, 48–49, 160, 210–11
Polish Film Chronicle, 203–4
Polish Journalists' Association (Stowarzyszenie Dziennikarzy Polskich), 26
Polishness, 17–18, 124, 187, 273–74
Polish opposition
   compromise within, 6–7, 9
   history of, 6, 26, 58, 116
   importance of Roman Catholicism for, 20–21, 159–60
   material culture of, 23–26, 33, 113, 154, 200–1, 216–17
   musicians in, 32, 48–50, 89, 90, 143–44, 178, 208–11
   nationalism within, 9, 116–17

Polish opposition (*cont.*)
   print culture of, 31–32, 34–35, 113–14, 121–22, 135–36, 243 (*see also* drugi obieg)
   religion and, 89, 156–57, 160
   social networks of, 39, 68, 201
   visual culture of, 1–2, 13, 23, 141, 153*f*, 168, 193–94, 211, 220, 230–31, 243, 250, 272–73
   women in, 89, 95, 98, 134, 218, 233
Polish Radio, 12–13, 17, 63–64, 71, 129–30, 220n.81
   Experimental Studio at, 49
Polish Television, 71, 72*f*, 119n.44
Polish United Workers Party (Polska Zjednoczona Partia Robotnicza, PZPR), 14–15, 50, 119, 125, 203
   Central Committee, 6–7, 15–16, 114, 228–29
   Department of Culture, 52–59, 53*t*, 199, 212
   membership, 26, 213
   Subcommittee on Music, 54–55, 212
   Subcommittee on Rozrywka and the Stage, 60
Polony, Leszek, 248, 270–71, 273–74
Pope John Paul II (Karol Wojtyła), 1–2, 27–28, 89, 155–56, 159–60, 164, 174–77, 193, 199–201, 214, 243, 248, 276–77
   and music, 154, 160–61, 217, 262–63, 277
Popiełuszko, Jerzy, 145
   body, 158, 168
   grave, 152–56, 163, 184–86, 197
   mourning of, 1–2, 152, 176, 249
   sermons, 36*f*, 148, 186–87 (*see also* "Masses for the Fatherland")
popular culture
   from the United States, 60, 62, 233
popular song, 11–12, 50, 58–59, 102–3, 136–38, 178
   as anthemic, 240–42
   See also vernacular song
Porter-Szűcs, Brian, 159, 261
postal service, 39, 82, 95, 250*f*, 250
posters, 75–77, 76*f*, 137–38, 237
Potter, Pamela, 239–40
Poznań, 213–15, 258–59
Praffdata, 237

Prague Spring, 9–10
prayer
   sound of, 130–31, 155–56, 186, 187–88, 259–60, 263–64
Preisner, Zbigniew, 27–28
presence, 113, 184, 192, 210–11, 226–27
   voice as, 146–47, 148, 163, 241
press. *See also* journalism
   conference, 184–86
   freedom of, 26, 35–38, 74, 121–22
printing press, 34–35, 40, 256
prison
   guards, 99–101
   space, 95, 98, 99–100
prizes, 63–64, 199, 213
   Nobel, 145–46
   Prix Italia, 129–30
   "Solidarity," 42, 43–44, 45*t*, 183
   Stalin, 43–44n.51
program music, 179–80, 184, 186, 276
program note, 186–87, 211, 253–54, 274–75
pronounciation, 58–59, 107, 121, 161–62, 166–67, 195, 223–24
propaganda, 10–11, 121
protest
   and hope, 111–14, 117–18, 127, 141, 233
   coordination of, 3–4, 114, 120, 163
   culture, 20, 107–9, 113, 135, 227, 231–32, 237
   demands, 116, 121–22, 141–42, 199–200
   music's efficacy for, 5–6, 58, 107, 228–29, 230–31, 241
   on street, 17, 142, 234, 240
   singing during, 77, 117–18, 122–23, 123*t*, 228–29, 234–36
   songs about, 67–71, 84–85, 99–100, 107–11, 141, 216
   sounds of, 111, 114, 224
   staged, 1–3, 78, 113, 114, 122, 219–20, 228, 240
proverb, 27–28
pseudonyms, 42n.50, 44–45n.53, 46, 48–49, 93, 219–20
public address, 31–32, 50, 114, 122, 131*t*, 156–57, 163, 169–71, 192–93, 204, 213
   emcee, 138–40, 174–76
public assembly, *see* assembly

public space, 15–16, 20, 70, 114, 150, 152, 169, 174–75, 203, 205–6, 234–35, 260–61
public sphere, 34–35, 41, 77, 240, 255, 260
punk, 5, 53–54, 61, 80–81n.42, 237

quiet, 163, 205
　fade-in/out, 27–28, 131–33, 134, 182–83, 266–68, 269–70, 278–79
　voices, 15, 68, 80, 145, 147, 167–68, 269–70
quotation, 9–10, 21–22, 93, 177, 200–1, 248, 265, 276n.133

radio, 29–30, 38–39, 70, 115, 122, 128–29, 182, 192–93
　as archive, 128–29, 203–4
Radio Free Europe (*Radio Wolnej Europy*), 28–29, 143–44, 178, 243, 248, 262–63
radio signal, 12–13, 40, 65–66, 110–11, 206–8, 227, 264–65
Radio Solidarity, 65–66, 84, 110–11, 128–30, 136, 143–44, 157, 203–4, 231–32, 242
Ratzinger, Joseph, 163
reading, 31, 107–9, 162
reading aloud, 17–18, 49–50, 90, 130–31, 131*t*, 148, 179, 186, 201–3
　performance of, 26, 71
Reagan, Ronald, 10
rebellion, 48–49
recitation, 85, 134, 161–62, 166, 180–82, 186–87, 218
recitative, *see* recitation
recognition, 224, 256–57
recollection, 13, 15–16, 78, 92, 165–68, 171–73, 221–23, 238–39
record industry, 29–30, 39, 47–48, 60, 61, 213, 265–66
　Polskie Nagrania (Polish Records), 58–59
recording studio, *see* studio production
reenactment, 152, 216
refrain, 13, 15, 90–92, 108–11, 124, 126, 142, 143–44, 224, 233, 234
　as slogan, 9, 119–20, 141, 240–41
　See also spoken mantra
Rehding, Alexander, 238–39
religious music, 160, 197–98, 256–57
　and commemoration, 152, 248

　and protest, 227, 240–41, 258–59
　Psalms as, 161–62, 174
　style in, 215–16
　Virgin Mary in, 133, 152, 160–61, 167–68, 174, 184, 186
repetition, 35–38, 85, 116–17, 166, 180, 187, 226–27
Review of Authentic Song (Przegląd Piosenki Prawdziwej), 13, 136–38, 221
revival, 90–92, 93, 110–11, 164–65, 256
revolution. *See also* uprisings
　French Revolution, 57–58, 199
　songs for, 124–25, 229
rhyme, 121, 251–52
rhythm, 124, 151–52, 187–88, 219–20, 259, 278
rock music, 48n.67, 49–50, 53–54, 80–81n.42, 160–61, 226–27, 240
Rodowicz, Maryla, 62–63
Rosaldo, Michelle, 168, 190–91
Rosiewicz, Andrzej, 178
rozrywka, *see* entertainment industry in Poland
Ruch Muzyczny (*Musical Movement*), 270

St. Stanisław Kostka Church, 152, 156–57, 163, 165–66, 168, 177–78, 183, 187, 249
salon
　literary, 82, 84
　musical, 80–81, 258
Salon of Independents (Salon Niezależnych), 81–82
samizdat, 34–35, 48–49
sanctuary, 80, 92, 149–50, 154, 166, 169–71, 180, 189–90, 233, 258–59
satellite technology, 10
SB (Służba Bezpieczeństwa, Security Service), 1–2, 23, 38–39, 40–41, 65–66, 80–81, 86, 100–1, 146–48, 152–54, 158, 168, 169–71, 186, 234–35
　apartment raids, 65, 71
Schmidt, Anna, 208–9
scouts, 27–28, 154, 235–36
second circulation, *see* drugi obieg
Second Vatican Council, 160–61, 163, 164
secularization, 159, 160, 169, 214–15, 261–62
Seehaber, Ruth, 198–99

Shostakovich, Dmitri, 40, 275–76
shouting, 17, 31–32, 113–14, 116–17, 122–23, 123*t*, 218–19, 229, 238–39, 279
Sienkiewicz, Henryk, 276–77
signature, 230–31
Sikora, Elżbieta, 223–24
Sikora, Tadeusz, 31–32
silence
   as absence or death, 78–79, 94, 155–56, 168
   as affective atmosphere, 70, 71, 87–89, 148, 224
   as historiographic trope, 9, 68–69, 85, 90, 103, 146–47n.3
   as impulse to create, 86, 94, 103
   as permission, 213
   as synonym for censorship, 11–12, 25, 143, 193, 204–5, 263–64
   cancelled concerts as, 69–70
   recorded, 28, 99–100
   See also minute of silence
simultaneity, 5–6, 22, 155
Sinatra, Frank, 12–13
singer-songwriters, 49–50, 97, 134, 221
singing
   as commemoration, 203, 234, 278
   as embodied, 70, 77, 241, 259–60
   as risk, 101, 167–68, 280
   critique of quality, 64–65
   collective, 49–50, 82–83, 86, 92, 95, 99, 113–14, 124, 155–56, 164, 238, 255
   faith and, 277
   forbidden, 46
   in detention, 94, 98–101
   performance practice, 27–28, 109, 138–40, 169–71, 182, 228–29
sirens, 201–3, 224
Skarżanka, Hanna, 163, 165–67, 171
Smith, Patti, 27–28
Snyder, Timothy, 174–75
social media, 107–9
social movements
   authenticity in, 120, 121, 136, 137–38, 171–73, 196–97
   Civil Rights Movement, 110–11, 231–32, 238n.11
   culture as model, 41, 42–43, 70
   leadership of, 196, 227
   opposition as, 6–7
   theory of, 3–6, 113–14

transnational mediation of, 107–9, 113–14, 128, 141, 223, 230–32, 237–38
socialist realism, 58–59n.101, 183–84, 238–39
soldiers, 78–79, 251, 253–54, 256–57
solidarity (as political concept), 3–4, 22, 127, 143–44, 200–1, 250
Solidarity (Solidarność)
   Party, 1–2
   Trade Union (NSZZ Solidarność), 6–7, 15, 41, 74–75, 108, 114, 136, 152–54, 153*f*, 178, 216–17
solitude, 108, 142–44
song
   as history, 19–20, 105–6, 109–10, 135, 226–27
   as protection, 229, 265–64
   family, 101
   "forbidden songs," 81–82, 105, 136–37
   lyrics, 64–65, 135, 150–51, 218–21, 237–38, 249, 255
   musicians' allegiance to, 49–50, 226
   patriotic songs, 90, 124, 152–54, 171–73, 251
   self-referentiality of, 141, 276
songbooks, 40, 216–17
   crafted in detention, 81–82, 95–97, 100–1, 109, 247
songwriting, 103, 173, 221–23, 231–32, 251–52
Sosa, Mercedes, 231–32
sovereignty, 9, 42–43, 111, 126, 148, 199–200, 240–41, 251–52, 256, 261
Soviet Union, 7–9, 31, 51, 89, 150, 234–35, 275–76
   Polish friendship with, 62, 199
sound
   and community, 111–12, 119, 120, 136–37, 149–50, 160, 269–70
   as affectively powerful, 166, 177, 196–97, 206–8, 223–24
   as labor, 32, 50, 93, 95–97, 100–1, 112–13, 135, 149–50, 182, 223, 226–27
   in fiction, 78–79, 276–77
   and intimacy, 72–74, 163, 188, 260
   synthesized, 150–52, 154, 182, 224
   vs. music, 69, 131–33
sound editing, 26, 40, 128, 150–51, 166, 203–4, 206–8, 223, 231–32

sound effects, 26–27, 30, 79, 86, 132n.81, 182, 223
sound recording
   as history, 113–14, 216–17
   as preservation, 135, 166, 216–17
   in detention, 95–97
   techniques, 26, 128, 150–51
soundscape, 70, 78–79, 117–18, 130–31, 260–61
speaking, 149–50, 157, 161–63, 164, 186
   eulogy, 176–77
speech act, 106, 109, 116–17, 141
Spivak, Gayatri, 240
spoken mantra, 35–38, 235–36
spontaneity, 111, 119–20, 123*t*, 135, 164–65, 206–8
stage presence, 61, 127–28, 138–40, 162, 233
stage production, 63, 166, 278–79
stalinism, 52–53, 58–59n.101, 183–84, 234
Stańko, Tomasz, 160–61
Staszewski, Kazik, *see* Kazik
State Song and Dance Ensembles, 121, 240
stenography, *see* transcription
"Sto lat," *see* "One Hundred Years"
stones
   as memorial, 155–56
   as weapons, 155–56, 158
storage, 38–39, 52–53
streets
   as theater, 6–7, 16, 18, 234–38
   crowds filling, 15–16, 77, 114, 209, 219–20
   empty, 70, 72–74, 80
strikes, 71, 74–75, 77, 114, 156–57, 197
   choreography, 116–17, 124, 193–94, 227, 242
Strzelecki, Paweł, 265–66
students, 84, 90–92, 136, 167–68, 177–78, 209–10, 229
studio production, 29–30, 131*t*, 150–51, 186, 223, 245
   stereo recording in, 130–31, 132*f*, 206–8, 270
subculture, 9, 133, 235–36
sung poetry, *see* poezja śpiewana
surveillance, 31–32, 78–79, 80–81, 157–58, 169–71, 189–90, 204, 209–10, 215–16, 233

sonic, 65–66, 86, 95–97, 99–101, 157–58, 168
symbols
   of nation, 71, 106, 174, 184, 269–70
   of opposition, 1–2, 23, 109–10, 136–37, 152–54, 240–41
symphony orchestra, 131–33, 197–98, 265, 275
Szamotul, Wacław z, 277
Szymanowski, Karol, 68
Szymański, Paweł, 68, 86–89

Tagore, Rabindranath, 91*t*
tamizdat, 34–35, 48–49
Tansman, Aleksander, 228, 269
tape
   cassettes (*see* cassette tape)
   circulation, 15, 28, 65–66, 129–30, 136–37, 173, 233, 271–72
   loops, 150–52
   music, 150–51, 177–78, 182, 223–24
   recording, 14–15, 26, 33, 40, 65–66, 113–14, 117–18, 118*f*, 158–59
telephone, 30, 31, 53–54
television, 9–11, 71, 72–74, 86, 106, 119, 151, 206–8
television sets, 122
tempo, *see* pace
testimony
   in death, 176–77, 220
   legal, 146–47, 234
   through music, 141
Thatcher, Margaret, 155–56
Thaw, 159–60, 197–98, 228–29
theater, 2–3, 31–32, 40, 49–50, 61, 251
   and the Roman Catholic Church, 165–66
   based on internment camp life, 86
   domestic, 82, 86
   in internment camps, 82–84
   pageantry, 120
Thompson, Robert, 183
timbre
   instrumental, 182–83, 187, 188
   vocal, 31, 63, 71–74, 87, 102–3, 124, 166–67, 175–76, 218–20, 223n.87
time
   historical, 13, 22, 154, 164, 221–23
   measurement of, 122, 179–80, 205–6, 217

time (cont.)
   music as measure of, 13, 134, 179–80, 223, 274
   theological, 154, 164
Tischner, Józef, 200–1
Tomaszewski, Mieczysław, 269–70
touring musicians, 29–30, 61, 69–70, 143–44, 233, 273
tourism, 103, 220–21
transcendence
   through music, 127–28, 177, 211, 258
transcription, 100, 101–3, 121–23, 146, 227, 237–38, 243
translation, 12–13, 40–41, 58–59, 89, 97, 109, 140, 161–62, 168, 171, 215–16, 233, 235n.3, 240, 256–57, 275n.128
Traugutt Philharmonic (*Filharmonia im. Traugutta*), 90, 98, 100–1, 161–62, 248, 259–60
Traugutt, Romuald, 164
trauma
   martial law as, 10, 72–74, 101, 158, 164, 223–24
   murder as, 176–77, 186, 188–89, 208–9, 216, 226
   musical, 178–79
   of Jerzy Popiełuszko's murderers, 146–47, 149*t*
   plane crash at Smolensk and, 278–79
   Second World War as, 7–9, 103–5, 177–78
   of Warsaw Uprising and song, 263–65
trial
   singing as evidence in, 234–35
truth, historical
   and deed, 165
   as heard, 72–74, 78–79, 176–77, 178–79
   as sung, 101, 136–38, 141–42
   as written, 85, 101, 121–22, 141–42
   embodied, 149–50, 154, 216
Twardowski, Romuald, 245

unison, *see* unity: musical
unity
   and listening, 163, 229
   musical, 2–4, 60, 110–11, 117–18, 124, 135, 143, 164–65, 182, 229, 237–39, 245, 269–70

   poetry and, 80
   social, 4, 5–6, 143, 149–50, 231–32, 238, 269–70
unofficial concerts, 49, 80, 108
unofficial culture, 33, 41, 45–48, 86–87, 140, 178
uprisings
   January Uprising, 83–84, 90, 164, 248, 263–64
   music in, 90–92, 249, 263–65
   November Uprising, 90
   Warsaw Uprising, 90, 141–42, 154, 217, 263–65, 278
US Information Agency, 10

vernacular song, 65–66, 95, 104, 117–18
   as subversive, 120, 121
victory sign, 23, 89, 168, 234, 235, 249, 250
Vilnius, 166
vinyl, 30, 121, 134, 151–52, 230–31, 245, 249
violence, 116
   during martial law, 74–75
   murder, 146–48, 158, 168
   musical representation of, 72–74, 151–52, 183
   sonic, 151–52, 183, 218–19, 280
virtuosity, 187–89
visiting
   as musical migration, 184, 262–63
   people in detention, 95–97, 99, 245
visual arts, 31–32, 86–87, 90–92, 174–75, 200–1
   see also logo; monument
vocal performance, *see* reading aloud; singing
vocal register, 124, 187–88
voice
   as political power, 145, 190–91, 192, 193–94, 196
   as technology, 147, 163, 187–88, 189–91, 218–19
   composer's, 184
   equivalence with agency, 145, 168, 193, 196–97
   in theological context, 148–50, 160, 161–62, 168
   recorded, 158–59
Voice of America, 128–29, 131–33n.81

voice-over, 10, 223
voice recognition technology, 38–39, 65–66
vowels, 15, 58–59, 259–60
Vysotsky, Vladimir, 140–41
waiting, 25, 100–1, 114, 115, 120, 133, 158, 179, 247
Wajda, Andrzej, 201
    and commemoration, 205, 208–9
    and Lech Wałęsa, 194–95, 210–11, 232–33
    and musicians, 109, 208–9
    Man of Iron (Człowiek z żelaza), 119n.44, 217–18, 223n.87, 230
Walentynowicz, Anna, 116–17, 124
Wałęsa, Lech, 49–50, 111, 116–17, 119, 123*t*, 127–28, 136–37, 145–46, 199–200, 203, 249
    as leader, 227–33
    singing, 243
Walicki, Andrzej, 193–94
war, 150
    martial law as, 10–11
    music and, 124–25, 251
    sounds of, 11, 197–98, 223, 275
Warsaw
    architecture, 52–53, 75–77
    concert halls, 15, 61, 75–77, 243
    during the Second World War, 103–4
    liberation of, 62–63
    rebuilding of, 105
    streets, 15–16, 105, 157, 174–75, 229, 234–35, 278–79
Warsaw Autumn Festival, 5, 56–57, 68n.3, 180–82, 213n.62, 274–75
    cancellation of, 69–70

Wawrzykowska-Wierciochowa, Dioniza, 254, 256
Weber, Max, 196
Week of Christian Culture, 43–44, 209–10
weeping, 175–76, 189–96, 205–6, 209, 248
"We Shall Overcome," 108
West-East Divan Orchestra, 4
Wick, Charles, 10, 12–13
Wieniawski, Henryk, 90, 91*t*
Wierzchowo prison, 98
winter, *see* cold
Wiśniewski, Grzegorz, 203–4
witness, 72–74, 77, 113, 119–21, 131*t*, 147, 199–200, 219–20, 235, 249
Wlodarski, Amy, 72–74
workers, 58–59, 63–64, 116–17, 152–54, 195–96, 199–201, 204, 227
Workers '80 (Robotnicy '80), 114, 124, 229n.103
Woytowicz, Stefania, 49–50, 89, 210n.48, 213
Wybicki, Józef, 124–25
Wyszyński, Stefan, 209, 213, 217

yelling, 27–28
youth culture, 60, 63, 84, 109, 178, 237, 276–77

Zajaczkowski, Andrzej, see *Workers '80*
Zembaty, Maciej, 97, 136–37, 209–10n.46
Ziembiński, Wojciech, 234–35
zine, 150

www.ingramcontent.com/pod-product-compliance
Ingram Content Group UK Ltd.
Pitfield, Milton Keynes, MK11 3LW, UK
UKHW042005230426
12048UKWH00009B/574